CW00832934

THE
CONSTITUTION
OF
INDIA

FP

Reprint 2024

FiNGERPRINT!

An imprint of Prakash Books India Pvt. Ltd

113/A, Darya Ganj,
New Delhi-110 002
Email: info@prakashbooks.com/sales@prakashbooks.com

⬛ Fingerprint Publishing
✖ @FingerprintP
⬛ @fingerprintpublishingbooks
www.fingerprintpublishing.com

ISBN: 978 93 5856 074 9

Text sourced from: https://legislative.gov.in/constitution-of-india/

INTRODUCTION TO THE TEXT

India is a diverse country with varying cultures, people, languages, and geography. Naturally, the history of the constitution of such a country is an interesting one. From a mere collection of statutes before the country gained independence to becoming the supreme law of India, the constitution has gone through substantial revisions and reworkings.

The Constitution of India lays down the framework and structure of India's government, along with its powers and directive principles and the fundamental rights and duties of its citizens. It is the longest written constitution in the world, whose drafting took 2 years, 11 months, and 18 days and cost 6.4 crore rupees. It draws heavily from the other constitutions in the world and contains 25 parts, comprising 448 articles and 12 schedules.

What we know today as the Constitution of India started as the Government of India Acts of 1919 and 1935. Even after getting independence from the British rule in 1947, India continued to be governed by the Government of India Acts of 1919 and 1935, as it was still a dominion of the United Kingdom.

The Government of India Act of 1919 was passed as a gesture of gratitude acknowledging India's role in World War I for Great Britain. This Act is the basic structure of the constitution that governs our country today. The main goal of this legislation was to increase the role of native Indians in mainstream politics and government. Under this act, the Imperial Legislative Council (ICL) was transformed into a bicameral legislature with an Upper House and a Lower House, which are known as the Rajya Sabha and the Lok Sabha respectively today. In addition to this, a High Commissioner with a London address was also established by the Act to represent India in the United Kingdom, and the system of dyarchy was introduced.

However, this Act provided next to no autonomy to Indian representatives in the government and was met with protests from the Indian National Congress (INC). As a result, the Government of India Act of 1935 was passed.

Thereafter, as the possibility of India becoming a sovereign country was becoming a reality, a Constituent Assembly with 296 representatives was chosen by the members of the provincial legislatures to draft the Constitution of India. Although the Indian National Congress held a majority in this assembly, it also consisted of representatives from the Muslim League, Scheduled Caste Federation, Indian Communist Party and Union Party, among others. The first meeting of this Constituent Assembly took place in December 1946.

Since framing the constitution was a complicated process, a number of committees were appointed by the assembly to tackle various aspects of the framing process. Some of these committees were the Union Powers Committee, Union Constitution Committee, and Committees on Fundamental Rights, among others. These committees worked tirelessly to produce the fundamentals of the constitution.

In October 1947, the first draft of the Indian Constitution was produced by the Advisory Branch of the Office of the Constituent Assembly with Sir B.N. Rau as the constitutional legal advisor. What went behind the making of this Draft Constitution was widespread research and a three series 'Constitutional Precedents' which consisted of principal texts from the constitutions of about 60 countries.

This draft constitution of India was submitted to the Constituent Assembly in February 1948 and was debated extensively. A special committee was formed to comb through the draft, and the suggestions made by it were again debated by the Drafting Committee.

After a clause-by-clause consideration, followed by the Second Reading and the Third Reading by the Assembly, the 243 items and 13 schedules of the draft constitution were changed to 395 articles and 8 schedules with necessary amendments. The legislature then moved, discussed, and rejected 2,473 of the total 7,635 amendments during its discussions on the revised drafted constitution.

On November 26, 1949, Dr B.R. Ambedkar, the Chairman of the Drafting Committee said, "that the constitution as settled by the assembly be passed." Thus, the constitution was adopted by the Constituent Assembly and this day is now celebrated as Constitution Day in India.

On January 26, 1950, the constitution came into effect in its entirety, and the Constituent Assembly became a **Provisional Parliament**. From this day on, with the constitution, India was now the Sovereign Democratic Republic of India.

In his closing remarks, Dr. Rajendra Prasad noted that they had been able to write a strong constitution that he was confident would benefit the nation. But he also said:

"If the people who are elected are capable and men of character and integrity, they would be able to make the best even of a defective constitution. If they are lacking in these, the constitution cannot help the country. After all, a constitution like a machine is a lifeless thing. It acquires life because of men who control it and operate it, and India needs today nothing more than a set of honest men who will have the interest of the country before them. There is a fissiparous tendency arising out of various elements in our life. We have communal differences, caste differences, language differences, provincial differences and so forth.

It requires men of strong character, men of vision, men who will not sacrifice the interests of the country at large for the sake of smaller groups and areas and who will rise over the prejudices which are born of these differences.

We can only hope that the country will throw up such men in abundance."

The making of the Constitution of India has always been a dynamic process. Today, the aim is to incorporate essential reforms to keep up with the times while preserving the pillars of the polity. Through judicial interpretations and constitutional amendments, the constitution, which is the driving force of our country, has been amended 104 times, making it one of the most amended constitutions in the world.

The original copy of the constitution was handwritten by the Indian calligrapher Prem Behari Narain Raizada and each page was decorated by renowned artists from all over the country. It is currently housed at the Library of the Parliament of India.

TIMELINE OF THE MAKING OF THE INDIAN CONSTITUTION

- **6 December 1946:** The Constitution Assembly was formed.
- **9 December 1946:** The first meeting of this Constitution Assembly was held in the constitution hall.
- **11 December 1946:** Rajendra Prasad was chosen as the Assembly's president, along with H. C. Mukherjee as vicepresident and, B. N. Rau as constitutional legal adviser.

- **13 December 1946:** Jawaharlal Nehru submitted a "Objective Resolution" outlining the fundamental ideas of the constitution. This is what we know today as the Preamble of the Constitution.
- **22 July 1947:** The national flag of India was adopted.
- **15 August 1947:** Indian subcontinent gained independence and was divided into the Dominion of India and the Dominion of Pakistan.
- **29 August 1947:** The Drafting Committee was appointed. The six members of this committee were K.M. Munshi, Muhammed Sadulla, Alladi Krishnaswamy Iyer, N. Gopalaswami Ayyangar, Devi Prasad Khaitan and BL Mitter. Dr B.R. Ambedkar was the chairman of this committee.
- **26 November 1949:** The Indian Constitution was adopted and ratified by the legislature.
- **24 January 1950:** Last meeting of the Constituent Assembly was held wherein the Constitution was signed and accepted.
- **26 January 1950:** The Constitution came into force and India was Sovereign Democratic Republic of India.

CONTENTS

Introduction to the Text   *3*

Preface   23

List of Abbreviations Used   25

Preamble   27

PART I

Articles

THE UNION AND ITS TERRITORY   29
1.   Name and territory of the Union.   29
2.   Admission or establishment of new States.   29
2A.   [Sikkim to be associated with the Union.—*Omitted*].   29
3.   Formation of new States and alteration of areas, boundaries or names of
        existing States.   29
4.   Laws made under articles 2 and 3 to provide for the amendment of the First and
        the Fourth Schedules and supplemental, incidental and consequential matters.   30

PART II

CITIZENSHIP   31
5.   Citizenship at the commencement of the Constitution.   31
6.   Rights of citizenship of certain persons who have migrated to India from Pakistan.   31
7.   Rights of citizenship of certain migrants to Pakistan.   32
8.   Rights of citizenship of certain persons of Indian origin residing outside India.   32
9.   Persons voluntarily acquiring citizenship of a foreign State not to be citizens.   32
10.   Continuance of the rights of citizenship.   32
11.   Parliament to regulate the right of citizenship by law.   32

PART III

FUNDAMENTAL RIGHTS   33

General

12.   Definition.   33
13.   Laws inconsistent with or in derogation of the fundamental rights.   33

Right to Equality

14.   Equality before law.   34
15.   Prohibition of discrimination on grounds of religion, race, caste, sex or place of birth.   34
16.   Equality of opportunity in matters of public employment.   35
17.   Abolition of Untouchability.   37
18.   Abolition of titles.   37

Right to Freedom

19.   Protection of certain rights regarding freedom of speech, etc.   37
20.   Protection in respect of conviction for offences.   39

21.	Protection of life and personal liberty.	39
21A.	Right to education.	39
22.	Protection against arrest and detention in certain cases.	39

Right against Exploitation

23.	Prohibition of traffic in human beings and forced labour.	41
24.	Prohibition of employment of children in factories, etc.	42

Right to Freedom of Religion

25.	Freedom of conscience and free profession, practice and propagation of religion.	42
26.	Freedom to manage religious affairs.	42
27.	Freedom as to payment of taxes for promotion of any particular religion.	43
28.	Freedom as to attendance at religious instruction or religious worship in certain educational institutions.	43

Cultural and Educational Rights

29.	Protection of interests of minorities.	43
30.	Right of minorities to establish and administer educational institutions.	43
31.	[Compulsory acquisition of property.—*Omitted*].	44

Saving of Certain Laws

31A.	Saving of laws providing for acquisition of estates, etc.	44
31B.	Validation of certain Acts and Regulations.	46
31C.	Saving of laws giving effect to certain directive principles.	46
31D.	[Saving of laws in respect of anti-national activities.—*Omitted*].	47

Right to Constitutional Remedies

32.	Remedies for enforcement of rights conferred by this Part.	47
32A.	[Constitutional validity of State laws not to be considered in proceedings under article 32.—*Omitted*].	47
33.	Power of Parliament to modify the rights conferred by this Part in their application to Forces, etc.	47
34.	Restriction on rights conferred by this Part while martial law is in force in any area.	48
35.	Legislation to give effect to the provisions of this Part.	48

PART IV

DIRECTIVE PRINCIPLES OF STATE POLICY		49
36.	Definition.	49
37.	Application of the principles contained in this Part.	49
38.	State to secure a social order for the promotion of welfare of the people.	49
39.	Certain principles of policy to be followed by the State.	50
39A.	Equal justice and free legal aid.	50
40.	Organisation of village panchayats.	50
41.	Right to work, to education and to public assistance in certain cases.	50
42.	Provision for just and humane conditions of work and maternity relief.	51
43.	Living wage, etc., for workers.	51
43A.	Participation of workers in management of industries.	51
43B.	Promotion of co-operative societies.	51
44.	Uniform civil code for the citizens.	51
45.	Provision for early childhood care and education to children below the age of six years.	51
46.	Promotion of educational and economic interests of Scheduled Castes, Scheduled Tribes and other weaker sections.	51
47.	Duty of the State to raise the level of nutrition and the standard of living and to improve public health.	52
48.	Organisation of agriculture and animal husbandry.	52
48A.	Protection and improvement of environment and safeguarding of forests and wild life.	52

49.	Protection of monuments and places and objects of national importance.	52
50.	Separation of judiciary from executive.	52
51.	Promotion of international peace and security.	52

PART IV A

FUNDAMENTAL DUTIES 53

51A.   Fundamental duties.   53

PART V

THE UNION 54

CHAPTER I.—THE EXECUTIVE
The President and Vice-President

52.	The President of India.	54
53.	Executive power of the Union.	54
54.	Election of President.	54
55.	Manner of election of President.	55
56.	Term of office of President.	56
57.	Eligibility for re-election.	56
58.	Qualifications for election as President.	56
59.	Conditions of President's office.	57
60.	Oath or affirmation by the President.	57
61.	Procedure for impeachment of the President.	58
62.	Time of holding election to fill vacancy in the office of President and the term of office of person elected to fill casual vacancy.	58
63.	The Vice-President of India.	58
64.	The Vice-President to be *ex officio* Chairman of the Council of States.	59
65.	The Vice-President to act as President or to discharge his functions during casual vacancies in the office, or during the absence, of President.	59
66.	Election of Vice-President.	59
67.	Term of office of Vice-President.	60
68.	Time of holding election to fill vacancy in the office of Vice-President and the term of office of person elected to fill casual vacancy.	61
69.	Oath or affirmation by the Vice-President.	61
70.	Discharge of President's functions in other contingencies.	61
71.	Matters relating to, or connected with, the election of a President or Vice-President.	61
72.	Power of President to grant pardons, etc., and to suspend, remit or commute sentences in certain cases.	62
73.	Extent of executive power of the Union.	62

Council of Ministers

74.	Council of Ministers to aid and advise President.	63
75.	Other provisions as to Ministers.	64

The Attorney-General for India

76.	Attorney-General for India.	64

Conduct of Government Business

77.	Conduct of business of the Government of India.	65
78.	Duties of Prime Minister as respects the furnishing of information to the President, etc.	65

CHAPTER II.—PARLIAMENT
General

79.	Constitution of Parliament.	66

80.	Composition of the Council of States.	66
81.	Composition of the House of the People.	67
82.	Readjustment after each census.	68
84.	Qualification for membership of Parliament.	69
85.	Sessions of Parliament, prorogation and dissolution.	70
86.	Right of President to address and send messages to Houses.	70
87.	Special address by the President.	70
88.	Rights of Ministers and Attorney-General as respects Houses.	71

Officers of Parliament

89.	The Chairman and Deputy Chairman of the Council of States.	71
90.	Vacation and resignation of, and removal from, the office of Deputy Chairman.	71
91.	Power of the Deputy Chairman or other person to perform the duties of the office of, or to act as, Chairman.	71
92.	The Chairman or the Deputy Chairman not to preside while a resolution for his removal from office is under consideration.	72
93.	The Speaker and Deputy Speaker of the House of the People.	72
94.	Vacation and resignation of, and removal from, the offices of Speaker and Deputy Speaker.	72
95.	Power of the Deputy Speaker or other person to perform the duties of the office of, or to act as, Speaker.	73
96.	The Speaker or the Deputy Speaker not to preside while a resolution for his removal from office is under consideration.	73
97.	Salaries and allowances of the Chairman and Deputy Chairman and the Speaker and Deputy Speaker.	74
98.	Secretariat of Parliament.	74

Conduct of Business

99.	Oath or affirmation by members.	74
100.	Voting in Houses, power of Houses to act notwithstanding vacancies and quorum.	74

Disqualifications of Members

101.	Vacation of seats.	75
102.	Disqualifications for membership.	76
103.	Decision on questions as to disqualifications of members.	77
104.	Penalty for sitting and voting before making oath or affirmation under article 188 or when not qualified or when disqualified.	77

*Powers, Privileges and Immunities of State
Legislatures and their Members*

105.	Powers, privileges, etc., of the Houses of Legislatures and of the members and committees thereof.	78
106.	Salaries and allowances of members.	79

Legislative Procedure

107.	Provisions as to introduction and passing of Bills.	79
108.	Joint sitting of both Houses in certain cases.	79
109.	Special procedure in respect of Money Bills.	81
110.	Definition of "Money Bills".	81
111.	Assent to Bills.	82

Procedure in Financial Matters

112.	Annual financial statement.	83
114.	Appropriation Bills.	85

115.	Supplementary, additional or excess grants.	85
116.	Votes on account, votes of credit and exceptional grants.	86
117.	Special provisions as to financial Bills.	86

Procedure Generally

118.	Rules of procedure.	87
119.	Regulation by law of procedure in Parliament in relation to financial business.	88
120.	Language to be used in Parliament.	88
121.	Restriction on discussion in Parliament.	88
122.	Courts not to inquire into proceedings of Parliament.	88

CHAPTER III.—LEGISLATIVE POWERS OF THE PRESIDENT

| 123. | Power of President to promulgate Ordinances during recess of Parliament. | 89 |

CHAPTER IV.—THE UNION JUDICIARY

124.	Establishment and constitution of Supreme Court.	90
124A.	National Judicial Appointments Commission.	91
124B.	Functions of Commission.	92
124C.	Power of Parliament to make law.	92
125.	Salaries, etc., of Judges.	93
126.	Appointment of acting Chief Justice.	93
127.	Appointment of ad hoc Judges.	93
128.	Attendance of retired Judges at sittings of the Supreme Court.	94
129.	Supreme Court to be a court of record.	94
130.	Seat of Supreme Court.	94
131.	Original jurisdiction of the Supreme Court.	94
131A.	[Exclusive jurisdiction of the Supreme Court in regard to questions as to constitutional validity of Central laws.—*Omitted*].	95
132.	Appellate jurisdiction of Supreme Court in appeals from High Courts in certain cases.	95
133.	Appellate jurisdiction of Supreme Court in appeals from High Courts in regard to civil matters.	96
134.	Appellate jurisdiction of Supreme Court in regard to criminal matters.	96
134A.	Certificate for appeal to the Supreme Court.	97
135.	Jurisdiction and powers of the Federal Court under existing law to be exercisable by the Supreme Court.	97
136.	Special leave to appeal by the Supreme Court.	97
137.	Review of judgments or orders by the Supreme Court.	98
138.	Enlargement of the jurisdiction of the Supreme Court.	98
139.	Conferment on the Supreme Court of powers to issue certain writs.	98
139A.	Transfer of certain cases.	98
140.	Ancillary powers of Supreme Court.	99
141.	Law declared by Supreme Court to be binding on all courts.	99
142.	Enforcement of decrees and orders of Supreme Court and orders as to discovery, etc.	99
143.	Power of President to consult Supreme Court.	99
144.	Civil and judicial authorities to act in aid of the Supreme Court.	100
144A.	[Special provisions as to disposal of questions relating to constitutional validity of laws.—*Omitted*].	100
145.	Rules of Court, etc.	100
146.	Officers and servants and the expenses of the Supreme Court.	102
147.	Interpretation.	102

CHAPTER V.—COMPTROLLER AND AUDITOR-GENERAL OF INDIA

148.	Comptroller and Auditor-General of India.	103
149.	Duties and powers of the Comptroller and Auditor-General.	104
150.	Form of accounts of the Union and of the States.	104
151.	Audit reports.	104

PART VI

THE STATES

105

CHAPTER I.—GENERAL

152.   Definition.   105

CHAPTER II.—THE EXECUTIVE
The Governor

153.   Governors of States.   105
154.   Executive power of State.   105
155.   Appointment of Governor.   105
156.   Term of office of Governor.   106
157.   Qualifications for appointment as Governor.   106
158.   Conditions of Governor's office.   106
159.   Oath or affirmation by the Governor.   106
160.   Discharge of the functions of the Governor in certain contingencies.   107
161.   Power of Governor to grant pardons, etc., and to suspend, remit or commute
       sentences in certain cases.   107
162.   Extent of executive power of State.   107

Council of Ministers

163.   Council of Ministers to aid and advise Governor.   107
164.   Other provisions as to Ministers.   108

The Advocate-General for the State

165.   Advocate-General for the State.   109

Conduct of Government Business

166.   Conduct of Business of the Government of a State.   110
167.   Duties of Chief Minister as respects the furnishing of information to Governor, etc.   110

CHAPTER III.—THE STATE LEGISLATURE
General

168.   Constitution of Legislatures in States.   111
169.   Abolition or creation of Legislative Councils in States.   111
[170. Composition of the Legislative Assemblies.   112
171.   Composition of the Legislative Councils.   113
172.   Duration of State Legislatures.   114
173.   Qualification for membership of the State Legislature.   115
174.   Sessions of the State Legislature, prorogation and dissolution.   115
175.   Right of Governor to address and send messages to the House or Houses.   116
176.   Special address by the Governor.   116
177.   Rights of Ministers and Advocate-General as respects the Houses.   116

Officers of the State Legislature

178.   The Speaker and Deputy Speaker of the Legislative Assembly.   117
179.   Vacation and resignation of, and removal from, the offices of Speaker and
       Deputy Speaker.   117
180.   Power of the Deputy Speaker or other person to perform the duties of
       the office of, or to act as, Speaker.   117
181.   The Speaker or the Deputy Speaker not to preside while a resolution for his removal from
       office is under consideration.   118
182.   The Chairman and Deputy Chairman of the Legislative Council.   118
183.   Vacation and resignation of, and removal from, the offices of Chairman and
       Deputy Chairman.   118

184. Power of the Deputy Chairman or other person to perform the duties of
the office of, or to act as, Chairman.   119

185. The Chairman or the Deputy Chairman not to preside while a resolution for
his removal from office is under consideration.   119

186. Salaries and allowances of the Speaker and Deputy Speaker and the Chairman
and Deputy Chairman.   119

187. Secretariat of State Legislature.   120

Conduct of Business

188. Oath or affirmation by members.   120

189. Voting in Houses, power of Houses to act notwithstanding vacancies and quorum.   120

Disqualifications of Members

190. Vacation of seats.   121

191. Disqualifications for membership.   122

192. Decision on questions as to disqualifications of members.   123

193. Penalty for sitting and voting before making oath or affirmation under article 188
or when not qualified or when disqualified.   123

Powers, Privileges and Immunities of State Legislatures and their Members

194. Powers, privileges, etc., of the Houses of Legislatures and of the members and
committees thereof.   124

195. Salaries and allowances of members.   125

Legislative Procedure

196. Provisions as to introduction and passing of Bills.   125

197. Restriction on powers of Legislative Council as to Bills other than Money Bills.   125

198. Special procedure in respect of Money Bills.   126

199. Definition of "Money Bills".   127

200. Assent to Bills.   128

201. Bills reserved for consideration.   129

Procedure in Financial Matters

202. Annual financial statement.   129

203. Procedure in Legislature with respect to estimates.   130

204. Appropriation Bills.   130

205. Supplementary, additional or excess grants.   131

206. Votes on account, votes of credit and exceptional grants.   132

207. Special provisions as to financial Bills.   132

Procedure Generally

208. Rules of procedure.   133

209. Regulation by law of procedure in the Legislature of the State in relation to
financial business.   133

210. Language to be used in the Legislature.   134

211. Restriction on discussion in the Legislature.   135

212. Courts not to inquire into proceedings of the Legislature.   135

CHAPTER IV.—LEGISLATIVE POWER OF THE GOVERNOR

213. Power of Governor to promulgate Ordinances during recess of Legislature.   135

CHAPTER V.—THE HIGH COURTS IN THE STATES

214. High Courts for States.   137

215. High Courts to be courts of record.   137

216. Constitution of High Courts.   137

217.	Appointment and conditions of the office of a Judge of a High Court.	137
218.	Application of certain provisions relating to Supreme Court to High Courts.	139
219.	Oath or affirmation by Judges of High Courts.	139
220.	Restriction on practice after being a permanent Judge.	139
221.	Salaries, etc., of Judges.	140
222.	Transfer of a Judge from one High Court to another.	140
223.	Appointment of acting Chief Justice.	140
224.	Appointment of additional and acting Judges.	141
224A.	Appointment of retired Judges at sittings of High Courts.	141
225.	Jurisdiction of existing High Courts.	142
226.	Power of High Courts to issue certain writs.	142
226A.	[Constitutional validity of Central laws not to be considered in proceedings under article 226.—*Omitted*].	144
227.	Power of superintendence over all courts by the High Court.	144
228.	Transfer of certain cases to High Court.	145
228A.	[Special provisions as to disposal of questions relating to constitutional validity of State laws.—*Omitted*].	145
229.	Officers and servants and the expenses of High Courts.	145
230.	Extension of jurisdiction of High Courts to Union territories.	146
231.	Establishment of a common High Court for two or more States.	146
232.	[Interpretation.—Articles 230, 231 and 232 subs. by articles 230 and 231]	147

CHAPTER VI.—SUBORDINATE COURTS

233.	Appointment of district judges.	147
233A.	Validation of appointments of, and judgments, etc., delivered by, certain district judges.	147
234.	Recruitment of persons other than district judges to the judicial service.	148
235.	Control over subordinate courts.	148
236.	Interpretation.	149
237.	Application of the provisions of this Chapter to certain class or classes of magistrates.	149

[PART VII—Omitted]

THE STATES IN PART B OF THE FIRST SCHEDULE

238.	[*Omitted*].	149

PART VIII

THE UNION TERRITORIES		150
239.	Administration of Union territories.	150
239A.	Creation of local Legislatures or Council of Ministers or both for certain Union territories.	150
239AA.	Special provisions with respect to Delhi.	151
239AB.	Provision in case of failure of constitutional machinery.	153
239B.	Power of administrator to promulgate Ordinances during recess of Legislature.	154
240.	Power of President to make regulations for certain Union territories.	155
241.	High Courts for Union territories.	156
242.	[Coorg.—*Omitted*].	157

PART IX

THE PANCHAYATS		157
243.	Definitions.	157
243A.	Gram Sabha.	158
243B.	Constitution of Panchayats.	158
243C.	Composition of Panchayats.	158

243D.   Reservation of seats.   159
243E.   Duration of Panchayats, etc.   160
243F.   Disqualifications for membership.   161
243G.   Powers, authority and responsibilities of Panchayats.   161
243H.   Powers to impose taxes by, and Funds of, the Panchayats.   162
243-I.   Constitution of Finance Commission to review financial position.   162
243J.   Audit of accounts of Panchayats.   163
243K.   Elections to the Panchayats.   163
243L.   Application to Union territories.   164
243M.   Part not to apply to certain areas.   164
243N.   Continuance of existing laws and Panchayats.   165
243-O.   Bar to interference by courts in electoral matters.   166

PART IX A

THE MUNICIPALITIES   166
243P.   Definitions.   166
243Q.   Constitution of Municipalities.   167
243R.   Composition of Municipalities.   167
243S.   Constitution and composition of Wards Committees, etc.   168
243T.   Reservation of seats.   168
243U.   Duration of Municipalities, etc.   169
243V.   Disqualifications for membership.   170
243W.   Powers, authority and responsibilities of Municipalities, etc.   170
243X.   Power to impose taxes by, and Funds of, the Municipalities.   171
243Y.   Finance Commission.   171
243Z.   Audit of accounts of Municipalities.   172
243ZA.   Elections to the Municipalities.   172
243ZB.   Application to Union territories.   172
243ZC.   Part not to apply to certain areas.   173
243ZD.   Committee for district planning.   173
243ZE.   Committee for Metropolitan planning.   174
243ZF.   Continuance of existing laws and Municipalities.   175
243ZG.   Bar to interference by courts in electoral matters.   176

PART IX B

THE CO-OPERATIVE SOCIETIES   176
243ZH.   Definitions.   176
243 ZI. Incorporation of co-operative societies.   177
243ZJ.   Number and term of members of board and its office bearers.   177
243ZK.   Election of members of board.   178
243ZL.   Supersession and suspension of board and interim management.   179
243ZM.   Audit of accounts of co-operative societies.   180
243ZN.   Convening of general body meetings.   180
243ZO.   Right of a member to get information.   180
243ZP.   Returns.   181
243ZQ.   Offences and penalties.   181
243ZR.   Application to multi-State co-operative societies.   182
243ZS.   Application to Union territories.   182
243ZT.   Continuance of existing laws.   182

PART X

THE SCHEDULED AND TRIBAL AREAS   183
244.   Administration of Scheduled Areas and Tribal Areas.   183
244A.   Formation of an autonomous State comprising certain tribal areas in Assam and creation
         of local Legislature or Council of Ministers or both therefor.   183

PART XI

RELATIONS BETWEEN THE UNION AND THE STATES   185

CHAPTER I.—LEGISLATIVE RELATIONS
Distribution of Legislative Powers

245.	Extent of laws made by Parliament and by the Legislatures of States.	185
246.	Subject-matter of laws made by Parliament and by the Legislatures of States.	185
246A.	Special provision with respect to goods and services tax.	186
247.	Power of Parliament to provide for the establishment of certain additional courts.	186
248.	Residuary powers of legislation.	186
249.	Power of Parliament to legislate with respect to a matter in the State List in the national interest.	186
250.	Power of Parliament to legislate with respect to any matter in the State List if a Proclamation of Emergency is in operation.	187
251.	Inconsistency between laws made by Parliament under articles 249 and 250 and laws made by the Legislatures of States.	188
252.	Power of Parliament to legislate for two or more States by consent and adoption of such legislation by any other State.	188
253.	Legislation for giving effect to international agreements.	188
254.	Inconsistency between laws made by Parliament and laws made by the Legislatures of States.	188
255.	Requirements as to recommendations and previous sanctions to be regarded as matters of procedure only.	189

CHAPTER II.—ADMINISTRATIVE RELATIONS
General

256.	Obligation of States and the Union.	190
257.	Control of the Union over States in certain cases.	190
257A.	[Assistance to States by deployment of armed forces or other forces of the Union.—*Omitted*].	191
258.	Power of the Union to confer powers, etc., on States in certain cases.	191
258A.	Power of the States to entrust functions to the Union.	191
259.	[Armed Forces in States in Part B of the First Schedule.—*Omitted*].	191
260.	Jurisdiction of the Union in relation to territories outside India.	192
261.	Public acts, records and judicial proceedings.	192

Disputes relating to Waters

262.	Adjudication of disputes relating to waters of inter-State rivers or river valleys.	192

Co-ordination between States

263.	Provisions with respect to an inter-State Council.	192

PART XII

FINANCE, PROPERTY, CONTRACTS AND SUITS   193

CHAPTER I.—FINANCE
General

264.	Interpretation.	193
265.	Taxes not to be imposed save by authority of law.	193
266.	Consolidated Funds and public accounts of India and of the States.	193
267.	Contingency Fund.	194

Distribution of Revenues between the Union and the States

268.	Duties levied by the Union but collected and appropriated by the States.	195

268A. [Service tax levied by Union and collected and appropriated by the Union and the States.—*Omitted*]. 195

269. Taxes levied and collected by the Union but assigned to the States. 195

269A. Levy and collection of goods and services tax in course of inter-State trade or commerce. 196

270. Taxes levied and distributed between the Union and the States. 197

271. Surcharge on certain duties and taxes for purposes of the Union. 198

272. [Taxes which are levied and collected by the Union and may be distributed between the Union and the States.—*Omitted*]. 198

273. Grants in lieu of export duty on jute and jute products. 198

274. Prior recommendation of President required to Bills affecting taxation in which States are interested. 198

275. Grants from the Union to certain States. 199

276. Taxes on professions, trades, callings and employments. 200

277. Savings. 201

278. [Agreement with States in Part B of the First Schedule with regard to certain financial matters.—*Omitted*]. 201

279. Calculation of "net proceeds", etc. 201

279A. Goods and Services Tax Council. 202

280. Finance Commission. 204

281. Recommendations of the Finance Commission. 205

Miscellaneous Financial Provisions

282. Expenditure defrayable by the Union or a State out of its revenues. 205

283. Custody, etc., of Consolidated Funds, Contingency Funds and moneys credited to the public accounts. 205

284. Custody of suitors' deposits and other moneys received by public servants and courts. 206

285. Exemption of property of the Union from State taxation. 206

286. Restrictions as to imposition of tax on the sale or purchase of goods. 207

287. Exemption from taxes on electricity. 207

288. Exemption from taxation by States in respect of water or electricity in certain cases. 208

289. Exemption of property and income of a State from Union taxation. 209

290. Adjustment in respect of certain expenses and pensions. 209

290A. Annual payment to certain Devaswom Funds. 210

291. [Privy purse sums of Rulers.—*Omitted*]. 210

CHAPTER II.—BORROWING

292. Borrowing by the Government of India. 210

293. Borrowing by States. 210

CHAPTER III.—PROPERTY, CONTRACTS, RIGHTS, LIABILITIES, OBLIGATIONS AND SUITS

294. Succession to property, assets, rights, liabilities and obligations in certain cases. 211

295. Succession to property, assets, rights, liabilities and obligations in other cases. 211

296. Property accruing by escheat or lapse or as bona vacantia. 212

297. Things of value within territorial waters or continental shelf and resources of the exclusive economic zone to vest in the Union. 213

298. Power to carry on trade, etc. 213

299. Contracts. 213

300. Suits and proceedings. 214

CHAPTER IV.—RIGHT TO PROPERTY

300A. Persons not to be deprived of property save by authority of law. 214

PART XIII

TRADE, COMMERCE AND INTERCOURSE WITHIN THE TERRITORY OF INDIA   215

301.	Freedom of trade, commerce and intercourse.	215
302.	Power of Parliament to impose restrictions on trade, commerce and intercourse.	215
303.	Restrictions on the legislative powers of the Union and of the States with regard to trade and commerce.	215
304.	Restrictions on trade, commerce and intercourse among States.	215
305.	Saving of existing laws and laws providing for State monopolies.	216
306.	[Power of certain States in Part B of the First Schedule to impose restrictions on trade and commerce.—*Omitted*].	216
307.	Appointment of authority for carrying out the purposes of articles 301 to 304.	216

PART XIV

SERVICES UNDER THE UNION AND THE STATES   217

CHAPTER I.—SERVICES

308.	Interpretation.	217
309.	Recruitment and conditions of service of persons serving the Union or a State.	217
310.	Tenure of office of persons serving the Union or a State.	217
311.	Dismissal, removal or reduction in rank of persons employed in civil capacities under the Union or a State.	218
312.	All-India services.	219
312A.	Power of Parliament to vary or revoke conditions of service of officers of certain services.	220
313.	Transitional provisions.	221
314.	[Provision for protection of existing officers of certain services.—*Omitted*].	221

CHAPTER II.—PUBLIC SERVICE COMMISSIONS

315.	Public Service Commissions for the Union and for the States.	221
316.	Appointment and term of office of members.	222
317.	Removal and suspension of a member of a Public Service Commission.	223
318.	Power to make regulations as to conditions of service of members and staff of the Commission.	224
319.	Prohibition as to the holding of offices by members of Commission on ceasing to be such members.	225
320.	Functions of Public Service Commissions.	226
321.	Power to extend functions of Public Service Commissions.	227
322.	Expenses of Public Service Commissions.	228
323.	Reports of Public Service Commissions.	228

PART XIV A

TRIBUNALS   229

323A.	Administrative tribunals.	229
323B.	Tribunals for other matters.	230

PART XV

ELECTIONS   232

324.	Superintendence, direction and control of elections to be vested in an Election Commission.	232
325.	No person to be ineligible for inclusion in, or to claim to be included in a special, electoral roll on grounds of religion, race, caste or sex.	233
326.	Elections to the House of the People and to the Legislative Assemblies of States to be on the basis of adult suffrage.	234
327.	Power of Parliament to make provision with respect to elections to Legislatures.	234

328. Power of Legislature of a State to make provision with respect to elections to such Legislature. 234

329. Bar to interference by courts in electoral matters. 234

329a. [Special provision as to elections to Parliament in the case of Prime Minister and Speaker.—*Omitted*]. 235

PART XVI

SPECIAL PROVISIONS RELATING TO CERTAIN CLASSES 235

330. Reservation of seats for Scheduled Castes and Scheduled Tribes in the House of the People. 235

331. Representation of the Anglo-Indian Community in the House of the People. 236

332. Reservation of seats for Scheduled Castes and Scheduled Tribes in the Legislative Assemblies of the States. 236

333. Representation of the Anglo-Indian community in the Legislative Assemblies of the States. 238

334. Reservation of seats and special representation to cease after certain period. 239

335. Claims of Scheduled Castes and Scheduled Tribes to services and posts. 239

336. Special provision for Anglo-Indian community in certain services. 240

337. Special provision with respect to educational grants for the benefit of Anglo-Indian community. 240

338. National Commission for Scheduled Castes. 241

338A. National Commission for Scheduled Tribes. 243

338B. National Commission for Backward Classes. 245

339. Control of the Union over the administration of Scheduled Areas and the welfare of Scheduled Tribes. 248

340. Appointment of a Commission to investigate the conditions of backward classes. 248

341. Scheduled Castes. 249

342. Scheduled Tribes. 249

342A. Socially and educationally backward classes. 250

PART XVII

OFFICIAL LANGUAGE 251

CHAPTER I.—LANGUAGE OF THE UNION

343. Official language of the Union. 251

344. Commission and Committee of Parliament on official language. 251

CHAPTER II.—REGIONAL LANGUAGES

345. Official language or languages of a State. 253

346. Official language for communication between one State and another or between a State and the Union. 253

347. Special provision relating to language spoken by a section of the population of a State. 253

CHAPTER III.—LANGUAGE OF THE SUPREME COURT, HIGH COURTS, ETC.

348. Language to be used in the Supreme Court and in the High Courts and for Acts, Bills, etc. 253

349. Special procedure for enactment of certain laws relating to language. 255

CHAPTER IV.—SPECIAL DIRECTIVES

350. Language to be used in representations for redress of grievances. 255

350A. Facilities for instruction in mother-tongue at primary stage. 255

350B. Special Officer for linguistic minorities. 255

351. Directive for development of the Hindi language. 256

PART XVIII

EMERGENCY PROVISIONS   256
352.   Proclamation of Emergency.   256
353.   Effect of Proclamation of Emergency.   259
354.   Application of provisions relating to distribution of revenues while a Proclamation
            of Emergency is in operation.   260
355.   Duty of the Union to protect States against external aggression and internal
            disturbance.   260
356.   Provisions in case of failure of constitutional machinery in States.   260
357.   Exercise of legislative powers under Proclamation issued under article 356.   263
358.   Suspension of provisions of article 19 during emergencies.   264
359.   Suspension of the enforcement of the rights conferred by Part III during
            emergencies.   265
359A.   [Application of this Part to the State of Punjab.—*Omitted*].   266
360.   Provisions as to financial emergency.   266

PART XIX

MISCELLANEOUS   268
361.   Protection of President and Governors and Rajpramukhs.   268
361A.   Protection of publication of proceedings of Parliament and State Legislatures. 269
361B.   Disqualification for appointment on remunerative political post.   269
362.   [Rights and privileges of Rulers of Indian States.—*Omitted*].   270
363.   Bar to interference by courts in disputes arising out of certain treaties, agreements, etc. 270
363A.   Recognition granted to Rulers of Indian States to cease and privy purses to be abolished. 271
364.   Special provisions as to major ports and aerodromes.   271
365.   Effect of failure to comply with, or to give effect to, directions given by the Union. 272
366.   Definitions.   272
367.   Interpretation.   276

PART XX

AMENDMENT OF THE CONSTITUTION   277
368.   Power of Parliament to amend the Constitution and procedure therefor.   277

PART XXI

TEMPORARY, TRANSITIONAL AND SPECIAL PROVISIONS   279
369.   Temporary power to Parliament to make laws with respect to certain matters in
            the State List as if they were matters in the Concurrent List.   279
370.   Temporary provisions with respect to the State of Jammu and Kashmir.   279
371.   Special provision with respect to the States of Maharashtra and Gujarat.   281
371A.   Special provision with respect to the State of Nagaland.   282
371B.   Special provision with respect to the State of Assam.   286
371C.   Special provision with respect to the State of Manipur.   287
371D.   Special provisions with respect to [the State of Andhra Pradesh or the State of
            Telangana.   287
371E.   Establishment of Central University in Andhra Pradesh.   291
371F.   Special provisions with respect to the State of Sikkim.   291
371G.   Special provision with respect to the State of Mizoram.   295
371H.   Special provision with respect to the State of Arunachal Pradesh.   295
371-I.   Special provision with respect to the State of Goa.   296
371J.   Special provisions with respect to the State of Karnataka.   296
372.   Continuance in force of existing laws and their adaptation.   297
372A.   Power of the President to adapt laws.   299
373.   Power of President to make order in respect of persons under preventive detention
            in certain cases.   299
374.   Provisions as to Judges of the Federal Court and proceedings pending in the
            Federal Court or before His Majesty in Council.   299

375.	Courts, authorities and officers to continue to function subject to the provisions of the Constitution.	300
376.	Provisions as to Judges of High Courts.	301
377.	Provisions as to Comptroller and Auditor-General of India.	301
378.	Provisions as to Public Service Commissions.	302
378A.	Special provision as to duration of Andhra Pradesh Legislative Assembly.	302
379.	[Provisions as to provisional Parliament and the Speaker and Deputy Speaker thereof.—*Omitted*].	303
380.	[Provision as to President.—*Omitted*].	303
381.	[Council of Ministers of the President.—*Omitted*].	303
382.	[Provisions as to provisional Legislatures for States in Part A of the First Schedule.—*Omitted*].	303
383.	[Provision as to Governors of Provinces.—*Omitted*].	303
384.	[Council of Ministers of the Governors.—*Omitted*].	303
385.	[Provision as to provisional Legislatures in States in Part B of the First Schedule.—*Omitted*].	303
386.	[Council of Ministers for States in Part B of the First Schedule.—*Omitted*].	303
387.	[Special provision as to determination of population for the purposes of certain elections.—*Omitted*].	303
388.	[Provisions as to the filling of casual vacancies in the provisional Parliament and provisional Legislatures of the States.—*Omitted*].	303
389.	[Provision as to Bills pending in the Dominion Legislatures and in the Legislatures of Provinces and Indian States.—*Omitted*].	303
390.	[Money received or raised or expenditure incurred between the commencement of the Constitution and the 31st day of March, 1950.—*Omitted*]	303
391.	[Power of the President to amend the First and Fourth Schedules in certain contingencies.—*Omitted*].	303
392.	Power of the President to remove difficulties.	304

PART XXII

SHORT TITLE, COMMENCEMENT, [AUTHORITATIVE TEXT IN HINDI] AND REPEALS		304
393.	Short title.	304
394.	Commencement.	304
394A.	Authoritative text in the Hindi language.	304
395.	Repeals.	305

SCHEDULE

FIRST SCHEDULE
I.	The States.	306
II.	The Union territories.	311

SECOND SCHEDULE
PART A—Provisions as to the President and the Governors of States	313
PART C—Provisions as to the Speaker and the Deputy Speaker of the House of the People and the Chairman and the Deputy Chairman of the Council of States and the Speaker and the Deputy Speaker of the Legislative Assembly and the Chairman and the Deputy Chairman of the Legislative Council of A State.	314
PART D—Provisions as to the Judges of the Supreme Court and of the High Courts.	315
PART E—Provisions as to the Comptroller and Auditor-General of India.	319

THIRD SCHEDULE
Forms of Oaths or Affirmations	320

FOURTH SCHEDULE
Allocation of seats in the Council of States	323

FIFTH SCHEDULE
Provisions as to the Administration and Control of Scheduled Areas and Scheduled Tribes	326
PART A—General	326
PART B—Administration and Control of Scheduled Areas and Scheduled Tribes	326

PART C—Scheduled Areas — 328
PART D—Amendment of the Schedule — 329

SIXTH SCHEDULE
Provisions as to the Administration of Tribal Areas in the States of Assam, Meghalaya,
Tripura and Mizoram — 330

SEVENTH SCHEDULE
List I—Union List — 359
List II—State List — 366
List III—Concurrent List — 370

EIGHTH SCHEDULE
Languages — 373

NINTH SCHEDULE
Validation of certain Acts and Regulations. — 374

TENTH SCHEDULE
Provisions as to disqualification on ground of defection. — 391

ELEVENTH SCHEDULE
Powers, authority and responsibilities of Panchayats. — 396

TWELFTH SCHEDULE
Powers, authority and responsibilities of Municipalities, etc. — 397

APPENDIX

APPENDIX I
The Constitution (One Hundredth Amendment) Act, 2015. — 398

APPENDIX II
The Constitution (Application to Jammu And Kashmir) Order, 2019. — 414

APPENDIX III
Declration Under Article 370(3) of the Constitution. — 415

PREFACE

In this edition, the text of the Constitution of India has been brought up-to-date by incorporating therein all the amendments up to the Constitution (One Hundred and Fifth Amendment) Act, 2021. The foot notes below the text indicate the Constitution Amendment Acts by which such amendments have been made.

The Constitution (One Hundredth Amendment) Act, 2015 containing details of acquired and transferred territories between the Governments of India and Bangladesh has been provided in APPENDIX I.

The Constitution (Application to Jammu and Kashmir) Order, 2019 and the declaration under article 370(3) of the Constitution have been provided respectively in Appendix II and Appendix III for reference.

Dr. Reeta Vasishta
New Delhi
Secretary to the Government of India

LIST OF ABBREVIATIONS USED

Art., arts	....	for Article, articles.
Cl., cls.	....	for Clause, clauses.
C.O.	....	for Constitution Order.
Ins.	....	for Inserted.
P., pp.	....	for Page, pages.
Pt.	....	for Part.
Rep.	....	for Repealed.
Ss., ss.	....	for Section, sections.
Sch.	....	for Schedule.
Subs.	....	for Substituted.
w.e.f.	....	for with effect from.
w.r.e.f.	....	for with retrospective effect from.

THE CONSTITUTION OF INDIA

PREAMBLE

WE, THE PEOPLE OF INDIA, having solemnly resolved to constitute India into a [1][SOVEREIGN SOCIALIST SECULAR DEMOCRATIC REPUBLIC] and to secure to all its citizens:

JUSTICE, social, economic and political;

LIBERTY of thought, expression, belief, faith and worship;

EQUALITY of status and of opportunity; and to promote among them all

FRATERNITY assuring the dignity of the individual and the [2][unity and integrity of the Nation];

IN OUR CONSTITUENT ASSEMBLY this twenty-sixth day of November, 1949, do HEREBY ADOPT, ENACT AND GIVE TO OURSELVES THIS CONSTITUTION.

---

1 Subs. by the Constitution (Forty-second Amendment) Act, 1976, s.2, for "SOVEREIGN DEMOCRATIC REPUBLIC" (w.e.f. 3-1-1977).

2 Subs. by s. 2, *ibid.*, for "Unity of the Nation" (w.e.f. 3-1-1977).

PART I

THE UNION AND ITS TERRITORY

1. **Name and territory of the Union.**—
   (1) India, that is Bharat, shall be a Union of States.
   [1][(2) The States and the territories thereof shall be as specified in the First Schedule.]
   (3) The territory of India shall comprise—
       (*a*) the territories of the States;
       [2][(*b*) the Union territories specified in the First Schedule; and]
       (*c*) such other territories as may be acquired.

2. **Admission or establishment of new States.**—Parliament may by law admit into the Union, or establish, new States on such terms and conditions as it thinks fit.

[3][**2A.** [*Sikkim to be associated with the Union.*].—Omitted *by the Constitution (Thirty-sixth Amendment) Act,* 1975, *s.* 5 (*w.e.f.* 26-4-1975).]

3. **Formation of new States and alteration of areas, boundaries or names of existing States.**—Parliament may by law—
   (*a*) form a new State by separation of territory from any State or by uniting two or more States or parts of States or by uniting any territory to a part of any State;
   (*b*) increase the area of any State;
   (*c*) diminish the area of any State;
   (*d*) alter the boundaries of any State;
   (*e*) alter the name of any State:

---

1 Subs. by the Constitution (Seventh Amendment) Act, 1956, s. 2, for cl. (2) (w.e.f. 1-11-1956).
2 Subs. by s. 2 *ibid*, for sub-clause (*b*) (w.e.f. 1-11-1956).
3 Ins. by the Constitution (Thirty-fifth Amendment) Act, 1974, s. 2 (w.e.f. 1-3-1975).

¹[Provided that no Bill for the purpose shall be introduced in either House of Parliament except on the recommendation of the President and unless, where the proposal contained in the Bill affects the area, boundaries or name of any of the States ²***, the Bill has been referred by the President to the Legislature of that State for expressing its views thereon within such period as may be specified in the reference or within such further period as the President may allow and the period so specified or allowed has expired.]

³[*Explanation I.*—In this article, in clauses (*a*) to (*e*), "State" includes a Union territory, but in the proviso, "State" does not include a Union territory.

Explanation II.—The power conferred on Parliament by clause (*a*) includes the power to form a new State or Union territory by uniting a part of any State or Union territory to any other State or Union territory.]

4.   **Laws made under articles 2 and 3 to provide for the amendment of the First and the Fourth Schedules and supplemental, incidental and consequential matters.**— (1) Any law referred to in article 2 or article 3 shall contain such provisions for the amendment of the First Schedule and the Fourth Schedule as may be necessary to give effect to the provisions of the law and may also contain such supplemental, incidental and consequential provisions (including provisions as to representation in Parliament and in the Legislature or Legislatures of the State or States affected by such law) as Parliament may deem necessary.

(2) No such law as aforesaid shall be deemed to be an amendment of this Constitution for the purposes of article 368.

---

1   Subs. by the Constitution (Fifth Amendment) Act, 1955, s. 2, for the proviso (w.e.f. 24-12-1955).
2   The words and letters "specified in Part A or Part B of the First Schedule" omitted by the Constitution (Seventh Amendment) Act, 1956, s. 29 and Sch. (w.e.f. 1-11-1956).
3   Ins. by the Constitution (Eighteenth Amendment) Act, 1966, s. 2 (w.e.f. 27-8-1966).

PART II

CITIZENSHIP

5.   **Citizenship at the commencement of the Constitution.**—At the commencement of this Constitution, every person who has his domicile in the territory of India and—

(*a*)   who was born in the territory of India; or

(*b*)   either of whose parents was born in the territory of India; or

(*c*)   who has been ordinarily resident in the territory of India for not less than five years immediately preceding such commencement,

shall be a citizen of India.

6.   **Rights of citizenship of certain persons who have migrated to India from Pakistan.**—Notwithstanding anything in article 5, a person who has migrated to the territory of India from the territory now included in Pakistan shall be deemed to be a citizen of India at the commencement of this Constitution if—

(*a*)   he or either of his parents or any of his grand-parents was born in India as defined in the Government of India Act, 1935 (as originally enacted); and

(*b*)   (*i*)   in the case where such person has so migrated before the nineteenth day of July, 1948, he has been ordinarily resident in the territory of India since the date of his migration, or

(*ii*)   in the case where such person has so migrated on or after the nineteenth day of July, 1948, he has been registered as a citizen of India by an officer appointed in that behalf by the Government of the Dominion of India on an application made by him therefor to such officer before the commencement of this Constitution in the form and manner prescribed by that Government:

Provided that no person shall be so registered unless he has been resident in the territory of India for at least six months immediately preceding the date of his application.

7. **Rights of citizenship of certain migrants to Pakistan.**— Notwithstanding anything in articles 5 and 6, a person who has after the first day of March, 1947, migrated from the territory of India to the territory now included in Pakistan shall not be deemed to be a citizen of India:

Provided that nothing in this article shall apply to a person who, after having so migrated to the territory now included in Pakistan, has returned to the territory of India under a permit for resettlement or permanent return issued by or under the authority of any law and every such person shall for the purposes of clause (*b*) of article 6 be deemed to have migrated to the territory of India after the nineteenth day of July, 1948.

8. **Rights of citizenship of certain persons of Indian origin residing outside India.**—Notwithstanding anything in article 5, any person who or either of whose parents or any of whose grand-parents was born in India as defined in the Government of India Act, 1935 (as originally enacted), and who is ordinarily residing in any country outside India as so defined shall be deemed to be a citizen of India if he has been registered as a citizen of India by the diplomatic or consular representative of India in the country where he is for the time being residing on an application made by him therefor to such diplomatic or consular representative, whether before or after the commencement of this Constitution, in the form and manner prescribed by the Government of the Dominion of India or the Government of India.

9. **Persons voluntarily acquiring citizenship of a foreign State not to be citizens.**—No person shall be a citizen of India by virtue of article 5, or be deemed to be a citizen of India by virtue of article 6 or article 8, if he has voluntarily acquired the citizenship of any foreign State.

10. **Continuance of the rights of citizenship.**—Every person who is or is deemed to be a citizen of India under any of the foregoing provisions of this Part shall, subject to the provisions of any law that may be made by Parliament, continue to be such citizen.

11. **Parliament to regulate the right of citizenship by law.**— Nothing in the foregoing provisions of this Part shall derogate

from the power of Parliament to make any provision with respect to the acquisition and termination of citizenship and all other matters relating to citizenship.

PART III

FUNDAMENTAL RIGHTS

General

12. **Definition.**—In this Part, unless the context otherwise requires, "the State" includes the Government and Parliament of India and the Government and the Legislature of each of the States and all local or other authorities within the territory of India or under the control of the Government of India.

13. **Laws inconsistent with or in derogation of the fundamental rights.**—(1) All laws in force in the territory of India immediately before the commencement of this Constitution, in so far as they are inconsistent with the provisions of this Part, shall, to the extent of such inconsistency, be void.

(2) The State shall not make any law which takes away or abridges the rights conferred by this Part and any law made in contravention of this clause shall, to the extent of the contravention, be void.

(3) In this article, unless the context otherwise requires,—

    (*a*) "law" includes any Ordinance, order, bye-law, rule, regulation, notification, custom or usage having in the territory of India the force of law;

    (*b*) "laws in force" includes laws passed or made by a Legislature or other competent authority in the territory of India before the commencement of this Constitution and not previously repealed, notwithstanding that any such law or any part thereof may not be then in operation either at all or in particular areas.

¹[(4) Nothing in this article shall apply to any amendment of this Constitution made under article 368.]

Right to Equality

14. **Equality before law.**—The State shall not deny to any person equality before the law or the equal protection of the laws within the territory of India.

15. **Prohibition of discrimination on grounds of religion, race, caste, sex or place of birth.**—(1) The State shall not discriminate against any citizen on grounds only of religion, race, caste, sex, place of birth or any of them.

(2) No citizen shall, on grounds only of religion, race, caste, sex, place of birth or any of them, be subject to any disability, liability, restriction or condition with regard to—

    (*a*)   access to shops, public restaurants, hotels and places of public entertainment; or

    (*b*)   the use of wells, tanks, bathing ghats, roads and places of public resort maintained wholly or partly out of State funds or dedicated to the use of the general public.

(3) Nothing in this article shall prevent the State from making any special provision for women and children.

²[(4) Nothing in this article or in clause (2) of article 29 shall prevent the State from making any special provision for the advancement of any socially and educationally backward classes of citizens or for the Scheduled Castes and the Scheduled Tribes.]

³[(5) Nothing in this article or in sub-clause (*g*) of clause (1) of article 19 shall prevent the State from making any special provision, by law, for the advancement of any socially and educationally backward classes of citizens or for the Scheduled Castes or the Scheduled Tribes in so far as such special provisions relate to their admission to educational institutions including private educational institutions, whether aided or unaided by the

---

1 Ins. by the Constitution (Twenty-fourth Amendment) Act, 1971, s. 2 (w.e.f. 5-11-1971).
2 Added by the Constitution (First Amendment) Act, 1951, s. 2 (w.e.f. 18-6-1951).
3 Ins. by the Constitution (Ninety-third Amendment) Act, 2005, s. 2 (w.e.f. 20-1-2006).

State, other than the minority educational institutions referred to in clause (1) of article 30.]

[1][(6) Nothing in this article or sub-clause (*g*) of clause (1) of article 19 or clause (2) of article 29 shall prevent the State from making,—

(*a*) any special provision for the advancement of any economically weaker sections of citizens other than the classes mentioned in clauses (4) and (5); and

(*b*) any special provision for the advancement of any economically weaker sections of citizens other than the classes mentioned in clauses (4) and (5) in so far as such special provisions relate to their admission to educational institutions including private educational institutions, whether aided or unaided by the State, other than the minority educational institutions referred to in clause (1) of article 30, which in the case of reservation would be in addition to the existing reservations and subject to a maximum of ten per cent. of the total seats in each category.

Explanation.—For the purposes of this article and article 16, "economically weaker sections" shall be such as may be notified by the State from time to time on the basis of family income and other indicators of economic disadvantage.]

16. Equality of opportunity in matters of public employment.—(1) There shall be equality of opportunity for all citizens in matters relating to employment or appointment to any office under the State.

(2) No citizen shall, on grounds only of religion, race, caste, sex, descent, place of birth, residence or any of them, be ineligible for, or discriminated against in respect of, any employment or office under the State.

(3) Nothing in this article shall prevent Parliament from making any law prescribing, in regard to a class or classes of employment or appointment to an office [2][under the Government of, or any

---

1 Ins. by the Constitution (One Hundred and Third Amendment) Act, 2019, s. 2 (w.e.f. 14-1-2019).
2 Subs. by the Constitution (Seventh Amendment) Act, 1956, s. 29 and Sch., for "under any State specified in the First Schedule or any local or other authority within its territory, any requirement as to residence within that State" (w.e.f. 1-11-1956).

local or other authority within, a State or Union territory, any requirement as to residence within that State or Union territory] prior to such employment or appointment.

(4) Nothing in this article shall prevent the State from making any provision for the reservation of appointments or posts in favour of any backward class of citizens which, in the opinion of the State, is not adequately represented in the services under the State.

[1][(4A) Nothing in this article shall prevent the State from making any provision for reservation [2][in matters of promotion, with consequential seniority, to any class] or classes of posts in the services under the State in favour of the Scheduled Castes and the Scheduled Tribes which, in the opinion of the State, are not adequately represented in the services under the State.]

[3][(4B) Nothing in this article shall prevent the State from considering any unfilled vacancies of a year which are reserved for being filled up in that year in accordance with any provision for reservation made under clause (4) or clause (4A) as a separate class of vacancies to be filled up in any succeeding year or years and such class of vacancies shall not be considered together with the vacancies of the year in which they are being filled up for determining the ceiling of fifty per cent. reservation on total number of vacancies of that year.]

(5) Nothing in this article shall affect the operation of any law which provides that the incumbent of an office in connection with the affairs of any religious or denominational institution or any member of the governing body thereof shall be a person professing a particular religion or belonging to a particular denomination.

[4][(6) Nothing in this article shall prevent the State from making any provision for the reservation of appointments or posts in

---

1 Ins. by the Constitution (Seventy-seventh Amendment) Act, 1995, s. 2 (w.e.f. 17-6-1995).
2 Subs. by the Constitution (Eighty-fifth Amendment) Act, 2001, s. 2, for certain words (retrospectively w.e.f. 17-6-1995).
3 Ins. by the Constitution (Eighty-first Amendment) Act, 2000, s. 2 (w.e.f. 9-6-2000).
4 Ins. by the Constitution (One Hundred and Third Amendment) Act, 2019, s. 3 (w.e.f. 14-1-2019).

favour of any economically weaker sections of citizens other than the classes mentioned in clause (4), in addition to the existing reservation and subject to a maximum of ten per cent. of the posts in each category.]

17. **Abolition of Untouchability.**—"Untouchability" is abolished and its practice in any form is forbidden. The enforcement of any disability arising out of "Untouchability" shall be an offence punishable in accordance with law.

18. **Abolition of titles.**—(1) No title, not being a military or academic distinction, shall be conferred by the State.

(2) No citizen of India shall accept any title from any foreign State.

(3) No person who is not a citizen of India shall, while he holds any office of profit or trust under the State, accept without the consent of the President any title from any foreign State.

(4) No person holding any office of profit or trust under the State shall, without the consent of the President, accept any present, emolument, or office of any kind from or under any foreign State.

Right to Freedom

19. **Protection of certain rights regarding freedom of speech, etc.—**

(1) All citizens shall have the right—

    (a) to freedom of speech and expression;

    (b) to assemble peaceably and without arms;

    (c) to form associations or unions[1] [or co-operative societies];

    (d) to move freely throughout the territory of India;

    (e) to reside and settle in any part of the territory of India; [2][and] [3][(/)****]

    (g) to practise any profession, or to carry on any occupation, trade or business.

---

1 Ins. by the Constitution (Ninety-seventh Amendment) Act, 2011, s. 2 (w.e.f. 8-2-2012).
2 Ins. by the Constitution (Forty-fourth Amendment) Act, 1978, s. 2 (w.e.f. 20-6-1979).
3 Sub-clause (f) omitted by s.2, *ibid.* (w.e.f. 20-6-1979).

[1][(2) Nothing in sub-clause (*a*) of clause (1) shall affect the operation of any existing law, or prevent the State from making any law, in so far as such law imposes reasonable restrictions on the exercise of the right conferred by the said sub-clause in the interests of 4[the sovereignty and integrity of India], the security of the State, friendly relations with foreign States, public order, decency or morality, or in relation to contempt of court, defamation or incitement to an offence.]

(3) Nothing in sub-clause (*b*) of the said clause shall affect the operation of any existing law in so far as it imposes, or prevent the State from making any law imposing, in the interests of 2[the sovereignty and integrity of India or] public order, reasonable restrictions on the exercise of the right conferred by the said sub-clause.

(4) Nothing in sub-clause (*c*) of the said clause shall affect the operation of any existing law in so far as it imposes, or prevent the State from making any law imposing, in the interests of 4[the sovereignty and integrity of India or] public order or morality, reasonable restrictions on the exercise of the right conferred by the said sub-clause.

(5) Nothing in 3[sub-clauses (*d*) and (*e*)] of the said clause shall affect the operation of any existing law in so far as it imposes, or prevent the State from making any law imposing, reasonable restrictions on the exercise of any of the rights conferred by the said sub-clauses either in the interests of the general public or for the protection of the interests of any Scheduled Tribe.

(6) Nothing in sub-clause (*g*) of the said clause shall affect the operation of any existing law in so far as it imposes, or prevent the State from making any law imposing, in the interests of the general public, reasonable restrictions on the exercise of the right conferred by the said sub-clause, and, in particular, 4[nothing in

---

1 Subs. by the Constitution (First Amendment) Act, 1951, s. 3, for cl. (2) (with retrospective effect).
2 Ins. by the Constitution (Sixteenth Amendment) Act, 1963, s. 2 (w.e.f. 5-10-1963).
3 Subs. by the Constitution (Forty-fourth Amendment) Act, 1978, s. 2, for "sub-clauses (*d*), (*e*) and (*f*)" (w.e.f. 20-6-1979).
4 Subs. by the Constitution (First Amendment) Act, 1951, s. 3, for certain words (w.e.f. 18-6-1951).

the said sub-clause shall affect the operation of any existing law in so far as it relates to, or prevent the State from making any law relating to,—

    (*i*) the professional or technical qualifications necessary for practising any profession or carrying on any occupation, trade or business, or

    (*ii*) the carrying on by the State, or by a corporation owned or controlled by the State, of any trade, business, industry or service, whether to the exclusion, complete or partial, of citizens or otherwise.]

20. **Protection in respect of conviction for offences.**—(1) No person shall be convicted of any offence except for violation of a law in force at the time of the commission of the Act charged as an offence, nor be subjected to a penalty greater than that which might have been inflicted under the law in force at the time of the commission of the offence.

(2) No person shall be prosecuted and punished for the same offence more than once.

(3) No person accused of any offence shall be compelled to be a witness against himself.

21. **Protection of life and personal liberty.**—No person shall be deprived of his life or personal liberty except according to procedure established by law.

¹[**21A.** **Right to education.**—The State shall provide free and compulsory education to all children of the age of six to fourteen years in such manner as the State may, by law, determine.]

22. **Protection against arrest and detention in certain cases.**— (1) No person who is arrested shall be detained in custody without being informed, as soon as may be, of the grounds for such arrest nor shall he be denied the right to consult, and to be defended by, a legal practitioner of his choice.

(2) Every person who is arrested and detained in custody shall be produced before the nearest magistrate within a period of twenty-four hours of such arrest excluding the time necessary for the journey from the place of arrest to the court of the

1 Ins. by the Constitution (Eighty-sixth Amendment) Act, 2002, s. 2 (w.e.f. 1-4-2010).

magistrate and no such person shall be detained in custody beyond the said period without the authority of a magistrate.

(3) Nothing in clauses (1) and (2) shall apply—

(a) to any person who for the time being is an enemy alien; or

(b) to any person who is arrested or detained under any law providing for preventive detention.

[1](4) No law providing for preventive detention shall authorise the detention of a person for a longer period than three months unless—

(a) an Advisory Board consisting of persons who are, or have been, or are qualified to be appointed as, Judges of a High Court has reported before the expiration of the said period of three months that there is in its opinion sufficient cause for such detention:

Provided that nothing in this sub-clause shall authorise the detention of any person beyond the maximum period prescribed by any law made by Parliament under sub-clause (b) of clause (7); or

(b) such person is detained in accordance with the provisions of any law made by Parliament under sub-clauses (a) and (b) of clause (7).

---

1 Cl. (4) shall stand substituted by the Constitution (Forty-fourth Amendment) Act, 1978, s. 3 (date yet to be notified) as—

"(4) No law providing for preventive detention shall authorise the detention of a person for a longer period than two months unless an Advisory Board constituted in accordance with the recommendations of the Chief Justice of the appropriate High Court has reported before the expiration of the said period of two months that there is in its opinion sufficient cause for such detention:

Provided that an Advisory Board shall consist of a Chairman and not less than two other members, and the Chairman shall be a serving Judge of the appropriate High Court and the other members shall be serving or retired Judges of any High Court:

Provided further that nothing in this clause shall authorise the detention of any person beyond the maximum period prescribed by any law made by Parliament under sub-clause (a) of clause (7).

Explanation.—In this clause, "appropriate High Court" means,—

(i) in the case of the detention of a person in pursuance of an order of detention made by the Government of India or an officer or authority subordinate to that Government, the High Court for the Union territory of Delhi;

(ii) in the case of the detention of a person in pursuance of an order of detention made by the Government of any State (other than a Union territory), the High Court for that State; and

(iii) in the case of the detention of a person in pursuance of an order of detention made by the administrator of a Union territory or an officer or authority subordinate to such administrator, such High Court as may be specified by or under any law made by Parliament in this behalf.".

(5) When any person is detained in pursuance of an order made under any law providing for preventive detention, the authority making the order shall, as soon as may be, communicate to such person the grounds on which the order has been made and shall afford him the earliest opportunity of making a representation against the order.

(6) Nothing in clause (5) shall require the authority making any such order as is referred to in that clause to disclose facts which such authority considers to be against the public interest to disclose.

(7) Parliament may by law prescribe—

[1](*a*) the circumstances under which, and the class or classes of cases in which, a person may be detained for a period longer than three months under any law providing for preventive detention without obtaining the opinion of an Advisory Board in accordance with the provisions of sub-clause (*a*) of clause (4);

[2](*b*) the maximum period for which any person may in any class or classes of cases be detained under any law providing for preventive detention; and

[3](*c*) the procedure to be followed by an Advisory Board in an inquiry under [4]sub-clause (*a*) of clause (4).

Right against Exploitation

23. **Prohibition of traffic in human beings and forced labour.—**
(1) Traffic in human beings and *beggar* and other similar forms of forced labour are prohibited and any contravention of this provision shall be an offence punishable in accordance with law.

(2) Nothing in this article shall prevent the State from imposing compulsory service for public purposes, and in imposing such

1 Sub-clause (*a*) shall stand omitted by the Constitution (Forty-fourth Amendment) Act, 1978, s. 3(*b*)(*i*) (date yet to be notified).
2 Sub-clause (*b*) shall stand re-lettered as sub-clause (*a*) by s. 3(*b*)(*ii*), *ibid.* (date yet to be notified).
3 Sub-clause (*c*) shall stand re-lettered as sub-clause (*b*) by s. 3(*b*)(*iii*), *ibid.* (date yet to be notified).
4 "sub-clause (*a*) of clause (4)" shall stand substituted as "clause (4)" by s. 3(*b*)(*iii*), *ibid.* (date yet to be notified).

service the State shall not make any discrimination on grounds only of religion, race, caste or class or any of them.

24. Prohibition of employment of children in factories, etc.— No child below the age of fourteen years shall be employed to work in any factory or mine or engaged in any other hazardous employment.

Right to Freedom of Religion

25. Freedom of conscience and free profession, practice and propagation of religion.—(1) Subject to public order, morality and health and to the other provisions of this Part, all persons are equally entitled to freedom of conscience and the right freely to profess, practice and propagate religion.

(2) Nothing in this article shall affect the operation of any existing law or prevent the State from making any law—

    (*a*) regulating or restricting any economic, financial, political or other secular activity which may be associated with religious practice;

    (*b*) providing for social welfare and reform or the throwing open of Hindu religious institutions of a public character to all classes and sections of Hindus.

Explanation I.—The wearing and carrying of *kirpans* shall be deemed to be included in the profession of the Sikh religion.

Explanation II.—In sub-clause (*b*) of clause (2), the reference to Hindus shall be construed as including a reference to persons professing the Sikh, Jaina or Buddhist religion, and the reference to Hindu religious institutions shall be construed accordingly.

26. Freedom to manage religious affairs.—Subject to public order, morality and health, every religious denomination or any section thereof shall have the right—

    (*a*) to establish and maintain institutions for religious and charitable purposes;

    (*b*) to manage its own affairs in matters of religion;

    (*c*) to own and acquire movable and immovable property; and

    (*d*) to administer such property in accordance with law.

27. **Freedom as to payment of taxes for promotion of any particular religion.**—No person shall be compelled to pay any taxes, the proceeds of which are specifically appropriated in payment of expenses for the promotion or maintenance of any particular religion or religious denomination.

28. **Freedom as to attendance at religious instruction or religious worship in certain educational institutions.**—(1) No religious instruction shall be provided in any educational institution wholly maintained out of State funds.

(2) Nothing in clause (1) shall apply to an educational institution which is administered by the State but has been established under any endowment or trust which requires that religious instruction shall be imparted in such institution.

(3) No person attending any educational institution recognised by the State or receiving aid out of State funds shall be required to take part in any religious instruction that may be imparted in such institution or to attend any religious worship that may be conducted in such institution or in any premises attached thereto unless such person or, if such person is a minor, his guardian has given his consent thereto.

Cultural and Educational Rights

29. **Protection of interests of minorities.**—(1) Any section of the citizens residing in the territory of India or any part thereof having a distinct language, script or culture of its own shall have the right to conserve the same.

(2) No citizen shall be denied admission into any educational institution maintained by the State or receiving aid out of State funds on grounds only of religion, race, caste, language or any of them.

30. **Right of minorities to establish and administer educational institutions.**—(1) All minorities, whether based on religion or language, shall have the right to establish and administer educational institutions of their choice.

[1](1A) In making any law providing for the compulsory acquisition of any property of an educational institution established and administered by a minority, referred to in clause (1), the State shall ensure that the amount fixed by or determined under such law for the acquisition of such property is such as would not restrict or abrogate the right guaranteed under that clause.]

(2) The State shall not, in granting aid to educational institutions, discriminate against any educational institution on the ground that it is under the management of a minority, whether based on religion or language.

[2]***

31. *[Compulsory acquisition of property.].—Omitted by the Constitution (Forty-fourth Amendment) Act, 1978, s. 6 (w.e.f. 20-6-1979).*

[3]*[Saving of Certain Laws]*

[4]**[31A. Saving of laws providing for acquisition of estates, etc.**—[5](1) Notwithstanding anything contained in article 13, no law providing for—

(a) the acquisition by the State of any estate or of any rights therein or the extinguishment or modification of any such rights, or

(b) the taking over of the management of any property by the State for a limited period either in the public interest or in order to secure the proper management of the property, or

(c) the amalgamation of two or more corporations either in the public interest or in order to secure the proper management of any of the corporations, or

(d) the extinguishment or modification of any rights of managing agents, secretaries and treasurers, managing

---

1 Ins. by the Constitution (Forty-fourth Amendment) Act, 1978, s. 4 (w.e.f. 20-6-1979).
2 Sub-heading "Right to Property" omitted by s. 5, *ibid.* (w.e.f. 20-6-1979).
3 Ins. by the Constitution (Forty-second Amendment) Act, 1976, s. 3 (w.e.f. 3-1-1977).
4 Ins. by the Constitution (First Amendment) Act, 1951, s. 4 (with retrospective effect).
5 Subs. by the Constitution (Fourth Amendment) Act, 1955, s. 3, for cl. (1) (with retrospective effect).

directors, directors or managers of corporations, or of any voting rights of shareholders thereof, or

(e) the extinguishment or modification of any rights accruing by virtue of any agreement, lease or licence for the purpose of searching for, or winning, any mineral or mineral oil, or the premature termination or cancellation of any such agreement, lease or licence,

shall be deemed to be void on the ground that it is inconsistent with, or takes away or abridges any of the rights conferred by [1][article 14 or article 19]:

Provided that where such law is a law made by the Legislature of a State, the provisions of this article shall not apply thereto unless such law, having been reserved for the consideration of the President, has received his assent:]

[2][Provided further that where any law makes any provision for the acquisition by the State of any estate and where any land comprised therein is held by a person under his personal cultivation, it shall not be lawful for the State to acquire any portion of such land as is within the ceiling limit applicable to him under any law for the time being in force or any building or structure standing thereon or appurtenant thereto, unless the law relating to the acquisition of such land, building or structure, provides for payment of compensation at a rate which shall not be less than the market value thereof.]

(2) In this article,—

[3][(a) the expression "estate" shall, in relation to any local area, have the same meaning as that expression or its local equivalent has in the existing law relating to land tenures in force in that area and shall also include—

(i) any *jagir*, *inam* or *muafi* or other similar grant and in the States of [4][Tamil Nadu] and Kerala, any *janmam* right;

---

1 Subs. by the Constitution (Forty-fourth Amendment) Act, 1978, s. 7, for "article 14, article 19 or article 31" (w.e.f. 20-6-1979).
2 Ins. by the Constitution (Seventeenth Amendment) Act, 1964, s. 2(i) (w.e.f. 20-6-1964).
3 Subs. by s.2(ii), *ibid.*, for sub-clause (a) (with retrospective effect).
4 Subs. by the Madras State (Alteration of Name) Act, 1968 (53 of 1968), s. 4, for "Madras" (w.e.f. 14-1-1969).

(*ii*) any land held under ryotwari settlement;

(*iii*) any land held or let for purposes of agriculture or for purposes ancillary thereto, including waste land, forest land, land for pasture or sites of buildings and other structures occupied by cultivators of land, agricultural labourers and village artisans;]

(*b*) the expression "rights", in relation to an estate, shall include any rights vesting in a proprietor, sub-proprietor, under-proprietor, tenure- holder, [1][*raiyat, under-raiyat*] or other intermediary and any rights or privileges in respect of land revenue.]

[2][**31B. Validation of certain Acts and Regulations.**—Without prejudice to the generality of the provisions contained in article 31A, none of the Acts and Regulations specified in the Ninth Schedule nor any of the provisions thereof shall be deemed to be void, or ever to have become void, on the ground that such Act, Regulation or provision is inconsistent with, or takes away or abridges any of the rights conferred by, any provisions of this Part, and notwithstanding any judgment, decree or order of any court or Tribunal to the contrary, each of the said Acts and Regulations shall, subject to the power of any competent Legislature to repeal or amend it, continue in force.]

[3][**31C. Saving of laws giving effect to certain directive principles.**— Notwithstanding anything contained in article 13, no law giving effect to the policy of the State towards securing [4][all or any of the principles laid down in Part IV] shall be deemed to be void on the ground that it is inconsistent with, or takes away or abridges any of the rights conferred by [5][article 14 or article 19;] [6][*and no law containing a declaration that it is for giving effect to such policy*

---

1 Ins. by the Constitution (Fourth Amendment) Act, 1955, s. 3 (with retrospective effect).
2 Ins. by the Constitution (First Amendment) Act, 1951, s. 5 (w.e.f. 18-6-1951).
3 Ins. by the Constitution (Twenty-fifth Amendment) Act, 1971, s. 3 (w.e.f. 20-4-1972).
4 Subs. by the Constitution (Forty-second Amendment) Act, 1976, s. 4, for "the principles specified in clause (*b*) or clause (*c*) of article 39" (w.e.f. 3-1-1977). Section 4 has been declared invalid by the Supreme Court in *Minerva Mills Ltd. and Others Vs Union of India and Others*, AIR 1980 SC 1789.
5 Subs. by the Constitution (Forty-fourth Amendment) Act, 1978, s. 8, for "article 14, article 19 or article 31" (w.e.f. 20-6-1979).
6 The words in italics struck down by the Supreme Court in *Kesavananda Bharati vs. State of Kerala*, AIR 1973, SC 1461.

shall be called in question in any court on the ground that it does not give effect to such policy]:

Provided that where such law is made by the Legislature of a State, the provisions of this article shall not apply thereto unless such law, having been reserved for the consideration of the President, has received his assent.]

¹**31D.** [*Saving of laws in respect of anti-national activities.*].—*Omitted by the Constitution (Forty-third Amendment) Act,*1977, *s.* 2 (*w.e.f.*13-4-1978).

Right to Constitutional Remedies

32. Remedies for enforcement of rights conferred by this Part.—(1) The right to move the Supreme Court by appropriate proceedings for the enforcement of the rights conferred by this Part is guaranteed.

(2) The Supreme Court shall have power to issue directions or orders or writs, including writs in the nature of *habeas corpus, mandamus,* prohibition, *quo warranto* and *certiorari,* whichever may be appropriate, for the enforcement of any of the rights conferred by this Part.

(3) Without prejudice to the powers conferred on the Supreme Court by clauses (1) and (2), Parliament may by law empower any other court to exercise within the local limits of its jurisdiction all or any of the powers exercisable by the Supreme Court under clause (2).

(4) The right guaranteed by this article shall not be suspended except as otherwise provided for by this Constitution.

²**32A.** [*Constitutional validity of State laws not to be considered in proceedings under article 32.*].—*Omitted by the Constitution (Forty-third Amendment) Act,* 1977, *s.* 3 (*w.e.f.* 13-4-1978).

³[**33. Power of Parliament to modify the rights conferred by this Part in their application to Forces, etc.**—Parliament may, by law, determine to what extent any of the rights conferred by this Part shall, in their application to,—

---

1 Ins. by the Constitution (Forty-second Amendment) Act, 1976, s. 5 (w.e.f. 3-1-1977).
2 Ins. by the Constitution (Forty-second Amendment) Act, 1976, s. 6 (w.e.f. 1-2-1977).
3 Subs. by the Constitution (Fiftieth Amendment) Act, 1984, s. 2, for art. 33 (w.e.f. 11-9-1984).

(*a*)   the members of the Armed Forces; or

(*b*)   the members of the Forces charged with the maintenance of public order; or

(*c*)   persons employed in any bureau or other organisation established by the State for purposes of intelligence or counter intelligence; or

(*d*)   person employed in, or in connection with, the telecommunication systems set up for the purposes of any Force, bureau or organisation referred to in clauses (*a*) to (*c*),

be restricted or abrogated so as to ensure the proper discharge of their duties and the maintenance of discipline among them.]

34.   **Restriction on rights conferred by this Part while martial law is in force in any area.**—Notwithstanding anything in the foregoing provisions of this Part, Parliament may by law indemnify any person in the service of the Union or of a State or any other person in respect of any act done by him in connection with the maintenance or restoration of order in any area within the territory of India where martial law was in force or validate any sentence passed, punishment inflicted, forfeiture ordered or other act done under martial law in such area.

35.   **Legislation to give effect to the provisions of this Part.**— Notwithstanding anything in this Constitution,—

(*a*)   Parliament shall have, and the Legislature of a State shall not have, power to make laws—

(*i*)   with respect to any of the matters which under clause (3) of article 16, clause (3) of article 32, article 33 and article 34 may be provided for by law made by Parliament; and

(*ii*)   for prescribing punishment for those acts which are declared to be offences under this Part,

and Parliament shall, as soon as may be after the commencement of this Constitution, make laws for prescribing punishment for the acts referred to in sub-clause (*ii*);

(*b*)   any law in force immediately before the commencement of this Constitution in the territory of India with respect to any of the matters referred to in sub-clause (*i*) of clause (*a*) or providing for punishment for any act referred to in sub-clause (*ii*) of that clause shall, subject to the terms thereof and to any adaptations and modifications that may be made therein under article 372, continue in force until altered or repealed or amended by Parliament.

Explanation.—In this article, the expression "law in force" has the same meaning as in article 372.

PART IV

DIRECTIVE PRINCIPLES OF STATE POLICY

36. **Definition.**—In this Part, unless the context otherwise requires, "the State" has the same meaning as in Part III.

37. **Application of the principles contained in this Part.**—The provisions contained in this Part shall not be enforceable by any court, but the principles therein laid down are nevertheless fundamental in the governance of the country and it shall be the duty of the State to apply these principles in making laws.

38. **State to secure a social order for the promotion of welfare of the people.**—[1][(1)] The State shall strive to promote the welfare of the people by securing and protecting as effectively as it may a social order in which justice, social, economic and political, shall inform all the institutions of the national life.

[2][(2) The State shall, in particular, strive to minimise the inequalities in income, and endeavour to eliminate inequalities in status, facilities and opportunities, not only amongst individuals but also amongst groups of people residing in different areas or engaged in different vocations.]

---

1 Art. 38 renumbered as cl. (1) by the Constitution (Forty-fourth Amendment) Act, 1978, s. 9 (w.e.f. 20-6-1979).
2 Ins. by s. 9, *ibid.* (w.e.f. 20-6-1979).

39. **Certain principles of policy to be followed by the State.**—The State shall, in particular, direct its policy towards securing—

(a) that the citizens, men and women equally, have the right to an adequate means of livelihood;

(b) that the ownership and control of the material resources of the community are so distributed as best to subserve the common good;

(c) that the operation of the economic system does not result in the concentration of wealth and means of production to the common detriment;

(d) that there is equal pay for equal work for both men and women;

(e) that the health and strength of workers, men and women, and the tender age of children are not abused and that citizens are not forced by economic necessity to enter avocations unsuited to their age or strength;

[1][(f) that children are given opportunities and facilities to develop in a healthy manner and in conditions of freedom and dignity and that childhood and youth are protected against exploitation and against moral and material abandonment.]

[2][**39A.** **Equal justice and free legal aid.**—The State shall secure that the operation of the legal system promotes justice, on a basis of equal opportunity, and shall, in particular, provide free legal aid, by suitable legislation or schemes or in any other way, to ensure that opportunities for securing justice are not denied to any citizen by reason of economic or other disabilities.]

40. **Organisation of village panchayats.**—The State shall take steps to organise village panchayats and endow them with such powers and authority as may be necessary to enable them to function as units of self-government.

41. **Right to work, to education and to public assistance in certain cases.**—The State shall, within the limits of its economic capacity and development, make effective provision for securing

---

1 Subs. by the Constitution (Forty-second Amendment) Act, 1976, s. 7, for cl. (f) (w.e.f. 3-1-1977).
2 Ins. by s. 8, *ibid.* (w.e.f. 3-1-1977).

the right to work, to education and to public assistance in cases of unemployment, old age, sickness and disablement, and in other cases of undeserved want.

42. **Provision for just and humane conditions of work and maternity relief.**—The State shall make provision for securing just and humane conditions of work and for maternity relief.

43. **Living wage, etc., for workers.**—The State shall endeavour to secure, by suitable legislation or economic organisation or in any other way, to all workers, agricultural, industrial or otherwise, work, a living wage, conditions of work ensuring a decent standard of life and full enjoyment of leisure and social and cultural opportunities and, in particular, the State shall endeavour to promote cottage industries on an individual or co-operative basis in rural areas.

[1][43A. **Participation of workers in management of industries.**—The State shall take steps, by suitable legislation or in any other way, to secure the participation of workers in the management of undertakings, establishments or other organisations engaged in any industry.]

[2][43B. **Promotion of co-operative societies.**—The State shall endeavour to promote voluntary formation, autonomous functioning, democratic control and professional management of co-operative societies.]

44. **Uniform civil code for the citizens.**—The State shall endeavour to secure for the citizens a uniform civil code throughout the territory of India.

[3][45. **Provision for early childhood care and education to children below the age of six years.**—The State shall endeavour to provide early childhood care and education for all children until they complete the age of six years.]

46. **Promotion of educational and economic interests of Scheduled Castes, Scheduled Tribes and other weaker sections.**—The State shall promote with special care the educational and economic interests of the weaker sections of

1 Ins. by s. 9, *ibid.* (w.e.f. 3-1-1977).
2 Ins. by the Constitution (Ninety-seventh Amendment) Act, 2011, s. 3 (w.e.f. 15-2-2012).
3 Subs. by the Constitution (Eighty-sixth Amendment) Act, 2002, s. 3, for art. 45 (w.e.f. 1-4-2010).

the people, and, in particular, of the Scheduled Castes and the Scheduled Tribes, and shall protect them from social injustice and all forms of exploitation.

47. Duty of the State to raise the level of nutrition and the standard of living and to improve public health.—The State shall regard the raising of the level of nutrition and the standard of living of its people and the improvement of public health as among its primary duties and, in particular, the State shall endeavour to bring about prohibition of the consumption except for medicinal purposes of intoxicating drinks and of drugs which are injurious to health.

48. Organisation of agriculture and animal husbandry.— The State shall endeavour to organise agriculture and animal husbandry on modern and scientific lines and shall, in particular, take steps for preserving and improving the breeds, and prohibiting the slaughter, of cows and calves and other milch and draught cattle.

¹[**48A. Protection and improvement of environment and safeguarding of forests and wild life.**—The State shall endeavour to protect and improve the environment and to safeguard the forests and wild life of the country.]

49. Protection of monuments and places and objects of national importance.—It shall be the obligation of the State to protect every monument or place or object of artistic or historic interest, ²[declared by or under law made by Parliament] to be of national importance, from spoliation, disfigurement, destruction, removal, disposal or export, as the case may be.

50. Separation of judiciary from executive.—The State shall take steps to separate the judiciary from the executive in the public services of the State.

51. Promotion of international peace and security.—The State shall endeavour to—

(*a*) promote international peace and security;

(*b*) maintain just and honourable relations between nations;

---

1 Ins. by the Constitution (Forty-second Amendment) Act, 1976, s. 10 (w.e.f. 3-1-1977).
2 Subs. by the Constitution (Seventh Amendment) Act, 1956, s. 27, for "declared by Parliament by law" (w.e.f. 1-11-1956).

(c) foster respect for international law and treaty obligations in the dealings of organised peoples with one another; and

(d) encourage settlement of international disputes by arbitration.

¹PART IV A

FUNDAMENTAL DUTIES

51A. **Fundamental duties.**—It shall be the duty of every citizen of India—

(a) to abide by the Constitution and respect its ideals and institutions, the National Flag and the National Anthem;

(b) to cherish and follow the noble ideals which inspired our national struggle for freedom;

(c) to uphold and protect the sovereignty, unity and integrity of India;

(d) to defend the country and render national service when called upon to do so;

(e) to promote harmony and the spirit of common brotherhood amongst all the people of India transcending religious, linguistic and regional or sectional diversities; to renounce practices derogatory to the dignity of women;

(f) to value and preserve the rich heritage of our composite culture;

(g) to protect and improve the natural environment including forests, lakes, rivers and wild life, and to have compassion for living creatures;

(h) to develop the scientific temper, humanism and the spirit of inquiry and reform;

(i) to safeguard public property and to abjure violence;

(j) to strive towards excellence in all spheres of individual

---

1 Ins. by the Constitution (Forty-second Amendment) Act, 1976, s. 11 (w.e.f. 3-1-1977).

and collective activity so that the nation constantly rises to higher levels of endeavour and achievement;]

[1][(*k*) who is a parent or guardian to provide opportunities for education to his child or, as the case may be, ward between the age of six and fourteen years.]

PART V

THE UNION

Chapter I.—The Executive

The President and Vice-President

52. **The President of India.**—There shall be a President of India.

53. **Executive power of the Union.**—(1) The executive power of the Union shall be vested in the President and shall be exercised by him either directly or through officers subordinate to him in accordance with this Constitution.

(2) Without prejudice to the generality of the foregoing provision, the supreme command of the Defence Forces of the Union shall be vested in the President and the exercise thereof shall be regulated by law.

(3) Nothing in this article shall—

(*a*) be deemed to transfer to the President any functions conferred by any existing law on the Government of any State or other authority; or

(*b*) prevent Parliament from conferring by law functions on authorities other than the President.

54. **Election of President.**—The President shall be elected by the members of an electoral college consisting of—

(*a*) the elected members of both Houses of Parliament; and

(*b*) the elected members of the Legislative Assemblies of the States.

---

1 Ins. by the Constitution (Eighty-sixth Amendment) Act, 2002, s. 4 (w.e.f. 1-4-2010).

¹[*Explanation.*—In this article and in article 55, "State" includes the National Capital Territory of Delhi and the Union territory of *Pondicherry.]

55. Manner of election of President.—(1) As far as practicable, there shall be uniformity in the scale of representation of the different States at the election of the President.

(2) For the purpose of securing such uniformity among the States *inter se* as well as parity between the States as a whole and the Union, the number of votes which each elected member of Parliament and of the Legislative Assembly of each State is entitled to cast at such election shall be determined in the following manner:—

    (*a*)   every elected member of the Legislative Assembly of a State shall have as many votes as there are multiples of one thousand in the quotient obtained by dividing the population of the State by the total number of the elected members of the Assembly;

    (*b*)   if, after taking the said multiples of one thousand, the remainder is not less than five hundred, then the vote of each member referred to in sub-clause (*a*) shall be further increased by one;

    (*c*)   each elected member of either House of Parliament shall have such number of votes as may be obtained by dividing the total number of votes assigned to the members of the Legislative Assemblies of the States under sub-clauses (*a*) and (*b*) by the total number of the elected members of both Houses of Parliament, fractions exceeding one-half being counted as one and other fractions being disregarded.

(3) The election of the President shall be held in accordance with the system of proportional representation by means of the single transferable vote and the voting at such election shall be by secret ballot.

---

1 Ins. by the Constitution (Seventieth Amendment) Act, 1992, s. 2 (w.e.f. 1-6-1995).
* Now Puducherry *vide* the Pondicherry (Alteration of Name) Act, 2006 (44 of 2006), s. 3 (w.e.f. 1-10-2006).

¹[*Explanation*.—In this article, the expression "population" means the population as ascertained at the last preceding census of which the relevant figures have been published:

Provided that the reference in this *Explanation* to the last preceding census of which the relevant figures have been published shall, until the relevant figures for the first census taken after the year ²[2026] have been published, be construed as a reference to the 1971 census.]

56. **Term of office of President**.—(1) The President shall hold office for a term of five years from the date on which he enters upon his office:

Provided that—

(*a*) the President may, by writing under his hand addressed to the Vice-President, resign his office;

(*b*) the President may, for violation of the Constitution, be removed from office by impeachment in the manner provided in article 61;

(*c*) the President shall, notwithstanding the expiration of his term, continue to hold office until his successor enters upon his office.

(2) Any resignation addressed to the Vice-President under clause (*a*) of the proviso to clause (1) shall forthwith be communicated by him to the Speaker of the House of the People.

57. **Eligibility for re-election**.—A person who holds, or who has held, office as President shall, subject to the other provisions of this Constitution, be eligible for re-election to that office.

58. **Qualifications for election as President**.—(1) No person shall be eligible for election as President unless he—

(*a*) is a citizen of India,

(*b*) has completed the age of thirty-five years, and

(*c*) is qualified for election as a member of the House of the People.

(2) A person shall not be eligible for election as President if he holds any office of profit under the Government of India or the

1 Subs. by the Constitution (Forty-second Amendment) Act, 1976, s. 12, for the *Explanation* (w.e.f. 3-1-1977).
2 Subs. by the Constitution (Eighty-fourth Amendment) Act, 2001, s. 2, for "2000" (w.e.f. 21-2-2002).

Government of any State or under any local or other authority subject to the control of any of the said Governments.

Explanation.—For the purposes of this article, a person shall not be deemed to hold any office of profit by reason only that he is the President or Vice-President of the Union or the Governor [1]*** of any State or is a Minister either for the Union or for any State.

59. **Conditions of President's office.**—(1) The President shall not be a member of either House of Parliament or of a House of the Legislature of any State, and if a member of either House of Parliament or of a House of the Legislature of any State be elected President, he shall be deemed to have vacated his seat in that House on the date on which he enters upon his office as President.

(2) The President shall not hold any other office of profit.

(3) The President shall be entitled without payment of rent to the use of his official residences and shall be also entitled to such emoluments, allowances and privileges as may be determined by Parliament by law and, until provision in that behalf is so made, such emoluments, allowances and privileges as are specified in the Second Schedule.

(4) The emoluments and allowances of the President shall not be diminished during his term of office.

60. **Oath or affirmation by the President.**—Every President and every person acting as President or discharging the functions of the President shall, before entering upon his office, make and subscribe in the presence of the Chief Justice of India or, in his absence, the senior-most Judge of the Supreme Court available, an oath or affirmation in the following form, that is to say—

"I, A.B., do $\frac{\text{swear in the name of God}}{\text{solemnly affirm}}$ that I will faithfully execute the office of President (or discharge the functions of the President) of India and will to the best of my ability preserve, protect and defend the Constitution and the law and that I will devote myself to the service and well-being of the people of India.".

---

1 The words "or Rajpramukh or Uparajpramukh" omitted by the Constitution (Seventh Amendment) Act, 1956, s. 29 and Sch. (w.e.f. 1-11-1956).

61.   **Procedure for impeachment of the President.**—(1) When a
President is to be impeached for violation of the Constitution,
the charge shall be preferred by either House of Parliament.

(2) No such charge shall be preferred unless—

> (*a*) the proposal to prefer such charge is contained in a
> resolution which has been moved after at least fourteen
> days' notice in writing signed by not less than one-fourth
> of the total number of members of the House has been
> given of their intention to move the resolution, and
>
> (*b*) such resolution has been passed by a majority of not
> less than two-thirds of the total membership of the
> House.

(3) When a charge has been so preferred by either House of
Parliament, the other House shall investigate the charge or cause
the charge to be investigated and the President shall have the
right to appear and to be represented at such investigation.

(4) If as a result of the investigation a resolution is passed by
a majority of not less than two-thirds of the total membership
of the House by which the charge was investigated or caused
to be investigated, declaring that the charge preferred against
the President has been sustained, such resolution shall have the
effect of removing the President from his office as from the date
on which the resolution is so passed.

62.   **Time of holding election to fill vacancy in the office of
President and the term of office of person elected to fill
casual vacancy.**—(1) An election to fill a vacancy caused by the
expiration of the term of office of President shall be completed
before the expiration of the term.

(2) An election to fill a vacancy in the office of President occurring
by reason of his death, resignation or removal, or otherwise shall
be held as soon as possible after, and in no case later than six
months from, the date of occurrence of the vacancy; and the
person elected to fill the vacancy shall, subject to the provisions
of article 56, be entitled to hold office for the full term of five
years from the date on which he enters upon his office.

63.   **The Vice-President of India.**—There shall be a Vice-President
of India.

64. **The Vice-President to be *ex officio* Chairman of the Council of States.**—The Vice-President shall be *ex officio* Chairman of the Council of the States and shall not hold any other office of profit: Provided that during any period when the Vice-President acts as President or discharges the functions of the President under article 65, he shall not perform the duties of the office of Chairman of the Council of States and shall not be entitled to any salary or allowance payable to the Chairman of the Council of States under article 97.

65. **The Vice-President to act as President or to discharge his functions during casual vacancies in the office, or during the absence, of President.**—(1) In the event of the occurrence of any vacancy in the office of the President by reason of his death, resignation or removal, or otherwise, the Vice-President shall act as President until the date on which a new President elected in accordance with the provisions of this Chapter to fill such vacancy enters upon his office.

(2) When the President is unable to discharge his functions owing to absence, illness or any other cause, the Vice-President shall discharge his functions until the date on which the President resumes his duties.

(3) The Vice-President shall, during, and in respect of, the period while he is so acting as, or discharging the functions of, President, have all the powers and immunities of the President and be entitled to such emoluments, allowances and privileges as may be determined by Parliament by law and, until provision in that behalf is so made, such emoluments, allowances and privileges as are specified in the Second Schedule.

66. **Election of Vice-President.**—(1) The Vice-President shall be elected by the [1][members of an electoral college consisting of the members of both Houses of Parliament] in accordance with the system of proportional representation by means of the single transferable vote and the voting at such election shall be by secret ballot.

---

1 Subs. by the Constitution (Eleventh Amendment) Act, 1961, s. 2, for "members of both Houses of Parliament assembled at a joint meeting" (w.e.f. 19-12-1961).

(2) The Vice-President shall not be a member of either House of Parliament or of a House of the Legislature of any State, and if a member of either House of Parliament or of a House of the Legislature of any State be elected Vice-President, he shall be deemed to have vacated his seat in that House on the date on which he enters upon his office as Vice-President.

(3) No person shall be eligible for election as Vice-President unless he—

    (a) is a citizen of India;

    (b) has completed the age of thirty-five years; and

    (c) is qualified for election as a member of the Council of States.

(4) A person shall not be eligible for election as Vice-President if he holds any office of profit under the Government of India or the Government of any State or under any local or other authority subject to the control of any of the said Governments.

Explanation.—For the purposes of this article, a person shall not be deemed to hold any office of profit by reason only that he is the President or Vice-President of the Union or the Governor [1]*** of any State or is a Minister either for the Union or for any State.

67. Term of office of Vice-President.—The Vice-President shall hold office for a term of five years from the date on which he enters upon his office:

Provided that—

    (a) a Vice-President may, by writing under his hand addressed to the President, resign his office;

    (b) a Vice-President may be removed from his office by a resolution of the Council of States passed by a majority of all the then members of the Council and agreed to by the House of the People; but no resolution for the purpose of this clause shall be moved unless at least fourteen days' notice has been given of the intention to move the resolution;

---

1 The words "or Rajpramukh or Uparajpramukh" omitted by the Constitution (Seventh Amendment) Act, 1956, s. 29 and Sch. (w.e.f. 1-11-1956).

(c) a Vice-President shall, notwithstanding the expiration of his term, continue to hold office until his successor enters upon his office.

68. Time of holding election to fill vacancy in the office of Vice-President and the term of office of person elected to fill casual vacancy.—(1) An election to fill a vacancy caused by the expiration of the term of office of Vice-President shall be completed before the expiration of the term.

(2) An election to fill a vacancy in the office of Vice-President occurring by reason of his death, resignation or removal, or otherwise shall be held as soon as possible after the occurrence of the vacancy, and the person elected to fill the vacancy shall, subject to the provisions of article 67, be entitled to hold office for the full term of five years from the date on which he enters upon his office.

69. Oath or affirmation by the Vice-President.—Every Vice-President shall, before entering upon his office, make and subscribe before the President, or some person appointed in that behalf by him, an oath or affirmation in the following form, that is to say—

"I, A.B., do $\dfrac{\text{swear in the name of God}}{\text{solemnly affirm}}$ that I will bear true faith and allegiance to the Constitution of India as by law established and that I will faithfully discharge the duty upon which I am about to enter.".

70. Discharge of President's functions in other contingencies.— Parliament may make such provision as it thinks fit for the discharge of the functions of the President in any contingency not provided for in this Chapter.

[1][**71. Matters relating to, or connected with, the election of a President or Vice-President.**—(1) All doubts and disputes arising out of or in connection with the election of a President or Vice-President shall be inquired into and decided by the Supreme Court whose decision shall be final.

---

1 Subs. by the Constitution (Thirty-ninth Amendment) Act, 1975, s. 2 (w.e.f 10-8-1975) and further subs. by the Constitution (Forty-fourth Amendment) Act, 1978, s. 10. (w.e.f. 20-6-1979).

(2) If the election of a person as President or Vice-President is declared void by the Supreme Court, acts done by him in the exercise and performance of the powers and duties of the office of President or Vice-President, as the case may be, on or before the date of the decision of the Supreme Court shall not be invalidated by reason of that declaration.

(3) Subject to the provisions of this Constitution, Parliament may by law regulate any matter relating to or connected with the election of a President or Vice-President.

(4) The election of a person as President or Vice-President shall not be called in question on the ground of the existence of any vacancy for whatever reason among the members of the electoral college electing him.]

72. **Power of President to grant pardons, etc., and to suspend, remit or commute sentences in certain cases.**—(1) The President shall have the power to grant pardons, reprieves, respites or remissions of punishment or to suspend, remit or commute the sentence of any person convicted of any offence—

   (*a*) in all cases where the punishment or sentence is by a Court Martial;

   (*b*) in all cases where the punishment or sentence is for an offence against any law relating to a matter to which the executive power of the Union extends;

   (*c*) in all cases where the sentence is a sentence of death.

(2) Nothing in sub-clause (*a*) of clause (1) shall affect the power conferred by law on any officer of the Armed Forces of the Union to suspend, remit or commute a sentence passed by a Court Martial.

(3) Nothing in sub-clause (*c*) of clause (1) shall affect the power to suspend, remit or commute a sentence of death exercisable by the Governor [1]*** of a State under any law for the time being in force.

73. **Extent of executive power of the Union.**—(1) Subject to the provisions of this Constitution, the executive power of the

---

1 The words "or Rajpramukh" omitted by the Constitution (Seventh Amendment) Act, 1956, s. 29 and Sch. (w.e.f. 1-11-1956).

Union shall extend—

(*a*) to the matters with respect to which Parliament has power to make laws; and

(*b*) to the exercise of such rights, authority and jurisdiction as are exercisable by the Government of India by virtue of any treaty or agreement:

Provided that the executive power referred to in sub-clause (*a*) shall not, save as expressly provided in this Constitution or in any law made by Parliament, extend in any State [1]*** to matters with respect to which the Legislature of the State has also power to make laws.

(2) Until otherwise provided by Parliament, a State and any officer or authority of a State may, notwithstanding anything in this article, continue to exercise in matters with respect to which Parliament has power to make laws for that State such executive power or functions as the State or officer or authority thereof could exercise immediately before the commencement of this Constitution.

Council of Ministers

74. **Council of Ministers to aid and advise President.**—[2][(1) There shall be a Council of Ministers with the Prime Minister at the head to aid and advise the President who shall, in the exercise of his functions, act in accordance with such advice:]
[3][Provided that the President may require the Council of Ministers to reconsider such advice, either generally or otherwise, and the President shall act in accordance with the advice tendered after such reconsideration.]

(2) The question whether any, and if so what, advice was tendered by Ministers to the President shall not be inquired into in any court.

1 The words and letters "specified in Part A or Part B of the First Schedule" omitted by the Constitution (Seventh Amendment) Act, 1956, s. 29 and Sch. (w.e.f. 1-11-1956).
2 Subs. by the Constitution (Forty-second Amendment) Act, 1976, s.13, for cl. (1) (w.e.f. 3-1-1977).
3 Ins. by the Constitution (Forty-fourth Amendment) Act, 1978, s. 11 (w.e.f. 20-6-1979).

75. **Other provisions as to Ministers.**—(1) The Prime Minister shall be appointed by the President and the other Ministers shall be appointed by the President on the advice of the Prime Minister.

[1][(1A) The total number of Ministers, including the Prime Minister, in the Council of Ministers shall not exceed fifteen per cent. of the total number of members of the House of the People.

(1B) A member of either House of Parliament belonging to any political party who is disqualified for being a member of that House under paragraph 2 of the Tenth Schedule shall also be disqualified to be appointed as a Minister under clause (1) for duration of the period commencing from the date of his disqualification till the date on which the term of his office as such member would expire or where he contests any election to either House of Parliament before the expiry of such period, till the date on which he is declared elected, whichever is earlier.]

(2) The Ministers shall hold office during the pleasure of the President.

(3) The Council of Ministers shall be collectively responsible to the House of the People.

(4) Before a Minister enters upon his office, the President shall administer to him the oaths of office and of secrecy according to the forms set out for the purpose in the Third Schedule.

(5) A Minister who for any period of six consecutive months is not a member of either House of Parliament shall at the expiration of that period cease to be a Minister.

(6) The salaries and allowances of Ministers shall be such as Parliament may from time to time by law determine and, until Parliament so determines, shall be as specified in the Second Schedule.

The Attorney-General for India

76. **Attorney-General for India.**—(1) The President shall appoint a person who is qualified to be appointed a Judge of the Supreme Court to be Attorney-General for India.

---

1 Ins. by the Constitution (Ninety-first Amendment) Act, 2003, s. 2 (w.e.f. 1-1-2004).

(2) It shall be the duty of the Attorney-General to give advice to the Government of India upon such legal matters, and to perform such other duties of a legal character, as may from time to time be referred or assigned to him by the President, and to discharge the functions conferred on him by or under this Constitution or any other law for the time being in force.

(3) In the performance of his duties the Attorney-General shall have right of audience in all courts in the territory of India.

(4) The Attorney-General shall hold office during the pleasure of the President, and shall receive such remuneration as the President may determine.

Conduct of Government Business

77. **Conduct of business of the Government of India.**—(1) All executive action of the Government of India shall be expressed to be taken in the name of the President.

(2) Orders and other instruments made and executed in the name of the President shall be authenticated in such manner as may be specified in rules[1] to be made by the President, and the validity of an order or instrument which is so authenticated shall not be called in question on the ground that it is not an order or instrument made or executed by the President.

(3) The President shall make rules for the more convenient transaction of the business of the Government of India, and for the allocation among Ministers of the said business.

[2](4) *   *   *   *

78. **Duties of Prime Minister as respects the furnishing of information to the President, etc.**—It shall be the duty of the Prime Minister—

   (a) to communicate to the President all decisions of the Council of Ministers relating to the administration of the affairs of the Union and proposals for legislation;

---

1 *See* notification No. S.O. 2297, dated the 3rd November, 1958, Gazette of India, Extraordinary, Pt. II, Sec. 3 (ii), p. 1315, as amended from time to time.

2 Cl. (4) was ins. by the Constitution (Forty-second Amendment) Act, 1976, s.14 (w.e.f. 3-1-1977) and omitted by the Constitution (Forty-fourth Amendment) Act, 1978, s. 12 (w.e.f. 20-6-1979).

(b) to furnish such information relating to the administration of the affairs of the Union and proposals for legislation as the President may call for; and

(c) if the President so requires, to submit for the consideration of the Council of Ministers any matter on which a decision has been taken by a Minister but which has not been considered by the Council.

Chapter II.—Parliament

General

79. Constitution of Parliament.—There shall be a Parliament for the Union which shall consist of the President and two Houses to be known respectively as the Council of States and the House of the People.

80. Composition of the Council of States.—(1) [1][2*** The Council of States] shall consist of—

(a) twelve members to be nominated by the President in accordance with the provisions of clause (3); and

(b) not more than two hundred and thirty-eight representatives of the States 3[and of the Union territories].

(2) The allocation of seats in the Council of States to be filled by representatives of the States 1[and of the Union territories] shall be in accordance with the provisions in that behalf contained in the Fourth Schedule.

(3) The members to be nominated by the President under sub-clause (a) of clause (1) shall consist of persons having special knowledge or practical experience in respect of such matters as the following, namely:—

Literature, science, art and social service.

---

1 Subs. by the Constitution (Thirty-fifth Amendment) Act, 1974, s. 3, for "The Council of States" (w.e.f. 1-3-1975).

2 The words "Subject to the provisions of paragraph 4 of the Tenth Schedule," omitted by the Constitution (Thirty-sixth Amendment) Act, 1975, s. 5 (w.e.f. 26-4-1975).

3 Added by the Constitution (Seventh Amendment) Act, 1956, s. 3 (w.e.f. 1-11-1956).

(4) The representatives of each State [1]*** in the Council of States shall be elected by the elected members of the Legislative Assembly of the State in accordance with the system of proportional representation by means of the single transferable vote.

(5) The representatives of the [2][Union territories] in the Council of States shall be chosen in such manner as Parliament may by law prescribe.

[3][**81. Composition of the House of the People.**—(1) [4][Subject to the provisions of article 331 [5]***], the House of the People shall consist of—

> (*a*) not more than [6][five hundred and thirty members] chosen by direct election from territorial constituencies in the States, and
>
> (*b*) not more than [7][twenty members] to represent the Union territories, chosen in such manner as Parliament may by law provide.

(2) For the purposes of sub-clause (*a*) of clause (1),—

> (*a*) there shall be allotted to each State a number of seats in the House of the People in such manner that the ratio between that number and the population of the State is, so far as practicable, the same for all States; and
>
> (*b*) each State shall be divided into territorial constituencies in such manner that the ratio between the population of each constituency and the number of seats allotted to it is, so far as practicable, the same throughout the State:

---

1 The words and letters "specified in Part A or Part B of the First Schedule" omitted by the Constitution (Seventh Amendment) Act, 1956, s. 3 (w.e.f. 1-11-1956).
2 Subs. by s. 3, *ibid*, for "States specified in Part C of First Schedule" (w.e.f. 1-11-1956).
3 Subs. by s. 4, *ibid*. for arts. 81 and 82 (w.e.f. 1-11-1956).
4 Subs. by the Constitution (Thirty-fifth Amendment) Act, 1974, s. 4, for "subject to the provisions of article 331" (w.e.f. 1-3-1975).
5 The words and figure "and paragraph 4 of the Tenth Schedule" omitted by the Constitution (Thirty-sixth Amendment) Act, 1975, s. 5 (w.e.f. 26-4-1975).
6 Subs. by the Goa, Daman and Diu Reorganisation Act, 1987 (18 of 1987), s. 63, for "five hundred and twenty-five members" (w.e.f. 30-5-1987).
7 Subs. by the Constitution (Thirty-first Amendment) Act, 1973, s. 2, for "twenty-five members" (w.e.f. 17-10-1973).

[Provided that the provisions of sub-clause (*a*) of this clause shall not be applicable for the purpose of allotment of seats in the House of the People to any State so long as the population of that State does not exceed six millions.]

(3) In this article, the expression "population" means the population as ascertained at the last preceding census of which the relevant figures have been published.

²[Provided that the reference in this clause to the last preceding census of which the relevant figures have been published shall, until the relevant figures for the first census taken after the year ³[2026] have been published, ⁴[be construed,—

> (*i*) for the purposes of sub-clause (*a*) of clause (2) and the proviso to that clause, as a reference to the 1971 census; and
>
> (ii) for the purposes of sub-clause (*b*) of clause (2) as a reference to the ⁵[2001] census.]]

82.   Readjustment after each census.—Upon the completion of each census, the allocation of seats in the House of the People to the States and the division of each State into territorial constituencies shall be readjusted by such authority and in such manner as Parliament may by law determine:

Provided that such readjustment shall not affect representation in the House of the People until the dissolution of the then existing House:

⁶[Provided further that such readjustment shall take effect from such date as the President may, by order, specify and until such readjustment takes effect, any election to the House may be held on the basis of the territorial constituencies existing before such readjustment:

Provided also that until the relevant figures for the first census

---

1   Ins. by s. 2, *ibid*. (w.e.f. 17-10-1973).
2   Added by the Constitution (Forty-second Amendment) Act, 1976, s. 15 (w.e.f. 3-1-1977).
3   Subs. by the Constitution (Eighty-fourth Amendment) Act, 2001, s. 3, for "2000" (w.e.f. 21-2-2002).
4   Subs. by s.3, *ibid*, for certain words (w.e.f. 21-2-2002).
5   Subs. by the Constitution (Eighty-seventh Amendment) Act, 2003, s. 2, for "1991" (w.e.f. 22-6-2003).
6   Ins. by the Constitution (Forty-second Amendment) Act, 1976, s. 16 (w.e.f. 3-1-1977).

taken after the year [1][2026] have been published, it shall not be necessary to [2][readjust—

    (*i*) the allocation of seats in the House of the People to the States as readjusted on the basis of the 1971 census; and

    (*ii*) the division of each State into territorial constituencies as may be readjusted on the basis of the [3][2001] census,

under this article.]]

83.   **Duration of Houses of Parliament.**—(1) The Council of States shall not be subject to dissolution, but as nearly as possible one-third of the members thereof shall retire as soon as may be on the expiration of every second year in accordance with the provisions made in that behalf by Parliament by law.

(2) The House of the People, unless sooner dissolved, shall continue for [4][five years] from the date appointed for its first meeting and no longer and the expiration of the said period of [1][five years] shall operate as a dissolution of the House:

Provided that the said period may, while a Proclamation of Emergency is in operation, be extended by Parliament by law for a period not exceeding one year at a time and not extending in any case beyond a period of six months after the Proclamation has ceased to operate.

84.   **Qualification for membership of Parliament.**—A person shall not be qualified to be chosen to fill a seat in Parliament unless he—

    [5][(*a*) is a citizen of India, and makes and subscribes before some person authorised in that behalf by the Election Commission an oath or affirmation according to the form set out for the purpose in the Third Schedule;]

1 Subs. by the Constitution (Eighty-fourth Amendment) Act, 2001, s. 4, for "2000" (w.e.f. 21-2-2002).
2 Subs. by s.4, *ibid.*, for certain words (w.e.f. 21-2-2002).
3 Subs. by the Constitution (Eighty-seventh Amendment) Act, 2003, s. 3, for "1991" (w.e.f. 22-6-2003).
4 Subs. by the Constitution (Forty-second Amendment) Act, 1976, s. 17, for "five years" (w.e.f. 3-1-1977) and further subs. by the Constitution (Forty-fourth Amendment) Act, 1978, s. 13, for "six years" (w.e.f. 20-6-1979).
5 Subs. by the Constitution (Sixteenth Amendment) Act, 1963, s. 3, for cl.(*a*) (w.e.f. 5-10-1963).

(*b*)   is, in the case of a seat in the Council of States, not less than thirty years of age and, in the case of a seat in the House of the People, not less than twenty-five years of age; and

(*c*)   possesses such other qualifications as may be prescribed in that behalf by or under any law made by Parliament.

[1][85.   **Sessions of Parliament, prorogation and dissolution.**—(1) The President shall from time to time summon each House of Parliament to meet at such time and place as he thinks fit, but six months shall not intervene between its last sitting in one session and the date appointed for its first sitting in the next session.

(2) The President may from time to time—

(*a*)   prorogue the Houses or either House;

(*b*)   dissolve the House of the People.]

86.   **Right of President to address and send messages to Houses.**—(1) The President may address either House of Parliament or both Houses assembled together, and for that purpose require the attendance of members.

(2) The President may send messages to either House of Parliament, whether with respect to a Bill then pending in Parliament or otherwise, and a House to which any message is so sent shall with all convenient dispatch consider any matter required by the message to be taken into consideration.

87.   **Special address by the President.**—(1) At the commencement of [2][the first session after each general election to the House of the People and at the commencement of the first session of each year] the President shall address both Houses of Parliament assembled together and inform Parliament of the causes of its summons.

(2) Provision shall be made by the rules regulating the procedure of either House for the allotment of time for discussion of the matters referred to in such address [3]***.

---

1   Subs. by the Constitution (First Amendment) Act, 1951, s. 6, for art. 85 (w.e.f. 18-6-1951).
2   Subs. by the Constitution (First Amendment) Act, 1951, s. 7, for "every session" (w.e.f. 18-6-1951).
3   The words "and for the precedence of such discussion over other business of the House" omitted by s. 7, *ibid.* (w.e.f. 18-6-1951).

88. **Rights of Ministers and Attorney-General as respects Houses.**—Every Minister and the Attorney-General of India shall have the right to speak in, and otherwise to take part in the proceedings of, either House, any joint sitting of the Houses, and any committee of Parliament of which he may be named a member, but shall not by virtue of this article be entitled to vote.

Officers of Parliament

89. **The Chairman and Deputy Chairman of the Council of States.**—(1) The Vice-President of India shall be *ex officio* Chairman of the Council of States.

(2) The Council of States shall, as soon as may be, choose a member of the Council to be Deputy Chairman thereof and, so often as the office of Deputy Chairman becomes vacant, the Council shall choose another member to be Deputy Chairman thereof.

90. **Vacation and resignation of, and removal from, the office of Deputy Chairman.**—A member holding office as Deputy Chairman of the Council of States—

(a) shall vacate his office if he ceases to be a member of the Council;

(b) may at any time, by writing under his hand addressed to the Chairman, resign his office; and

(c) may be removed from his office by a resolution of the Council passed by a majority of all the then members of the Council:

Provided that no resolution for the purpose of clause *(c)* shall be moved unless at least fourteen days' notice has been given of the intention to move the resolution.

91. **Power of the Deputy Chairman or other person to perform the duties of the office of, or to act as, Chairman.**—(1) While the office of Chairman is vacant, or during any period when the Vice-President is acting as, or discharging the functions of, President, the duties of the office shall be performed by the Deputy Chairman, or, if the office of Deputy Chairman is also vacant, by such member of the Council of States as the President may appoint for the purpose.

(2) During the absence of the Chairman from any sitting of the Council of States the Deputy Chairman, or, if he is also absent, such person as may be determined by the rules of procedure of the Council, or, if no such person is present, such other person as may be determined by the Council, shall act as Chairman.

92. **The Chairman or the Deputy Chairman not to preside while a resolution for his removal from office is under consideration.**—(1) At any sitting of the Council of States, while any resolution for the removal of the Vice-President from his office is under consideration, the Chairman, or while any resolution for the removal of the Deputy Chairman from his office is under consideration, the Deputy Chairman, shall not, though he is present, preside, and the provisions of clause (2) of article 91 shall apply in relation to every such sitting as they apply in relation to a sitting from which the Chairman, or, as the case may be, the Deputy Chairman, is absent.

(2) The Chairman shall have the right to speak in, and otherwise to take part in the proceedings of, the Council of States while any resolution for the removal of the Vice-President from his office is under consideration in the Council, but, notwithstanding anything in article 100, shall not be entitled to vote at all on such resolution or on any other matter during such proceedings.

93. **The Speaker and Deputy Speaker of the House of the People.**—The House of the People shall, as soon as may be, choose two members of the House to be respectively Speaker and Deputy Speaker thereof and, so often as the office of Speaker or Deputy Speaker becomes vacant, the House shall choose another member to be Speaker or Deputy Speaker, as the case may be.

94. **Vacation and resignation of, and removal from, the offices of Speaker and Deputy Speaker.**—A member holding office as Speaker or Deputy Speaker of the House of the People—

　　(a) shall vacate his office if he ceases to be a member of the House of the People;

　　(b) may at any time, by writing under his hand addressed, if such member is the Speaker, to the Deputy Speaker, and if such member is the Deputy Speaker, to the Speaker, resign his office; and

72

(c) may be removed from his office by a resolution of the House of the People passed by a majority of all the then members of the House:

Provided that no resolution for the purpose of clause (c) shall be moved unless at least fourteen days' notice has been given of the intention to move the resolution:

Provided further that, whenever the House of the People is dissolved, the Speaker shall not vacate his office until immediately before the first meeting of the House of the People after the dissolution.

95. **Power of the Deputy Speaker or other person to perform the duties of the office of, or to act as, Speaker.**—(1) While the office of Speaker is vacant, the duties of the office shall be performed by the Deputy Speaker or, if the office of Deputy Speaker is also vacant, by such member of the House of the People as the President may appoint for the purpose.

(2) During the absence of the Speaker from any sitting of the House of the People the Deputy Speaker or, if he is also absent, such person as may be determined by the rules of procedure of the House, or, if no such person is present, such other person as may be determined by the House, shall act as Speaker.

96. **The Speaker or the Deputy Speaker not to preside while a resolution for his removal from office is under consideration.**—(1) At any sitting of the House of the People, while any resolution for the removal of the Speaker from his office is under consideration, the Speaker, or while any resolution for the removal of the Deputy Speaker from his office is under consideration, the Deputy Speaker, shall not, though he is present, preside, and the provisions of clause (2) of article 95 shall apply in relation to every such sitting as they apply in relation to a sitting from which the Speaker, or, as the case may be, the Deputy Speaker, is absent.

(2) The Speaker shall have the right to speak in, and otherwise to take part in the proceedings of, the House of the People while any resolution for his removal from office is under consideration in the House and shall, notwithstanding anything in article 100, be entitled to vote only in the first instance on such resolution or

on any other matter during such proceedings but not in the case of an equality of votes.

97. **Salaries and allowances of the Chairman and Deputy Chairman and the Speaker and Deputy Speaker.**—There shall be paid to the Chairman and the Deputy Chairman of the Council of States, and to the Speaker and the Deputy Speaker of the House of the People, such salaries and allowances as may be respectively fixed by Parliament by law and, until provision in that behalf is so made, such salaries and allowances as are specified in the Second Schedule.

98. **Secretariat of Parliament.**—(1) Each House of Parliament shall have a separate secretarial staff:

Provided that nothing in this clause shall be construed as preventing the creation of posts common to both Houses of Parliament.

(2) Parliament may by law regulate the recruitment, and the conditions of service of persons appointed, to the secretarial staff of either House of Parliament.

(3) Until provision is made by Parliament under clause (2), the President may, after consultation with the Speaker of the House of the People or the Chairman of the Council of States, as the case may be, make rules regulating the recruitment, and the conditions of service of persons appointed, to the secretarial staff of the House of the People or the Council of States, and any rules so made shall have effect subject to the provisions of any law made under the said clause.

Conduct of Business

99. **Oath or affirmation by members.**—Every member of either House of Parliament shall, before taking his seat, make and subscribe before the President, or some person appointed in that behalf by him, an oath or affirmation according to the form set out for the purpose in the Third Schedule.

100. **Voting in Houses, power of Houses to act notwithstanding vacancies and quorum.**—(1) Save as otherwise provided in this Constitution, all questions at any sitting of either House or

joint sitting of the Houses shall be determined by a majority of votes of the members present and voting, other than the Speaker or person acting as Chairman or Speaker.

The Chairman or Speaker, or person acting as such, shall not vote in the first instance, but shall have and exercise a casting vote in the case of an equality of votes.

(2) Either House of Parliament shall have power to act notwithstanding any vacancy in the membership thereof, and any proceedings in Parliament shall be valid notwithstanding that it is discovered subsequently that some person who was not entitled so to do sat or voted or otherwise took part in the proceedings.

[1][(3) Until Parliament by law otherwise provides, the quorum to constitute a meeting of either House of Parliament shall be one-tenth of the total number of members of the House.

(4) If at any time during a meeting of a House there is no quorum, it shall be the duty of the Chairman or Speaker, or person acting as such, either to adjourn the House or to suspend the meeting until there is a quorum.]

Disqualifications of Members

101. Vacation of seats.—(1) No person shall be a member of both Houses of Parliament and provision shall be made by Parliament by law for the vacation by a person who is chosen a member of both Houses of his seat in one House or the other.

(2) No person shall be a member both of Parliament and of a House of the Legislature of a State [2]***, and if a person is chosen a member both of Parliament and of a House of the Legislature of [3][a State], then, at the expiration of such period as may be specified in rules* made by the President, that person's seat

---

1 Cls. (3) and (4) omitted by the Constitution (Forty-second Amendment) Act, 1973, s. 18 (date not notified). This amendment was omitted by the Constitution (Forty-fourth Amendment) Act, 1978, s. 45 (w.e.f. 20-6-1979).

2 The words and letters "specified in Part A or Part B of the First Schedule" omitted by the Constitution (Seventh Amendment) Act, 1956, s. 29 and Sch. (w.e.f. 1-11-1956).

3 Subs. by s. 29 and Sch., *ibid.*, for "such a State" (w.e.f. 1-11-1956).

* *See* the Prohibition of Simultaneous Membership Rules, 1950, published with the Ministry of Law, notification No. F. 46/50-C, dated the 26th January, 1950, Gazette of India, Extraordinary, P. 678.

in Parliament shall become vacant, unless he has previously resigned his seat in the Legislature of the State.

(3) If a member of a House of the Legislature of a State—

(*a*) becomes subject to any of the disqualifications mentioned in [1][clause (1) or clause (2) of article 191]; or

[2][(*b*) resigns his seat by writing under his hand addressed to the speaker or the Chairman, as the case may be, and his resignation is accepted by the Speaker or the Chairman, as the case may be,]

his seat shall thereupon become vacant:

[3][Provided that in the case of any resignation referred to in sub-clause (*b*), if from information received or otherwise and after making such inquiry as he thinks fit, the Speaker or the Chairman, as the case may be, is satisfied that such resignation is not voluntary or genuine, he shall not accept such resignation.]

(4) If for a period of sixty days a member of a House of the Legislature of a State is without permission of the House absent from all meetings thereof, the House may declare his seat vacant:

Provided that in computing the said period of sixty days no account shall be taken of any period during which the House is prorogued or is adjourned for more than four consecutive days.

102. **Disqualifications for membership.**—(1) A person shall be disqualified for being chosen as, and for being, a member of the Legislative Assembly or Legislative Council of a State—

[4][(*a*) if he holds any office of profit under the Government of India or the Government of any State specified in the First Schedule, other than an office declared by the Legislature of the State by law not to disqualify its holder;]

1 Subs. by the Constitution (Fifty-second Amendment) Act, 1985, s. 4, for "clause (*1*) of article 191" (w.e.f. 1-3-1985).

2 Subs. by the Constitution (Thirty-third Amendment) Act, 1974, s. 3 (w.e.f. 19-5-1974).

3 Ins. by s. 3, *ibid.* (w.e.f. 19-5-1974).

4 Subs. by the Constitution (Forty-second Amendment) Act, 1976, s. 32 to read as "(*a*) if he holds any such office of profit under the Government of India or the Government of any State specified in the First Schedule as is declared by Parliament by law to disqualify its holder" (date not notified). This amendment was omitted by the Constitution (Forty-fourth Amendment) Act, 1978, s. 45 (w.e.f. 20-6-1979).

(*b*) if he is of unsound mind and stands so declared by a competent court;

(*c*) if he is an undischarged insolvent;

(*d*) if he is not a citizen of India, or has voluntarily acquired the citizenship of a foreign State, or is under any acknowledgment of allegiance or adherence to a foreign State;

(*e*) if he is so disqualified by or under any law made by Parliament.

[1][*Explanation.*—For the purposes of this clause], a person shall not be deemed to hold an office of profit under the Government of India or the Government of any State specified in the First Schedule by reason only that he is a Minister either for the Union or for such State.

[2][(2) A person shall be disqualified for being a member of the Legislative Assembly or Legislative Council of a State if he is so disqualified under the Tenth Schedule.]

[3][**103.   Decision on questions as to disqualifications of members.**— (1) If any question arises as to whether a member of a House of the Legislature of a State has become subject to any of the disqualifications mentioned in clause (1) of article 191, the question shall be referred for the decision of the Governor and his decision shall be final.

(2) Before giving any decision on any such question, the Governor shall obtain the opinion of the Election Commission and shall act according to such opinion.]

104.   Penalty for sitting and voting before making oath or affirmation under article 188 or when not qualified or when disqualified.—If a person sits or votes as a member of the Legislative Assembly or the Legislative Council of a State before he has complied with the requirements of article 188, or when

---

1 Subs. by the Constitution (Fifty-second Amendment) Act, 1985, s. 5, for "(2) For the purposes of this article" (w.e.f. 1-3-1985).

2 Ins. by s. 5, *ibid.* (w.e.f. 1-3-1985).

3 Subs. by the Constitution (Forty-second Amendment) Act, 1976, s. 33, for art. 192 (w.e.f. 3-1-1977) and further subs. by the Constitution (Forty-fourth Amendment) Act, 1978, s. 25, for art. 192 (w.e.f. 20-6-1979).

he knows that he is not qualified or that he is disqualified for membership thereof, or that he is prohibited from so doing by the provisions of any law made by Parliament or the Legislature of the State, he shall be liable in respect of each day on which he so sits or votes to a penalty of five hundred rupees to be recovered as a debt due to the State.

Powers, Privileges and Immunities of
State Legislatures and their Members

105. Powers, privileges, etc., of the Houses of Legislatures and of the members and committees thereof.—(1) Subject to the provisions of this Constitution and to the rules and standing orders regulating the procedure of the Legislature, there shall be freedom of speech in the Legislature of every State.

(2) No member of the Legislature of a State shall be liable to any proceedings in any court in respect of anything said or any vote given by him in the Legislature or any committee thereof, and no person shall be so liable in respect of the publication by or under the authority of a House of such a Legislature of any report, paper, votes or proceedings.

[1][(3) In other respects, the powers, privileges and immunities of a House of the Legislature of a State, and of the members and the committees of a House of such Legislature, shall be such as may from time to time be defined by the Legislature by law, and, until so defined, [2][shall be those of that House and of its members and committees immediately before the coming into force of section 26 of the Constitution (Forty-fourth Amendment) Act, 1978].

(4) The provisions of clauses (1), (2) and (3) shall apply in relation to persons who by virtue of this Constitution have the right to speak in, and otherwise to take part in the proceedings of, a

---

1 Subs. by the Constitution (Forty-second Amendment) Act, 1976, s. 21 (date not notified). This amendment was omitted by the Constitution (Forty-fourth Amendment) Act, 1978, s. 45 (w.e.f. 20-6-1979).

2 Subs. by the Constitution (Forty-fourth Amendment) Act, 1978, s. 26, for certain words (w.e.f. 20-6-1979).

House of the Legislature of a State or any committee thereof as they apply in relation to members of that Legislature.

106. Salaries and allowances of members.—Members of the Legislative Assembly and the Legislative Council of a State shall be entitled to receive such salaries and allowances as may from time to time be determined, by the Legislature of the State by law and, until provision in that respect is so made, salaries and allowances at such rates and upon such conditions as were immediately before the commencement of this Constitution applicable in the case of members of the Legislative Assembly of the corresponding Province.

Legislative Procedure

107. Provisions as to introduction and passing of Bills.—(1) Subject to the provisions of articles 198 and 207 with respect to Money Bills and other financial Bills, a Bill may originate in either House of the Legislature of a State which has a Legislative Council.

(2) Subject to the provisions of articles 197 and 198, a Bill shall not be deemed to have been passed by the Houses of the Legislature of a State having a Legislative Council unless it has been agreed to by both Houses, either without amendment or with such amendments only as are agreed to by both Houses.

(3) A Bill pending in the Legislature of a State shall not lapse by reason of the prorogation of the House or Houses thereof.

(4) A Bill pending in the Legislative Council of a State which has not been passed by the Legislative Assembly shall not lapse on a dissolution of the Assembly.

(5) A Bill which is pending in the Legislative Assembly of a State, or which having been passed by the Legislative Assembly is pending in the Legislative Council, shall lapse on a dissolution of the Assembly.

108. Joint sitting of both Houses in certain cases.—(1) If after a Bill has been passed by one House and transmitted to the other House—

(*a*) the Bill is rejected by the other House; or

79

(*b*) the Houses have finally disagreed as to the amendments to be made in the Bill; or

(*c*) more than six months elapse from the date of the reception of the Bill by the other House without the Bill being passed by it,

the President may, unless the Bill has elapsed by reason of a dissolution of the House of the People, notify to the Houses by message if they are sitting or by public notification if they are not sitting, his intention to summon them to meet in a joint sitting for the purpose of deliberating and voting on the Bill:

Provided that nothing in this clause shall apply to a Money Bill.

(2) In reckoning any such period of six months as is referred to in clause (1), no account shall be taken of any period during which the House referred to in sub-clause (*c*) of that clause is prorogued or adjourned for more than four consecutive days.

(3) Where the President has under clause (1) notified his intention of summoning the Houses to meet in a joint sitting, neither House shall proceed further with the Bill, but the President may at any time after the date of his notification summon the Houses to meet in a joint sitting for the purpose specified in the notification and, if he does so, the Houses shall meet accordingly.

(4) If at the joint sitting of the two Houses the Bill, with such amendments, if any, as are agreed to in joint sitting, is passed by a majority of the total number of members of both Houses present and voting, it shall be deemed for the purposes of this Constitution to have been passed by both Houses:

Provided that at a joint sitting—

(*a*) if the Bill, having been passed by one House, has not been passed by the other House with amendments and returned to the House in which it originated, no amendment shall be proposed to the Bill other than such amendments (if any) as are made necessary by the delay in the passage of the Bill;

(*b*) if the Bill has been so passed and returned, only such amendments as aforesaid shall be proposed to the Bill and such other amendments as are relevant to the matters with respect to which the Houses have not agreed;

and the decision of the person presiding as to the amendments which are admissible under this clause shall be final.

(5) A joint sitting may be held under this article and a Bill passed thereat, notwithstanding that a dissolution of the House of the People has intervened since the President notified his intention to summon the Houses to meet therein.

109. **Special procedure in respect of Money Bills.**—(1) A Money Bill shall not be introduced in the Council of States.

(2) After a Money Bill has been passed by the House of the People it shall be transmitted to the Council of States for its recommendations and the Council of States shall within a period of fourteen days from the date of its receipt of the Bill return the Bill to the House of the People with its recommendations and the House of the People may thereupon either accept or reject all or any of the recommendations of the Council of States.

(3) If the House of the People accepts any of the recommendations of the Council of States, the Money Bill shall be deemed to have been passed by both Houses with the amendments recommended by the Council of States and accepted by the House of the People.

(4) If the House of the People does not accept any of the recommendations of the Council of States, the Money Bill shall be deemed to have been passed by both Houses in the form in which it was passed by the House of the People without any of the amendments recommended by the Council of States.

(5) If a Money Bill passed by the House of the People and transmitted to the Council of States for its recommendations is not returned to the House of the People within the said period of fourteen days, it shall be deemed to have been passed by both Houses at the expiration of the said period in the form in which it was passed by the House of the People.

110. **Definition of "Money Bills".**—(1) For the purposes of this Chapter, a Bill shall be deemed to be a Money Bill if it contains only provisions dealing with all or any of the following matters, namely:—

    (*a*) the imposition, abolition, remission, alteration or regulation of any tax;

(b)   the regulation of the borrowing of money or the giving of any guarantee by the Government of India, or the amendment of the law with respect to any financial obligations undertaken or to be undertaken by the Government of India;

(c)   the custody of the Consolidated Fund or the Contingency Fund of India, the payment of moneys into or the withdrawal of moneys from any such Fund;

(d)   the appropriation of moneys out of the Consolidated Fund of India;

(e)   the declaring of any expenditure to be expenditure charged on the Consolidated Fund of India or the increasing of the amount of any such expenditure;

(f)   the receipt of money on account of the Consolidated Fund of India or the public account of India or the custody or issue of such money or the audit of the accounts of the Union or of a State; or

(g)   any matter incidental to any of the matters specified in sub-clauses (a) to (f).

(2) A Bill shall not be deemed to be a Money Bill by reason only that it provides for the imposition of fines or other pecuniary penalties, or for the demand or payment of fees for licences or fees for services rendered, or by reason that it provides for the imposition, abolition, remission, alteration or regulation of any tax by any local authority or body for local purposes.

(3) If any question arises whether a Bill is a Money Bill or not, the decision of the Speaker of the House of the People thereon shall be final.

(4) There shall be endorsed on every Money Bill when it is transmitted to the Council of States under article 109, and when it is presented to the President for assent under article 111, the certificate of the Speaker of the House of the People signed by him that it is a Money Bill.

111.   **Assent to Bills.**—When a Bill has been passed by the Houses of Parliament, it shall be presented to the President, and the President shall declare either that he assents to the Bill, or that he withholds assent therefrom:

Provided that the President may, as soon as possible after the presentation to him of a Bill for assent, return the Bill if it is not a Money Bill to the Houses with a message requesting that they will reconsider the Bill or any specified provisions thereof and, in particular, will consider the desirability of introducing any such amendments as he may recommend in his message, and when a Bill is so returned, the Houses shall reconsider the Bill accordingly, and if the Bill is passed again by the Houses with or without amendment and presented to the President for assent, the President shall not withhold assent therefrom.

Procedure in Financial Matters

112. **Annual financial statement.**—(1) The President shall in respect of every financial year cause to be laid before both the Houses of Parliament a statement of the estimated receipts and expenditure of the Government of India for that year, in this Part referred to as the "annual financial statement".

(2) The estimates of expenditure embodied in the annual financial statement shall show separately—

    (*a*) the sums required to meet expenditure described by this Constitution as expenditure charged upon the Consolidated Fund of India; and

    (*b*) the sums required to meet other expenditure proposed to be made from the Consolidated Fund of India,

and shall distinguish expenditure on revenue account from other expenditure.

(3) The following expenditure shall be expenditure charged on the Consolidated Fund of India—

    (*a*) the emoluments and allowances of the President and other expenditure relating to his office;

    (*b*) the salaries and allowances of the Chairman and the Deputy Chairman of the Council of States and the Speaker and the Deputy Speaker of the House of the People;

    (*c*) debt charges for which the Government of India is liable including interest, sinking fund charges and redemption charges, and other expenditure relating to the raising of loans and the service and redemption of debt;

(*d*) (*i*) the salaries, allowances and pensions payable to or in respect of Judges of the Supreme Court;

(*ii*) the pensions payable to or in respect of Judges of the Federal Court;

(*iii*) the pensions payable to or in respect of Judges of any High Court which exercises jurisdiction in relation to any area included in the territory of India or which at any time before the commencement of this Constitution exercised jurisdiction in relation to any area included in ¹[a Governor's Province of the Dominion of India];

(*e*) the salary, allowances and pension payable to or in respect of the Comptroller and Auditor-General of India;

(*f*) any sums required to satisfy any judgment, decree or award of any court or arbitral tribunal;

(*g*) any other expenditure declared by this Constitution or by Parliament by law to be so charged.

113. Procedure in Parliament with respect to estimates.—(1) So much of the estimates as relates to expenditure charged upon the Consolidated Fund of India shall not be submitted to the vote of Parliament, but nothing in this clause shall be construed as preventing the discussion in either House of Parliament of any of those estimates.

(2) So much of the said estimates as relates to other expenditure shall be submitted in the form of demands for grants to the House of the People, and the House of the People shall have power to assent, or to refuse to assent, to any demand, or to assent to any demand subject to a reduction of the amount specified therein.

(3) No demand for a grant shall be made except on the recommendation of the President.

---

1 Subs. by the Constitution (Seventh Amendment) Act, 1956, s. 29 and Sch., for "a Province corresponding to a State specified in Part A of the First Schedule" (w.e.f. 1-11-1956).

114. **Appropriation Bills.**—(1) As soon as may be after the grants under article 113 have been made by the House of the People, there shall be introduced a Bill to provide for the appropriation out of the Consolidated Fund of India of all moneys required to meet—

(*a*) the grants so made by the House of the People; and

(*b*) the expenditure charged on the Consolidated Fund of India but not exceeding in any case the amount shown in the statement previously laid before Parliament.

(2) No amendment shall be proposed to any such Bill in either House of Parliament which will have the effect of varying the amount or altering the destination of any grant so made or of varying the amount of any expenditure charged on the Consolidated Fund of India, and the decision of the person presiding as to whether an amendment is inadmissible under this clause shall be final.

(3) Subject to the provisions of articles 115 and 116, no money shall be withdrawn from the Consolidated Fund of India except under appropriation made by law passed in accordance with the provisions of this article.

115. **Supplementary, additional or excess grants.**—(1) The President shall—

(*a*) if the amount authorised by any law made in accordance with the provisions of article 114 to be expended for a particular service for the current financial year is found to be insufficient for the purposes of that year or when a need has arisen during the current financial year for supplementary or additional expenditure upon some new service not contemplated in the annual financial statement for that year, or

(*b*) if any money has been spent on any service during a financial year in excess of the amount granted for that service and for that year,

cause to be laid before both the Houses of Parliament another statement showing the estimated amount of that expenditure or cause to be presented to the House of the People a demand for such excess, as the case may be.

(2) The provisions of articles 112, 113 and 114 shall have effect in relation to any such statement and expenditure or demand and also to any law to be made authorising the appropriation of moneys out of the Consolidated Fund of India to meet such expenditure or the grant in respect of such demand as they have effect in relation to the annual financial statement and the expenditure mentioned therein or to a demand for a grant and the law to be made for the authorisation of appropriation of moneys out of the Consolidated Fund of India to meet such expenditure or grant.

116. **Votes on account, votes of credit and exceptional grants.**— (1) Notwithstanding anything in the foregoing provisions of this Chapter, the House of the People shall have power—

    (*a*) to make any grant in advance in respect of the estimated expenditure for a part of any financial year pending the completion of the procedure prescribed in article 113 for the voting of such grant and the passing of the law in accordance with the provisions of article 114 in relation to that expenditure;

    (*b*) to make a grant for meeting an unexpected demand upon the resources of India when on account of the magnitude or the indefinite character of the service the demand cannot be stated with the details ordinarily given in an annual financial statement;

    (*c*) to make an exceptional grant which forms no part of the current service of any financial year,

and Parliament shall have power to authorise by law the withdrawal of moneys from the Consolidated Fund of India for the purposes for which the said grants are made.

(2) The provisions of articles 113 and 114 shall have effect in relation to the making of any grant under clause (1) and to any law to be made under that clause as they have effect in relation to the making of a grant with regard to any expenditure mentioned in the annual financial statement and the law to be made for the authorisation of appropriation of moneys out of the Consolidated Fund of India to meet such expenditure.

117. **Special provisions as to financial Bills.**—(1) A Bill or amendment making provision for any of the matters specified

in sub-clauses (*a*) to (*f*) of clause (1) of article 110 shall not be introduced or moved except on the recommendation of the President and a Bill making such provision shall not be introduced in the Council of States:

Provided that no recommendation shall be required under this clause for the moving of an amendment making provision for the reduction or abolition of any tax.

(2) A Bill or amendment shall not be deemed to make provision for any of the matters aforesaid by reason only that it provides for the imposition of fines or other pecuniary penalties, or for the demand or payment of fees for licences or fees for services rendered, or by reason that it provides for the imposition, abolition, remission, alteration or regulation of any tax by any local authority or body for local purposes.

(3) A Bill which, if enacted and brought into operation, would involve expenditure from the Consolidated Fund of India shall not be passed by either House of Parliament unless the President has recommended to that House the consideration of the Bill.

Procedure Generally

118. **Rules of procedure.**—(1) Each House of Parliament may make rules for regulating, subject to the provisions of this Constitution, its procedure* and the conduct of its business.

(2) Until rules are made under clause (1), the rules of procedure and standing orders in force immediately before the commencement of this Constitution with respect to the Legislature of the Dominion of India shall have effect in relation to Parliament subject to such modifications and adaptations as may be made therein by the Chairman of the Council of States or the Speaker of the House of the People, as the case may be.

(3) The President, after consultation with the Chairman of the Council of States and the Speaker of the House of the People,

---

* The brackets and words "(including the quorum to constitute a meeting of the House" ins. by the Constitution (Forty-second Amendment) Act, 1976, s. 22 (date not notified). This amendment was omitted by the Constitution (Forty-fourth Amendment) Act, 1978, s. 45 (w.e.f. 20-6-1979).

may make rules as to the procedure with respect to joint sittings of, and communications between, the two Houses.

(4) At a joint sitting of the two Houses the Speaker of the House of the People, or in his absence such person as may be determined by rules of procedure made under clause (3), shall preside.

119. **Regulation by law of procedure in Parliament in relation to financial business.**— Parliament may, for the purpose of the timely completion of financial business, regulate by law the procedure of, and the conduct of business in, each House of Parliament in relation to any financial matter or to any Bill for the appropriation of moneys out of the Consolidated Fund of India, and, if and so far as any provision of any law so made is inconsistent with any rule made by a House of Parliament under clause (1) of article 118 or with any rule or standing order having effect in relation to Parliament under clause (2) of that article, such provision shall prevail.

120. **Language to be used in Parliament.**—(1) Notwithstanding anything in Part XVII, but subject to the provisions of article 348, business in Parliament shall be transacted in Hindi or in English:

Provided that the Chairman of the Council of States or Speaker of the House of the People, or person acting as such, as the case may be, may permit any member who cannot adequately express himself in Hindi or in English to address the House in his mother-tongue.

(2) Unless Parliament by law otherwise provides, this article shall, after the expiration of a period of fifteen years from the commencement of this Constitution, have effect as if the words "or in English" were omitted therefrom.

121. **Restriction on discussion in Parliament.**—No discussion shall take place in Parliament with respect to the conduct of any Judge of the Supreme Court or of a High Court in the discharge of his duties except upon a motion for presenting an address to the President praying for the removal of the Judge as hereinafter provided.

122. **Courts not to inquire into proceedings of Parliament.**— (1) The validity of any proceedings in Parliament shall not be

called in question on the ground of any alleged irregularity of procedure.

(2) No officer or member of Parliament in whom powers are vested by or under this Constitution for regulating procedure or the conduct of business, or for maintaining order, in Parliament shall be subject to the jurisdiction of any court in respect of the exercise by him of those powers.

Chapter III.—Legislative Powers of the President

123. Power of President to promulgate Ordinances during recess of Parliament.—(1) If at any time, except when both Houses of Parliament are in session, the President is satisfied that circumstances exist which render it necessary for him to take immediate action, he may promulgate such Ordinances as the circumstances appear to him to require.

(2) An Ordinance promulgated under this article shall have the same force and effect as an Act of Parliament, but every such Ordinance—

    (a) shall be laid before both Houses of Parliament and shall cease to operate at the expiration of six weeks from the reassembly of Parliament, or, if before the expiration of that period resolutions disapproving it are passed by both Houses, upon the passing of the second of those resolutions; and

    (b) may be withdrawn at any time by the President.

Explanation.—Where the Houses of Parliament are summoned to reassemble on different dates, the period of six weeks shall be reckoned from the later of those dates for the purposes of this clause.

(3) If and so far as an Ordinance under this article makes any provision which Parliament would not under this Constitution be competent to enact, it shall be void.

[1](4)*   *   *   *   *

---

1 Ins. by the Constitution (Thirty-eighth Amendment) Act, 1975, s. 2 (with retrospective effect) and omitted by the Constitution (Forty-fourth Amendment) Act, 1978, s. 16 (w.e.f. 20-6-1979).

* Now "thirty-three" *vide* the Supreme Court (Number of Judges) Amendment Act, 2019 (37 of 2019), s. 2 (w.e.f. 9-8-2019).

Chapter IV.—The Union Judiciary

124. Establishment and constitution of Supreme Court.—(1) There shall be a Supreme Court of India consisting of a Chief Justice of India and, until Parliament by law prescribes a larger number, of not more than ˙[seven] other Judges.

(2) Every Judge of the Supreme Court shall be appointed by the President by warrant under his hand and seal [1][on the recommendation of the National Judicial Appointments Commission referred to in article 124A] and shall hold office until he attains the age of sixty-five years:

[2][*   *   *   *   *]]

[3][Provided that]—

  (a) a Judge may, by writing under his hand addressed to the President, resign his office;

  (b) a Judge may be removed from his office in the manner provided in clause (4).

[4][(2A) The age of a Judge of the Supreme Court shall be determined by such authority and in such manner as Parliament may by law provide.]

(3) A person shall not be qualified for appointment as a Judge of the Supreme Court unless he is a citizen of India and—

  (a) has been for at least five years a Judge of a High Court or of two or more such Courts in succession; or

  (b) has been for at least ten years an advocate of a High Court or of two or more such Courts in succession; or

---

1 Subs. by the Constitution (Ninety-ninth Amendment) Act, 2014, s. 2, for "after consultation with such of the Judges of the Supreme Court and of the High Court in the States as the President may deem necessary for the purpose" (w.e.f. 13-4-2015). This amendment has been struck down by the Supreme Court in the case of Supreme Court Advocates-on-Record Association and another Vs. Union of India in its judgment dated 16-10-2015, AIR 2016 SC 117.

2 The first proviso was omitted by s. 2, *ibid.* (w.e.f. 13-4-2015). The proviso was as under:— "Provided that in the case of appointment of a Judge other than the Chief Justice, the Chief Justice of India shall always be consulted:". This amendment has been struck down by the Supreme Court in the case of Supreme Court Advocates-on-Record Association and another Vs. Union of India in its judgment dated 16-10-2015, AIR 2016 SC 117.

3 Subs. by s. 2, *ibid.* for "provided further that" (w.e.f.13-4-2015). This amendment has been struck down by the Supreme Court in the Supreme Court Advocates-on-Record Association and another Vs Union of India judgment dated 16-10-2015, AIR 2016 SC 117.

4 Ins. by the Constitution (Fifteenth Amendment) Act, 1963, s. 2 (w.e.f. 5-10-1963).

(c) is, in the opinion of the President, a distinguished jurist.

Explanation I.—In this clause "High Court" means a High Court which exercises, or which at any time before the commencement of this Constitution exercised, jurisdiction in any part of the territory of India.

Explanation II.—In computing for the purpose of this clause the period during which a person has been an advocate, any period during which a person has held judicial office not inferior to that of a district judge after he became an advocate shall be included.

(4) A Judge of the Supreme Court shall not be removed from his office except by an order of the President passed after an address by each House of Parliament supported by a majority of the total membership of that House and by a majority of not less than two-thirds of the members of that House present and voting has been presented to the President in the same session for such removal on the ground of proved misbehaviour or incapacity.

(5) Parliament may by law regulate the procedure for the presentation of an address and for the investigation and proof of the misbehaviour or incapacity of a Judge under clause (4).

(6) Every person appointed to be a Judge of the Supreme Court shall, before he enters upon his office, make and subscribe before the President, or some person appointed in that behalf by him, an oath or affirmation according to the form set out for the purpose in the Third Schedule.

(7) No person who has held office as a Judge of the Supreme Court shall plead or act in any court or before any authority within the territory of India.

[124A. **National Judicial Appointments Commission.**—(1) There shall be a Commission to be known as the National Judicial Appointments Commission consisting of the following, namely:—

(a) the Chief Justice of India, Chairperson, *ex officio*;

---

1 Ins. by the Constitution (Ninety-ninth Amendment) Act, 2014, s. 3 (w.e.f. 13-4-2015). This amendment has been struck down by the Supreme Court in the case of Supreme Court Advocates- on-Record Association and another Vs Union of India in its judgment dated 16-10-2015, AIR 2016 SC 117.

(*b*) two other senior Judges of the Supreme Court next to the Chief Justice of India—Members, *ex officio*;

(*c*) the Union Minister in charge of Law and Justice—Member, *ex officio*;

(*d*) two eminent persons to be nominated by the committee consisting of the Prime Minister, the Chief Justice of India and the Leader of Opposition in the House of the People or where there is no such Leader of Opposition, then, the Leader of single largest Opposition Party in the House of the People—Members:

Provided that one of the eminent person shall be nominated from amongst the persons belonging to the Scheduled Castes, the Scheduled Tribes, Other Backward Classes, Minorities or Women:

Provided further that an eminent person shall be nominated for a period of three years and shall not be eligible for renomination.

(2) No act or proceedings of the National Judicial Appointments Commission shall be questioned or be invalidated merely on the ground of the existence of any vacancy or defect in the constitution of the Commission.

124B. **Functions of Commission.**—It shall be the duty of the National Judicial Appointments Commission to—

(*a*) recommend persons for appointment as Chief Justice of India, Judges of the Supreme Court, Chief Justices of High Courts and other Judges of High Courts;

(*b*) recommend transfer of Chief Justices and other Judges of High Courts from one High Court to any other High Court; and

(*c*) ensure that the person recommended is of ability and integrity.

124C. **Power of Parliament to make law.**—Parliament may, by law, regulate the procedure for the appointment of Chief Justice of India and other Judges of the Supreme Court and Chief Justices and other Judges of High Courts and empower the Commission to lay down by regulations the procedure for the discharge of its functions, the manner of selection of persons for appointment and such other matters as may be considered necessary by it.]

125. **Salaries, etc., of Judges.**—[1][(1) There shall be paid to the Judges of the Supreme Court such salaries as may be determined by Parliament by law and, until provision in that behalf is so made, such salaries as are specified in the Second Schedule.]

(2) Every Judge shall be entitled to such privileges and allowances and to such rights in respect of leave of absence and pension as may from time to time be determined by or under law made by Parliament and, until so determined, to such privileges, allowances and rights as are specified in the Second Schedule:

Provided that neither the privileges nor the allowances of a Judge nor his rights in respect of leave of absence or pension shall be varied to his disadvantage after his appointment.

126. **Appointment of acting Chief Justice.**—When the office of Chief Justice of India is vacant or when the Chief Justice is, by reason of absence or otherwise, unable to perform the duties of his office, the duties of the office shall be performed by such one of the other Judges of the Court as the President may appoint for the purpose.

127. **Appointment of *ad hoc* Judges.**—(1) If at any time there should not be a quorum of the Judges of the Supreme Court available to hold or continue any session of the Court, [2][the National Judicial Appointments Commission on a reference made to it by the Chief Justice of India, may with the previous consent of the President] and after consultation with the Chief Justice of the High Court concerned, request in writing the attendance at the sittings of the Court, as an *ad hoc* Judge, for such period as may be necessary, of a Judge of a High Court duly qualified for appointment as a Judge of the Supreme Court to be designated by the Chief Justice of India.

---

1 Subs. by the Constitution (Fifty-fourth Amendment) Act, 1986, s. 2, for cl. (1) (w.e.f. 1-4-1986).
2 Subs. by the Constitution (Ninety-ninth Amendment) Act, 2014, s. 4, for "the Chief Justice of India may, with the previous consent of the President" (w.e.f. 13-4-2015). This amendment has been struck down by the Supreme Court in the case of Supreme Court Advocates-on-Record Association and another vs. Union of India in its judgment dated 16-10-2015, AIR 2016 SC 117.

(2) It shall be the duty of the Judge who has been so designated, in priority to other duties of his office, to attend the sittings of the Supreme Court at the time and for the period for which his attendance is required, and while so attending he shall have all the jurisdiction, powers and privileges, and shall discharge the duties, of a Judge of the Supreme Court.

128. Attendance of retired Judges at sittings of the Supreme Court.—Notwithstanding anything in this Chapter, [1][the National Judicial Appointments Commission] may at any time, with the previous consent of the President, request any person who has held the office of a Judge of the Supreme Court or of the Federal Court [2][or who has held the office of a Judge of a High Court and is duly qualified for appointment as a Judge of the Supreme Court] to sit and act as a Judge of the Supreme Court, and every such person so requested shall, while so sitting and acting, be entitled to such allowances as the President may by order determine and have all the jurisdiction, powers and privileges of, but shall not otherwise be deemed to be, a Judge of that Court:

Provided that nothing in this article shall be deemed to require any such person as aforesaid to sit and act as a Judge of that Court unless he consents so to do.

129. Supreme Court to be a court of record.—The Supreme Court shall be a court of record and shall have all the powers of such a court including the power to punish for contempt of itself.

130. Seat of Supreme Court.—The Supreme Court shall sit in Delhi or in such other place or places, as the Chief Justice of India may, with the approval of the President, from time to time, appoint.

131. Original jurisdiction of the Supreme Court.—Subject to the provisions of this Constitution, the Supreme Court shall, to the exclusion of any other court, have original jurisdiction in any dispute—

(*a*) between the Government of India and one or more States; or

---

1 Subs. by s. 5, *ibid.*, for "the Chief Justice of India" (w.e.f. 13-4-2015). This amendment has been struck down by the Supreme Court in the case of Supreme Court Advocates-on-Record Association and another Vs. Union of India in its judgment dated 16-10-2015, AIR 2016 SC 117.
2 Ins. by the Constitution (Fifteenth Amendment) Act, 1963, s.3 (w.e.f. 5-10-1963).

(b) between the Government of India and any State or States on one side and one or more other States on the other; or

(c) between two or more States,

if and in so far as the dispute involves any question (whether of law or fact) on which the existence or extent of a legal right depends:

[1][Provided that the said jurisdiction shall not extend to a dispute arising out of any treaty, agreement, covenant, engagement, *sanad* or other similar instrument which, having been entered into or executed before the commencement of this Constitution, continues in operation after such commencement, or which provides that the said jurisdiction shall not extend to such a dispute.]

[2][**131A.** *Exclusive jurisdiction of the Supreme Court in regard to questions as to constitutional validity of Central laws.*].—*Omitted by the Constitution (Forty-third Amendment) Act, 1977, s. 4 (w.e.f. 13-4-1978).*

132. **Appellate jurisdiction of Supreme Court in appeals from High Courts in certain cases.**—(1) An appeal shall lie to the Supreme Court from any judgment, decree or final order of a High Court in the territory of India, whether in a civil, criminal or other proceeding, [3][if the High Court certifies under article 134A] that the case involves a substantial question of law as to the interpretation of this Constitution.

[4](2) *   *   *   *   *

(3) Where such a certificate is given, [2]*** any party in the case may appeal to the Supreme Court on the ground that any such question as aforesaid has been wrongly decided [5]***.

Explanation.—For the purposes of this article, the expression "final order" includes an order deciding an issue which, if

---

1 Subs. by the Constitution (Seventh Amendment) Act, 1956, s. 5, for the proviso (w.e.f. 1-11-1956).
2 Ins. by the Constitution (Forty-second Amendment) Act, 1976, s. 23 (w.e.f. 1-2-1977).
3 Subs. by the Constitution (Forty-fourth Amendment) Act, 1978, s. 17, for "if the High Court certifies" (w.e.f. 1-8-1979).
4 Cl. (2) omitted by the Constitution (Forty-fourth Amendment) Act, 1978, s. 17, for "if the High Court certifies" (w.e.f. 1-8-1979).
5 Certain words omitted by s. 17, *ibid.* (w.e.f. 1-8-1979).

decided in favour of the appellant, would be sufficient for the final disposal of the case.

133. Appellate jurisdiction of Supreme Court in appeals from High Courts in regard to civil matters.—[1][(1) An appeal shall lie to the Supreme Court from any judgment, decree or final order in a civil proceeding of a High Court in the territory of India [2][if the High Court certifies under article 134A—]

(a) that the case involves a substantial question of law of general importance; and

(b) that in the opinion of the High Court the said question needs to be decided by the Supreme Court.]

(2) Notwithstanding anything in article 132, any party appealing to the Supreme Court under clause (1) may urge as one of the grounds in such appeal that a substantial question of law as to the interpretation of this Constitution has been wrongly decided.

(3) Notwithstanding anything in this article, no appeal shall, unless Parliament by law otherwise provides, lie to the Supreme Court from the judgment, decree or final order of one Judge of a High Court.

134. Appellate jurisdiction of Supreme Court in regard to criminal matters.—(1) An appeal shall lie to the Supreme Court from any judgment, final order or sentence in a criminal proceeding of a High Court in the territory of India if the High Court—

(a) has on appeal reversed an order of acquittal of an accused person and sentenced him to death; or

(b) has withdrawn for trial before itself any case from any court subordinate to its authority and has in such trial convicted the accused person and sentenced him to death; or

(c) [3][certifies under article 134A] that the case is a fit one for appeal to the Supreme Court:

Provided that an appeal under sub-clause (c) shall lie subject to such provisions as may be made in that behalf under clause (1)

---

1 Subs. by the Constitution (Thirtieth Amendment) Act, 1972, s. 2, for cl. (1) (w.e.f. 27-2-1973).
2 Subs. by the Constitution (Forty-fourth Amendment) Act, 1978, s.18, for "if the High Court certifies.—" (w.e.f. 1-8-1979).
3 Subs. by s. 19, *ibid.*, for "certifies" (w.e.f. 1-8-1979).

of article 145 and to such conditions as the High Court may establish or require.

(2) Parliament may by law confer on the Supreme Court any further powers to entertain and hear appeals from any judgment, final order or sentence in a criminal proceeding of a High Court in the territory of India subject to such conditions and limitations as may be specified in such law.

¹[**134A. Certificate for appeal to the Supreme Court.**—Every High Court, passing or making a judgment, decree, final order, or sentence, referred to in clause (1) of article 132 or clause (1) of article 133, or clause (1) of article 134,—

    (*a*) may, if it deems fit so to do, on its own motion; and

    (*b*) shall, if an oral application is made, by or on behalf of the party aggrieved, immediately after the passing or making of such judgment, decree, final order or sentence,

determine, as soon as may be after such passing or making, the question whether a certificate of the nature referred to in clause (1) of article 132, or clause (1) of article 133 or, as the case may be, sub-clause (*c*) of clause (1) of article 134, may be given in respect of that case.]

135. **Jurisdiction and powers of the Federal Court under existing law to be exercisable by the Supreme Court.**—Until Parliament by law otherwise provides, the Supreme Court shall also have jurisdiction and powers with respect to any matter to which the provisions of article 133 or article 134 do not apply if jurisdiction and powers in relation to that matter were exercisable by the Federal Court immediately before the commencement of this Constitution under any existing law.

136. **Special leave to appeal by the Supreme Court.**—(1) Notwithstanding anything in this Chapter, the Supreme Court may, in its discretion, grant special leave to appeal from any judgment, decree, determination, sentence or order in any cause or matter passed or made by any court or tribunal in the territory of India.

---

1 Ins. by the Constitution (Forty-fourth Amendment) Act, 1978, s. 20 (w.e.f. 1-8-1979).

(2) Nothing in clause (1) shall apply to any judgment, determination, sentence or order passed or made by any court or tribunal constituted by or under any law relating to the Armed Forces.

137. Review of judgments or orders by the Supreme Court.— Subject to the provisions of any law made by Parliament or any rules made under article 145, the Supreme Court shall have power to review any judgment pronounced or order made by it.

138. Enlargement of the jurisdiction of the Supreme Court.— (1) The Supreme Court shall have such further jurisdiction and powers with respect to any of the matters in the Union List as Parliament may by law confer.

(2) The Supreme Court shall have such further jurisdiction and powers with respect to any matter as the Government of India and the Government of any State may by special agreement confer, if Parliament by law provides for the exercise of such jurisdiction and powers by the Supreme Court.

139. Conferment on the Supreme Court of powers to issue certain writs.—Parliament may by law confer on the Supreme Court power to issue directions, orders or writs, including writs in the nature of *habeas corpus, mandamus,* prohibition, *quo warranto* and *certiorari,* or any of them, for any purposes other than those mentioned in clause (2) of article 32.

[1][**139A. Transfer of certain cases.**—[2][(1) Where cases involving the same or substantially the same questions of law are pending before the Supreme Court and one or more High Courts or before two or more High Courts and the Supreme Court is satisfied on its own motion or on an application made by the Attorney-General of India or by a party to any such case that such questions are substantial questions of general importance, the Supreme Court may withdraw the case or cases pending before the High Court or the High Courts and dispose of all the cases itself:

Provided that the Supreme Court may after determining the said questions of law return any case so withdrawn together with a

---

1 Ins. by the Constitution (Forty-second Amendment) Act, 1976, s. 24 (w.e.f. 1-2-1977).
2 Subs. by the Constitution (Forty-fourth Amendment) Act, 1978, s. 21, for cl. (1) (w.e.f. 1-8-1979).

copy of its judgment on such questions to the High Court from which the case has been withdrawn, and the High Court shall on receipt thereof, proceed to dispose of the case in conformity with such judgment.]

(2) The Supreme Court may, if it deems it expedient so to do for the ends of justice, transfer any case, appeal or other proceedings pending before any High Court to any other High Court.]

140. **Ancillary powers of Supreme Court.**—Parliament may by law make provision for conferring upon the Supreme Court such supplemental powers not inconsistent with any of the provisions of this Constitution as may appear to be necessary or desirable for the purpose of enabling the Court more effectively to exercise the jurisdiction conferred upon it by or under this Constitution.

141. **Law declared by Supreme Court to be binding on all courts.**— The law declared by the Supreme Court shall be binding on all courts within the territory of India.

142. **Enforcement of decrees and orders of Supreme Court and orders as to discovery, etc.**—(1) The Supreme Court in the exercise of its jurisdiction may pass such decree or make such order as is necessary for doing complete justice in any cause or matter pending before it, and any decree so passed or order so made shall be enforceable throughout the territory of India in such manner as may be prescribed by or under any law made by Parliament and, until provision in that behalf is so made, in such manner as the President may by order[1] prescribe.

(2) Subject to the provisions of any law made in this behalf by Parliament, the Supreme Court shall, as respects the whole of the territory of India, have all and every power to make any order for the purpose of securing the attendance of any person, the discovery or production of any documents, or the investigation or punishment of any contempt of itself.

143. **Power of President to consult Supreme Court.**—(1) If at any time it appears to the President that a question of law or fact has arisen, or is likely to arise, which is of such a nature and of such public importance that it is expedient to obtain the opinion of

---

1 *See* the Supreme Court (Decrees and Orders) Enforcement Order, 1954 (C.O. 47).

the Supreme Court upon it, he may refer the question to that Court for consideration and the Court may, after such hearing as it thinks fit, report to the President its opinion thereon.

(2) The President may, notwithstanding anything in [1]*** the proviso to article 131, refer a dispute of the kind mentioned in the [2][said proviso] to the Supreme Court for opinion and the Supreme Court shall, after such hearing as it thinks fit, report to the President its opinion thereon.

144. **Civil and judicial authorities to act in aid of the Supreme Court.**—All authorities, civil and judicial, in the territory of India shall act in aid of the Supreme Court.

[3][**144A.** *[Special provisions as to disposal of questions relating to constitutional validity of laws.].—Omitted by the Constitution (Forty-third Amendment) Act,* 1977, *s.* 5 *(w.e.f.* 13-4-1978).]

145. **Rules of Court, etc.**—(1) Subject to the provisions of any law made by Parliament, the Supreme Court may from time to time, with the approval of the President, make rules for regulating generally the practice and procedure of the Court including—

(*a*) rules as to the persons practising before the Court;

(*b*) rules as to the procedure for hearing appeals and other matters pertaining to appeals including the time within which appeals to the Court are to be entered;

(*c*) rules as to the proceedings in the Court for the enforcement of any of the rights conferred by Part III; [4][(*cc*) rules as to the proceedings in the Court under [5][article 139A];]

(*d*) rules as to the entertainment of appeals under sub-clause (*c*) of clause (1) of article 134;

(*e*) rules as to the conditions subject to which any judgment pronounced or order made by the Court may be reviewed and the procedure for such review

---

1 The words, brackets and figure "clause (i) of" omitted by the Constitution (Seventh Amendment) Act, 1956, s. 29 and Sch. (w.e.f. 1-11-1956).

2 Subs. by s. 29 and Sch., *ibid.*, for "said clause" (w.e.f. 1-11-1956).

3 Ins. by the Constitution (Forty-second Amendment) Act, 1976, s. 25 (w.e.f. 1-2-1977).

4 Ins. by the Constitution (Forty-second Amendment) Act, 1976, s. 26 (w.e.f. 1-2-1977).

5 Subs. by the Constitution (Forty-third Amendment) Act, 1977, s. 6, for "articles 131A and 139A" (w.e.f. 13-4-1978).

including the time within which applications to the Court for such review are to be entered;

(*f*) rules as to the costs of and incidental to any proceedings in the Court and as to the fees to be charged in respect of proceedings therein;

(*g*) rules as to the granting of bail;

(*h*) rules as to stay of proceedings;

(*i*) rules providing for the summary determination of any appeal which appears to the Court to be frivolous or vexatious or brought for the purpose of delay;

(*j*) rules as to the procedure for inquiries referred to in clause (1) of article 317.

(2) Subject to the ¹[provisions of ²*** clause (3)], rules made under this article may fix the minimum number of Judges who are to sit for any purpose, and may provide for the powers of single Judges and Division Courts.

(3) ³[****The minimum number] of Judges who are to sit for the purpose of deciding any case involving a substantial question of law as to the interpretation of this Constitution or for the purpose of hearing any reference under article 143 shall be five: Provided that, where the Court hearing an appeal under any of the provisions of this Chapter other than article 132 consists of less than five Judges and in the course of the hearing of the appeal the Court is satisfied that the appeal involves a substantial question of law as to the interpretation of this Constitution the determination of which is necessary for the disposal of the appeal, such Court shall refer the question for opinion to a Court constituted as required by this clause for the purpose of deciding any case involving such a question and shall on receipt of the opinion dispose of the appeal in conformity with such opinion.

---

1 Subs. by the Constitution (Forty-second Amendment) Act, 1976, s. 26, for "provisions of clause (3)" (w.e.f. 1-2-1977).
2 Certain words omitted by the Constitution (Forty-third Amendment) Act, 1977, s. 6 (w.e.f. 13-4-1978).
3 Subs. by the Constitution (Forty-second Amendment) Act, 1976, s. 26, for "The minimum number" (w.e.f. 1-2-1977).

(4) No judgment shall be delivered by the Supreme Court save in open Court, and no report shall be made under article 143 save in accordance with an opinion also delivered in open Court.

(5) No judgment and no such opinion shall be delivered by the Supreme Court save with the concurrence of a majority of the Judges present at the hearing of the case, but nothing in this clause shall be deemed to prevent a Judge who does not concur from delivering a dissenting judgment or opinion.

146. **Officers and servants and the expenses of the Supreme Court.**—(1) Appointments of officers and servants of the Supreme Court shall be made by the Chief Justice of India or such other Judge or officer of the Court as he may direct:

Provided that the President may by rule require that in such cases as may be specified in the rule, no person not already attached to the Court shall be appointed to any office connected with the Court, save after consultation with the Union Public Service Commission.

(2) Subject to the provisions of any law made by Parliament, the conditions of service of officers and servants of the Supreme Court shall be such as may be prescribed by rules made by the Chief Justice of India or by some other Judge or officer of the Court authorised by the Chief Justice of India to make rules for the purpose:

Provided that the rules made under this clause shall, so far as they relate to salaries, allowances, leave or pensions, require the approval of the President.

(3) The administrative expenses of the Supreme Court, including all salaries, allowances and pensions payable to or in respect of the officers and servants of the Court, shall be charged upon the Consolidated Fund of India, and any fees or other moneys taken by the Court shall form part of that Fund.

147. **Interpretation.**—In this Chapter and in Chapter V of Part VI, references to any substantial question of law as to the interpretation of this Constitution shall be construed as including references to any substantial question of law as to the interpretation of the Government of India Act, 1935 (including any enactment amending or supplementing that Act), or of any

Order in Council or order made thereunder, or of the Indian Independence Act, 1947, or of any order made thereunder.

Chapter V.—Comptroller and Auditor-General of India

148.   **Comptroller and Auditor-General of India.**—(1) There shall be a Comptroller and Auditor-General of India who shall be appointed by the President by warrant under his hand and seal and shall only be removed from office in like manner and on the like grounds as a Judge of the Supreme Court.

(2) Every person appointed to be the Comptroller and Auditor-General of India shall, before he enters upon his office, make and subscribe before the President, or some person appointed in that behalf by him, an oath or affirmation according to the form set out for the purpose in the Third Schedule.

(3) The salary and other conditions of service of the Comptroller and Auditor-General shall be such as may be determined by Parliament by law and, until they are so determined, shall be as specified in the Second Schedule:

Provided that neither the salary of a Comptroller and Auditor-General nor his rights in respect of leave of absence, pension or age of retirement shall be varied to his disadvantage after his appointment.

(4) The Comptroller and Auditor-General shall not be eligible for further office either under the Government of India or under the Government of any State after he has ceased to hold his office.

(5) Subject to the provisions of this Constitution and of any law made by Parliament, the conditions of service of persons serving in the Indian Audit and Accounts Department and the administrative powers of the Comptroller and Auditor-General shall be such as may be prescribed by rules made by the President after consultation with the Comptroller and Auditor-General.

(6) The administrative expenses of the office of the Comptroller and Auditor-General, including all salaries, allowances and pensions payable to or in respect of persons serving in that office, shall be charged upon the Consolidated Fund of India.

149. **Duties and powers of the Comptroller and Auditor-General.**—The Comptroller and Auditor-General shall perform such duties and exercise such powers in relation to the accounts of the Union and of the States and of any other authority or body as may be prescribed by or under any law made by Parliament and, until provision in that behalf is so made, shall perform such duties and exercise such powers in relation to the accounts of the Union and of the States as were conferred on or exercisable by the Auditor-General of India immediately before the commencement of this Constitution in relation to the accounts of the Dominion of India and of the Provinces respectively.

¹[150. **Form of accounts of the Union and of the States.**—The accounts of the Union and of the States shall be kept in such form as the President may, ²[on the advice of] the Comptroller and Auditor-General of India, prescribe.]

151. **Audit reports.**—(1) The reports of the Comptroller and Auditor-General of India relating to the accounts of the Union shall be submitted to the President, who shall cause them to be laid before each House of Parliament.

(2) The reports of the Comptroller and Auditor-General of India relating to the accounts of a State shall be submitted to the Governor ³*** of the State, who shall cause them to be laid before the Legislature of the State.

---

1 Subs. by the Constitution (Forty-second Amendment) Act, 1976, s. 27, for art.150 (w.e.f. 1-4-1977).

2 Subs. by the Constitution (Forty-fourth Amendment) Act, 1978, s. 22, for "after consultation with" (w.e.f. 20-6-1979).

3 The words "or Rajpramukh" omitted by the Constitution (Seventh Amendment) Act, 1956, s. 29 and Sch. (w.e.f. 1-11-1956).

PART VI

THE STATES [1]***

Chapter I.—General

152. **Definition.**—In this Part, unless the context otherwise requires, the expression "State" [2][does not include the State of Jammu and Kashmir].

Chapter II.—The Executive

The Governor

153. **Governors of States.**—There shall be a Governor for each State: [3][Provided that nothing in this article shall prevent the appointment of the same person as Governor for two or more States.]

154. **Executive power of State.**—(1) The executive power of the State shall be vested in the Governor and shall be exercised by him either directly or through officers subordinate to him in accordance with this Constitution.

(2) Nothing in this article shall—

    (*a*)   be deemed to transfer to the Governor any functions conferred by any existing law on any other authority; or

    (*b*)   prevent Parliament or the Legislature of the State from conferring by law functions on any authority subordinate to the Governor.

155. **Appointment of Governor.**—The Governor of a State shall be appointed by the President by warrant under his hand and seal.

---

1 The words "IN PART A OF THE FIRST SCHEDULE" omitted by the Constitution (Seventh Amendment) Act, 1956, s. 29 and Sch. (w.e.f. 1-11-1956).

2 Subs. by s. 29 and Sch. *ibid.*, for "means a State specified in Part A of the First Schedule" (w.e.f. 1-11-1956).

3 Added by s. 6, *ibid.* (w.e.f. 1-11-1956).

156. **Term of office of Governor.**—(1) The Governor shall hold office during the pleasure of the President.

(2) The Governor may, by writing under his hand addressed to the President, resign his office.

(3) Subject to the foregoing provisions of this article, a Governor shall hold office for a term of five years from the date on which he enters upon his office:

Provided that a Governor shall, notwithstanding the expiration of his term, continue to hold office until his successor enters upon his office.

157. **Qualifications for appointment as Governor.**—No person shall be eligible for appointment as Governor unless he is a citizen of India and has completed the age of thirty-five years.

158. **Conditions of Governor's office.**—(1) The Governor shall not be a member of either House of Parliament or of a House of the Legislature of any State specified in the First Schedule, and if a member of either House of Parliament or of a House of the Legislature of any such State be appointed Governor, he shall be deemed to have vacated his seat in that House on the date on which he enters upon his office as Governor.

(2) The Governor shall not hold any other office of profit.

(3) The Governor shall be entitled without payment of rent to the use of his official residences and shall be also entitled to such emoluments, allowances and privileges as may be determined by Parliament by law and, until provision in that behalf is so made, such emoluments, allowances and privileges as are specified in the Second Schedule.

[1](3A) Where the same person is appointed as Governor of two or more States, the emoluments and allowances payable to the Governor shall be allocated among the States in such proportion as the President may by order determine.]

(4) The emoluments and allowances of the Governor shall not be diminished during his term of office.

159. **Oath or affirmation by the Governor.**—Every Governor and every person discharging the functions of the Governor

---

1 Ins. by the Constitution (Seventh Amendment) Act, 1956, s. 7 (w.e.f. 1-11-1956).

shall, before entering upon his office, make and subscribe in the presence of the Chief Justice of the High Court exercising jurisdiction in relation to the State, or, in his absence, the senior most Judge of that Court available, an oath or affirmation in the following form, that is to say—

"I, A. B., do $\dfrac{\text{swear in the name of God}}{\text{solemnly affirm}}$ that I will faithfully execute the office of Governor (or discharge the functions of the Governor) of .... (*name of the State*) and will to the best of my ability preserve, protect and defend the Constitution and the law and that I will devote myself to the service and well-being of the people of .... (*name of the State*).".

160. **Discharge of the functions of the Governor in certain contingencies.**—The President may make such provision as he thinks fit for the discharge of the functions of the Governor of a State in any contingency not provided for in this Chapter.

161. **Power of Governor to grant pardons, etc., and to suspend, remit or commute sentences in certain cases.**—The Governor of a State shall have the power to grant pardons, reprieves, respites or remissions of punishment or to suspend, remit or commute the sentence of any person convicted of any offence against any law relating to a matter to which the executive power of the State extends.

162. **Extent of executive power of State.**—Subject to the provisions of this Constitution, the executive power of a State shall extend to the matters with respect to which the Legislature of the State has power to make laws:

Provided that in any matter with respect to which the Legislature of a State and Parliament have power to make laws, the executive power of the State shall be subject to, and limited by, the executive power expressly conferred by this Constitution or by any law made by Parliament upon the Union or authorities thereof.

Council of Ministers

163. **Council of Ministers to aid and advise Governor.**—(1) There shall be a Council of Ministers with the Chief Minister at the head

to aid and advise the Governor in the exercise of his functions, except in so far as he is by or under this Constitution required to exercise his functions or any of them in his discretion.

(2) If any question arises whether any matter is or is not a matter as respects which the Governor is by or under this Constitution required to act in his discretion, the decision of the Governor in his discretion shall be final, and the validity of anything done by the Governor shall not be called in question on the ground that he ought or ought not to have acted in his discretion.

(3) The question whether any, and if so what, advice was tendered by Ministers to the Governor shall not be inquired into in any court.

164.   **Other provisions as to Ministers.**—(1) The Chief Minister shall be appointed by the Governor and the other Ministers shall be appointed by the Governor on the advice of the Chief Minister, and the Ministers shall hold office during the pleasure of the Governor:

Provided that in the States of [1][Chhattisgarh, Jharkhand], Madhya Pradesh and [2][Odisha] there shall be a Minister in charge of tribal welfare who may in addition be in charge of the welfare of the Scheduled Castes and backward classes or any other work.

[3][(1A) The total number of Ministers, including the Chief Minister, in the Council of Ministers in a State shall not exceed fifteen per cent. of the total number of members of the Legislative Assembly of that State:

Provided that the number of Ministers, including the Chief Minister in a State shall not be less than twelve:

Provided further that where the total number of Ministers including the Chief Minister in the Council of Ministers in any State at the commencement of the Constitution (Ninety-first Amendment) Act, 2003 exceeds the said fifteen per cent. or the number specified in the first proviso, as the case may be, then the total number of Ministers in that State shall be brought in

---

1   Subs. by the Constitution (Ninety-fourth Amendment) Act, 2006, s. 2, for "Bihar" (w.e.f. 12-6-2006).

2   Subs. by the Orissa (Alteration of Name) Act, 2011 (15 of 2011), s. 4, for "Orissa" (w.e.f. 1-11-2011).

3   Ins. by the Constitution (Ninety-first Amendment) Act, 2003, s. 3 (w.e.f. 1-1-2004).

conformity with the provisions of this clause within six months from such date [1] as the President may by public notification appoint.

(1B) A member of the Legislative Assembly of a State or either House of the Legislature of a State having Legislative Council belonging to any political party who is disqualified for being a member of that House under paragraph 2 of the Tenth Schedule shall also be disqualified to be appointed as a Minister under clause (1) for duration of the period commencing from the date of his disqualification till the date on which the term of his office as such member would expire or where he contests any election to the Legislative Assembly of a State or either House of the Legislature of a State having Legislative Council, as the case may be, before the expiry of such period, till the date on which he is declared elected, whichever is earlier.]

(2) The Council of Ministers shall be collectively responsible to the Legislative Assembly of the State.

(3) Before a Minister enters upon his office, the Governor shall administer to him the oaths of office and of secrecy according to the forms set out for the purpose in the Third Schedule.

(4) A Minister who for any period of six consecutive months is not a member of the Legislature of the State shall at the expiration of that period cease to be a Minister.

(5) The salaries and allowances of Ministers shall be such as the Legislature of the State may from time to time by law determine and, until the Legislature of the State so determines, shall be as specified in the Second Schedule.

The Advocate-General for the State

165. **Advocate-General for the State.**—(1) The Governor of each State shall appoint a person who is qualified to be appointed a Judge of a High Court to be Advocate-General for the State.

(2) It shall be the duty of the Advocate-General to give advice to the Government of the State upon such legal matters, and to

---

1 7-1-2004, *vide* notification number S.O. 21(E), dated 7-1-2004.

perform such other duties of a legal character, as may from time to time be referred or assigned to him by the Governor, and to discharge the functions conferred on him by or under this Constitution or any other law for the time being in force.

(3) The Advocate-General shall hold office during the pleasure of the Governor, and shall receive such remuneration as the Governor may determine.

Conduct of Government Business

166. Conduct of Business of the Government of a State.—(1) All executive action of the Government of a State shall be expressed to be taken in the name of the Governor.

(2) Orders and other instruments made and executed in the name of the Governor shall be authenticated in such manner as may be specified in rules to be made by the Governor, and the validity of an order or instrument which is so authenticated shall not be called in question on the ground that it is not an order or instrument made or executed by the Governor.

(3) The Governor shall make rules for the more convenient transaction of the business of the Government of the State, and for the allocation among Ministers of the said business in so far as it is not business with respect to which the Governor is by or under this Constitution required to act in his discretion.

[1](4)*　　*　　*　　*　　*

167. Duties of Chief Minister as respects the furnishing of information to Governor, etc.—It shall be the duty of the Chief Minister of each State—

(a)　to communicate to the Governor of the State all decisions of the Council of Ministers relating to the administration of the affairs of the State and proposals for legislation;

(b)　to furnish such information relating to the administration of the affairs of the State and proposals for legislation as the Governor may call for; and

---

1 Ins. by the Constitution (Forty-second Amendment) Act, 1976, s. 28 (w.e.f. 3-1-1977) and omitted by the Constitution (Forty-fourth Amendment) Act, 1978, s. 23 (w.e.f. 20-6-1979).

(*c*)   if the Governor so requires, to submit for the consideration of the Council of Ministers any matter on which a decision has been taken by a Minister but which has not been considered by the Council.

Chapter III.—The State Legislature
General

168.   **Constitution of Legislatures in States.**—(1) For every State there shall be a Legislature which shall consist of the Governor, and—

(*a*)   in the States of ¹*** ²[Andhra Pradesh], Bihar, ³*** ⁴[Madhya Pradesh], ⁵*** ⁶[Maharashtra], ⁷[Karnataka], ⁸*** ⁹[¹⁰[Tamil Nadu, Telangana]] ¹¹[and Uttar Pradesh], two Houses;

(*b*)   in other States, one House.

(2) Where there are two Houses of the Legislature of a State, one shall be known as the Legislative Council and the other as the Legislative Assembly, and where there is only one House, it shall be known as the Legislative Assembly.

169.   **Abolition or creation of Legislative Councils in States.**—(1) Notwithstanding anything in article 168, Parliament may by law

---

1   The words "Andhra Pradesh," omitted by the Andhra Pradesh Legislative Council (Abolition) Act, 1985 (34 of 1985), s. 4 (w.e.f. 1-6-1985).
2   Ins. by the Andhra Pradesh Legislative Council Act, 2005 (1 of 2006), s. 3 (w.e.f. 30-3-2007).
3   The word "Bombay" omitted by the Bombay Reorganisation Act, 1960 (11 of 1960) s. 20 (w.e.f. 1-5-1960).
4   Ins. by the Constitution (Seventh Amendment) Act, 1956, s. 8 (w.e.f. 1-11-1956).
5   The words "Tamil Nadu," omitted by the Tamil Nadu Legislative Council (Abolition) Act, 1986 (40 of 1986), s. 4 (w.e.f. 1-11-1986).
6   Ins. by the Bombay Reorganisation Act, 1960 (11 of 1960), s. 20 (w.e.f. 1-5-1960).
7   Subs. by the Mysore State (Alteration of Name) Act, 1973 (31 of 1973), s. 4, for "Mysore" (w.e.f. 1-11-1973), which was inserted by the Constitution (Seventh Amendment) Act, 1956, s. 8(1) (w.e.f. 1 11 1956).
8   The word, "Punjab," omitted by the Punjab Legislative Council (Abolition) Act, 1969 (46 of 1969), s. 4 (w.e.f. 7-1-1970).
9   The words "Tamil Nadu" ins. by the Tamil Nadu Legislative Council Act, 2010 (16 of 2010), s. 3 (date not yet notified).
10 Subs. by the Andhra Pradesh Reorganisation Act, 2014 (6 of 2014), s. 96, for "Tamil Nadu" (w.e.f. 2-6-2014).
11 Subs. by the West Bengal Legislative Council (Abolition) Act, 1969 (20 of 1969), s. 4 for "Uttar Pradesh and West Bengal" (w.e.f. 1-8-1969).

provide for the abolition of the Legislative Council of a State having such a Council or for the creation of such a Council in a State having no such Council, if the Legislative Assembly of the State passes a resolution to that effect by a majority of the total membership of the Assembly and by a majority of not less than two-thirds of the members of the Assembly present and voting.

(2) Any law referred to in clause (1) shall contain such provisions for the amendment of this Constitution as may be necessary to give effect to the provisions of the law and may also contain such supplemental, incidental and consequential provisions as Parliament may deem necessary.

(3) No such law as aforesaid shall be deemed to be an amendment of this Constitution for the purposes of article 368.

[1][170.   **Composition of the Legislative Assemblies.**—(1) Subject to the provisions of article 333, the Legislative Assembly of each State shall consist of not more than five hundred, and not less than sixty, members chosen by direct election from territorial constituencies in the State.

(2) For the purposes of clause (1), each State shall be divided into territorial constituencies in such manner that the ratio between the population of each constituency and the number of seats allotted to it shall, so far as practicable, be the same throughout the State.

[2][*Explanation.*—In this clause, the expression "population" means the population as ascertained at the last preceding census of which the relevant figures have been published:

Provided that the reference in this *Explanation* to the last preceding census of which the relevant figures have been published shall, until the relevant figures for the first census taken after the year [3][2026] have been published, be construed as a reference to the [4][2001] census.]

1   Subs. by the Constitution (Seventh Amendment) Act, 1956, s. 9, for art. 170 (w.e.f. 1-11-1956).
2   Subs. by the Constitution (Forty-second Amendment) Act, 1976, s. 29, for the *Explanation* (w.e.f. 3-1-1977).
3   Subs. by the Constitution (Eighty-fourth Amendment) Act, 2001, s. 5, for "2000" (w.e.f. 21-2-2002).
4   Subs. by the Constitution (Eighty-seventh Amendment) Act, 2003, s. 4, for "1991" (w.e.f. 22-6-2003). The figures "1991" were substituted for the original figures "1971" by the Constitution (Eighty fourth Amendment) Act, 2001, s. 5 (w.e.f. 21-2-2002).

(3) Upon the completion of each census, the total number of seats in the Legislative Assembly of each State and the division of each State into territorial constituencies shall be readjusted by such authority and in such manner as Parliament may by law determine:

Provided that such readjustment shall not affect representation in the Legislative Assembly until the dissolution of the then existing Assembly:

[1][Provided further that such readjustment shall take effect from such date as the President may, by order, specify and until such readjustment takes effect, any election to the Legislative Assembly may be held on the basis of the territorial constituencies existing before such readjustment:

Provided also that until the relevant figures for the first census taken after the year [1][2026] have been published, it shall not be necessary to [2][readjust—

(*i*) the total number of seats in the Legislative Assembly of each State as readjusted on the basis of the 1971 census; and

(*ii*) the division of such State into territorial constituencies as may be readjusted on the basis of the [2][2001] census, under this clause.]

171. Composition of the Legislative Councils.—(1) The total number of members in the Legislative Council of a State having such a Council shall not exceed [3][one-third] of the total number of members in the Legislative Assembly of that State:

Provided that the total number of members in the Legislative Council of a State shall in no case be less than forty.

(2) Until Parliament by law otherwise provides, the composition of the Legislative Council of a State shall be as provided in clause (3).

(3) Of the total number of members of the Legislative Council of a State—

---

1 Ins. by the Constitution (Forty-second Amendment) Act, 1976, s. 29 (w.e.f. 3-1-1977).
2 Subs. by the Constitution (Eighty-fourth Amendment) Act, 2001, s. 5, for certain words (w.e.f. 21-2-2002).
3 Subs. by the Constitution (Seventh Amendment) Act, 1956, s. 10, for "one-fourth" (w.e.f. 1-11-1956).

(*a*) as nearly as may be, one-third shall be elected by electorates consisting of members of municipalities, district boards and such other local authorities in the State as Parliament may by law specify;

(*b*) as nearly as may be, one-twelfth shall be elected by electorates consisting of persons residing in the State who have been for at least three years graduates of any university in the territory of India or have been for at least three years in possession of qualifications prescribed by or under any law made by Parliament as equivalent to that of a graduate of any such university;

(*c*) as nearly as may be, one-twelfth shall be elected by electorates consisting of persons who have been for at least three years engaged in teaching in such educational institutions within the State, not lower in standard than that of a secondary school, as may be prescribed by or under any law made by Parliament;

(*d*) as nearly as may be, one-third shall be elected by the members of the Legislative Assembly of the State from amongst persons who are not members of the Assembly;

(*e*) the remainder shall be nominated by the Governor in accordance with the provisions of clause (5).

(4) The members to be elected under sub-clauses (*a*), (*b*) and (*c*) of clause (3) shall be chosen in such territorial constituencies as may be prescribed by or under any law made by Parliament, and the elections under the said sub-clauses and under sub-clause (*d*) of the said clause shall be held in accordance with the system of proportional representation by means of the single transferable vote.

(5) The members to be nominated by the Governor under sub-clause (*e*) of clause (3) shall consist of persons having special knowledge or practical experience in respect of such matters as the following, namely:—

Literature, science, art, co-operative movement and social service.

172. Duration of State Legislatures.—(1) Every Legislative Assembly of every State, unless sooner dissolved, shall continue for [1][five years] from the date appointed for its first meeting and no longer and the expiration of the said period of [1][five years] shall operate as a dissolution of the Assembly:

Provided that the said period may, while a Proclamation of Emergency is in operation, be extended by Parliament by law for a period not exceeding one year at a time and not extending in any case beyond a period of six months after the Proclamation has ceased to operate.

(2) The Legislative Council of a State shall not be subject to dissolution, but as nearly as possible one-third of the members thereof shall retire as soon as may be on the expiration of every second year in accordance with the provisions made in that behalf by Parliament by law.

173. **Qualification for membership of the State Legislature.**—A person shall not be qualified to be chosen to fill a seat in the Legislature of a State unless he—

[2][(a) is a citizen of India, and makes and subscribes before some person authorised in that behalf by the Election Commission an oath or affirmation according to the form set out for the purpose in the Third Schedule;]

(b) is, in the case of a seat in the Legislative Assembly, not less than twenty-five years of age and, in the case of a seat in the Legislative Council, not less than thirty years of age; and

(c) possesses such other qualifications as may be prescribed in that behalf by or under any law made by Parliament.

[3][174. **Sessions of the State Legislature, prorogation and dissolution.**—(1) The Governor shall from time to time summon the House or each House of the Legislature of the State to meet at such time and place as he thinks fit, but six months shall not intervene between its last sitting in one session and the date appointed for its first sitting in the next session.

---

1 Subs. by the Constitution (Forty-second Amendment) Act, 1976, s. 30, for "five years" (w.e.f. 3-1-1977) and further subs. by the Constitution (Forty-fourth Amendment) Act, 1978, s. 24, for "six years" (w.e.f. 6-9-1979).
2 Subs. by the Constitution (Sixteenth Amendment) Act, 1963, s. 4, for cl. (a) (w.e.f. 5-10-1963).
3 Subs. by the Constitution (First Amendment) Act, 1951, s. 8, for art.174 (w.e.f. 18-6-1951).

(2) The Governor may from time to time—

    (*a*)   prorogue the House or either House;

    (*b*)   dissolve the Legislative Assembly.]

175. **Right of Governor to address and send messages to the House or Houses.**—(1) The Governor may address the Legislative Assembly or, in the case of a State having a Legislative Council, either House of the Legislature of the State, or both Houses assembled together, and may for that purpose require the attendance of members.

(2) The Governor may send messages to the House or Houses of the Legislature of the State, whether with respect to a Bill then pending in the Legislature or otherwise, and a House to which any message is so sent shall with all convenient despatch consider any matter required by the message to be taken into consideration.

176. **Special address by the Governor.**—(1) At the commencement of [1][the first session after each general election to the Legislative Assembly and at the commencement of the first session of each year], the Governor shall address the Legislative Assembly or, in the case of a State having a Legislative Council, both Houses assembled together and inform the Legislature of the causes of its summons.

(2) Provision shall be made by the rules regulating the procedure of the House or either House for the allotment of time for discussion of the matters referred to in such address [2]***.

177. **Rights of Ministers and Advocate-General as respects the Houses.**—Every Minister and the Advocate-General for a State shall have the right to speak in, and otherwise to take part in the proceedings of, the Legislative Assembly of the State or, in the case of a State having a Legislative Council, both Houses, and to speak in, and otherwise to take part in the proceedings of, any committee of the Legislature of which he may be named a member, but shall not, by virtue of this article, be entitled to vote.

Officers of the State Legislature

---

1 Subs. by s. 9, *ibid.*, for "every session" (w.e.f. 18-6-1951).
2 The words "and for the precedence of such discussion over other business of the House" omitted by s. 9, *ibid.* (w.e.f. 18-6-1951).

178. **The Speaker and Deputy Speaker of the Legislative Assembly.**—Every Legislative Assembly of a State shall, as soon as may be, choose two members of the Assembly to be respectively Speaker and Deputy Speaker thereof and, so often as the office of Speaker or Deputy Speaker becomes vacant, the Assembly shall choose another member to be Speaker or Deputy Speaker, as the case may be.

179. **Vacation and resignation of, and removal from, the offices of Speaker and Deputy Speaker.**—A member holding office as Speaker or Deputy Speaker of an Assembly—

    (*a*) shall vacate his office if he ceases to be a member of the Assembly;

    (*b*) may at any time by writing under his hand addressed, if such member is the Speaker, to the Deputy Speaker, and if such member is the Deputy Speaker, to the Speaker, resign his office; and

    (*c*) may be removed from his office by a resolution of the Assembly passed by a majority of all the then members of the Assembly:

Provided that no resolution for the purpose of clause (*c*) shall be moved unless at least fourteen days' notice has been given of the intention to move the resolution:

Provided further that, whenever the Assembly is dissolved, the Speaker shall not vacate his office until immediately before the first meeting of the Assembly after the dissolution.

180. **Power of the Deputy Speaker or other person to perform the duties of the office of, or to act as, Speaker.**—(1) While the office of Speaker is vacant, the duties of the office shall be performed by the Deputy Speaker or, if the office of Deputy Speaker is also vacant, by such member of the Assembly as the Governor may appoint for the purpose.

(2) During the absence of the Speaker from any sitting of the Assembly the Deputy Speaker or, if he is also absent, such person as may be determined by the rules of procedure of the Assembly, or, if no such person is present, such other person as may be determined by the Assembly, shall act as Speaker.

181. **The Speaker or the Deputy Speaker not to preside while a resolution for his removal from office is under consideration.**—(1) At any sitting of the Legislative Assembly, while any resolution for the removal of the Speaker from his office is under consideration, the Speaker, or while any resolution for the removal of the Deputy Speaker from his office is under consideration, the Deputy Speaker, shall not, though he is present, preside, and the provisions of clause (2) of article 180 shall apply in relation to every such sitting as they apply in relation to a sitting from which the Speaker or, as the case may be, the Deputy Speaker, is absent.

(2) The Speaker shall have the right to speak in, and otherwise to take part in the proceedings of, the Legislative Assembly while any resolution for his removal from office is under consideration in the Assembly and shall, notwithstanding anything in article 189, be entitled to vote only in the first instance on such resolution or on any other matter during such proceedings but not in the case of an equality of votes.

182. **The Chairman and Deputy Chairman of the Legislative Council.**—The Legislative Council of every State having such Council shall, as soon as may be, choose two members of the Council to be respectively Chairman and Deputy Chairman thereof and, so often as the office of Chairman or Deputy Chairman becomes vacant, the Council shall choose another member to be Chairman or Deputy Chairman, as the case may be.

183. **Vacation and resignation of, and removal from, the offices of Chairman and Deputy Chairman.**—A member holding office as Chairman or Deputy Chairman of a Legislative Council—

    (a) shall vacate his office if he ceases to be a member of the Council;

    (b) may at any time by writing under his hand addressed, if such member is the Chairman, to the Deputy Chairman, and if such member is the Deputy Chairman, to the Chairman, resign his office; and

    (c) may be removed from his office by a resolution of the Council passed by a majority of all the then members of the Council:

Provided that no resolution for the purpose of clause (*c*) shall be moved unless at least fourteen days' notice has been given of the intention to move the resolution.

184. **Power of the Deputy Chairman or other person to perform the duties of the office of, or to act as, Chairman.**—(1) While the office of Chairman is vacant, the duties of the office shall be performed by the Deputy Chairman or, if the office of Deputy Chairman is also vacant, by such member of the Council as the Governor may appoint for the purpose.

(2) During the absence of the Chairman from any sitting of the Council the Deputy Chairman or, if he is also absent, such person as may be determined by the rules of procedure of the Council, or, if no such person is present, such other person as may be determined by the Council, shall act as Chairman.

185. **The Chairman or the Deputy Chairman not to preside while a resolution for his removal from office is under consideration.**—(1) At any sitting of the Legislative Council, while any resolution for the removal of the Chairman from his office is under consideration, the Chairman, or while any resolution for the removal of the Deputy Chairman from his office is under consideration, the Deputy Chairman, shall not, though he is present, preside, and the provisions of clause (2) of article 184 shall apply in relation to every such sitting as they apply in relation to a sitting from which the Chairman or, as the case may be, the Deputy Chairman is absent.

(2) The Chairman shall have the right to speak in, and otherwise to take part in the proceedings of, the Legislative Council while any resolution for his removal from office is under consideration in the Council and shall, notwithstanding anything in article 189, be entitled to vote only in the first instance on such resolution or on any other matter during such proceedings but not in the case of an equality of votes.

186. **Salaries and allowances of the Speaker and Deputy Speaker and the Chairman and Deputy Chairman.**—There shall be paid to the Speaker and the Deputy Speaker of the Legislative Assembly, and to the Chairman and the Deputy Chairman of the Legislative Council, such salaries and allowances as may be

respectively fixed by the Legislature of the State by law and, until provision in that behalf is so made, such salaries and allowances as are specified in the Second Schedule.

187. **Secretariat of State Legislature.**—(1) The House or each House of the Legislature of a State shall have a separate secretarial staff: Provided that nothing in this clause shall, in the case of the Legislature of a State having a Legislative Council, be construed as preventing the creation of posts common to both Houses of such Legislature.

(2) The Legislature of a State may by law regulate the recruitment, and the conditions of service of persons appointed, to the secretarial staff of the House or Houses of the Legislature of the State.

(3) Until provision is made by the Legislature of the State under clause (2), the Governor may, after consultation with the Speaker of the Legislative Assembly or the Chairman of the Legislative Council, as the case may be, make rules regulating the recruitment, and the conditions of service of persons appointed, to the secretarial staff of the Assembly or the Council, and any rules so made shall have effect subject to the provisions of any law made under the said clause.

Conduct of Business

188. **Oath or affirmation by members.**—Every member of the Legislative Assembly or the Legislative Council of a State shall, before taking his seat, make and subscribe before the Governor, or some person appointed in that behalf by him, an oath or affirmation according to the form set out for the purpose in the Third Schedule.

189. **Voting in Houses, power of Houses to act notwithstanding vacancies and quorum.**—(1) Save as otherwise provided in this Constitution, all questions at any sitting of a House of the Legislature of a State shall be determined by a majority of votes of the members present and voting, other than the Speaker or Chairman, or person acting as such.

The Speaker or Chairman, or person acting as such, shall not vote in the first instance, but shall have and exercise a casting vote in the case of an equality of votes.

(2) A House of the Legislature of a State shall have power to act notwithstanding any vacancy in the membership thereof, and any proceedings in the Legislature of a State shall be valid notwithstanding that it is discovered subsequently that some person who was not entitled so to do sat or voted or otherwise took part in the proceedings.

[1][(3) Until the Legislature of the State by law otherwise provides, the quorum to constitute a meeting of a House of the Legislature of a State shall be ten members or one-tenth of the total number of members of the House, whichever is greater.

(4) If at any time during a meeting of the Legislative Assembly or the Legislative Council of a State there is no quorum, it shall be the duty of the Speaker or Chairman, or person acting as such, either to adjourn the House or to suspend the meeting until there is a quorum.]

Disqualifications of Members

190. **Vacation of seats.**—(1) No person shall be a member of both Houses of the Legislature of a State and provision shall be made by the Legislature of the State by law for the vacation by a person who is chosen a member of both Houses of his seat in one house or the other.

(2) No person shall be a member of the Legislatures of two or more States specified in the First Schedule and if a person is chosen a member of the Legislatures of two or more such States, then, at the expiration of such period as may be specified in rules[2] made by the President, that person's seat in the Legislatures of

---

1 Omitted by the Constitution (Forty-second Amendment) Act, 1976, s. 31 (date not notified). This amendment was omitted by the Constitution (Forty-fourth Amendment) Act, 1978, s. 45 (w.e.f. 20-6-1979).

2 *See* the Prohibition of Simultaneous Membership Rules, 1950 published by the Ministry of Law Notification number F. 46/50-C, dated the 26th January, 1950, Gazette of India, Extraordinary, p. 678.

all such States shall become vacant, unless he has previously resigned his seat in the Legislatures of all but one of the States.

(3) If a member of a House of the Legislature of a State—

(*a*) becomes subject to any of the disqualifications mentioned in [1][clause (1) or clause (2) of article 191]; or

[2][(*b*) resigns his seat by writing under his hand addressed to the speaker or the Chairman, as the case may be, and his resignation is accepted by the Speaker or the Chairman, as the case may be,]

his seat shall thereupon become vacant:

[3][Provided that in the case of any resignation referred to in sub-clause (*b*), if from information received or otherwise and after making such inquiry as he thinks fit, the Speaker or the Chairman, as the case may be, is satisfied that such resignation is not voluntary or genuine, he shall not accept such resignation.]

(4) If for a period of sixty days a member of a House of the Legislature of a State is without permission of the House absent from all meetings thereof, the House may declare his seat vacant: Provided that in computing the said period of sixty days no account shall be taken of any period during which the House is prorogued or is adjourned for more than four consecutive days.

191. Disqualifications for membership.—(1) A person shall be disqualified for being chosen as, and for being, a member of the Legislative Assembly or Legislative Council of a State—

[4][(*a*) if he holds any office of profit under the Government of India or the Government of any State specified in the First Schedule, other than an office declared by the Legislature of the State by law not to disqualify its holder;]

---

1 Subs. by the Constitution (Fifty-second Amendment) Act, 1985, s. 4, for "clause (*1*) of article 191" (w.e.f. 1-3-1985).

2 Subs. by the Constitution (Thirty-third Amendment) Act, 1974, s. 3 (w.e.f. 19-5-1974).

3 Ins. by s. 3, *ibid.* (w.e.f. 19-5-1974).

4 Subs. by the Constitution (Forty-second Amendment) Act, 1976, s. 32 to read as "(a) if he holds any such office of profit under the Government of India or the Government of any State specified in the First Schedule as is declared by Parliament by law to disqualify its holder" (date not notified). This amendment was omitted by the Constitution (Forty-fourth Amendment) Act, 1978, s. 45 (w.e.f. 20-6-1979).

(b) if he is of unsound mind and stands so declared by a competent court;

(c) if he is an undischarged insolvent;

(d) if he is not a citizen of India, or has voluntarily acquired the citizenship of a foreign State, or is under any acknowledgment of allegiance or adherence to a foreign State;

(e) if he is so disqualified by or under any law made by Parliament.

¹[*Explanation.*—For the purposes of this clause], a person shall not be deemed to hold an office of profit under the Government of India or the Government of any State specified in the First Schedule by reason only that he is a Minister either for the Union or for such State.

²[(2) A person shall be disqualified for being a member of the Legislative Assembly or Legislative Council of a State if he is so disqualified under the Tenth Schedule.]

³[192. **Decision on questions as to disqualifications of members.**— (1) If any question arises as to whether a member of a House of the Legislature of a State has become subject to any of the disqualifications mentioned in clause (1) of article 191, the question shall be referred for the decision of the Governor and his decision shall be final.

(2) Before giving any decision on any such question, the Governor shall obtain the opinion of the Election Commission and shall act according to such opinion.]

193. **Penalty for sitting and voting before making oath or affirmation under article 188 or when not qualified or when disqualified.**—If a person sits or votes as a member of the Legislative Assembly or the Legislative Council of a State before he has complied with the requirements of article 188, or when

---

1 Subs. by the Constitution (Fifty-second Amendment) Act, 1985, s. 5, for "(2) For the purposes of this article" (w.e.f. 1-3-1985).

2 Ins. by s. 5, *ibid.* (w.e.f. 1-3-1985).

3 Subs. by the Constitution (Forty-second Amendment) Act, 1976, s. 33, for art. 192 (w.e.f. 3-1-1977) and further subs. by the Constitution (Forty-fourth Amendment) Act, 1978, s. 25, for art. 192 (w.e.f. 20-6-1979).

he knows that he is not qualified or that he is disqualified for membership thereof, or that he is prohibited from so doing by the provisions of any law made by Parliament or the Legislature of the State, he shall be liable in respect of each day on which he so sits or votes to a penalty of five hundred rupees to be recovered as a debt due to the State.

Powers, Privileges and Immunities of
State Legislatures and their Members

194. Powers, privileges, etc., of the Houses of Legislatures and of the members and committees thereof.—(1) Subject to the provisions of this Constitution and to the rules and standing orders regulating the procedure of the Legislature, there shall be freedom of speech in the Legislature of every State.

(2) No member of the Legislature of a State shall be liable to any proceedings in any court in respect of anything said or any vote given by him in the Legislature or any committee thereof, and no person shall be so liable in respect of the publication by or under the authority of a House of such a Legislature of any report, paper, votes or proceedings.

[1][(3) In other respects, the powers, privileges and immunities of a House of the Legislature of a State, and of the members and the committees of a House of such Legislature, shall be such as may from time to time be defined by the Legislature by law, and, until so defined, [2][shall be those of that House and of its members and committees immediately before the coming into force of section 26 of the Constitution (Forty-fourth Amendment) Act, 1978].

---

1 Subs. by the Constitution (Forty-second Amendment) Act, 1976, s. 34 to read as follows.:
"(3) In other respects, the powers, privileges and immunities of a House of the Legislature of a State, and of the members and the committees of a House of such Legislature, shall be those of that House, and of its members and Committees, at the commencement of section 34 of the Constitution (Forty-second Amendment) Act, 1976, and as may be evolved by such House of the House of the People, and of its members and committees where such House is the Legislative Assembly and in accordance with those of the Council of States, and of its members and committees where such House is the Legislative Council." (date not notified). This amendment was omitted by the Constitution (Forty-fourth Amendment) Act, 1978, s. 45 (w.e.f. 19-6-1979)."
2 Subs. by the Constitution (Forty-fourth Amendment) Act, 1978, s. 26, for certain words (w.e.f. 20-6-1979).

(4) The provisions of clauses (1), (2) and (3) shall apply in relation to persons who by virtue of this Constitution have the right to speak in, and otherwise to take part in the proceedings of, a House of the Legislature of a State or any committee thereof as they apply in relation to members of that Legislature.

195. **Salaries and allowances of members.**—Members of the Legislative Assembly and the Legislative Council of a State shall be entitled to receive such salaries and allowances as may from time to time be determined, by the Legislature of the State by law and, until provision in that respect is so made, salaries and allowances at such rates and upon such conditions as were immediately before the commencement of this Constitution applicable in the case of members of the Legislative Assembly of the corresponding Province.

Legislative Procedure

196. **Provisions as to introduction and passing of Bills.**—(1) Subject to the provisions of articles 198 and 207 with respect to Money Bills and other financial Bills, a Bill may originate in either House of the Legislature of a State which has a Legislative Council.

(2) Subject to the provisions of articles 197 and 198, a Bill shall not be deemed to have been passed by the Houses of the Legislature of a State having a Legislative Council unless it has been agreed to by both Houses, either without amendment or with such amendments only as are agreed to by both Houses.

(3) A Bill pending in the Legislature of a State shall not lapse by reason of the prorogation of the House or Houses thereof.

(4) A Bill pending in the Legislative Council of a State which has not been passed by the Legislative Assembly shall not lapse on a dissolution of the Assembly.

(5) A Bill which is pending in the Legislative Assembly of a State, or which having been passed by the Legislative Assembly is pending in the Legislative Council, shall lapse on a dissolution of the Assembly.

197. **Restriction on powers of Legislative Council as to Bills other than Money Bills.**—(1) If after a Bill has been passed by the Legislative Assembly of a State having a Legislative Council and transmitted to the Legislative Council—

(a) the Bill is rejected by the Council; or

(b) more than three months elapse from the date on which the Bill is laid before the Council without the Bill being passed by it; or

(c) the Bill is passed by the Council with amendments to which the Legislative Assembly does not agree;

the Legislative Assembly may, subject to the rules regulating its procedure, pass the Bill again in the same or in any subsequent session with or without such amendments, if any, as have been made, suggested or agreed to by the Legislative Council and then transmit the Bill as so passed to the Legislative Council.

(2) If after a Bill has been so passed for the second time by the Legislative Assembly and transmitted to the Legislative Council—

(a) the Bill is rejected by the Council; or

(b) more than one-month elapses from the date on which the Bill is laid before the Council without the Bill being passed by it; or

(c) the Bill is passed by the Council with amendments to which the Legislative Assembly does not agree;

the Bill shall be deemed to have been passed by the Houses of the Legislature of the State in the form in which it was passed by the Legislative Assembly for the second time with such amendments, if any, as have been made or suggested by the Legislative Council and agreed to by the Legislative Assembly.

(3) Nothing in this article shall apply to a Money Bill.

198. **Special procedure in respect of Money Bills.**—(1) A Money Bill shall not be introduced in a Legislative Council.

(2) After a Money Bill has been passed by the Legislative Assembly of a State having a Legislative Council, it shall be transmitted to the Legislative Council for its recommendations, and the Legislative Council shall within a period of fourteen days from the date of its receipt of the Bill return the Bill to the Legislative Assembly with its recommendations, and the Legislative Assembly may thereupon either accept or reject all or any of the recommendations of the Legislative Council.

(3) If the Legislative Assembly accepts any of the recommendations of the Legislative Council, the Money Bill shall be deemed to have been passed by both Houses with the amendments recommended by the Legislative Council and accepted by the Legislative Assembly.

(4) If the Legislative Assembly does not accept any of the recommendations of the Legislative Council, the Money Bill shall be deemed to have been passed by both Houses in the form in which it was passed by the Legislative Assembly without any of the amendments recommended by the Legislative Council.

(5) If a Money Bill passed by the Legislative Assembly and transmitted to the Legislative Council for its recommendations is not returned to the Legislative Assembly within the said period of fourteen days, it shall be deemed to have been passed by both Houses at the expiration of the said period in the form in which it was passed by the Legislative Assembly.

199. **Definition of "Money Bills".**—(1) For the purposes of this Chapter, a Bill shall be deemed to be a Money Bill if it contains only provisions dealing with all or any of the following matters, namely:—

(a) the imposition, abolition, remission, alteration or regulation of any tax;

(b) the regulation of the borrowing of money or the giving of any guarantee by the State, or the amendment of the law with respect to any financial obligations undertaken or to be undertaken by the State;

(c) the custody of the Consolidated Fund or the Contingency Fund of the State, the payment of moneys into or the withdrawal of moneys from any such Fund;

(d) the appropriation of moneys out of the Consolidated Fund of the State;

(e) the declaring of any expenditure to be expenditure charged on the Consolidated Fund of the State, or the increasing of the amount of any such expenditure;

(f) the receipt of money on account of the Consolidated Fund of the State or the public account of the State or the custody or issue of such money; or

(g) any matter incidental to any of the matters specified in sub-clauses (*a*) to (*f*).

(2) A Bill shall not be deemed to be a Money Bill by reason only that it provides for the imposition of fines or other pecuniary penalties, or for the demand or payment of fees for licences or fees for services rendered, or by reason that it provides for the imposition, abolition, remission, alteration or regulation of any tax by any local authority or body for local purposes.

(3) If any question arises whether a Bill introduced in the Legislature of a State which has a Legislative Council is a Money Bill or not, the decision of the Speaker of the Legislative Assembly of such State thereon shall be final.

(4) There shall be endorsed on every Money Bill when it is transmitted to the Legislative Council under article 198, and when it is presented to the Governor for assent under article 200, the certificate of the Speaker of the Legislative Assembly signed by him that it is a Money Bill.

200.   **Assent to Bills.**—When a Bill has been passed by the Legislative Assembly of a State or, in the case of a State having a Legislative Council, has been passed by both Houses of the Legislature of the State, it shall be presented to the Governor and the Governor shall declare either that he assents to the Bill or that he withholds assent therefrom or that he reserves the Bill for the consideration of the President:

Provided that the Governor may, as soon as possible after the presentation to him of the Bill for assent, return the Bill if it is not a Money Bill together with a message requesting that the House or Houses will reconsider the Bill or any specified provisions thereof and, in particular, will consider the desirability of introducing any such amendments as he may recommend in his message and, when a Bill is so returned, the House or Houses shall reconsider the Bill accordingly, and if the Bill is passed again by the House or Houses with or without amendment and presented to the Governor for assent, the Governor shall not withhold assent therefrom:

Provided further that the Governor shall not assent to, but shall reserve for the consideration of the President, any Bill which in the opinion of the Governor would, if it became law, so derogate from the powers of the High Court as to endanger the position which that Court is by this Constitution designed to fill.

201. Bills reserved for consideration.—When a Bill is reserved by a Governor for the consideration of the President, the President shall declare either that he assents to the Bill or that he withholds assent therefrom:

Provided that, where the Bill is not a Money Bill, the President may direct the Governor to return the Bill to the House or, as the case may be, the Houses of the Legislature of the State together with such a message as is mentioned in the first proviso to article 200 and, when a Bill is so returned, the House or Houses shall reconsider it accordingly within a period of six months from the date of receipt of such message and, if it is again passed by the House or Houses with or without amendment, it shall be presented again to the President for his consideration.

Procedure in Financial Matters

202. Annual financial statement.—(1) The Governor shall in respect of every financial year cause to be laid before the House or Houses of the Legislature of the State a statement of the estimated receipts and expenditure of the State for that year, in this Part referred to as the "annual financial statement".

(2) The estimates of expenditure embodied in the annual financial statement shall show separately—

(*a*) the sums required to meet expenditure described by this Constitution as expenditure charged upon the Consolidated Fund of the State; and

(*b*) the sums required to meet other expenditure proposed to be made from the Consolidated Fund of the State;

and shall distinguish expenditure on revenue account from other expenditure.

(3) The following expenditure shall be expenditure charged on the Consolidated Fund of each State—

(*a*) the emoluments and allowances of the Governor and other expenditure relating to his office;

129

(*b*) the salaries and allowances of the Speaker and the Deputy Speaker of the Legislative Assembly and, in the case of a State having a Legislative Council, also of the Chairman and the Deputy Chairman of the Legislative Council;

(*c*) debt charges for which the State is liable including interest, sinking fund charges and redemption charges, and other expenditure relating to the raising of loans and the service and redemption of debt;

(*d*) expenditure in respect of the salaries and allowances of Judges of any High Court;

(*e*) any sums required to satisfy any judgment, decree or award of any court or arbitral tribunal;

(*f*) any other expenditure declared by this Constitution, or by the Legislature of the State by law, to be so charged.

203. **Procedure in Legislature with respect to estimates.**—(1) So much of the estimates as relates to expenditure charged upon the Consolidated Fund of a State shall not be submitted to the vote of the Legislative Assembly, but nothing in this clause shall be construed as preventing the discussion in the Legislature of any of those estimates.

(2) So much of the said estimates as relates to other expenditure shall be submitted in the form of demands for grants to the Legislative Assembly, and the Legislative Assembly shall have power to assent, or to refuse to assent, to any demand, or to assent to any demand subject to a reduction of the amount specified therein.

(3) No demand for a grant shall be made except on the recommendation of the Governor.

204. **Appropriation Bills.**—(1) As soon as may be after the grants under article 203 have been made by the Assembly, there shall be introduced a Bill to provide for the appropriation out of the Consolidated Fund of the State of all moneys required to meet—

(*a*) the grants so made by the Assembly; and

(*b*) the expenditure charged on the Consolidated Fund of the State but not exceeding in any case the amount shown in the statement previously laid before the House or Houses.

(2) No amendment shall be proposed to any such Bill in the House or either House of the Legislature of the State which will have the effect of varying the amount or altering the destination of any grant so made or of varying the amount of any expenditure charged on the Consolidated Fund of the State, and the decision of the person presiding as to whether an amendment is inadmissible under this clause shall be final.

(3) Subject to the provisions of articles 205 and 206, no money shall be withdrawn from the Consolidated Fund of the State except under appropriation made by law passed in accordance with the provisions of this article.

205. Supplementary, additional or excess grants.—(1) The Governor shall—

    (*a*) if the amount authorised by any law made in accordance with the provisions of article 204 to be expended for a particular service for the current financial year is found to be insufficient for the purposes of that year or when a need has arisen during the current financial year for supplementary or additional expenditure upon some new service not contemplated in the annual financial statement for that year, or

    (*b*) if any money has been spent on any service during a financial year in excess of the amount granted for that service and for that year,

cause to be laid before the House or the Houses of the Legislature of the State another statement showing the estimated amount of that expenditure or cause to be presented to the Legislative Assembly of the State a demand for such excess, as the case may be.

(2) The provisions of articles 202, 203 and 204 shall have effect in relation to any such statement and expenditure or demand and also to any law to be made authorising the appropriation of moneys out of the Consolidated Fund of the State to meet such expenditure or the grant in respect of such demand as they have effect in relation to the annual financial statement and the expenditure mentioned therein or to a demand for a grant and the law to be made for the authorisation of appropriation of

moneys out of the Consolidated Fund of the State to meet such expenditure or grant.

206. **Votes on account, votes of credit and exceptional grants.**—(1) Notwithstanding anything in the foregoing provisions of this Chapter, the Legislative Assembly of a State shall have power—

(a) to make any grant in advance in respect of the estimated expenditure for a part of any financial year pending the completion of the procedure prescribed in article 203 for the voting of such grant and the passing of the law in accordance with the provisions of article 204 in relation to that expenditure;

(b) to make a grant for meeting an unexpected demand upon the resources of the State when on account of the magnitude or the indefinite character of the service the demand cannot be stated with the details ordinarily given in an annual financial statement;

(c) to make an exceptional grant which forms no part of the current service of any financial year;

and the Legislature of the State shall have power to authorise by law the withdrawal of moneys from the Consolidated Fund of the State for the purposes for which the said grants are made.

(2) The provisions of articles 203 and 204 shall have effect in relation to the making of any grant under clause (1) and to any law to be made under that clause as they have effect in relation to the making of a grant with regard to any expenditure mentioned in the annual financial statement and the law to be made for the authorisation of appropriation of moneys out of the Consolidated Fund of the State to meet such expenditure.

207. **Special provisions as to financial Bills.**—(1) A Bill or amendment making provision for any of the matters specified in sub-clauses *(a)* to *(f)* of clause (1) of article 199 shall not be introduced or moved except on the recommendation of the Governor, and a Bill making such provision shall not be introduced in a Legislative Council:

Provided that no recommendation shall be required under this clause for the moving of an amendment making provision for the reduction or abolition of any tax.

(2) A Bill or amendment shall not be deemed to make provision for any of the matters aforesaid by reason only that it provides for the imposition of fines or other pecuniary penalties, or for the demand or payment of fees for licences or fees for services rendered, or by reason that it provides for the imposition, abolition, remission, alteration or regulation of any tax by any local authority or body for local purposes.

(3) A Bill which, if enacted and brought into operation, would involve expenditure from the Consolidated Fund of a State shall not be passed by a House of the Legislature of the State unless the Governor has recommended to that House the consideration of the Bill.

Procedure Generally

208. **Rules of procedure.**—(1) A House of the Legislature of a State may make rules for regulating, subject to the provisions of this Constitution, its procedure* and the conduct of its business.

(2) Until rules are made under clause (1), the rules of procedure and standing orders in force immediately before the commencement of this Constitution with respect to the Legislature for the corresponding Province shall have effect in relation to the Legislature of the State subject to such modifications and adaptations as may be made therein by the Speaker of the Legislative Assembly, or the Chairman of the Legislative Council, as the case may be.

(3) In a State having a Legislative Council the Governor, after consultation with the Speaker of the Legislative Assembly and the Chairman of the Legislative Council, may make rules as to the procedure with respect to communications between the two Houses.

209. **Regulation by law of procedure in the Legislature of the State in relation to financial business.**—The Legislature of a

---

* The brackets and words "(including the quorum to constitute a meeting of the House)" ins. by the Constitution (Forty-second Amendment) Act, 1976, s. 35 (date not notified). This amendment was omitted by the Constitution (Forty-fourth Amendment) Act, 1978, s. 45 (w.e.f. 20-6-1979).

State may, for the purpose of the timely completion of financial business, regulate by law the procedure of, and the conduct of business in, the House or Houses of the Legislature of the State in relation to any financial matter or to any Bill for the appropriation of moneys out of the Consolidated Fund of the State, and, if and so far as any provision of any law so made is inconsistent with any rule made by the House or either House of the Legislature of the State under clause (1) of article 208 or with any rule or standing order having effect in relation to the Legislature of the State under clause (2) of that article, such provision shall prevail.

210. Language to be used in the Legislature.—(1) Notwithstanding anything in Part XVII, but subject to the provisions of article 348, business in the Legislature of a State shall be transacted in the official language or languages of the State or in Hindi or in English:

Provided that the Speaker of the Legislative Assembly or Chairman of the Legislative Council, or person acting as such, as the case may be, may permit any member who cannot adequately express himself in any of the languages aforesaid to address the House in his mother-tongue.

(2) Unless the Legislature of the State by law otherwise provides, this article shall, after the expiration of a period of fifteen years from the commencement of this Constitution, have effect as if the words "or in English" were omitted therefrom:

[1][Provided that in relation to the [2][Legislatures of the States of Himachal Pradesh, Manipur, Meghalaya and Tripura] this clause shall have effect as if for the words "fifteen years" occurring therein, the words "twenty-five years" were substituted:]

[3][Provided further that in relation to the [4][Legislatures of the States of [5][Arunachal Pradesh, Goa and Mizoram]], this clause

---

1 Ins. by the State of Himachal Pradesh Act, 1970 (53 of 1970), s. 46 (w.e.f. 25-1-1971).
2 Subs. by the North-Eastern Areas (Reorganisation) Act, 1971 (81 of 1971), s. 71, for "Legislature of the State of Himachal Pradesh" (w.e.f. 21-1-1972).
3 Ins. by the State of Mizoram Act, 1986 (34 of 1986), s. 39 (w.e.f. 20-2-1987).
4 Subs. by the State of Arunachal Pradesh Act, 1986 (69 of 1986), s. 42, for "Legislature of the State of Mizoram" (w.e.f. 20-2-1987).
5 Subs. by the Goa, Daman and Diu Reorganisation Act, 1987 (18 of 1987), s. 63, for "Arunachal Pradesh and Mizoram" (w.e.f. 30-5-1987).

shall have effect as if for the words "fifteen years" occurring therein, the words "forty years" were substituted.]

211. Restriction on discussion in the Legislature.—No discussion shall take place in the Legislature of a State with respect to the conduct of any Judge of the Supreme Court or of a High Court in the discharge of his duties.

212. Courts not to inquire into proceedings of the Legislature.— (1) The validity of any proceedings in the Legislature of a State shall not be called in question on the ground of any alleged irregularity of procedure.

(2) No officer or member of the Legislature of a State in whom powers are vested by or under this Constitution for regulating procedure or the conduct of business, or for maintaining order, in the Legislature shall be subject to the jurisdiction of any court in respect of the exercise by him of those powers.

Chapter IV.—Legislative Power of the Governor

213. Power of Governor to promulgate Ordinances during recess of Legislature.—(1) If at any time, except when the Legislative Assembly of a State is in session, or where there is a Legislative Council in a State, except when both Houses of the Legislature are in session, the Governor is satisfied that circumstances exist which render it necessary for him to take immediate action, he may promulgate such Ordinances as the circumstances appear to him to require:

Provided that the Governor shall not, without instructions from the President, promulgate any such Ordinance if—

(a) a Bill containing the same provisions would under this Constitution have required the previous sanction of the President for the introduction thereof into the Legislature; or

(b) he would have deemed it necessary to reserve a Bill containing the same provisions for the consideration of the President; or

(c) an Act of the Legislature of the State containing the same provisions would under this Constitution have been invalid unless, having been reserved for the consideration of the President, it had received the assent of the President.

(2) An Ordinance promulgated under this article shall have the same force and effect as an Act of the Legislature of the State assented to by the Governor, but every such Ordinance—

(a) shall be laid before the Legislative Assembly of the State, or where there is a Legislative Council in the State, before both the Houses, and shall cease to operate at the expiration of six weeks from the reassembly of the Legislature, or if before the expiration of that period a resolution disapproving it is passed by the Legislative Assembly and agreed to by the Legislative Council, if any, upon the passing of the resolution or, as the case may be, on the resolution being agreed to by the Council; and

(b) may be withdrawn at any time by the Governor.

Explanation.—Where the Houses of the Legislature of a State having a Legislative Council are summoned to reassemble on different dates, the period of six weeks shall be reckoned from the later of those dates for the purposes of this clause.

(3) If and so far as an Ordinance under this article makes any provision which would not be valid if enacted in an Act of the Legislature of the State assented to by the Governor, it shall be void:

Provided that, for the purposes of the provisions of this Constitution relating to the effect of an Act of the Legislature of a State which is repugnant to an Act of Parliament or an existing law with respect to a matter enumerated in the Concurrent List, an Ordinance promulgated under this article in pursuance of instructions from the President shall be deemed to be an Act of the Legislature of the State which has been reserved for the consideration of the President and assented to by him.

[1](4)*   *   *   *

---

1 Cl. (4) was ins. by the Constitution (Thirty-eighth Amendment) Act, 1975, s. 3 (with retrospective effect) and omitted by the Constitution (Forty-fourth Amendment) Act, 1978, s. 27 (w.e.f. 20-6-1979).

Chapter V.—The High Courts in the States

214. **High Courts for States.**—[2]*** There shall be a High Court for each State.

[1](2)*   *   *   *

[2](3)*   *   *   *

215. **High Courts to be courts of record.**—Every High Court shall be a court of record and shall have all the powers of such a court including the power to punish for contempt of itself.

216. **Constitution of High Courts.**—Every High Court shall consist of a Chief Justice and such other Judges as the President may from time to time deem it necessary to appoint.

[3]*   *   *   *   *

217. **Appointment and conditions of the office of a Judge of a High Court.**—(1) Every Judge of a High Court shall be appointed by the President by warrant under his hand and seal [4][on the recommendation of the National Judicial Appointments Commission referred to in article 124A], and the Governor of the State, and, in the case of appointment of a Judge other than the Chief Justice, the Chief Justice of the High Court, [5][shall hold office, in the case of an additional or acting Judge, as provided in article 224, and in any other case, until he attains the age of [6][sixty-two years:]]

Provided that—

    (*a*) a Judge may, by writing under his hand addressed to the President, resign his office;

---

1 The bracket and figure "(1)" omitted by the Constitution (Seventh Amendment) Act, 1956, s. 29 and Sch. (w.e.f. 1-11-1956).

2 Cls. (2) and (3) omitted by s. 29 and Sch., *ibid.* (w.e.f. 1-11-1956).

3 Proviso omitted by the Constitution (Seventh Amendment) Act, 1956, s. 11 (w.e.f. 1-11-1956).

4 Subs. by the Constitution (Ninety-ninth Amendment) Act, 2014, s. 6, for "after consultation with the Chief Justice of India, the Governor of the State, and, in the case of appointment of a Judge other than the Chief Justice, the Chief Justice of the High Court" (w.e.f. 13-4-2015). This amendment has been struck down by the Supreme Court in the case of Supreme Court Advocates-on-Record Association and Another Vs. Union of India in its judgment dated 16-10-2015, AIR 2016 SC 117.

5 Subs. by the Constitution (Seventh Amendment) Act, 1956, s. 12, for "shall hold office until he attains the age of sixty years" (w.e.f. 1-11-1956).

6 Subs. by the Constitution (Fifteenth Amendment) Act, 1963, s. 4(*a*), for "sixty years" (w.e.f. 5-10-1963).

(*b*) a Judge may be removed from his office by the President in the manner provided in clause (4) of article 124 for the removal of a Judge of the Supreme Court;

(*c*) the office of a Judge shall be vacated by his being appointed by the President to be a Judge of the Supreme Court or by his being transferred by the President to any other High Court within the territory of India.

(2) A person shall not be qualified for appointment as a Judge of a High Court unless he is a citizen of India and—

(*a*) has for at least ten years held a judicial office in the territory of India; or

(*b*) has for at least ten years been an advocate of a High Court [1]*** or of two or more such Courts in succession.[2]***

[2][(c) * * * * *

Explanation.—For the purposes of this clause—

[3][(*a*) in computing the period during which a person has held judicial office in the territory of India, there shall be included any period, after he has held any judicial office, during which the person has been an advocate of a High Court or has held the office of a member of a tribunal or any post, under the Union or a State, requiring special knowledge of law;]

[4][(*aa*)]in computing the period during which a person has been an advocate of a High Court, there shall be included any period during which the person [5][has held judicial office or the office of a member of a tribunal or any post, under the Union or a State, requiring special knowledge of law] after he became an advocate;

---

1 The words "in any State specified in the First Schedule" omitted by the Constitution (Seventh Amendment) Act, 1956, s. 29 and Sch. (w.e.f. 1-11-1956).

2 The word "or" and sub-clause (c) were ins. by the Constitution (Forty-second Amendment) Act, 1976, s. 36 (w.e.f. 3-1-1977) and omitted by the Constitution (Forty-fourth Amendment) Act, 1978, s. 28 (w.e.f. 20-6-1979).

3 Ins. by the Constitution (Forty-fourth Amendment) Act, 1978. s. 28 (w.e.f. 20-6-1979).

4 Cl. (a) re-lettered as cl. (aa) by the Constitution (Forty-fourth Amendment) Act, 1978, s. 28 (w.e.f. 20-6-1979).

5 Subs. by the Constitution (Forty-second Amendment) Act, 1976, s. 36, for "has held judicial office" (w.e.f. 3-1-1977).

(*b*) in computing the period during which a person has held judicial office in the territory of India or been an advocate of a High Court, there shall be included any period before the commencement of this Constitution during which he has held judicial office in any area which was comprised before the fifteenth day of August, 1947, within India as defined by the Government of India Act, 1935, or has been an advocate of any High Court in any such area, as the case may be.

[1][(3) If any question arises as to the age of a Judge of a High Court, the question shall be decided by the President after consultation with the Chief Justice of India and the decision of the President shall be final.]

218. **Application of certain provisions relating to Supreme Court to High Courts.**—The provisions of clauses (4) and (5) of article 124 shall apply in relation to a High Court as they apply in relation to the Supreme Court with the substitution of references to the High Court for references to the Supreme Court.

219. **Oath or affirmation by Judges of High Courts.**—Every person appointed to be a Judge of a High Court [2]*** shall, before he enters upon his office, make and subscribe before the Governor of the State, or some person appointed in that behalf by him, an oath or affirmation according to the form set out for the purpose in the Third Schedule.

[3][**220.** **Restriction on practice after being a permanent Judge.**—No person who, after the commencement of this Constitution, has held office as a permanent Judge of a High Court shall plead or act in any court or before any authority in India except the Supreme Court and the other High Courts.

Explanation.—In this article, the expression "High Court" does not include a High Court for a State specified in Part B of the

---

1 Ins. by the Constitution (Fifteenth Amendment) Act, 1963, s. 4(*b*), (with retrospective effect).
2 The words "in a State" omitted by the Constitution (Seventh Amendment) Act, 1956, s. 29 and Sch. (w.e.f. 1-11-1956).
3 Subs. by s. 13, *ibid.* (w.e.f. 1-11-1956).

First Schedule as it existed before the commencement[1] of the Constitution (Seventh Amendment) Act, 1956.]

221. **Salaries, etc., of Judges.**—[2][(1) There shall be paid to the Judges of each High Court such salaries as may be determined by Parliament by law and, until provision in that behalf is so made, such salaries as are specified in the Second Schedule.]

(2) Every Judge shall be entitled to such allowances and to such rights in respect of leave of absence and pension as may from time to time be determined by or under law made by Parliament and, until so determined, to such allowances and rights as are specified in the Second Schedule:

Provided that neither the allowances of a Judge nor his rights in respect to leave of absence or pension shall be varied to his disadvantage after his appointment.

222. **Transfer of a Judge from one High Court to another.**—(1) The President may, [3][on the recommendation of the National Judicial Appointments Commission referred to in article 124A], transfer a Judge from one High Court to any other High Court [4]***.

[5][(2) When a Judge has been or is so transferred, he shall, during the period he serves, after the commencement of the Constitution (Fifteenth Amendment) Act, 1963, as a Judge of the other High Court, be entitled to receive in addition to his salary such compensatory allowance as may be determined by Parliament by law and, until so determined, such compensatory allowance as the President may by order fix.]

223. **Appointment of acting Chief Justice.**—When the office of Chief Justice of a High Court is vacant or when any such

---

1 1st November, 1956.

2 Subs. by the Constitution (Fifty-fourth Amendment) Act, 1986, s. 3, for clause (1) (w.e.f. 1-4-1986).

3 Subs. by the Constitution (Ninety-ninth Amendment) Act, 2014, s. 7, for "after consultation with the Chief Justice of India" (w.e.f. 13-4-2015). This amendment has been struck down by the Supreme Court in the case of *Supreme Court Advocates-on- Record Association and Another Vs. Union of India* in its judgment dated 16-10-2015, AIR 2016 SC 117.

4 The words "within the territory of India" omitted by the Constitution (Seventh Amendment) Act, 1956, s. 14 (w.e.f. 1-11-1956).

5 Ins. by the Constitution (Fifteenth Amendment) Act, 1963, s. 5 (w.e.f. 5-10-1963). Original cl. (2) was omitted by the Constitution (Seventh Amendment) Act, 1956, s. 14 (w.e.f. 1-11-1956).

Chief Justice is, by reason of absence or otherwise, unable to perform the duties of his office, the duties of the office shall be performed by such one of the other Judges of the Court as the President may appoint for the purpose.

¹[**224. Appointment of additional and acting Judges.**—(1) If by reason of any temporary increase in the business of a High Court or by reason of arrears of work therein, it appears to the President that the number of the Judges of that Court should be for the time being increased, ²[the President may, in consultation with the National Judicial Appointments Commission, appoint] duly qualified persons to be additional Judges of the Court for such period not exceeding two years as he may specify.

(2) When any Judge of a High Court other than the Chief Justice is by reason of absence or for any other reason unable to perform the duties of his office or is appointed to act temporarily as Chief Justice, ³[the President may, in consultation with the National Judicial Appointments Commission, appoint] a duly qualified person to act as a Judge of that Court until the permanent Judge has resumed his duties.

(3) No person appointed as an additional or acting Judge of a High Court shall hold office after attaining the age of ⁴[sixty-two years].]

⁵[**224A. Appointment of retired Judges at sittings of High Courts.**— Notwithstanding anything in this Chapter, ⁶[the National

---

1 Subs. by the Constitution (Seventh Amendment) Act, 1956, s. 15 for art. 224 (w.e.f. 1-11-1956).

2 Subs. by the Constitution (Ninety-ninth Amendment) Act, 2014, s. 8, for "the President may appoint" (w.e.f. 13-4-2015). This amendment has been struck down, by the Supreme Court in the case of Supreme Court *Advocates-on-Record Association* and Another *Vs. Union of India* in its judgment, dated 16-10-2015, AIR 2016 SC 117.

3 Subs. by the Constitution (Ninety-ninth Amendment) Act, 2014, s. 8 for "the President may appoint" (w.e.f. 13-4-2015). This amendment has been struck down by the Supreme Court in the case of Supreme Court *Advocates-on-Record Association and Another Vs. Union of India* in its judgment, dated 16-10-2015, AIR 2016 SC 117.

4 Subs. by the Constitution (Fifteenth Amendment) Act, 1963, s. 6, for "sixty years" (w.e.f. 5-10-1963).

5 Ins. by s. 7, *ibid.* (w.e.f. 5-10-1963).

6 Subs. by the Constitution (Ninety-ninth Amendment) Act, 2014, s. 9, for "the Chief Justice of a High Court for any State may at any time, with the previous consent of the President" (w.e.f. 13-4-2015). This amendment has been struck down by the Supreme Court in the case of Supreme Court *Advocates-on-Record Association and Another Vs. Union of India* in its judgment dated 16-10-2015, AIR 2016 SC 117.

Judicial Appointments Commission on a reference made to it by the Chief Justice of a High Court for any State, may with the previous consent of the President], request any person who has held the office of a Judge of that Court or of any other High Court to sit and act as a Judge of the High Court for that State, and every such person so requested shall, while so sitting and acting, be entitled to such allowances as the President may by order determine and have all the jurisdiction, powers and privileges of, but shall not otherwise be deemed to be, a Judge of that High Court:

Provided that nothing in this article shall be deemed to require any such person as aforesaid to sit and act as a Judge of that High Court unless he consents so to do.]

225. **Jurisdiction of existing High Courts.**—Subject to the provisions of this Constitution and to the provisions of any law of the appropriate Legislature made by virtue of powers conferred on that Legislature by this Constitution, the jurisdiction of, and the law administered in, any existing High Court, and the respective powers of the Judges thereof in relation to the administration of justice in the Court, including any power to make rules of Court and to regulate the sittings of the Court and of members thereof sitting alone or in Division Courts, shall be the same as immediately before the commencement of this Constitution:

[1][Provided that any restriction to which the exercise of original jurisdiction by any of the High Courts with respect to any matter concerning the revenue or concerning any act ordered or done in the collection thereof was subject immediately before the commencement of this Constitution shall no longer apply to the exercise of such jurisdiction.]

[2][226. **Power of High Courts to issue certain writs.**—(1) Notwithstanding anything in article 32 [3]***, every High Court shall have power, throughout the territories in relation to which

---

1 Omitted by the Constitution (Forty-second Amendment) Act, 1976, s. 37 (w.e.f. 1-2-1977) and subsequently ins. by the Constitution (Forty-fourth Amendment) Act, 1978, s. 29 (w.e.f. 20-6-1979).

2 Subs. by the Constitution (Forty-second Amendment) Act, 1976, s. 38 for art. 226 (w.e.f. 1-2-1977).

3 The words, figures and letters "but subject to the provisions of article 131A and article 226A" omitted by the Constitution (Forty-third Amendment) Act, 1977, s. 7 (w.e.f. 13-4-1978).

it exercises jurisdiction, to issue to any person or authority, including in appropriate cases, any Government, within those territories directions, orders or writs, including [1][writs in the nature of *habeas corpus, mandamus,* prohibition, *quo warranto* and *certiorari,* or any of them, for the enforcement of any of the rights conferred by Part III and for any other purpose.]

(2) The power conferred by clause (1) to issue directions, orders or writs to any Government, authority or person may also be exercised by any High Court exercising jurisdiction in relation to the territories within which the cause of action, wholly or in part, arises for the exercise of such power, notwithstanding that the seat of such Government or authority or the residence of such person is not within those territories.

[2][(3) Where any party against whom an interim order, whether by way of injunction or stay or in any other manner, is made on, or in any proceedings relating to, a petition under clause (1), without—

(a) furnishing to such party copies of such petition and all documents in support of the plea for such interim order; and

(b) giving such party an opportunity of being heard,

makes an application to the High Court for the vacation of such order and furnishes a copy of such application to the party in whose favour such order has been made or the counsel of such party, the High Court shall dispose of the application within a period of two weeks from the date on which it is received or from the date on which the copy of such application is so furnished, whichever is later, or where the High Court is closed on the last day of that period, before the expiry of the next day afterwards on which the High Court is open; and if the application is not so disposed of, the interim order shall, on the expiry of that period, or, as the case may be, the expiry of the said next day, stand vacated.]

---

1 Subs. by the Constitution (Forty-fourth Amendment) Act, 1978, s. 30, for the portion beginning with "writs in the nature of *habeas corpus, mandamus, prohibition, quo warranto and certiorari,* or any of them" and ending with "such illegality has resulted in substantial failure of justice." (w.e.f. 1-8-1979).

2 Subs. by s.30, *ibid.,* for cls. (3), (4), (5) and (6) (w.e.f. 1-8-1979).

[1][(4) The power conferred on a High Court by this article shall not be in derogation of the power conferred on the Supreme Court by clause (2) of article 32.]

[2][**226A.** *Constitutional validity of Central laws not to be considered in proceedings under article 226.*].—*Omitted by the Constitution (Forty-third Amendment) Act, 1977, s. 8 (w.e.f. 13-4-1978).*

227. Power of superintendence over all courts by the High Court.— [3][(1) Every High Court shall have superintendence over all courts and tribunals throughout the territories in relation to which it exercises jurisdiction.]

(2) Without prejudice to the generality of the foregoing provision, the High Court may—

    (*a*) call for returns from such courts;

    (*b*) make and issue general rules and prescribe forms for regulating the practice and proceedings of such courts; and

    (*c*) prescribe forms in which books, entries and accounts shall be kept by the officers of any such courts.

(3) The High Court may also settle tables of fees to be allowed to the sheriff and all clerks and officers of such courts and to attorneys, advocates and pleaders practising therein:

Provided that any rules made, forms prescribed or tables settled under clause (2) or clause (3) shall not be inconsistent with the provision of any law for the time being in force, and shall require the previous approval of the Governor.

(4) Nothing in this article shall be deemed to confer on a High Court powers of superintendence over any court or tribunal constituted by or under any law relating to the Armed Forces.

[4](5) *   *   *   *

---

1 Cl. (7) renumbered as cl. (4) by the Constitution (Forty-fourth Amendment) Act, 1978, s. 30 (w.e.f. 1-8-1979).

2 Ins. by the Constitution (Forty-second Amendment) Act, 1976, s. 39 (w.e.f. 1-2-1977).

3 Subs. by the Constitution (Forty-second Amendment) Act, 1976, s. 40, for cl. (1) (w.e.f. 1-2-1977) and further subs. by the Constitution (Forty-fourth Amendment) Act, 1978, s. 31, for cl. (1) (w.e.f. 20-6-1979).

4 Cl. (5) was ins. by the Constitution (Forty-second Amendment) Act, 1976, s. 40 (w.e.f. 1-2-1977) and omitted by the Constitution (Forty-fourth Amendment) Act, 1978, s. 31 (w.e.f. 20-6-1979).

228. **Transfer of certain cases to High Court.**—If the High Court is satisfied that a case pending in a court subordinate to it involves a substantial question of law as to the interpretation of this Constitution the determination of which is necessary for the disposal of the case, [1][it shall withdraw the case and [2]*** may—]

(a) either dispose of the case itself, or

(b) determine the said question of law and return the case to the court from which the case has been so withdrawn together with a copy of its judgment on such question, and the said court shall on receipt thereof proceed to dispose of the case in conformity with such judgment.

[3][**228A.** *Special provisions as to disposal of questions relating to constitutional validity of State laws*].—*Omitted by the Constitution (Forty- third Amendment) Act,* 1977, *s.* 10 (w.e.f. 13-4-1978*).

229. **Officers and servants and the expenses of High Courts.**—(1) Appointments of officers and servants of a High Court shall be made by the Chief Justice of the Court or such other Judge or officer of the Court as he may direct:

Provided that the Governor of the State [4]*** may by rule require that in such cases as may be specified in the rule no person not already attached to the Court shall be appointed to any office connected with the Court save after consultation with the State Public Service Commission.

(2) Subject to the provisions of any law made by the Legislature of the State, the conditions of service of officers and servants of a High Court shall be such as may be prescribed by rules made by the Chief Justice of the Court or by some other Judge or officer of the Court authorised by the Chief Justice to make rules for the purpose:

---

1 Subs. by the Constitution (Forty-second Amendment) Act, 1976, s. 41, for "it shall withdraw the case and may—" (w.e.f. 1-2-1977).

2 The words, figures and letter, "subject to the provisions of article 131A," omitted by the Constitution (Forty-third Amendment) Act, 1977, s. 9 (w.e.f. 13-4-1978).

3 Ins. by the Constitution (Forty-second Amendment) Act, 1976, s. 42 (w.e.f. 1-2-1977).

4 The words "in which the High Court has its principal seat" omitted by the Constitution (Seventh Amendment) Act, 1956, s. 29 and Sch. (w.e.f. 1-11-1956).

Provided that the rules made under this clause shall, so far as they relate to salaries, allowances, leave or pensions, require the approval of the Governor of the State ¹***.

(3) The administrative expenses of a High Court, including all salaries, allowances and pensions payable to or in respect of the officers and servants of the Court, shall be charged upon the Consolidated Fund of the State, and any fees or other moneys taken by the Court shall form part of that Fund.

¹[**230. Extension of jurisdiction of High Courts to Union territories.**—(1) Parliament may by law extend the jurisdiction of a High Court to, or exclude the jurisdiction of a High Court from, any Union territory.

(2) Where the High Court of a State exercises jurisdiction in relation to a Union territory,—

    (*a*) nothing in this Constitution shall be construed as empowering the Legislature of the State to increase, restrict or abolish that jurisdiction; and

    (*b*) the reference in article 227 to the Governor shall, in relation to any rules, forms or tables for subordinate courts in that territory, be construed as a reference to the President.

231. Establishment of a common High Court for two or more States.—(1) Notwithstanding anything contained in the preceding provisions of this Chapter, Parliament may by law establish a common High Court for two or more States or for two or more States and a Union territory.

(2) In relation to any such High Court,—

    ²(*a*)   *   *   *   *   *

    (*b*) the reference in article 227 to the Governor shall, in relation to any rules, forms or tables for subordinate courts, be construed as a reference to the Governor

---

1 Subs. by s. 16, *ibid.*, for arts. 230, 231 and 232 (w.e.f. 1-11-1956).

2 Sub-clause (a) omitted by the Constitution (Ninety-ninth Amendment) Act, 2014, s. 10 (w.e.f. 13-4-2015). This amendment has been struck down by the Supreme Court *vide its order the* 16-10-2015 in the *Supreme Court Advocates-on-Record Association and Another Vs. Union of India reported* AIR 2016 SC 117. Before amendment, sub-clause (a) was as under:—

"(a) the reference in article 217 to the Governor of the State shall be construed as reference to the Governors of all the States in relation to which the High Court exercises jurisdiction;".

of the State in which the subordinate courts are situate; and

(c) the references in articles 219 and 229 to the State shall be construed as a reference to the State in which the High Court has its principal seat:

Provided that if such principal seat is in a Union territory, the references in articles 219 and 229 to the Governor, Public Service Commission, Legislature and Consolidated Fund of the State shall be construed respectively as references to the President, Union Public Service Commission, Parliament and Consolidated Fund of India.]

[**232.** *Interpretation.—Articles 230, 231 and 232 subs. by articles 230 and 231 by the Constitution (Seventh Amendment) Act, 1956, s. 16 (w.e.f. 1-11-1956)].*

Chapter VI.—Subordinate Courts

233. Appointment of district judges.—(1) Appointments of persons to be, and the posting and promotion of, district judges in any State shall be made by the Governor of the State in consultation with the High Court exercising jurisdiction in relation to such State.

(2) A person not already in the service of the Union or of the State shall only be eligible to be appointed a district judge if he has been for not less than seven years an advocate or a pleader and is recommended by the High Court for appointment.

[**233A. Validation of appointments of, and judgments, etc., delivered by, certain district judges.**—Notwithstanding any judgment, decree or order of any court,—

(a) (i) no appointment of any person already in the judicial service of a State or of any person who has been for not less than seven years an advocate or a pleader, to be a district judge in that State, and

(ii) no posting, promotion or transfer of any such person as a district judge,

---

1 Ins. by the Constitution (Twentieth Amendment) Act, 1966, s. 2 (w.e.f. 22-12-1966).

made at any time before the commencement of the Constitution (Twentieth Amendment) Act, 1966, otherwise than in accordance with the provisions of article 233 or article 235 shall be deemed to be illegal or void or ever to have become illegal or void by reason only of the fact that such appointment, posting, promotion or transfer was not made in accordance with the said provisions;

(b) no jurisdiction exercised, no judgment, decree, sentence or order passed or made, and no other act or proceeding done or taken, before the commencement of the Constitution (Twentieth Amendment) Act, 1966 by, or before, any person appointed, posted, promoted or transferred as a district judge in any State otherwise than in accordance with the provisions of article 233 or article 235 shall be deemed to be illegal or invalid or ever to have become illegal or invalid by reason only of the fact that such appointment, posting, promotion or transfer was not made in accordance with the said provisions.]

234. **Recruitment of persons other than district judges to the judicial service.**—Appointments of persons other than district judges to the judicial service of a State shall be made by the Governor of the State in accordance with rules made by him in that behalf after consultation with the State Public Service Commission and with the High Court exercising jurisdiction in relation to such State.

235. **Control over subordinate courts.**—The control over district courts and courts subordinate thereto including the posting and promotion of, and the grant of leave to, persons belonging to the judicial service of a State and holding any post inferior to the post of district judge shall be vested in the High Court, but nothing in this article shall be construed as taking away from any such person any right of appeal which he may have under the law regulating the conditions of his service or as authorising the High Court to deal with him otherwise than in accordance with the conditions of his service prescribed under such law.

236. **Interpretation.**—In this Chapter—

(*a*) the expression "district judge" includes judge of a city civil court, additional district judge, joint district judge, assistant district judge, chief judge of a small cause court, chief presidency magistrate, additional chief presidency magistrate, sessions judge, additional sessions judge and assistant sessions Judge;

(*b*) the expression "judicial service" means a service consisting exclusively of persons intended to fill the post of district judge and other civil judicial posts inferior to the post of district judge.

237. **Application of the provisions of this Chapter to certain class or classes of magistrates.**—The Governor may by public notification direct that the foregoing provisions of this Chapter and any rules made thereunder shall with effect from such date as may be fixed by him in that behalf apply in relation to any class or classes of magistrates in the State as they apply in relation to persons appointed to the judicial service of the State subject to such exceptions and modifications as may be specified in the notification.

*[PART VII

[*THE STATES IN PART B OF THE FIRST SCHEDULE*].

---

* Omitted by the Constitution (Seventh Amendment) Act, 1956, s. 29 and Sch. (w.e.f. 1-11-1956)

PART VIII

¹[THE UNION TERRITORIES]

²[**239. Administration of Union territories.**—(1) Save as otherwise provided by Parliament by law, every Union territory shall be administered by the President acting, to such extent as he thinks fit, through an administrator to be appointed by him with such designation as he may specify.

(2) Notwithstanding anything contained in Part VI, the President may appoint the Governor of a State as the administrator of an adjoining Union territory, and where a Governor is so appointed, he shall exercise his functions as such administrator independently of his Council of Ministers.]

³[**239A. Creation of local Legislatures or Council of Ministers or both for certain Union territories.**—(1) Parliament may by law create ⁴[for the Union territory of ⁵[Puducherry]]—

    (*a*) a body, whether elected or partly nominated and partly elected, to function as a Legislature for the Union territory, or

    (*b*) a Council of Ministers,

or both with such constitution, powers and functions, in each case, as may be specified in the law.

(2) Any such law as is referred to in clause (1) shall not be deemed to be an amendment of this Constitution for the purposes of article 368 notwithstanding that it contains any provision which amends or has the effect of amending this Constitution.]

---

1 Subs. by the Constitution (Seventh Amendment) Act, 1956, s. 17, for the heading "THE STATES IN PART C OF THE FIRST SCHEDULE" (w.e.f. 1-11-1956).

2 Subs. by s. 17, *ibid.*, for art. 239 (w.e.f. 1-11-1956).

3 Ins. by the Constitution (Fourteenth Amendment) Act, 1962, s. 4 (w.e.f. 28-12-1962). This article 239A has been made applicable to Union territory of Jammu and Kashmir by the Jammu and Kashmir Reorganisation Act, 2019 (34 of 2019) s. 13 (w.e.f. 31-10-2019).

4 Subs. by the Goa, Daman and Diu Reorganisation Act, 1987 (18 of 1987) s. 63, for "for any of the Union territories of Goa, Daman and Diu and Pondicherry" (w.e.f. 30-5-1987).

5 Subs. by the Pondicherry (Alteration of Name) Act, 2006 (44 of 2006), s. 4, for "Pondicherry" (w.e.f. 1-10-2006).

[239AA. **Special provisions with respect to Delhi.**—(1) As from the date of commencement of the Constitution (Sixty-ninth Amendment) Act, 1991, the Union territory of Delhi shall be called the National Capital Territory of Delhi (hereafter in this Part referred to as the National Capital Territory) and the administrator thereof appointed under article 239 shall be designated as the Lieutenant Governor.

(2) (*a*) There shall be a Legislative Assembly for the National Capital Territory and the seats in such Assembly shall be filled by members chosen by direct election from territorial constituencies in the National Capital Territory.

(*b*) The total number of seats in the Legislative Assembly, the number of seats reserved for Scheduled Castes, the division of the National Capital Territory into territorial constituencies (including the basis for such division) and all other matters relating to the functioning of the Legislative Assembly shall be regulated by law made by Parliament.

(*c*) The provisions of articles 324 to 327 and 329 shall apply in relation to the National Capital Territory, the Legislative Assembly of the National Capital Territory and the members thereof as they apply, in relation to a State, the Legislative Assembly of a State and the members thereof respectively; and any reference in articles 326 and 329 to "appropriate Legislature" shall be deemed to be a reference to Parliament.

(3) (*a*) Subject to the provisions of this Constitution, the Legislative Assembly shall have power to make laws for the whole or any part of the National Capital Territory with respect to any of the matters enumerated in the State List or in the Concurrent List in so far as any such matter is applicable to Union territories except matters with respect to Entries 1, 2 and 18 of the State List and

---

1 Arts. 239AA and 239 AB ins. by the Constitution (Sixty-ninth Amendment) Act, 1991, s. 2 (w.e.f. 1-2-1992).

151

Entries 64, 65 and 66 of that List in so far as they relate to the said Entries 1, 2 and 18.

(b) Nothing in sub-clause (a) shall derogate from the powers of Parliament under this Constitution to make laws with respect to any matter for a Union territory or any part thereof.

(c) If any provision of a law made by the Legislative Assembly with respect to any matter is repugnant to any provision of a law made by Parliament with respect to that matter, whether passed before or after the law made by the Legislative Assembly, or of an earlier law, other than a law made by the Legislative Assembly, then, in either case, the law made by Parliament, or, as the case may be, such earlier law, shall prevail and the law made by the Legislative Assembly shall, to the extent of the repugnancy, be void:

Provided that if any such law made by the Legislative Assembly has been reserved for the consideration of the President and has received his assent, such law shall prevail in the National Capital Territory:

Provided further that nothing in this sub-clause shall prevent Parliament from enacting at any time any law with respect to the same matter including a law adding to, amending, varying or repealing the law so made by the Legislative Assembly.

(4) There shall be a Council of Ministers consisting of not more than ten per cent. of the total number of members in the Legislative Assembly, with the Chief Minister at the head to aid and advise the Lieutenant Governor in the exercise of his functions in relation to matters with respect to which the Legislative Assembly has power to make laws, except in so far as he is, by or under any law, required to act in his discretion:

Provided that in the case of difference of opinion between the Lieutenant Governor and his Ministers on any matter, the Lieutenant Governor shall refer it to the President for decision and act according to the decision given thereon by the President and pending such decision it shall be competent for the Lieutenant Governor in any case where the matter, in his opinion, is so urgent that it is necessary for him to take immediate action, to take such action or to give such direction in the matter as he deems necessary.

(5) The Chief Minister shall be appointed by the President and other Ministers shall be appointed by the President on the advice of the Chief Minister and the Ministers shall hold office during the pleasure of the President.

(6) The Council of Ministers shall be collectively responsible to the Legislative Assembly.

¹[(7) (*a*)] Parliament may, by law, make provisions for giving effect to, or supplementing the provisions contained in the foregoing clauses and for all matters incidental or consequential thereto.

²[(*b*) Any such law as is referred to in sub-clause (*a*) shall not be deemed to be an amendment of this Constitution for the purposes of article 368 notwithstanding that it contains any provision which amends or has the effect of amending, this Constitution.]

(8) The provisions of article 239B shall, so far as may be, apply in relation to the National Capital Territory, the Lieutenant Governor and the Legislative Assembly, as they apply in relation to the Union territory of ³[Puducherry], the administrator and its Legislature, respectively; and any reference in that article to "clause (1) of article 239A" shall be deemed to be a reference to this article or article 239AB, as the case may be.

239AB. Provision in case of failure of constitutional machinery.— If the President, on receipt of a report from the Lieutenant Governor or otherwise, is satisfied—

(*a*) that a situation has arisen in which the administration of the National Capital Territory cannot be carried on in accordance with the provisions of article 239AA or of any law made in pursuance of that article; or

(*b*) that for the proper administration of the National Capital Territory it is necessary or expedient so to do,

---

1 Subs. by the Constitution (Seventieth Amendment) Act, 1992, s. 3, for "(7)" (w.e.f. 21-12-1991).
2 Ins. by s. 3, *ibid.* (w.e.f. 21-12-1991).
3 Subs. by the Pondicherry (Alteration of Name) Act, 2006 (44 of 2006), s. 4, for "Pondicherry" (w.e.f. 1-10-2006).

the President may by order suspend the operation of any provision of article 239AA or of all or any of the provisions of any law made in pursuance of that article for such period and subject to such conditions as may be specified in such law and make such incidental and consequential provisions as may appear to him to be necessary or expedient for administering the National Capital Territory in accordance with the provisions of article 239 and article 239AA.]

[239B. **Power of administrator to promulgate Ordinances during recess of Legislature.**—(1) If at any time, except when the Legislature of [the Union territory of [Puducherry]] is in session, the administrator thereof is satisfied that circumstances exist which render it necessary for him to take immediate action, he may promulgate such Ordinances as the circumstances appear to him to require:

Provided that no such Ordinance shall be promulgated by the administrator except after obtaining instructions from the President in that behalf:

Provided further that whenever the said Legislature is dissolved, or its functioning remains suspended on account of any action taken under any such law as is referred to in clause (1) of article 239A, the administrator shall not promulgate any Ordinance during the period of such dissolution or suspension.

(2) An Ordinance promulgated under this article in pursuance of instructions from the President shall be deemed to be an Act of the Legislature of the Union territory which has been duly enacted after complying with the provisions in that behalf contained in any such law as is referred to in clause (1) of article 239A, but every such Ordinance—

        (a) shall be laid before the Legislature of the Union territory and shall cease to operate at the expiration of six weeks from the reassembly of the Legislature

---

1 Ins. by the Constitution (Twenty-seventh Amendment) Act, 1971, s. 3 (w.e.f. 30-12-1971).
2 Subs. by the Goa, Daman and Diu Reorganisation Act, 1987 (18 of 1987) s. 63, for "a Union territory referred to in clause (1) article 239A" (w.e.f. 30-5-1987).
3 Subs. by the Pondicherry (Alteration of Name) Act, 2006 (44 of 2006), s. 4, for "Pondicherry" (w.e.f. 1-10-2006).

or if, before the expiration of that period, a resolution disapproving it is passed by the Legislature, upon the passing of the resolution; and

(b) may be withdrawn at any time by the administrator after obtaining instructions from the President in that behalf.

(3) If and so far as an Ordinance under this article makes any provision which would not be valid if enacted in an Act of the Legislature of the Union territory made after complying with the provisions in that behalf contained in any such law as is referred to in clause (1) of article 239A, it shall be void.]

[1](4) *   *   *   *

[2][**240. Power of President to make regulations for certain Union territories.**—(1) The President may make regulations for the peace, progress and good government of the Union territory of—

(a)   the Andaman and Nicobar Islands;

[3][(b) Lakshadweep;]

[4][(c) Dadra and Nagar Haveli and Daman and Diu;]

[5][(d) ****;]

[6][(e) [7][Puducherry];]

[8](f) *   *   *

[9](g) *   *   *

---

1   Clause (4) ins. by the Constitution (Thirty-eighth Amendment) Act, 1975, s. 4 (with retrospective effect). This amendment was omitted by the Constitution (Forty-fourth Amendment) Act, 1978, s. 32 (w.e.f. 20-6-1979).

2   Subs. by the Constitution (Seventh Amendment) Act, 1956, s.17, for art. 240 (w.e.f. 1-11-1956).

3   Subs. by the Laccadive, Minicoy and Amindivi Islands (Alteration of Name) Act, 1973 (34 of 1973), s. 4, for entry (b) (w.e.f. 1-11-1973).

4   Subs. by the Dadra and Nagar Haveli and Daman and Diu (Merger of Union territories) Act, 2019 (44 of 2019) s. 4(i) (w.e.f. 26-1-2020) for entry (c) which was ins. by the Constitution (Tenth Amendment) Act, 1961, s.3 (w.e.f. 11-8-1961).

5   Omitted by the Dadra and Nagar Haveli and Daman and Diu (Merger of Union territories) Act, 2019 (44 of 2019) s. 4(ii) (w.e.f. 26-1-2020)

6   Ins. by the Constitution (Fourteenth Amendment) Act, 1962, s. 5 (retrospectively w.e.f. 16-8-1962, vide s.7).

7   Subs. by the Pondicherry (Alteration of Name) Act, 2006 (44 of 2006), s. 4 for "Pondicherry" (w.e.f. 1-10-2006).

8   The entry (f) relating to Mizoram omitted by the State of Mizoram Act, 1986 (34 of 1986), s. 39 (w.e.f. 20-2-1987).

9   The entry (g) relating to Arunachal Pradesh omitted by the State of Arunachal Pradesh Act, 1986 (69 of 1986), s. 42 (w.e.f. 20-2-1987).

¹[Provided that when any body is created under article 239A to function as a Legislature for the Union territory of ⁶[Puducherry], the President shall not make any regulation for the peace, progress and good government of that Union territory with effect from the date appointed for the first meeting of the Legislature:]

²[Provided further that whenever the body functioning as a Legislature for the Union territory of ³[Puducherry] is dissolved, or the functioning of that body as such Legislature remains suspended on account of any action taken under any such law as is referred to in clause (1) of article 239A, the President may, during the period of such dissolution or suspension, make regulations for the peace, progress and good government of that Union territory.]

(2) Any regulation so made may repeal or amend any Act made by Parliament or ⁴[any other law], which is for the time being applicable to the Union territory and, when promulgated by the President, shall have the same force and effect as an Act of Parliament which applies to that territory.]

241. **High Courts for Union territories**—(1) Parliament may by law constitute a High Court for a ⁵[Union territory] or declare any court in any ⁶[such territory] to be a High Court for all or any of the purposes of this Constitution.

(2) The provisions of Chapter V of Part VI shall apply in relation to every High Court referred to in clause (1) as they apply in relation to a High Court referred to in article 214 subject to such modifications or exceptions as Parliament may by law provide.

⁷[(3) Subject to the provisions of this Constitution and to the provisions of any law of the appropriate Legislature made by virtue of powers conferred on that Legislature by or under

1 Ins. by the Constitution (Fourteenth Amendment) Act, 1962, s. 5 (w.e.f. 28-12-1962).
2 Ins. by the Constitution (Twenty-seventh Amendment) Act, 1971, s. 4 (w.e.f. 15-2-1972).
3 Subs. by the Pondicherry (Alteration of Name) Act, 2006 (44 of 2006), s. 4, for "Pondicherry" (w.e.f. 1-10-2006).
4 Subs. by the Constitution (Twenty-seventh Amendment) Act, 1971, s.4, for "any existing law" (w.e.f. 15-2-1972).
5 Subs. by the Constitution (Seventh Amendment) Act, 1956, s. 29 and Sch., for "State specified in Part C of the First Schedule" (w.e.f. 1-11-1956).
6 Subs. by s. 29 and Sch., *ibid.*, for "such State" (w.e.f. 1-11-1956).
7 Subs. by s. 29 and Sch., *ibid.*, for cls. (3) and (4) (w.e.f. 1-11-1956).

this Constitution, every High Court exercising jurisdiction immediately before the commencement of the Constitution (Seventh Amendment) Act, 1956, in relation to any Union territory shall continue to exercise such jurisdiction in relation to that territory after such commencement.

(4) Nothing in this article derogates from the power of Parliament to extend or exclude the jurisdiction of a High Court for a State to, or from, any Union territory or part thereof.]

242. *[Coorg].—Omitted by the Constitution (Seventh Amendment) Act,* 1956, *s. 29 and Sch.*(w.e.f. 1-11-1956).

[1]PART IX

THE PANCHAYATS

243. **Definitions.**—In this Part, unless the context otherwise requires,—

(a) "district" means a district in a State;

(b) "Gram Sabha" means a body consisting of persons registered in the electoral rolls relating to a village comprised within the area of Panchayat at the village level;

(c) "intermediate level" means a level between the village and district levels specified by the Governor of a State by public notification to be the intermediate level for the purposes of this Part;

(d) "Panchayat" means an institution (by whatever name called) of self-government constituted under article 243B, for the rural areas;

(e) "Panchayat area" means the territorial area of a Panchayat;

---

1 Original Part IX relating to "The territories in Part D of the First Schedule and other territories not specified in that Schedule" was omitted by the Constitution (Seventh Amendment) Act, 1956, s. 29 and Sch. (w.e.f. 1-11-1956) and subsequently ins. by the Constitution (Seventy-third Amendment) Act, 1992, s. 2 (w.e.f. 24-4-1993).

(*f*) "Population" means the population as ascertained at the last preceding census of which the relevant figures have been published;

(*g*) "village" means a village specified by the Governor by public notification to be a village for the purposes of this Part and includes a group of villages so specified.

243A. **Gram Sabha.**—A Gram Sabha may exercise such powers and perform such functions at the village level as the Legislature of a State may, by law, provide.

243B. **Constitution of Panchayats.**—(1) There shall be constituted in every State, Panchayats at the village, intermediate and district levels in accordance with the provisions of this Part.

(2) Notwithstanding anything in clause (1), Panchayats at the intermediate level may not be constituted in a State having a population not exceeding twenty lakhs.

243C. **Composition of Panchayats.**—(1) Subject to the provisions of this Part, the Legislature of a State may, by law, make provisions with respect to the composition of Panchayats:

Provided that the ratio between the population of the territorial area of a Panchayat at any level and the number of seats in such Panchayat to be filled by election shall, so far as practicable, be the same throughout the State.

(2) All the seats in a Panchayat shall be filled by persons chosen by direct election from territorial constituencies in the Panchayat area and, for this purpose, each Panchayat area shall be divided into territorial constituencies in such manner that the ratio between the population of each constituency and the number of seats allotted to it shall, so far as practicable, be the same throughout the Panchayat area.

(3) The Legislature of a State may, by law, provide for the representation—

(*a*) of the Chairpersons of the Panchayats at the village level, in the Panchayats at the intermediate level or, in the case of a State not having Panchayats at the intermediate level, in the Panchayats at the district level;

(*b*) of the Chairpersons of the Panchayats at the intermediate level, in the Panchayats at the district level;

(c) of the members of the House of the People and the members of the Legislative Assembly of the State representing constituencies which comprise wholly or partly a Panchayat area at a level other than the village level, in such Panchayat;

(d) of the members of the Council of States and the members of the Legislative Council of the State, where they are registered as electors within—

    (i) a Panchayat area at the intermediate level, in Panchayat at the intermediate level;

    (ii) a Panchayat area at the district level, in Panchayat at the district level.

(4) The Chairperson of a Panchayat and other members of a Panchayat whether or not chosen by direct election from territorial constituencies in the Panchayat area shall have the right to vote in the meetings of the Panchayats.

(5) The Chairperson of—

(a) a Panchayat at the village level shall be elected in such manner as the Legislature of a State may, by law, provide; and

(b) a Panchayat at the intermediate level or district level shall be elected by, and from amongst, the elected members thereof.

243D. Reservation of seats.—(1) Seats shall be reserved for—

(a) the Scheduled Castes; and

(b) the Scheduled Tribes,

in every Panchayat and the number of seats so reserved shall bear, as nearly as may be, the same proportion to the total number of seats to be filled by direct election in that Panchayat as the population of the Scheduled Castes in that Panchayat area or of the Scheduled Tribes in that Panchayat area bears to the total population of that area and such seats may be allotted by rotation to different constituencies in a Panchayat.

(2) Not less than one-third of the total number of seats reserved under clause (1) shall be reserved for women belonging to the Scheduled Castes or, as the case may be, the Scheduled Tribes.

(3) Not less than one-third (including the number of seats reserved for women belonging to the Scheduled Castes and the Scheduled Tribes) of the total number of seats to be filled by direct election in every Panchayat shall be reserved for women and such seats may be allotted by rotation to different constituencies in a Panchayat.

(4) The offices of the Chairpersons in the Panchayats at the village or any other level shall be reserved for the Scheduled Castes, the Scheduled Tribes and women in such manner as the Legislature of a State may, by law, provide:

Provided that the number of offices of Chairpersons reserved for the Scheduled Castes and the Scheduled Tribes in the Panchayats at each level in any State shall bear, as nearly as may be, the same proportion to the total number of such offices in the Panchayats at each level as the population of the Scheduled Castes in the State or of the Scheduled Tribes in the State bears to the total population of the State:

Provided further that not less than one-third of the total number of offices of Chairpersons in the Panchayats at each level shall be reserved for women:

Provided also that the number of offices reserved under this clause shall be allotted by rotation to different Panchayats at each level.

(5) The reservation of seats under clauses (1) and (2) and the reservation of offices of Chairpersons (other than the reservation for women) under clause (4) shall cease to have effect on the expiration of the period specified in article 334.

(6) Nothing in this Part shall prevent the Legislature of a State from making any provision for reservation of seats in any Panchayat or offices of Chairpersons in the Panchayats at any level in favour of backward class of citizens.

243E. **Duration of Panchayats, etc.**—(1) Every Panchayat, unless sooner dissolved under any law for the time being in force, shall continue for five years from the date appointed for its first meeting and no longer.

(2) No amendment of any law for the time being in force shall have the effect of causing dissolution of a Panchayat at any level,

which is functioning immediately before such amendment, till the expiration of its duration specified in clause (1).

(3) An election to constitute a Panchayat shall be completed—

   (a)   before the expiry of its duration specified in clause (1);

   (b)   before the expiration of a period of six months from the date of its dissolution:

Provided that where the remainder of the period for which the dissolved Panchayat would have continued is less than six months, it shall not be necessary to hold any election under this clause for constituting the Panchayat for such period.

(4) A Panchayat constituted upon the dissolution of a Panchayat before the expiration of its duration shall continue only for the remainder of the period for which the dissolved Panchayat would have continued under clause (1) had it not been so dissolved.

243F.   **Disqualifications for membership.**—(1) A person shall be disqualified for being chosen as, and for being, a member of a Panchayat—

   (a)   if he is so disqualified by or under any law for the time being in force for the purposes of elections to the Legislature of the State concerned:

   Provided that no person shall be disqualified on the ground that he is less than twenty-five years of age, if he has attained the age of twenty-one years;

   (b)   if he is so disqualified by or under any law made by the Legislature of the State.

(2) If any question arises as to whether a member of a Panchayat has become subject to any of the disqualifications mentioned in clause (1), the question shall be referred for the decision of such authority and in such manner as the Legislature of a State may, by law, provide.

243G.   **Powers, authority and responsibilities of Panchayats.**— Subject to the provisions of this Constitution, the Legislature of a State may, by law, endow the Panchayats with such powers and authority as may be necessary to enable them to function as institutions of self-government and such law may contain provisions for the devolution of powers and responsibilities upon

Panchayats at the appropriate level, subject to such conditions as may be specified therein, with respect to—

(a) the preparation of plans for economic development and social justice;

(b) the implementation of schemes for economic development and social justice as may be entrusted to them including those in relation to the matters listed in the Eleventh Schedule.

243H. Powers to impose taxes by, and Funds of, the Panchayats.— The Legislature of a State may, by law,—

(a) authorise a Panchayat to levy, collect and appropriate such taxes, duties, tolls and fees in accordance with such procedure and subject to such limits;

(b) assign to a Panchayat such taxes, duties, tolls and fees levied and collected by the State Government for such purposes and subject to such conditions and limits;

(c) provide for making such grants-in-aid to the Panchayats from the Consolidated Fund of the State; and

(d) provide for constitution of such Funds for crediting all moneys received, respectively, by or on behalf of the Panchayats and also for the withdrawal of such moneys therefrom,

as may be specified in the law.

243-I. Constitution of Finance Commission to review financial position.—(1) The Governor of a State shall, as soon as may be within one year from the commencement of the Constitution (Seventy-third Amendment) Act, 1992, and thereafter at the expiration of every fifth year, constitute a Finance Commission to review the financial position of the Panchayats and to make recommendations to the Governor as to—

(a) the principles which should govern—

(i) the distribution between the State and the Panchayats of the net proceeds of the taxes, duties, tolls and fees leviable by the State, which may be divided between them under this Part and the allocation between the Panchayats at all levels of their respective shares of such proceeds;

(*ii*) the determination of the taxes, duties, tolls and fees which may be assigned to, or appropriated by, the Panchayats;

(*iii*) the grants-in-aid to the Panchayats from the Consolidated Fund of the State;

(*b*) the measures needed to improve the financial position of the Panchayats;

(*c*) any other matter referred to the Finance Commission by the Governor in the interests of sound finance of the Panchayats.

(2) The Legislature of a State may, by law, provide for the composition of the Commission, the qualifications which shall be requisite for appointment as members thereof and the manner in which they shall be selected.

(3) The Commission shall determine their procedure and shall have such powers in the performance of their functions as the Legislature of the State may, by law, confer on them.

(4) The Governor shall cause every recommendation made by the Commission under this article together with an explanatory memorandum as to the action taken thereon to be laid before the Legislature of the State.

243J. **Audit of accounts of Panchayats.**—The Legislature of a State may, by law, make provisions with respect to the maintenance of accounts by the Panchayats and the auditing of such accounts.

243K. **Elections to the Panchayats.**—(1) The superintendence, direction and control of the preparation of electoral rolls for, and the conduct of, all elections to the Panchayats shall be vested in a State Election Commission consisting of a State Election Commissioner to be appointed by the Governor.

(2) Subject to the provisions of any law made by the Legislature of a State, the conditions of service and tenure of office of the State Election Commissioner shall be such as the Governor may by rule determine:

Provided that the State Election Commissioner shall not be removed from his office except in like manner and on the like grounds as a Judge of a High Court and the conditions of service

163

of the State Election Commissioner shall not be varied to his disadvantage after his appointment.

(3) The Governor of a State shall, when so requested by the State Election Commission, make available to the State Election Commission such staff as may be necessary for the discharge of the functions conferred on the State Election Commission by clause (1).

(4) Subject to the provisions of this Constitution, the Legislature of a State may, by law, make provision with respect to all matters relating to, or in connection with, elections to the Panchayats.

243L. **Application to Union territories.**—The provisions of this Part shall apply to the Union territories and shall, in their application to a Union territory, have effect as if the references to the Governor of a State were references to the Administrator of the Union territory appointed under article 239 and references to the Legislature or the legislative Assembly of a State were references, in relation to a Union territory having a Legislative Assembly, to that Legislative Assembly:

Provided that the President may, by public notification, direct that the provisions of this Part shall apply to any Union territory or part thereof subject to such exceptions and modifications as he may specify in the notification.

243M. **Part not to apply to certain areas.**—(1) Nothing in this Part shall apply to the Scheduled Areas referred to in clause (1), and the tribal areas referred to in clause (2), of article 244.

(2) Nothing in this Part shall apply to—

    (*a*) the States of Nagaland, Meghalaya and Mizoram;

    (*b*) the hill areas in the State of Manipur for which District Councils exist under any law for the time being in force.

(3) Nothing in this Part—

    (*a*) relating to Panchayats at the district level shall apply to the hill areas of the District of Darjeeling in the State of West Bengal for which Darjeeling Gorkha Hill Council exists under any law for the time being in force;

(*b*) shall be construed to affect the functions and powers of the Darjeeling Gorkha Hill Council constituted under such law.

[(3A) Nothing in article 243D, relating to reservation of seats for the Scheduled Castes, shall apply to the State of Arunachal Pradesh.]

(4) Notwithstanding anything in this Constitution,—

(*a*) the Legislature of a State referred to in sub-clause (*a*) of clause (2) may, by law, extend this Part to that State, except the areas, if any, referred to in clause (1), if the Legislative Assembly of that State passes a resolution to that effect by a majority of the total membership of that House and by a majority of not less than two-thirds of the members of that House present and voting;

(*b*) Parliament may, by law, extend the provisions of this Part to the Scheduled Areas and the tribal areas referred to in clause (1) subject to such exceptions and modifications as may be specified in such law, and no such law shall be deemed to be an amendment of this Constitution for the purposes of article 368.

243N. Continuance of existing laws and Panchayats.— Notwithstanding anything in this Part, any provision of any law relating to Panchayats in force in a State immediately before the commencement of the Constitution (Seventy-third Amendment) Act, 1992, which is inconsistent with the provisions of this Part, shall continue to be in force until amended or repealed by a competent Legislature or other competent authority or until the expiration of one year from such commencement, whichever is earlier:

Provided that all the Panchayats existing immediately before such commencement shall continue till the expiration of their duration, unless sooner dissolved by a resolution passed to that effect by the Legislative Assembly of that State or, in the case of a State having a Legislative Council, by each House of the Legislature of that State.

---

1 Ins. by the Constitution (Eighty-third Amendment) Act, 2000, s. 2 (w.e.f. 8-9-2000).

243-O. Bar to interference by courts in electoral matters.—
Notwithstanding anything in this Constitution,—

    (*a*) the validity of any law relating to the delimitation of constituencies or the allotment of seats to such constituencies, made or purporting to be made under article 243K, shall not be called in question in any court;

    (*b*) no election to any Panchayat shall be called in question except by an election petition presented to such authority and in such manner as is provided for by or under any law made by the Legislature of a State.

¹PART IX A

THE MUNICIPALITIES

243P. Definitions.—In this Part, unless the context otherwise requires,—

    (*a*) "Committee" means a Committee constituted under article 243S;

    (*b*) "district" means a district in a State;

    (*c*) "Metropolitan area" means an area having a population of ten lakhs or more, comprised in one or more districts and consisting of two or more Municipalities or Panchayats or other contiguous areas, specified by the Governor by public notification to be a Metropolitan area for the purposes of this Part;

    (*d*) "Municipal area" means the territorial area of a Municipality as is notified by the Governor;

    (*e*) "Municipality" means an institution of self-government constituted under article 243Q;

    (*f*) "Panchayat" means a Panchayat constituted under article 243B;

---

1 Part IX A ins. by the Constitution (Seventy-fourth Amendment) Act, 1992, s. 2 (w.e.f. 1-6-1993).

(g) "population" means the population as ascertained at the last preceding census of which the relevant figures have been published.

243Q. Constitution of Municipalities.—(1) There shall be constituted in every State,—

(a) a Nagar Panchayat (by whatever name called) for a transitional area, that is to say, an area in transition from a rural area to an urban area;

(b) a Municipal Council for a smaller urban area; and

(c) a Municipal Corporation for a larger urban area, in accordance with the provisions of this Part:

Provided that a Municipality under this clause may not be constituted in such urban area or part thereof as the Governor may, having regard to the size of the area and the municipal services being provided or proposed to be provided by an industrial establishment in that area and such other factors as he may deem fit, by public notification, specify to be an industrial township.

(2) In this article, "a transitional area", "a smaller urban area" or "a larger urban area" means such area as the Governor may, having regard to the population of the area, the density of the population therein, the revenue generated for local administration, the percentage of employment in non- agricultural activities, the economic importance or such other factors as he may deem fit, specify by public notification for the purposes of this Part.

243R. Composition of Municipalities.—(1) Save as provided in clause (2), all the seats in a Municipality shall be filled by persons chosen by direct election from the territorial constituencies in the Municipal area and for this purpose each Municipal area shall be divided into territorial constituencies to be known as wards.

(2) The Legislature of a State may, by law, provide—

(a) for the representation in a Municipality of—

(i) persons having special knowledge or experience in Municipal administration;

(ii) the members of the House of the People and the members of the Legislative Assembly of the

State representing constituencies which comprise wholly or partly the Municipal area;

(*iii*) the members of the Council of States and the members of the Legislative Council of the State registered as electors within the Municipal area;

(*iv*) the Chairpersons of the Committees constituted under clause (5) of article 243S:

Provided that the persons referred to in paragraph (*i*) shall not have the right to vote in the meetings of the Municipality;

(*b*) the manner of election of the Chairperson of a Municipality.

243S. Constitution and composition of Wards Committees, etc.— (1) There shall be constituted Wards Committees, consisting of one or more wards, within the territorial area of a Municipality having a population of three lakhs or more.

(2) The Legislature of a State may, by law, make provision with respect to—

(*a*) the composition and the territorial area of a Wards Committee;

(*b*) the manner in which the seats in a Wards Committee shall be filled.

(3) A member of a Municipality representing a ward within the territorial area of the Wards Committee shall be a member of that Committee.

(4) Where a Wards Committee consists of—

(*a*) one ward, the member representing that ward in the Municipality; or

(*b*) two or more wards, one of the members representing such wards

in the Municipality elected by the members of the Wards Committee, shall be the Chairperson of that Committee.

(5) Nothing in this article shall be deemed to prevent the Legislature of a State from making any provision for the constitution of Committees in addition to the Wards Committees.

243T. Reservation of seats.—(1) Seats shall be reserved for the Scheduled Castes and the Scheduled Tribes in every Municipality and the number of seats so reserved shall bear, as nearly as may be, the same proportion to the total number of seats to be filled by direct election in that Municipality as the population of the Scheduled Castes in the Municipal area or of the Scheduled Tribes in the Municipal area bears to the total population of that area and such seats may be allotted by rotation to different constituencies in a Municipality.

(2) Not less than one-third of the total number of seats reserved under clause (1) shall be reserved for women belonging to the Scheduled Castes or, as the case may be, the Scheduled Tribes.

(3) Not less than one-third (including the number of seats reserved for women belonging to the Scheduled Castes and the Scheduled Tribes) of the total number of seats to be filled by direct election in every Municipality shall be reserved for women and such seats may be allotted by rotation to different constituencies in a Municipality.

(4) The offices of Chairpersons in the Municipalities shall be reserved for the Scheduled Castes, the Scheduled Tribes and women in such manner as the Legislature of a State may, by law, provide.

(5) The reservation of seats under clauses (1) and (2) and the reservation of offices of Chairpersons (other than the reservation for women) under clause (4) shall cease to have effect on the expiration of the period specified in article 334.

(6) Nothing in this Part shall prevent the Legislature of a State from making any provision for reservation of seats in any Municipality or offices of Chairpersons in the Municipalities in favour of backward class of citizens.

243U. Duration of Municipalities, etc.—(1) Every Municipality, unless sooner dissolved under any law for the time being in force, shall continue for five years from the date appointed for its first meeting and no longer:

Provided that a Municipality shall be given a reasonable opportunity of being heard before its dissolution.

(2) No amendment of any law for the time being in force shall have the effect of causing dissolution of a Municipality at any level, which is functioning immediately before such amendment, till the expiration of its duration specified in clause (1).

(3) An election to constitute a Municipality shall be completed,—

    (*a*) before the expiry of its duration specified in clause (1);

    (*b*) before the expiration of a period of six months from the date of its dissolution:

Provided that where the remainder of the period for which the dissolved Municipality would have continued is less than six months, it shall not be necessary to hold any election under this clause for constituting the Municipality for such period.

(4) A Municipality constituted upon the dissolution of a Municipality before the expiration of its duration shall continue only for the remainder of the period for which the dissolved Municipality would have continued under clause (2) had it not been so dissolved.

243V. **Disqualifications for membership.**—(1) A person shall be disqualified for being chosen as, and for being, a member of a Municipality—

    (*a*) if he is so disqualified by or under any law for the time being in force for the purposes of elections to the Legislature of the State concerned:

Provided that no person shall be disqualified on the ground that he is less than twenty-five years of age, if he has attained the age of twenty-one years;

    (*b*) if he is so disqualified by or under any law made by the Legislature of the State.

(2) If any question arises as to whether a member of a Municipality has become subject to any of the disqualifications mentioned in clause (1), the question shall be referred for the decision of such authority and in such manner as the Legislature of a State may, by law, provide.

243W. **Powers, authority and responsibilities of Municipalities, etc.**—Subject to the provisions of this Constitution, the Legislature of a State may, by law, endow—

    (*a*) the Municipalities with such powers and authority as may be necessary to enable them to function as institutions of self-government and such law may contain provisions for the devolution of powers and responsibilities upon Municipalities, subject to such conditions as may be specified therein, with respect to—

    (*i*)   the preparation of plans for economic development and social justice;

    (*ii*) the performance of functions and the implementation of schemes as may be entrusted to them including those in relation to the matters listed in the Twelfth Schedule;

  (*b*) the Committees with such powers and authority as may be necessary to enable them to carry out the responsibilities conferred upon them including those in relation to the matters listed in the Twelfth Schedule.

243X.   **Power to impose taxes by, and Funds of, the Municipalities.**— The Legislature of a State may, by law,—

  (*a*) authorise a Municipality to levy, collect and appropriate such taxes, duties, tolls and fees in accordance with such procedure and subject to such limits;

  (*b*) assign to a Municipality such taxes, duties, tolls and fees levied and collected by the State Government for such purposes and subject to such conditions and limits;

  (*c*) provide for making such grants-in-aid to the Municipalities from the Consolidated Fund of the State; and

  (*d*) provide for constitution of such Funds for crediting all moneys received, respectively, by or on behalf of the Municipalities and also for the withdrawal of such moneys therefrom,

as may be specified in the law.

243Y.   **Finance Commission.**—(1) The Finance Commission constituted under article 243-I shall also review the financial position of the Municipalities and make recommendations to the Governor as to—

  (*a*) the principles which should govern—

    (*i*)   the distribution between the State and the Municipalities of the net proceeds of the taxes, duties, tolls and fees leviable by the State, which may be divided between them under this Part and the allocation between the Municipalities at all levels of their respective shares of such proceeds;

(*ii*) the determination of the taxes, duties, tolls and fees which may be assigned to, or appropriated by, the Municipalities;

(*iii*) the grants-in-aid to the Municipalities from the Consolidated Fund of the State;

(*b*) the measures needed to improve the financial position of the Municipalities;

(*c*) any other matter referred to the Finance Commission by the Governor in the interests of sound finance of the Municipalities.

(2) The Governor shall cause every recommendation made by the Commission under this article together with an explanatory memorandum as to the action taken thereon to be laid before the Legislature of the State.

243Z. Audit of accounts of Municipalities.—The Legislature of a State may, by law, make provisions with respect to the maintenance of accounts by the Municipalities and the auditing of such accounts.

243ZA. Elections to the Municipalities.—(1) The superintendence, direction and control of the preparation of electoral rolls for, and the conduct of, all elections to the Municipalities shall be vested in the State Election Commission referred to in article 243K.

(2) Subject to the provisions of this Constitution, the Legislature of a State may, by law, make provision with respect to all matters relating to, or in connection with, elections to the Municipalities.

243ZB. Application to Union territories.—The provisions of this Part shall apply to the Union territories and shall, in their application to a Union territory, have effect as if the references to the Governor of a State were references to the Administrator of the Union territory appointed under article 239 and references to the Legislature or the Legislative Assembly of a State were references in relation to a Union territory having a Legislative Assembly, to that Legislative Assembly:

172

Provided that the President may, by public notification, direct that the provisions of this Part shall apply to any Union territory or part thereof subject to such exceptions and modifications as he may specify in the notification.

243ZC. Part not to apply to certain areas.—(1) Nothing in this Part shall apply to the Scheduled Areas referred to in clause (1), and the tribal areas referred to in clause (2) of article 244.

(2) Nothing in this Part shall be construed to affect the functions and powers of the Darjeeling Gorkha Hill Council constituted under any law for the time being in force for the hill areas of the district of Darjeeling in the State of West Bengal.

(3) Notwithstanding anything in this Constitution, Parliament may, by law, extend the provisions of this Part to the Scheduled Areas and the tribal areas referred to in clause (1) subject to such exceptions and modifications as may be specified in such law, and no such law shall be deemed to be an amendment of this Constitution for the purposes of article 368.

243ZD. Committee for district planning.—(1) There shall be constituted in every State at the district level a District Planning Committee to consolidate the plans prepared by the Panchayats and the Municipalities in the district and to prepare a draft development plan for the district as a whole.

(2) The Legislature of a State may, by law, make provision with respect to—

    (*a*) the composition of the District Planning Committees;

    (*b*) the manner in which the seats in such Committees shall be filled:

Provided that not less than four-fifths of the total number of members of such Committee shall be elected by, and from amongst, the elected members of the Panchayat at the district level and of the Municipalities in the district in proportion to the ratio between the population of the rural areas and of the urban areas in the district;

    (*c*) the functions relating to district planning which may be assigned to such Committees;

    (*d*) the manner in which the Chairpersons of such Committees shall be chosen.

(3) Every District Planning Committee shall, in preparing the draft development plan,—

    (*a*) have regard to—

        (*i*) matters of common interest between the Panchayats and the Municipalities including spatial planning, sharing of water and other physical and natural resources, the integrated development of infrastructure and environmental conservation;

        (*ii*) the extent and type of available resources whether financial or otherwise;

    (*b*) consult such institutions and organisations as the Governor may, by order, specify.

(4) The Chairperson of every District Planning Committee shall forward the development plan, as recommended by such Committee, to the Government of the State.

243ZE. Committee for Metropolitan planning.—(1) There shall be constituted in every Metropolitan area a Metropolitan Planning Committee to prepare a draft development plan for the Metropolitan area as a whole.

(2) The Legislature of a State may, by law, make provision with respect to—

    (*a*) the composition of the Metropolitan Planning Committees;

    (*b*) the manner in which the seats in such Committees shall be filled:

Provided that not less than two-thirds of the members of such Committee shall be elected by, and from amongst, the elected members of the Municipalities and Chairpersons of the Panchayats in the Metropolitan area in proportion to the ratio between the population of the Municipalities and of the Panchayats in that area;

    (*c*) the representation in such Committees of the Government of India and the Government of the State and of such organisations and institutions as may be deemed necessary for carrying out the functions assigned to such Committees;

(*d*) the functions relating to planning and coordination for the Metropolitan area which may be assigned to such Committees;

(*e*) the manner in which the Chairpersons of such Committees shall be chosen.

(3) Every Metropolitan Planning Committee shall, in preparing the draft development plan,—

(*a*) have regard to—

(*i*) the plans prepared by the Municipalities and the Panchayats in the Metropolitan area;

(*ii*) matters of common interest between the Municipalities and the Panchayats, including coordinated spatial planning of the area, sharing of water and other physical and natural resources, the integrated development of infrastructure and environmental conservation;

(*iii*) the overall objectives and priorities set by the Government of India and the Government of the State;

(*iv*) the extent and nature of investments likely to be made in the Metropolitan area by agencies of the Government of India and of the Government of the State and other available resources whether financial or otherwise;

(*b*) consult such institutions and organisations as the Governor may, by order, specify.

(4) The Chairperson of every Metropolitan Planning Committee shall forward the development plan, as recommended by such Committee, to the Government of the State.

243ZF. Continuance of existing laws and Municipalities.— Notwithstanding anything in this Part, any provision of any law relating to Municipalities in force in a State immediately before the commencement of the Constitution (Seventy-fourth Amendment) Act, 1992, which is inconsistent with the provisions of this Part, shall continue to be in force until amended or repealed by a competent Legislature or other competent authority or until the expiration of one year from such commencement, whichever is earlier:

Provided that all the Municipalities existing immediately before such commencement shall continue till the expiration of their duration, unless sooner dissolved by a resolution passed to that effect by the Legislative Assembly of that State or, in the case of a State having a Legislative Council, by each House of the Legislature of that State.

243ZG. Bar to interference by courts in electoral matters.— Notwithstanding anything in this Constitution,—

    (*a*) the validity of any law relating to the delimitation of constituencies or the allotment of seats to such constituencies, made or purporting to be made under article 243ZA shall not be called in question in any court;

    (*b*) no election to any Municipality shall be called in question except by an election petition presented to such authority and in such manner as is provided for by or under any law made by the Legislature of a State.]

¹[PART IX B

THE CO-OPERATIVE SOCIETIES

243ZH. Definitions.—In this Part, unless the context otherwise requires,—

    (*a*) "authorised person" means a person referred to as such in article 243ZQ;

    (*b*) "board" means the board of directors or the governing body of a co-operative society, by whatever name called, to which the direction and control of the management of the affairs of a society is entrusted to;

---

1 Part IXB ins. by the Constitution (Ninety-seventh Amendment) Act, 2011, s. 4 (w.e.f. 15-2-2012).

(c) "co-operative society" means a society registered or deemed to be registered under any law relating to co-operative societies for the time being in force in any State;

(d) "multi-State co-operative society" means a society with objects not confined to one State and registered or deemed to be registered under any law for the time being in force relating to such co-operatives;

(e) "office bearer" means a President, Vice-President, Chairperson, Vice-Chairperson, Secretary or Treasurer, of a co-operative society and includes any other person to be elected by the board of any co-operative society;

(f) "Registrar" means the Central Registrar appointed by the Central Government in relation to the multi-State co-operative societies and the Registrar for co-operative societies appointed by the State Government under the law made by the Legislature of a State in relation to co-operative societies;

(g) "State Act" means any law made by the Legislature of a State;

(h) "State level co-operative society" means a co-operative society having its area of operation extending to the whole of a State and defined as such in any law made by the Legislature of a State.

243 ZI. Incorporation of co-operative societies.—Subject to the provisions of this Part, the Legislature of a State may, by law, make provisions with respect to the incorporation, regulation and winding up of co-operative societies based on the principles of voluntary formation, democratic member-control, member-economic participation and autonomous functioning.

243ZJ. Number and term of members of board and its office bearers.—(1) The board shall consist of such number of directors as may be provided by the Legislature of a State, by law:

Provided that the maximum number of directors of a co-operative society shall not exceed twenty-one:

Provided further that the Legislature of a State shall, by law, provide for the reservation of one seat for the Scheduled Castes or the Scheduled Tribes and two seats for women on board of every co-operative society consisting of individuals as members and having members from such class of category of persons.

(2) The term of office of elected members of the board and its office bearers shall be five years from the date of election and the term of office bearers shall be conterminous with the term of the board:

Provided that the board may fill a casual vacancy on the board by nomination out of the same class of members in respect of which the casual vacancy has arisen, if the term of office of the board is less than half of its original term.

(3) The Legislature of a State shall, by law, make provisions for co-option of persons to be members of the board having experience in the field of banking, management, finance or specialisation in any other field relating to the objects and activities undertaken by the co-operative society, as members of the board of such society:

Provided that the number of such co-opted members shall not exceed two in addition to twenty-one directors specified in the first proviso to clause (1):

Provided further that such co-opted members shall not have the right to vote in any election of the co-operative society in their capacity as such member or to be eligible to be elected as office bearers of the board:

Provided also that the functional directors of a co-operative society shall also be the members of the board and such members shall be excluded for the purpose of counting the total number of directors specified in the first proviso to clause (1).

243ZK. Election of members of board.—(1) Notwithstanding anything contained in any law made by the Legislature of a State, the election of a board shall be conducted before the expiry of the term of the board so as to ensure that the newly elected members of the board assume office immediately on the expiry of the term of the office of members of the outgoing board.

(2) The superintendence, direction and control of the preparation of electoral rolls for, and the conduct of, all elections to a co-operative society shall vest in such an authority or body, as may be provided by the Legislature of a State, by law:

Provided that the Legislature of a State may, by law, provide for the procedure and guidelines for the conduct of such elections.

243ZL. **Supersession and suspension of board and interim management.**—(1) Notwithstanding anything contained in any law for the time being in force, no board shall be superseded or kept under suspension for a period exceeding six months:

Provided that the board may be superseded or kept under suspension in a case—

(*i*)   of its persistent default; or

(*ii*) of negligence in the performance of its duties; or

(*iii*) the board has committed any act prejudicial to the interests of the co-operative society or its members; or

(*iv*) there is stalemate in the constitution or functions of the board; or

(*v*) the authority or body as provided by the Legislature of a State, by law, under clause (2) of article 243ZK, has failed to conduct elections in accordance with the provisions of the State Act:

Provided further that the board of any such co-operative society shall not be superseded or kept under suspension where there is no Government shareholding or loan or financial assistance or any guarantee by the Government:

Provided also that in case of a co-operative society carrying on the business of banking, the provisions of the Banking Regulation Act, 1949 shall also apply:

Provided also that in case of a co-operative society, other than a multi-State co-operative society, carrying on the business of banking, the provisions of this clause shall have the effect as if for the words "six months", the words "one year" had been substituted.

(2) In case of supersession of a board, the administrator appointed to manage the affairs of such co-operative society shall arrange for conduct of elections within the period specified in clause (1) and handover the management to the elected board.

(3) The Legislature of a State may, by law, make provisions for the conditions of service of the administrator.

243ZM. Audit of accounts of co-operative societies.—(1) The Legislature of a State may, by law, make provisions with respect to the maintenance of accounts by the co-operative societies and the auditing of such accounts at least once in each financial year. (2) The Legislature of a State shall, by law, lay down the minimum qualifications and experience of auditors and auditing firms that shall be eligible for auditing accounts of the co-operative societies. (3) Every co-operative society shall cause to be audited by an auditor or auditing firms referred to in clause (2) appointed by the general body of the co-operative society:

Provided that such auditors or auditing firms shall be appointed from a panel approved by a State Government or an authority authorised by the State Government in this behalf.

(4) The accounts of every co-operative society shall be audited within six months of the close of the financial year to which such accounts relate.

(5) The audit report of the accounts of an apex co-operative society, as may be defined by the State Act, shall be laid before the State Legislature in the manner, as may be provided by the State Legislature, by law.

243ZN. Convening of general body meetings.—The Legislature of a State may, by law, make provisions that the annual general body meeting of every co-operative society shall be convened within a period of six months of close of the financial year to transact the business as may be provided in such law.

243ZO. Right of a member to get information.—(1) The Legislature of a State may, by law, provide for access to every member of a co-operative society to the books, information and accounts of the co-operative society kept in regular transaction of its business with such member.

(2) The Legislature of a State may, by law, make provisions to ensure the participation of members in the management of the co-operative society providing minimum requirement of attending meetings by the members and utilising the minimum level of services as may be provided in such law.

(3) The Legislature of a State may, by law, provide for co-operative education and training for its members.

243ZP. Returns.—Every co-operative society shall file returns, within six months of the close of every financial year, to the authority designated by the State Government including the following matters, namely:—

    (*a*) annual report of its activities;

    (*b*) its audited statement of accounts;

    (*c*) plan for surplus disposal as approved by the general body of the co-operative society;

    (*d*) list of amendments to the bye-laws of the co-operative society, if any;

    (*e*) declaration regarding date of holding of its general body meeting and conduct of elections when due; and

    (*f*) any other information required by the Registrar in pursuance of any of the provisions of the State Act.

243ZQ. Offences and penalties.—(1) The Legislature of a State may, by law, make provisions for the offences relating to the co-operative societies and penalties for such offences.

(2) A law made by the Legislature of a State under clause (1) shall include the commission of the following act or omission as offences, namely:—

    (*a*) a co-operative society or an officer or member thereof wilfully makes a false return or furnishes false information, or any person wilfully not furnishes any information required from him by a person authorised in this behalf under the provisions of the State Act;

    (*b*) any person wilfully or without any reasonable excuse disobeys any summons, requisition or lawful written order issued under the provisions of the State Act;

    (*c*) any employer who, without sufficient cause, fails to pay to a co-operative society amount deducted by him from its employee within a period of fourteen days from the date on which such deduction is made;

    (*d*) any officer or custodian who wilfully fails to handover custody of books, accounts, documents, records, cash, security and other property belonging to a co-operative society of which he is an officer or custodian, to an authorised person; and

(e) whoever, before, during or after the election of members of the board or office bearers, adopts any corrupt practice.

243ZR. Application to multi-State co-operative societies.—The provisions of this Part shall apply to the multi-State co-operative societies subject to the modification that any reference to "Legislature of a State", "State Act" or "State Government" shall be construed as a reference to "Parliament", "Central Act" or "the Central Government" respectively.

243ZS. Application to Union territories.—The provisions of this Part shall apply to the Union territories and shall, in their application to a Union territory, having no Legislative Assembly as if the references to the Legislature of a State were a reference to the administrator thereof appointed under article 239 and, in relation to a Union territory having a Legislative Assembly, to that Legislative Assembly:

Provided that the President may, by notification in the Official Gazette, direct that the provisions of this Part shall not apply to any Union territory or part thereof as he may specify in the notification.

243ZT. Continuance of existing laws.— Notwithstanding anything in this Part, any provision of any law relating to co-operative societies in force in a State immediately before the commencement of the Constitution (Ninety-seventh Amendment) Act, 2011, which is inconsistent with the provisions of this Part, shall continue to be in force until amended or repealed by a competent Legislature or other competent authority or until the expiration of one year from such commencement, whichever is less.]

PART X

THE SCHEDULED AND TRIBAL AREAS

244. Administration of Scheduled Areas and Tribal Areas.—
(1) The provisions of the Fifth Schedule shall apply to the administration and control of the Scheduled Areas and Scheduled Tribes in any State [1]*** other than [2][the States of Assam, [3][, [4][Meghalaya, Tripura and Mizoram]]].

(2) The provisions of the Sixth Schedule shall apply to the administration of the tribal areas in [2][the States of Assam, [3][, [5][Meghalaya, Tripura and Mizoram]]].

[6][**244A. Formation of an autonomous State comprising certain tribal areas in Assam and creation of local Legislature or Council of Ministers or both therefor.**—(1) Notwithstanding anything in this Constitution, Parliament may, by law, form within the State of Assam an autonomous State comprising (whether wholly or in part) all or any of the tribal areas specified in [7][Part I] of the table appended to paragraph 20 of the Sixth Schedule and create therefor—

    (*a*) a body, whether elected or partly nominated and partly elected, to function as a Legislature for the autonomous State, or

    (*b*) a Council of Ministers,

or both with such constitution, powers and functions, in each case, as may be specified in the law.

---

1 The words and letters "specified in Part A or Part B of the First Schedule" omitted by the Constitution (Seventh Amendment) Act, 1956, s. 29 and Sch. (w.e.f. 1-11-1956).

2 Subs. by the North-Eastern Areas (Reorganisation) Act, 1971 (81 of 1971), s. 71, for "the State of Assam" (w.e.f. 21-1-1972).

3 Subs. by the Constitution (Forty-ninth Amendment) Act, 1984, s. 2, for "and Meghalaya" (w.e.f. 1-4-1985).

4 Subs. by the State of Mizoram Act, 1986 (34 of 1986), s. 39, for "Meghalaya and Tripura" (w.e.f. 20-2-1987).

5 Subs. by s. 39, *ibid.*, for "Meghalaya and Tripura and the Union territory of Mizoram". (w.e.f. 20-2-1987).

6 Ins. by the Constitution (Twenty-second Amendment) Act, 1969, s. 2 (w.e.f. 25-9-1969).

7 Subs. by the North-Eastern Areas (Reorganisation) Act, 1971 (81 of 1971), s. 71, for "Part A" (w.e.f. 21-1-1972).

(2) Any such law as is referred to in clause (1) may, in particular,—

(*a*) specify the matters enumerated in the State List or the Concurrent List with respect to which the Legislature of the autonomous State shall have power to make laws for the whole or any part thereof, whether to the exclusion of the Legislature of the State of Assam or otherwise;

(*b*) define the matters with respect to which the executive power of the autonomous State shall extend;

(*c*) provide that any tax levied by the State of Assam shall be assigned to the autonomous State in so far as the proceeds thereof are attributable to the autonomous State;

(*d*) provide that any reference to a State in any article of this Constitution shall be construed as including a reference to the autonomous State; and

(*e*) make such supplemental, incidental and consequential provisions as may be deemed necessary.

(3) An amendment of any such law as aforesaid in so far as such amendment relates to any of the matters specified in sub-clause (*a*) or sub-clause (*b*) of clause (2) shall have no effect unless the amendment is passed in each House of Parliament by not less than two-thirds of the members present and voting.

(4) Any such law as is referred to in this article shall not be deemed to be an amendment of this Constitution for the purposes of article 368 notwithstanding that it contains any provision which amends or has the effect of amending this Constitution.]

PART XI

RELATIONS BETWEEN THE UNION AND THE STATES

Chapter I.—Legislative Relations

Distribution of Legislative Powers

245. Extent of laws made by Parliament and by the Legislatures of States.—(1) Subject to the provisions of this Constitution, Parliament may make laws for the whole or any part of the territory of India, and the Legislature of a State may make laws for the whole or any part of the State.

(2) No law made by Parliament shall be deemed to be invalid on the ground that it would have extra-territorial operation.

246. Subject-matter of laws made by Parliament and by the Legislatures of States.—(1) Notwithstanding anything in clauses (2) and (3), Parliament has exclusive power to make laws with respect to any of the matters enumerated in List I in the Seventh Schedule (in this Constitution referred to as the "Union List").

(2) Notwithstanding anything in clause (3), Parliament, and, subject to clause (1), the Legislature of any State ¹*** also, have power to make laws with respect to any of the matters enumerated in List III in the Seventh Schedule (in this Constitution referred to as the "Concurrent List").

(3) Subject to clauses (1) and (2), the Legislature of any State ¹*** has exclusive power to make laws for such State or any part thereof with respect to any of the matters enumerated in List II in the Seventh Schedule (in this Constitution referred to as the "State List").

---

1 The words and letters "specified in Part A or Part B of the First Schedule" omitted by the Constitution (Seventh Amendment) Act, 1956, s. 29 and Sch. (w.e.f. 1-11-1956).

(4) Parliament has power to make laws with respect to any matter for any part of the territory of India not included ¹[in a State] notwithstanding that such matter is a matter enumerated in the State List.

²[**246A. Special provision with respect to goods and services tax.**— (1) Notwithstanding anything contained in articles 246 and 254, Parliament, and, subject to clause (2), the Legislature of every State, have power to make laws with respect to goods and services tax imposed by the Union or by such State.

(2) Parliament has exclusive power to make laws with respect to goods and services tax where the supply of goods, or of services, or both takes place in the course of inter-State trade or commerce.

Explanation.—The provisions of this article, shall, in respect of goods and services tax referred to in clause (5) of article 279A, take effect from the date recommended by the Goods and Services Tax Council.]

247. Power of Parliament to provide for the establishment of certain additional courts.—Notwithstanding anything in this Chapter, Parliament may by law provide for the establishment of any additional courts for the better administration of laws made by Parliament or of any existing laws with respect to a matter enumerated in the Union List.

248. Residuary powers of legislation.—(1) ³[Subject to article 246A, Parliament] has exclusive power to make any law with respect to any matter not enumerated in the Concurrent List or State List.

(2) Such power shall include the power of making any law imposing a tax not mentioned in either of those Lists.

249. Power of Parliament to legislate with respect to a matter in the State List in the national interest.—(1) Notwithstanding anything in the foregoing provisions of this Chapter, if the Council of States has declared by resolution supported by not less than two-thirds of the members present and voting that it is necessary

---

1 Subs. by s. 29 and Sch., *ibid.*, for "in Part A or Part B of the First Schedule" (w.e.f. 1-11-1956).
2 Ins. by the Constitution (One Hundred and First Amendment) Act, 2016, s. 2 (w.e.f. 16-9-2016).
3 Subs. by the Constitution (One Hundred and First Amendment) Act, 2016, s. 3, for "Parliament" (w.e.f. 16-9-2016).

or expedient in the national interest that Parliament should make laws with respect to [1][goods and services tax provided under article 246A or] any matter enumerated in the State List specified in the resolution, it shall be lawful for Parliament to make laws for the whole or any part of the territory of India with respect to that matter while the resolution remains in force.

(2) A resolution passed under clause (1) shall remain in force for such period not exceeding one year as may be specified therein:

Provided that, if and so often as a resolution approving the continuance in force of any such resolution is passed in the manner provided in clause (1), such resolution shall continue in force for a further period of one year from the date on which under this clause it would otherwise have ceased to be in force.

(3) A law made by Parliament which Parliament would not but for the passing of a resolution under clause (1) have been competent to make shall, to the extent of the incompetency, cease to have effect on the expiration of a period of six months after the resolution has ceased to be in force, except as respects things done or omitted to be done before the expiration of the said period.

250. Power of Parliament to legislate with respect to any matter in the State List if a Proclamation of Emergency is in operation.—(1) Notwithstanding anything in this Chapter, Parliament shall, while a Proclamation of Emergency is in operation, have power to make laws for the whole or any part of the territory of India with respect to [2][goods and services tax provided under article 246A or] any of the matters enumerated in the State List.

(2) A law made by Parliament which Parliament would not but for the issue of a Proclamation of Emergency have been competent to make shall, to the extent of the incompetency, cease to have effect on the expiration of a period of six months after the Proclamation has ceased to operate, except as respects things done or omitted to be done before the expiration of the said period.

---

1 Ins. by s. 4, *ibid.* (w.e.f. 16-9-2016).
2 Ins. by the Constitution (One Hundred and First Amendment) Act, 2016, s. 5 (w.e.f. 16-9-2016).

251. **Inconsistency between laws made by Parliament under articles 249 and 250 and laws made by the Legislatures of States.**—Nothing in articles 249 and 250 shall restrict the power of the Legislature of a State to make any law which under this Constitution it has power to make, but if any provision of a law made by the Legislature of a State is repugnant to any provision of a law made by Parliament which Parliament has under either of the said articles power to make, the law made by Parliament, whether passed before or after the law made by the Legislature of the State, shall prevail, and the law made by the Legislature of the State shall to the extent of the repugnancy, but so long only as the law made by Parliament continues to have effect, be inoperative.

252. **Power of Parliament to legislate for two or more States by consent and adoption of such legislation by any other State.**—(1) If it appears to the Legislatures of two or more States to be desirable that any of the matters with respect to which Parliament has no power to make laws for the States except as provided in articles 249 and 250 should be regulated in such States by Parliament by law, and if resolutions to that effect are passed by all the Houses of the Legislatures of those States, it shall be lawful for Parliament to pass an act for regulating that matter accordingly, and any Act so passed shall apply to such States and to any other State by which it is adopted afterwards by resolution passed in that behalf by the House or, where there are two Houses, by each of the Houses of the Legislature of that State.

(2) Any Act so passed by Parliament may be amended or repealed by an Act of Parliament passed or adopted in like manner but shall not, as respects any State to which it applies, be amended or repealed by an Act of the Legislature of that State.

253. **Legislation for giving effect to international agreements.**—Notwithstanding anything in the foregoing provisions of this Chapter, Parliament has power to make any law for the whole or any part of the territory of India for implementing any treaty, agreement or convention with any other country or countries or any decision made at any international conference, association or other body.

254. **Inconsistency between laws made by Parliament and laws made by the Legislatures of States.**—(1) If any provision of

a law made by the Legislature of a State is repugnant to any provision of a law made by Parliament which Parliament is competent to enact, or to any provision of an existing law with respect to one of the matters enumerated in the Concurrent List, then, subject to the provisions of clause (2), the law made by Parliament, whether passed before or after the law made by the Legislature of such State, or, as the case may be, the existing law, shall prevail and the law made by the Legislature of the State shall, to the extent of the repugnancy, be void.

(2) Where a law made by the Legislature of a State [1]*** with respect to one of the matters enumerated in the Concurrent List contains any provision repugnant to the provisions of an earlier law made by Parliament or an existing law with respect to that matter, then, the law so made by the Legislature of such State shall, if it has been reserved for the consideration of the President and has received his assent, prevail in that State:

Provided that nothing in this clause shall prevent Parliament from enacting at any time any law with respect to the same matter including a law adding to, amending, varying or repealing the law so made by the Legislature of the State.

255. Requirements as to recommendations and previous sanctions to be regarded as matters of procedure only.—No Act of Parliament or of the Legislature of a State [1]***, and no provision in any such Act, shall be invalid by reason only that some recommendation or previous sanction required by this Constitution was not given, if assent to that Act was given—

(a) where the recommendation required was that of the Governor, either by the Governor or by the President;

(b) where the recommendation required was that of the Rajpramukh, either by the Rajpramukh or by the President;

(c) where the recommendation or previous sanction required was that of the President, by the President.

---

1 The words and letters "specified in Part A or Part B of the First Schedule" omitted by the Constitution (Seventh Amendment) Act, 1956, s. 29 and Sch. (w.e.f. 1-11-1956).

Chapter II.—Administrative Relations
General

256. **Obligation of States and the Union.**—The executive power of every State shall be so exercised as to ensure compliance with the laws made by Parliament and any existing laws which apply in that State, and the executive power of the Union shall extend to the giving of such directions to a State as may appear to the Government of India to be necessary for that purpose.

257. **Control of the Union over States in certain cases.**—(1) The executive power of every State shall be so exercised as not to impede or prejudice the exercise of the executive power of the Union, and the executive power of the Union shall extend to the giving of such directions to a State as may appear to the Government of India to be necessary for that purpose.

(2) The executive power of the Union shall also extend to the giving of directions to a State as to the construction and maintenance of means of communication declared in the direction to be of national or military importance:

Provided that nothing in this clause shall be taken as restricting the power of Parliament to declare highways or waterways to be national highways or national waterways or the power of the Union with respect to the highways or waterways so declared or the power of the Union to construct and maintain means of communication as part of its functions with respect to naval, military and air force works.

(3) The executive power of the Union shall also extend to the giving of directions to a State as to the measures to be taken for the protection of the railways within the State.

(4) Where in carrying out any direction given to a State under clause (2) as to the construction or maintenance of any means of communication or under clause (3) as to the measures to be taken for the protection of any railway, costs have been incurred in excess of those which would have been incurred in the discharge of the normal duties of the State if such direction had not been given, there shall be paid by the Government of India to the State such sum as may be agreed, or, in default of agreement, as may

be determined by an arbitrator appointed by the Chief Justice of India, in respect of the extra costs so incurred by the State.

¹[**257A.** [*Assistance to States by deployment of armed forces or other forces of the Union*].—*Omitted by the Constitution (Forty-fourth Amendment) Act, 1978, s. 33 (w.e.f. 20-6-1979).*]

258. Power of the Union to confer powers, etc., on States in certain cases.—(1) Notwithstanding anything in this Constitution, the President may, with the consent of the Government of a State, entrust either conditionally or unconditionally to that Government or to its officers functions in relation to any matter to which the executive power of the Union extends.

(2) A law made by Parliament which applies in any State may, notwithstanding that it relates to a matter with respect to which the Legislature of the State has no power to make laws, confer powers and impose duties, or authorise the conferring of powers and the imposition of duties, upon the State or officers and authorities thereof.

(3) Where by virtue of this article powers and duties have been conferred or imposed upon a State or officers or authorities thereof, there shall be paid by the Government of India to the State such sum as may be agreed, or, in default of agreement, as may be determined by an arbitrator appointed by the Chief Justice of India, in respect of any extra costs of administration incurred by the State in connection with the exercise of those powers and duties.

²[**258A. Power of the States to entrust functions to the Union.**—Notwithstanding anything in this Constitution, the Governor of a State may, with the consent of the Government of India, entrust either conditionally or unconditionally to that Government or to its officers functions in relation to any matter to which the executive power of the State extends.]

[**259.** *Armed Forces in States in Part B of the First Schedule.*].— *Omitted by the Constitution (Seventh Amendment) Act, 1956, s. 29 and Sch. (w.e.f. 1-11-1956).*

---

1 Ins. by the Constitution (Forty-second Amendment) Act, 1976, s. 43 (w.e.f. 3-1-1977).
2 Ins. by the Constitution (Seventh Amendment) Act, 1956, s. 18 (w.e.f. 1-11-1956).

260. **Jurisdiction of the Union in relation to territories outside India.**—The Government of India may by agreement with the Government of any territory not being part of the territory of India undertake any executive, legislative or judicial functions vested in the Government of such territory, but every such agreement shall be subject to, and governed by, any law relating to the exercise of foreign jurisdiction for the time being in force.

261. **Public acts, records and judicial proceedings.**—(1) Full faith and credit shall be given throughout the territory of India to public acts, records and judicial proceedings of the Union and of every State.

(2) The manner in which and the conditions under which the acts, records and proceedings referred to in clause (1) shall be proved and the effect thereof determined shall be as provided by law made by Parliament.

(3) Final judgments or orders delivered or passed by civil courts in any part of the territory of India shall be capable of execution anywhere within that territory according to law.

Disputes relating to Waters

262. **Adjudication of disputes relating to waters of inter-State rivers or river valleys.**—(1) Parliament may by law provide for the adjudication of any dispute or complaint with respect to the use, distribution or control of the waters of, or in, any inter-State river or river valley.

(2) Notwithstanding anything in this Constitution, Parliament may by law provide that neither the Supreme Court nor any other court shall exercise jurisdiction in respect of any such dispute or complaint as is referred to in clause (1).

Co-ordination between States

263. **Provisions with respect to an inter-State Council.**—If at any time it appears to the President that the public interests would be served by the establishment of a Council charged with the duty of—

(*a*) inquiring into and advising upon disputes which may have arisen between States;

(*b*) investigating and discussing subjects in which some or all of the States, or the Union and one or more of the States, have a common interest; or

(*c*) making recommendations upon any such subject and, in particular, recommendations for the better co-ordination of policy and action with respect to that subject,

it shall be lawful for the President by order to establish such a Council, and to define the nature of the duties to be performed by it and its organisation and procedure.

PART XII

FINANCE, PROPERTY, CONTRACTS AND SUITS

Chapter I.—Finance
General

[1][264.   **Interpretation.**—In this Part, "Finance Commission" means a Finance Commission constituted under article 280.]

265.   **Taxes not to be imposed save by authority of law.**—No tax shall be levied or collected except by authority of law.

266.   **Consolidated Funds and public accounts of India and of the States.**—(1) Subject to the provisions of article 267 and to the provisions of this Chapter with respect to the assignment of the whole or part of the net proceeds of certain taxes and duties to States, all revenues received by the Government of India, all loans raised by that Government by the issue of treasury bills, loans or ways and means advances and all moneys received by that

---

1   Subs. by the Constitution (Seventh Amendment) Act, 1956, s. 29 and Sch., for art. 264 (w.e.f. 1-11-1956).

Government in repayment of loans shall form one consolidated fund to be entitled "the Consolidated Fund of India", and all revenues received by the Government of a State, all loans raised by that Government by the issue of treasury bills, loans or ways and means advances and all moneys received by that Government in repayment of loans shall form one consolidated fund to be entitled "the Consolidated Fund of the State".

(2) All other public moneys received by or on behalf of the Government of India or the Government of a State shall be credited to the public account of India or the public account of the State, as the case may be.

(3) No moneys out of the Consolidated Fund of India or the Consolidated Fund of a State shall be appropriated except in accordance with law and for the purposes and in the manner provided in this Constitution.

267. **Contingency Fund.**—(1) Parliament may by law establish a Contingency Fund in the nature of an imprest to be entitled "the Contingency Fund of India" into which shall be paid from time to time such sums as may be determined by such law, and the said Fund shall be placed at the disposal of the President to enable advances to be made by him out of such Fund for the purposes of meeting unforeseen expenditure pending authorisation of such expenditure by Parliament by law under article 115 or article 116.

(2) The Legislature of a State may by law establish a Contingency Fund in the nature of an imprest to be entitled "the Contingency Fund of the State" into which shall be paid from time to time such sums as may be determined by such law, and the said Fund shall be placed at the disposal of the Governor [1]*** of the State to enable advances to be made by him out of such Fund for the purposes of meeting unforeseen expenditure pending authorisation of such expenditure by the Legislature of the State by law under article 205 or article 206.

---

1 The words "or Rajpramukh" omitted by the Constitution (Seventh Amendment) Act, 1956, s. 29 and Sch. (w.e.f. 1-11-1956).

Distribution of Revenues between the Union and the States

268. Duties levied by the Union but collected and appropriated by the States.—(1) Such stamp duties [1]*** as are mentioned in the Union List shall be levied by the Government of India but shall be collected—

    (*a*)   in the case where such duties are leviable within any [2][Union territory], by the Government of India, and

    (*b*)   in other cases, by the States within which such duties are respectively leviable.

(2) The proceeds in any financial year of any such duty leviable within any State shall not form part of the Consolidated Fund of India, but shall be assigned to that State.

[3]**268A.** *[Service tax levied by Union and collected and appropriated by the Union and the States.].—Omitted by the Constitution (One Hundred and First Amendment) Act, 2016, s. 7 (w.e.f. 16-9-2016).*

269. Taxes levied and collected by the Union but assigned to the States.—[4][(1) Taxes on the sale or purchase of goods and taxes on the consignment of goods [5][except as provided in article 269A] shall be levied and collected by the Government of India but shall be assigned and shall be deemed to have been assigned to the States on or after the 1st day of April, 1996 in the manner provided in clause (2).

Explanation.—For the purposes of this clause,—

    (*a*)   the expression "taxes on the sale or purchase of goods" shall mean taxes on sale or purchase of goods other than newspapers, where such sale or purchase takes place in the course of inter-State trade or commerce;

    (*b*)   the expression "taxes on the consignment of goods" shall mean taxes on the consignment of goods (whether the consignment is to the person making it or to any

---

1 The words "and such duties of excise on medicinal and toilet preparations" omitted by the Constitution (One Hundred and First Amendment) Act, 2016, s. 6, (w.e.f. 16-9-2016).

2 Subs. by the Constitution (Seventh Amendment) Act, 1956, s. 29 and Sch., for "State Specified in Part C of the First Schedule" (w.e.f. 1-11-1956).

3 Ins. by the Constitution (Eighty-eighth Amendment) Act, 2003, s. 2 (date not notified).

4 Subs. by the Constitution (Eightieth Amendment) Act, 2000. s. 2, for cls. (1) and (2) (w.e.f. 9-6-2000).

5 Ins. by the Constitution (One Hundred and First Amendment) Act, 2016 s. 8, (w.e.f. 16-9-2016).

other person), where such consignment takes place in the course of inter-State trade or commerce.

(2) The net proceeds in any financial year of any such tax, except in so far as those proceeds represent proceeds attributable to Union territories, shall not form part of the Consolidated Fund of India, but shall be assigned to the States within which that tax is leviable in that year, and shall be distributed among those States in accordance with such principles of distribution as may be formulated by Parliament by law.]

[1][(3) Parliament may by law formulate principles for determining when a [2][sale or purchase of, or consignment of goods] takes place in the course of inter-State trade or commerce.]

[3][**269A. Levy and collection of goods and services tax in course of inter-State trade or commerce.**— (1) Goods and services tax on supplies in the course of inter-State trade or commerce shall be levied and collected by the Government of India and such tax shall be apportioned between the Union and the States in the manner as may be provided by Parliament by law on the recommendations of the Goods and Services Tax Council.

Explanation.—For the purposes of this clause, supply of goods, or of services, or both in the course of import into the territory of India shall be deemed to be supply of goods, or of services, or both in the course of inter- State trade or commerce.

(2) The amount apportioned to a State under clause (1) shall not form part of the Consolidated Fund of India.

(3) Where an amount collected as tax levied under clause (1) has been used for payment of the tax levied by a State under article 246A, such amount shall not form part of the Consolidated Fund of India.

(4) Where an amount collected as tax levied by a State under article 246A has been used for payment of the tax levied under clause (1), such amount shall not form part of the Consolidated Fund of the State.

---

1 Ins. by the Constitution (Sixth Amendment) Act, 1956, s. 3 (w.e.f. 11-9-1956).
2 Subs. by the Constitution (Forty-sixth Amendment) Act, 1982. s. 2, for "sale or purchase of goods" (w.e.f. 2-2-1983).
3 Ins. by the Constitution (One Hundred and First Amendment) Act, 2016, s. 9 (w.e.f. 16-9-2016).

(5) Parliament may, by law, formulate the principles for determining the place of supply, and when a supply of goods, or of services, or both takes place in the course of inter-State trade or commerce.]

¹[270.   **Taxes levied and distributed between the Union and the States.**—(1) All taxes and duties referred to in the Union List, except the duties and taxes referred to in ²[articles 268, 269 and 269A], respectively, surcharge on taxes and duties referred to in article 271 and any cess levied for specific purposes under any law made by Parliament shall be levied and collected by the Government of India and shall be distributed between the Union and the States in the manner provided in clause (2).

³[(1A) The tax collected by the Union under clause (1) of article 246A shall also be distributed between the Union and the States in the manner provided in clause (2).

(1B) The tax levied and collected by the Union under clause (2) of article 246A and article 269A, which has been used for payment of the tax levied by the Union under clause (1) of article 246A, and the amount apportioned to the Union under clause (1) of article 269A, shall also be distributed between the Union and the States in the manner provided in clause (2).]

(2) Such percentage, as may be prescribed, of the net proceeds of any such tax or duty in any financial year shall not form part of the Consolidated Fund of India, but shall be assigned to the States within which that tax or duty is leviable in that year, and shall be distributed among those States in such manner and from such time as may be prescribed in the manner provided in clause (3).

(3) In this article, "prescribed" means, —

  (*i*) until a Finance Commission has been constituted, prescribed by the President by order, and

  (*ii*) after a Finance Commission has been constituted, prescribed by the President by order after considering the recommendations of the Finance Commission.]

---

1 Subs. by the Constitution (Eightieth Amendment) Act, 2000, s. 3, for art. 270 (w.e.f. 1-4-1996).
2 Subs. by the Constitution (Eighty-eighth Amendment) Act, 2003, s. 3, for "articles 268 and 269" (date not notified) and further subs. by the Constitution (One Hundred and First Amendment) Act, 2016, s. 10, for "arts. 268, 268A and 269" (w.e.f. 16-9-2016).
3 Ins. by s. 10, *ibid*. (w.e.f. 16-9-2016).

271. Surcharge on certain duties and taxes for purposes of the Union.—Notwithstanding anything in articles 269 and 270, Parliament may at any time increase any of the duties or taxes referred to in those articles [1][except the goods and services tax under article 246A,] by a surcharge for purposes of the Union and the whole proceeds of any such surcharge shall form part of the Consolidated Fund of India.

[272. *Taxes which are levied and collected by the Union and may be distributed between the Union and the States.*].—*Omitted by the Constitution (Eightieth Amendment) Act, 2000, s. 4.* (w.e.f. 9-6-2000).

273. Grants in lieu of export duty on jute and jute products.—(1) There shall be charged on the Consolidated Fund of India in each year as grants-in-aid of the revenues of the States of Assam, Bihar, [2][Odisha] and West Bengal, in lieu of assignment of any share of the net proceeds in each year of export duty on jute and jute products to those States, such sums as may be prescribed.

(2) The sums so prescribed shall continue to be charged on the Consolidated Fund of India so long as any export duty on jute or jute products continues to be levied by the Government of India or until the expiration of ten years from the commencement of this Constitution whichever is earlier.

(3) In this article, the expression "prescribed" has the same meaning as in article 270.

274. Prior recommendation of President required to Bills affecting taxation in which States are interested.—(1) No Bill or amendment which imposes or varies any tax or duty in which States are interested, or which varies the meaning of the expression "agricultural income" as defined for the purposes of the enactments relating to Indian income-tax, or which affects the principles on which under any of the foregoing provisions of this Chapter moneys are or may be distributable to States, or which imposes any such surcharge for the purposes of the Union as is mentioned in the foregoing provisions of this Chapter, shall

---

1 Ins. by the Constitution (One Hundred and First Amendment) Act, 2016, s. 11 (w.e.f. 16-9-2016).

2 Subs. by the Orissa (Alteration of Name) Act, 2011 (15 of 2011), s. 5, for "Orissa" (w.e.f. 1-11-2011).

be introduced or moved in either House of Parliament except on the recommendation of the President.

(2) In this article, the expression "tax or duty in which States are interested" means—

    (*a*) a tax or duty the whole or part of the net proceeds whereof are assigned to any State; or

    (*b*) a tax or duty by reference to the net proceeds whereof sums are for the time being payable out of the Consolidated Fund of India to any State.

275.   **Grants from the Union to certain States.**—(1) Such sums as Parliament may by law provide shall be charged on the Consolidated Fund of India in each year as grants-in-aid of the revenues of such States as Parliament may determine to be in need of assistance, and different sums may be fixed for different States: Provided that there shall be paid out of the Consolidated Fund of India as grants-in-aid of the revenues of a State such capital and recurring sums as may be necessary to enable that State to meet the costs of such schemes of development as may be undertaken by the State with the approval of the Government of India for the purpose of promoting the welfare of the Scheduled Tribes in that State or raising the level of administration of the Scheduled Areas therein to that of the administration of the rest of the areas of that State:

Provided further that there shall be paid out of the Consolidated Fund of India as grants-in-aid of the revenues of the State of Assam sums, capital and recurring, equivalent to—

    (*a*) the average excess of expenditure over the revenues during the two years immediately preceding the commencement of this Constitution in respect of the administration of the tribal areas specified in [1][Part I] of the table appended to paragraph 20 of the Sixth Schedule; and

    (*b*) the costs of such schemes of development as may be undertaken by that State with the approval of the

---

1 Subs. by the North-Eastern Areas (Reorganisation) Act, 1971 (81 of 1971) s. 71, for "Part A" (w.e.f. 21-1-1972).

Government of India for the purpose of raising the level of administration of the said areas to that of the administration of the rest of the areas of that State.

[1][(1A) On and from the formation of the autonomous State under article 244A,—

(i) any sums payable under clause (a) of the second proviso to clause (1) shall, if the autonomous State comprises all the tribal areas referred to therein, be paid to the autonomous State, and, if the autonomous State comprises only some of those tribal areas, be apportioned between the State of Assam and the autonomous State as the President may, by order, specify;

(ii) there shall be paid out of the Consolidated Fund of India as grants-in-aid of the revenues of the autonomous State sums, capital and recurring, equivalent to the costs of such schemes of development as may be undertaken by the autonomous State with the approval of the Government of India for the purpose of raising the level of administration of that State to that of the administration of the rest of the State of Assam.]

(2) Until provision is made by Parliament under clause (1), the powers conferred on Parliament under that clause shall be exercisable by the President by order and any order made by the President under this clause shall have effect subject to any provision so made by Parliament:

Provided that after a Finance Commission has been constituted no order shall be made under this clause by the President except after considering the recommendations of the Finance Commission.

276. Taxes on professions, trades, callings and employments.— (1) Notwithstanding anything in article 246, no law of the Legislature of a State relating to taxes for the benefit of the State or of a municipality, district board, local board or other local authority therein in respect of professions, trades, callings or

---

1 Ins. by the Constitution (Twenty-second Amendment) Act, 1969, s. 3 (w.e.f. 25-9-1969).

employments shall be invalid on the ground that it relates to a tax on income.

(2) The total amount payable in respect of any one person to the State or to any one municipality, district board, local board or other local authority in the State by way of taxes on professions, trades, callings and employments shall not exceed [1][two thousand and five hundred rupees] per annum.

[2]*　　*　*　　*

(3) The power of the Legislature of a State to make laws as aforesaid with respect to taxes on professions, trades, callings and employments shall not be construed as limiting in any way the power of Parliament to make laws with respect to taxes on income accruing from or arising out of professions, trades, callings and employments.

277. **Savings.**—Any taxes, duties, cesses or fees which, immediately before the commencement of this Constitution, were being lawfully levied by the Government of any State or by any municipality or other local authority or body for the purposes of the State, municipality, district or other local area may, notwithstanding that those taxes, duties, cesses or fees are mentioned in the Union List, continue to be levied and to be applied to the same purposes until provision to the contrary is made by Parliament by law.

278. *[Agreement with States in Part B of the First Schedule with regard to certain financial matters].—Omitted by the Constitution (Seventh Amendment) Act, 1956, s. 29 and Sch. (*w.e.f. 1-11-1956*).*

279. **Calculation of "net proceeds", etc.**—(1) In the foregoing provisions of this Chapter, "net proceeds" means in relation to any tax or duty the proceeds thereof reduced by the cost of collection, and for the purposes of those provisions the net proceeds of any tax or duty, or of any part of any tax or duty, in or attributable to any area shall be ascertained and certified by the Comptroller and Auditor-General of India, whose certificate shall be final.

1　Subs. by the Constitution (Sixtieth Amendment) Act, 1988, s. 2, for "two hundred and fifty rupees" (w.e.f. 20-12-1988).

2　Proviso omitted by s.2, *ibid.* (w.e.f. 20-12-1988).

(2) Subject as aforesaid, and to any other express provision of this Chapter, a law made by Parliament or an order of the President may, in any case where under this Part the proceeds of any duty or tax are, or may be, assigned to any State, provide for the manner in which the proceeds are to be calculated, for the time from or at which and the manner in which any payments are to be made, for the making of adjustments between one financial year and another, and for any other incidental or ancillary matters.

¹[**279A. Goods and Services Tax Council.**—(1) The President shall, within sixty days from the date of commencement of the Constitution (One Hundred and First Amendment) Act, 2016, by order, constitute a Council to be called the Goods and Services Tax Council.

(2) The Goods and Services Tax Council shall consist of the following members, namely:—

(*a*) the Union Finance Minister — Chairperson;

(*b*) the Union Minister of State in charge of Revenue or Finance — Member;

(*c*) the Minister in charge of Finance or Taxation or any other Minister nominated by each State Government— Members.

(3) The Members of the Goods and Services Tax Council referred to in sub-clause (c) of clause (2) shall, as soon as may be, choose one amongst themselves to be the Vice-Chairperson of the Council for such period as they may decide.

(4) The Goods and Services Tax Council shall make recommendations to the Union and the States on—

(*a*) the taxes, cesses and surcharges levied by the Union, the States and the local bodies which may be subsumed in the goods and services tax;

(*b*) the goods and services that may be subjected to, or exempted from, the goods and services tax;

(*c*) model Goods and Services Tax Laws, principles of levy,

---

1 Ins. by the Constitution (One Hundred and First Amendment) Act, 2016, s. 12 (w.e.f. 12-9-2016).

apportionment of Goods and Services Tax levied on supplies in the course of inter-State trade or commerce under article 269A and the principles that govern the place of supply;

(d) the threshold limit of turnover below which goods and services may be exempted from goods and services tax;

(e) the rates including floor rates with bands of goods and services tax;

(f) any special rate or rates for a specified period, to raise additional resources during any natural calamity or disaster;

(g) special provision with respect to the States of Arunachal Pradesh, Assam, Jammu and Kashmir, Manipur, Meghalaya, Mizoram, Nagaland, Sikkim, Tripura, Himachal Pradesh and Uttarakhand; and

(h) any other matter relating to the goods and services tax, as the Council may decide.

(5) The Goods and Services Tax Council shall recommend the date on which the goods and services tax be levied on petroleum crude, high speed diesel, motor spirit (commonly known as petrol), natural gas and aviation turbine fuel.

(6) While discharging the functions conferred by this article, the Goods and Services Tax Council shall be guided by the need for a harmonised structure of goods and services tax and for the development of a harmonised national market for goods and services.

(7) One-half of the total number of Members of the Goods and Services Tax Council shall constitute the quorum at its meetings.

(8) The Goods and Services Tax Council shall determine the procedure in the performance of its functions.

(9) Every decision of the Goods and Services Tax Council shall be taken at a meeting, by a majority of not less than three-fourths of the weighted votes of the members present and voting, in accordance with the following principles, namely:—

(a) the vote of the Central Government shall have a weightage of one-third of the total votes cast, and

(b) the votes of all the State Governments taken together shall have a weightage of two-thirds of the total votes cast,

in that meeting.

(10) No act or proceedings of the Goods and Services Tax Council shall be invalid merely by reason of—

(a) any vacancy in, or any defect in, the constitution of the Council; or

(b) any defect in the appointment of a person as a Member of the Council; or

(c) any procedural irregularity of the Council not affecting the merits of the case.

(11) The Goods and Services Tax Council shall establish a mechanism to adjudicate any dispute—

(a) between the Government of India and one or more States; or

(b) between the Government of India and any State or States on one side and one or more other States on the other side; or

(c) between two or more States,

arising out of the recommendations of the Council or implementation thereof.]

280. **Finance Commission.**—(1) The President shall, within two years from the commencement of this Constitution and thereafter at the expiration of every fifth year or at such earlier time as the President considers necessary, by order constitute a Finance Commission which shall consist of a Chairman and four other members to be appointed by the President.

(2) Parliament may by law determine the qualifications which shall be requisite for appointment as members of the Commission and the manner in which they shall be selected.

(3) It shall be the duty of the Commission to make recommendations to the President as to—

(a) the distribution between the Union and the States of the net proceeds of taxes which are to be, or may be, divided between them under this Chapter and the allocation between the States of the respective shares of such proceeds;

(b) the principles which should govern the grants-in-aid of the revenues of the States out of the Consolidated Fund of India;

[1][(bb) the measures needed to augment the Consolidated Fund of a State to supplement the resources of the Panchayats in the State on the basis of the recommendations made by the Finance Commission of the State;]

[2][(c) the measures needed to augment the Consolidated Fund of a State to supplement the resources of the Municipalities in the State on the basis of the recommendations made by the Finance Commission of the State;]

[3][(d)] any other matter referred to the Commission by the President in the interests of sound finance.

(4) The Commission shall determine their procedure and shall have such powers in the performance of their functions as Parliament may by law confer on them.

281. Recommendations of the Finance Commission.—The President shall cause every recommendation made by the Finance Commission under the provisions of this Constitution together with an explanatory memorandum as to the action taken thereon to be laid before each House of Parliament.

Miscellaneous Financial Provisions

282. Expenditure defrayable by the Union or a State out of its revenues.—The Union or a State may make any grants for any public purpose, notwithstanding that the purpose is not one with respect to which Parliament or the Legislature of the State, as the case may be, may make laws.

283. Custody, etc., of Consolidated Funds, Contingency Funds and moneys credited to the public accounts.—(1) The

---

1 Ins. by the Constitution (Seventy-third Amendment) Act, 1992, s. 3 (w.e.f. 24-4-1993).
2 Ins. by the Constitution (Seventy-fourth Amendment) Act, 1992, s. 3 (w.e.f. 1-6-1993).
3 Sub-clause (c) re-lettered as sub-clause (d) by s. 3, *ibid.* (w.e.f. 1-6-1993).

custody of the Consolidated Fund of India and the Contingency Fund of India, the payment of moneys into such Funds, the withdrawal of moneys therefrom, the custody of public moneys other than those credited to such Funds received by or on behalf of the Government of India, their payment into the public account of India and the withdrawal of moneys from such account and all other matters connected with or ancillary to matters aforesaid shall be regulated by law made by Parliament, and, until provision in that behalf is so made, shall be regulated by rules made by the President.

(2) The custody of the Consolidated Fund of a State and the Contingency Fund of a State, the payment of moneys into such Funds, the withdrawal of moneys therefrom, the custody of public moneys other than those credited to such Funds received by or on behalf of the Government of the State, their payment into the public account of the State and the withdrawal of moneys from such account and all other matters connected with or ancillary to matters aforesaid shall be regulated by law made by the Legislature of the State, and, until provision in that behalf is so made, shall be regulated by rules made by the Governor [1]*** of the State.

284. **Custody of suitors' deposits and other moneys received by public servants and courts.**—All moneys received by or deposited with—

(*a*) any officer employed in connection with the affairs of the Union or of a State in his capacity as such, other than revenues or public moneys raised or received by the Government of India or the Government of the State, as the case may be, or

(*b*) any court within the territory of India to the credit of any cause, matter, account or persons,

shall be paid into the public account of India or the public account of State, as the case may be.

285. **Exemption of property of the Union from State taxation.**—
(1) The property of the Union shall, save in so far as Parliament

---

1 The words "or Rajpramukh" omitted by the Constitution (Seventh Amendment) Act, 1956, s. 29 and Sch. (w.e.f. 1-11-1956).

may by law otherwise provide, be exempt from all taxes imposed by a State or by any authority within a State.

(2) Nothing in clause (1) shall, until Parliament by law otherwise provides, prevent any authority within a State from levying any tax on any property of the Union to which such property was immediately before the commencement of this Constitution liable or treated as liable, so long as that tax continues to be levied in that State.

286. Restrictions as to imposition of tax on the sale or purchase of goods.—(1) No law of a State shall impose, or authorise the imposition of, a tax on ¹[the supply of goods or of services or both, where such supply takes place]—

    (*a*) outside the State; or

    (*b*) in the course of the import of the ²[goods or services or both] into, or export of the ²[goods or services or both] out of, the territory of India.

³[*   * *   *]

⁴[(2) Parliament may by law formulate principles for determining when a ⁵[supply of goods or of services or both] in any of the ways mentioned in clause (1).

⁶[(3) *   * *   *]

287. Exemption from taxes on electricity.—Save in so far as Parliament may by law otherwise provide, no law of a State shall impose, or authorise the imposition of, a tax on the consumption or sale of electricity (whether produced by a Government or other persons) which is—

    (*a*) consumed by the Government of India, or sold to the Government of India for consumption by that Government; or

---

1 Subs. by the Constitution (One Hundred and First Amendment) Act, 2016, s. 13, for "the sale or purchase of goods where such sale or purchase takes place" (w.e.f. 16-9-2016).
2 Subs. by s. 13 (i)(B), *ibid.*, for "goods" (w.e.f. 16-9-2016).
3 *Explanation* to cl. (1) omitted by the Constitution (Sixth Amendment) Act, 1956, s. 4 (w.e.f. 11-9-1956).
4 Subs. by s.4, *ibid.*, for cls. (2) and (3) (w.e.f. 11-9-1956).
5 Subs. by the Constitution (One Hundred and First Amendment) Act, 2016, s. 13(ii), for "sale or purchase of goods takes place" (w.e.f. 16-9-2016).
6 Cl. (3) omitted by s. 13 (iii), *ibid.* (w.e.f. 16-9-2016).

(*b*) consumed in the construction, maintenance or operation of any railway by the Government of India or a railway company operating that railway, or sold to that Government or any such railway company for consumption in the construction, maintenance or operation of any railway,

and any such law imposing, or authorising the imposition of, a tax on the sale of electricity shall secure that the price of electricity sold to the Government of India for consumption by that Government, or to any such railway company as aforesaid for consumption in the construction, maintenance or operation of any railway, shall be less by the amount of the tax than the price charged to other consumers of a substantial quantity of electricity.

288. **Exemption from taxation by States in respect of water or electricity in certain cases.**—(1) Save in so far as the President may by order otherwise provide, no law of a State in force immediately before the commencement of this Constitution shall impose, or authorise the imposition of, a tax in respect of any water or electricity stored, generated, consumed, distributed or sold by any authority established by any existing law or any law made by Parliament for regulating or developing any inter-State river or river-valley.

Explanation.—The expression "law of a State in force" in this clause shall include a law of a State passed or made before the commencement of this Constitution and not previously repealed, notwithstanding that it or parts of it may not be then in operation either at all or in particular areas.

(2) The Legislature of a State may by law impose, or authorise the imposition of, any such tax as is mentioned in clause (1), but no such law shall have any effect unless it has, after having been reserved for the consideration of the President, received his assent; and if any such law provides for the fixation of the rates and other incidents of such tax by means of rules or orders to be made under the law by any authority, the law shall provide for the previous consent of the President being obtained to the making of any such rule or order.

289. **Exemption of property and income of a State from Union taxation.**—(1) The property and income of a State shall be exempt from Union taxation.

(2) Nothing in clause (1) shall prevent the Union from imposing, or authorising the imposition of, any tax to such extent, if any, as Parliament may by law provide in respect of a trade or business of any kind carried on by, or on behalf of, the Government of a State, or any operations connected therewith, or any property used or occupied for the purposes of such trade or business, or any income accruing or arising in connection therewith.

(3) Nothing in clause (2) shall apply to any trade or business, or to any class of trade or business, which Parliament may by law declare to be incidental to the ordinary functions of Government.

290. **Adjustment in respect of certain expenses and pensions.**— Where under the provisions of this Constitution the expenses of any court or Commission, or the pension payable to or in respect of a person who has served before the commencement of this Constitution under the Crown in India or after such commencement in connection with the affairs of the Union or of a State, are charged on the Consolidated Fund of India or the Consolidated Fund of a State, then, if—

(a) in the case of a charge on the Consolidated Fund of India, the court or Commission serves any of the separate needs of a State, or the person has served wholly or in part in connection with the affairs of a State; or

(b) in the case of a charge on the Consolidated Fund of a State, the court or Commission serves any of the separate needs of the Union or another State, or the person has served wholly or in part in connection with the affairs of the Union or another State,

there shall be charged on and paid out of the Consolidated Fund of the State or, as the case may be, the Consolidated Fund of India or the Consolidated Fund of the other State, such contribution in respect of the expenses or pension as may be agreed, or as may in default of agreement be determined by an arbitrator to be appointed by the Chief Justice of India.

¹[**290A. Annual payment to certain Devaswom Funds.**—A sum of forty-six lakhs and fifty thousand rupees shall be charged on, and paid out of, the Consolidated Fund of the State of Kerala every year to the Travancore Devaswom Fund; and a sum of thirteen lakhs and fifty thousand rupees shall be charged on, and paid out of, the Consolidated Fund of the State of ²[Tamil Nadu] every year to the Devaswom Fund established in that State for the maintenance of Hindu temples and shrines in the territories transferred to that State on the 1st day of November, 1956, from the State of Travancore-Cochin.]

291. [*Privy purse sums of Rulers.*].—*Omitted by the Constitution (Twenty-sixth Amendment) Act, 1971, s. 2 (w.e.f. 28-12-1971).*

Chapter II.—Borrowing

292. Borrowing by the Government of India.—The executive power of the Union extends to borrowing upon the security of the Consolidated Fund of India within such limits, if any, as may from time to time be fixed by Parliament by law and to the giving of guarantees within such limits, if any, as may be so fixed.

293. Borrowing by States.—(1) Subject to the provisions of this article, the executive power of a State extends to borrowing within the territory of India upon the security of the Consolidated Fund of the State within such limits, if any, as may from time to time be fixed by the Legislature of such State by law and to the giving of guarantees within such limits, if any, as may be so fixed.

(2) The Government of India may, subject to such conditions as may be laid down by or under any law made by Parliament, make loans to any State or, so long as any limits fixed under article 292 are not exceeded, give guarantees in respect of loans raised by any State, and any sums required for the purpose of making such loans shall be charged on the Consolidated Fund of India.

(3) A State may not without the consent of the Government of India raise any loan if there is still outstanding any part of a

---

1 Ins. by the Constitution (Seventh Amendment) Act, 1956, s. 19 (w.e.f. 1-11-1956).
2 Subs. by the Madras State (Alteration of Name) Act, 1968 (53 of 1968), s. 4, for "Madras" (w.e.f. 14-1-1969).

loan which has been made to the State by the Government of India or by its predecessor Government, or in respect of which a guarantee has been given by the Government of India or by its predecessor Government.

(4) A consent under clause (3) may be granted subject to such conditions, if any, as the Government of India may think fit to impose.

Chapter III.—Property, Contracts, Rights, Liabilities, Obligations and Suits

294. **Succession to property, assets, rights, liabilities and obligations in certain cases.**—As from the commencement of this Constitution—

(*a*) all property and assets which immediately before such commencement were vested in His Majesty for the purposes of the Government of the Dominion of India and all property and assets which immediately before such commencement were vested in His Majesty for the purposes of the Government of each Governor's Province shall vest respectively in the Union and the corresponding State, and

(*b*) all rights, liabilities and obligations of the Government of the Dominion of India and of the Government of each Governor's Province, whether arising out of any contract or otherwise, shall be the rights, liabilities and obligations respectively of the Government of India and the Government of each corresponding State,

subject to any adjustment made or to be made by reason of the creation before the commencement of this Constitution of the Dominion of Pakistan or of the Provinces of West Bengal, East Bengal, West Punjab and East Punjab.

295. **Succession to property, assets, rights, liabilities and obligations in other cases.**—(1) As from the commencement of this Constitution—

(*a*) all property and assets which immediately before such commencement were vested in any Indian State corresponding to a State specified in Part B of the First Schedule shall vest in the Union, if the purposes for which such property and assets were held immediately before such commencement will thereafter be purposes of the Union relating to any of the matters enumerated in the Union List, and

(b) all rights, liabilities and obligations of the Government of any Indian State corresponding to a State specified in Part B of the First Schedule, whether arising out of any contract or otherwise, shall be the rights, liabilities and obligations of the Government of India, if the purposes for which such rights were acquired or liabilities or obligations were incurred before such commencement will thereafter be purposes of the Government of India relating to any of the matters enumerated in the Union List,

subject to any agreement entered into in that behalf by the Government of India with the Government of that State.

(2) Subject as aforesaid, the Government of each State specified in Part B of the First Schedule shall, as from the commencement of this Constitution, be the successor of the Government of the corresponding Indian State as regards all property and assets and all rights, liabilities and obligations, whether arising out of any contract or otherwise, other than those referred to in clause (1).

296. **Property accruing by escheat or lapse or as *bona vacantia*.—** Subject as hereinafter provided, any property in the territory of India which, if this Constitution had not come into operation, would have accrued to His Majesty or, as the case may be, to the Ruler of an Indian State by escheat or lapse, or as *bona vacantia* for want of a rightful owner, shall, if it is property situate in a State, vest in such State, and shall, in any other case, vest in the Union: Provided that any property which at the date when it would have so accrued to His Majesty or to the Ruler of an Indian State was in the possession or under the control of the Government of India or the Government of a State shall, according as the purposes for which it was then used or held were purposes of the Union or of a State, vest in the Union or in that State.

Explanation.—In this article, the expressions "Ruler" and "Indian State" have the same meanings as in article 363.

¹[**297.** **Things of value within territorial waters or continental shelf and resources of the exclusive economic zone to vest in the Union**.—(1) All lands, minerals and other things of value underlying the ocean within the territorial waters, or the continental shelf, or the exclusive economic zone, of India shall vest in the Union and be held for the purposes of the Union.

(2) All other resources of the exclusive economic zone of India shall also vest in the Union and be held for the purposes of the Union.

(3) The limits of the territorial waters, the continental shelf, the exclusive economic zone, and other maritime zones, of India shall be such as may be specified, from time to time, by or under any law made by Parliament.]

²[**298.** **Power to carry on trade, etc.**—The executive power of the Union and of each State shall extend to the carrying on of any trade or business and to the acquisition, holding and disposal of property and the making of contracts for any purpose:

Provided that—

(*a*) the said executive power of the Union shall, in so far as such trade or business or such purpose is not one with respect to which Parliament may make laws, be subject in each State to legislation by the State; and

(*b*) the said executive power of each State shall, in so far as such trade or business or such purpose is not one with respect to which the State Legislature may make laws, be subject to legislation by Parliament.]

299. **Contracts.**—(1) All contracts made in the exercise of the executive power of the Union or of a State shall be expressed to be made by the President, or by the Governor ³*** of the State, as the case may be, and all such contracts and all assurances of property made in the exercise of that power shall be executed

---

1 Subs. by the Constitution (Fortieth Amendment) Act, 1976, s. 2 (w.e.f. 27-5-1976).

2 Subs. by the Constitution (Seventh Amendment) Act, 1956, s. 20 (w.e.f. 1-11-1956).

3 The words "or the Rajpramukh" omitted by the Constitution (Seventh Amendment) Act, 1956, s. 29 and Sch. (w.e.f. 1-11-1956).

on behalf of the President or the Governor [1]*** by such persons and in such manner as he may direct or authorise.

(2) Neither the President nor the Governor [1]*** shall be personally liable in respect of any contract or assurance made or executed for the purposes of this Constitution, or for the purposes of any enactment relating to the Government of India heretofore in force, nor shall any person making or executing any such contract or assurance on behalf of any of them be personally liable in respect thereof.

300. **Suits and proceedings.**—(1) The Government of India may sue or be sued by the name of the Union of India and the Government of a State may sue or be sued by the name of the State and may, subject to any provisions which may be made by Act of Parliament or of the Legislature of such State enacted by virtue of powers conferred by this Constitution, sue or be sued in relation to their respective affairs in the like cases as the Dominion of India and the corresponding Provinces or the corresponding Indian States might have sued or been sued if this Constitution had not been enacted.

(2) If at the commencement of this Constitution—

(a) any legal proceedings are pending to which the Dominion of India is a party, the Union of India shall be deemed to be substituted for the Dominion in those proceedings; and

(b) any legal proceedings are pending to which a Province or an Indian State is a party, the corresponding State shall be deemed to be substituted for the Province or the Indian State in those proceedings.

[2][Chapter IV.—Right To Property

300A. **Persons not to be deprived of property save by authority of law.**— No person shall be deprived of his property save by authority of law.]

---

1 The words "nor the Rajpramukh" omitted by s. 29 and Sch., *ibid.* (w.e.f. 1-11-1956).
2 Ins. by the Constitution (Forty-fourth Amendment) Act, 1978, s. 34 (w.e.f. 20-6-1979).

PART XIII

TRADE, COMMERCE AND INTERCOURSE WITHIN THE TERRITORY OF INDIA

301. **Freedom of trade, commerce and intercourse.**—Subject to the other provisions of this Part, trade, commerce and intercourse throughout the territory of India shall be free.

302. **Power of Parliament to impose restrictions on trade, commerce and intercourse.**—Parliament may by law impose such restrictions on the freedom of trade, commerce or intercourse between one State and another or within any part of the territory of India as may be required in the public interest.

303. **Restrictions on the legislative powers of the Union and of the States with regard to trade and commerce.**—(1) Notwithstanding anything in article 302, neither Parliament nor the Legislature of a State shall have power to make any law giving, or authorising the giving of, any preference to one State over another, or making, or authorising the making of, any discrimination between one State and another, by virtue of any entry relating to trade and commerce in any of the Lists in the Seventh Schedule.

(2) Nothing in clause (1) shall prevent Parliament from making any law giving, or authorising the giving of, any preference or making, or authorising the making of, any discrimination if it is declared by such law that it is necessary to do so for the purpose of dealing with a situation arising from scarcity of goods in any part of the territory of India.

304. **Restrictions on trade, commerce and intercourse among States.**—Notwithstanding anything in article 301 or article 303, the Legislature of a State may by law—

(a) impose on goods imported from other States ¹[or the Union territories] any tax to which similar goods manufactured or produced in that State are subject, so, however, as not

---

1 Ins. by the Constitution (Seventh Amendment) Act, 1956, s. 29 and Sch. (w.e.f. 1-11-1956).

to discriminate between goods so imported and goods so manufactured or produced; and

(b) impose such reasonable restrictions on the freedom of trade, commerce or intercourse with or within that State as may be required in the public interest:

Provided that no Bill or amendment for the purposes of clause (b) shall be introduced or moved in the Legislature of a State without the previous sanction of the President.

¹[305. **Saving of existing laws and laws providing for State monopolies.**—Nothing in articles 301 and 303 shall affect the provisions of any existing law except in so far as the President may by order otherwise direct; and nothing in article 301 shall affect the operation of any law made before the commencement of the Constitution (Fourth Amendment) Act, 1955, in so far as it relates to, or prevent Parliament or the Legislature of a State from making any law relating to, any such matter as is referred to in sub-clause (ii) of clause (6) of article 19.]

306. *[Power of certain States in Part B of the First Schedule to impose restrictions on trade and commerce.].—Omitted by the Constitution (Seventh Amendment) Act, 1956, s. 29 and Sch.(w.e.f.1-11-1956).*

307. **Appointment of authority for carrying out the purposes of articles 301 to 304.**—Parliament may by law appoint such authority as it considers appropriate for carrying out the purposes of articles 301, 302, 303 and 304, and confer on the authority so appointed such powers and such duties as it thinks necessary.

---

1   Subs. by the Constitution (Fourth Amendment) Act, 1955, s. 4, for art. 305 (w.e.f. 27-4-1955).

PART XIV

SERVICES UNDER
THE UNION AND THE STATES

Chapter I.— Services

308. **Interpretation.**—In this Part, unless the context otherwise requires, the expression "State" [1][does not include the State of Jammu and Kashmir].

309. **Recruitment and conditions of service of persons serving the Union or a State.**—Subject to the provisions of this Constitution, Acts of the appropriate Legislature may regulate the recruitment, and conditions of service of persons appointed, to public services and posts in connection with the affairs of the Union or of any State:

Provided that it shall be competent for the President or such person as he may direct in the case of services and posts in connection with the affairs of the Union, and for the Governor [2]*** of a State or such person as he may direct in the case of services and posts in connection with the affairs of the State, to make rules regulating the recruitment, and the conditions of service of persons appointed, to such services and posts until provision in that behalf is made by or under an Act of the appropriate Legislature under this article, and any rules so made shall have effect subject to the provisions of any such Act.

310. **Tenure of office of persons serving the Union or a State.**—(1) Except as expressly provided by this Constitution, every person who is a member of a defence service or of a civil service of the Union or of an all-India service or holds any post connected with defence or any civil post under the Union holds office during the pleasure of the President, and every person who is a member of a

---

1 Subs. by the Constitution (Seventh Amendment) Act, 1956, s. 29 and Sch., for "means a State specified in Part A or Part B of the First Schedule" (w.e.f. 1-11-1956).
2 The words "or Rajpramukh" omitted by s.29 and Sch., *ibid* (w.e.f. 1-11-1956).

civil service of a State or holds any civil post under a State holds office during the pleasure of the Governor [1]*** of the State.

(2) Notwithstanding that a person holding a civil post under the Union or a State holds office during the pleasure of the President or, as the case may be, of the Governor [1]*** of the State, any contract under which a person, not being a member of a defence service or of an all-India service or of a civil service of the Union or a State, is appointed under this Constitution to hold such a post may, if the President or the Governor [2]***, as the case may be, deems it necessary in order to secure the services of a person having special qualifications, provide for the payment to him of compensation, if before the expiration of an agreed period that post is abolished or he is, for reasons not connected with any misconduct on his part, required to vacate that post.

311. Dismissal, removal or reduction in rank of persons employed in civil capacities under the Union or a State.—(1) No person who is a member of a civil service of the Union or an all-India service or a civil service of a State or holds a civil post under the Union or a State shall be dismissed or removed by an authority subordinate to that by which he was appointed.

[3][(2) No such person as aforesaid shall be dismissed or removed or reduced in rank except after an inquiry in which he has been informed of the charges against him and given a reasonable opportunity of being heard in respect of those charges [4]****:

[5][Provided that where it is proposed after such inquiry, to impose upon him any such penalty, such penalty may be imposed on the basis of the evidence adduced during such inquiry and it shall not be necessary to give such person any opportunity of making representation on the penalty proposed:

Provided further that this clause shall not apply—]

---

1 The words "or, as the case may be, the Rajpramukh" omitted by s.29 and Sch., *ibid.* (w.e.f. 1-11-1956).
2 The words "or the Rajpramukh" omitted by s.29 and Sch., *ibid.* (w.e.f. 1-11-1956).
3 Subs. by the Constitution (Fifteenth Amendment) Act, 1963, s. 10, for cls. (2) and (3) (w.e.f. 5-10-1963).
4 Certain words omitted by the Constitution (Forty-second Amendment) Act, 1976, s. 44 (w.e.f. 3-1-1977).
5 Subs. by s. 44, *ibid.*, for certain words (w.e.f. 3-1-1977).

(*a*) where a person is dismissed or removed or reduced in rank on the ground of conduct which has led to his conviction on a criminal charge; or

(*b*) where the authority empowered to dismiss or remove a person or to reduce him in rank is satisfied that for some reason, to be recorded by that authority in writing, it is not reasonably practicable to hold such inquiry; or

(*c*) where the President or the Governor, as the case may be, is satisfied that in the interest of the security of the State it is not expedient to hold such inquiry.

(3) If, in respect of any such person as aforesaid, a question arises whether it is reasonably practicable to hold such inquiry as is referred to in clause (2), the decision thereon of the authority empowered to dismiss or remove such person or to reduce him in rank shall be final.]

312. All-India services.—(1) Notwithstanding anything in ¹[Chapter VI of Part VI or Part XI], if the Council of States has declared by resolution supported by not less than two-thirds of the members present and voting that it is necessary or expedient in the national interest so to do, Parliament may by law provide for the creation of one or more all India services ²[(including an all-India judicial service)] common to the Union and the States, and, subject to the other provisions of this Chapter, regulate the recruitment, and the conditions of service of persons appointed, to any such service.

(2) The services known at the commencement of this Constitution as the Indian Administrative Service and the Indian Police Service shall be deemed to be services created by Parliament under this article.

²[(3) The all-India judicial service referred to in clause (1) shall not include any post inferior to that of a district judge as defined in article 236.

(4) The law providing for the creation of the all-India judicial service aforesaid may contain such provisions for the

---

1 Subs. by the Constitution (Forty-second Amendment) Act, 1976, s. 45, for "Part XI" (w.e.f. 3-1-1977).
2 Ins. by s. 45, *ibid.* (w.e.f. 3-1-1977).

amendment of Chapter VI of Part VI as may be necessary for giving effect to the provisions of that law and no such law shall be deemed to be an amendment of this Constitution for the purposes of article 368.]

¹[**312A. Power of Parliament to vary or revoke conditions of service of officers of certain services.**—(1) Parliament may by law—

(*a*) vary or revoke, whether prospectively or retrospectively, the conditions of services as respects remuneration, leave and pension and the rights as respects disciplinary matters of persons who, having been appointed by the Secretary of State or Secretary of State in Council to a civil service of the Crown in India before the commencement of this Constitution, continue on and after the commencement of the Constitution (Twenty-eighth Amendment) Act, 1972, to serve under the Government of India or of a State in any service or post;

(*b*) vary or revoke, whether prospectively or retrospectively, the conditions of service as respects pension of persons who, having been appointed by the Secretary of State or Secretary of State in Council to a civil service of the Crown in India before the commencement of this Constitution, retired or otherwise ceased to be in service at any time before the commencement of the Constitution (Twenty-eighth Amendment) Act, 1972:

Provided that in the case of any such person who is holding or has held the office of the Chief Justice or other Judge of the Supreme Court or a High Court, the Comptroller and Auditor-General of India, the Chairman or other member of the Union or a State Public Service Commission or the Chief Election Commissioner, nothing in sub-clause (*a*) or sub-clause (*b*) shall be construed as empowering Parliament to vary or revoke, after his appointment to such post, the conditions of his service to his disadvantage except in so far as such conditions of service are applicable to him by reason of his being a person appointed by

---

1 Ins. by the Constitution (Twenty-eighth Amendment) Act, 1972, s. 2 (w.e.f. 29-8-1972).

the Secretary of State or Secretary of State in Council to a civil service of the Crown in India.

(2) Except to the extent provided for by Parliament by law under this article, nothing in this article shall affect the power of any Legislature or other authority under any other provision of this Constitution to regulate the conditions of service of persons referred to in clause (1).

(3) Neither the Supreme Court nor any other court shall have jurisdiction in—

> (a) any dispute arising out of any provision of, or any endorsement on, any covenant, agreement or other similar instrument which was entered into or executed by any person referred to in clause (1), or arising out of any letter issued to such person, in relation to his appointment to any civil service of the Crown in India or his continuance in service under the Government of the Dominion of India or a Province thereof;
>
> (b) any dispute in respect of any right, liability or obligation under article 314 as originally enacted.

(4) The provisions of this article shall have effect notwithstanding anything in article 314 as originally enacted or in any other provision of this Constitution.]

313. Transitional provisions.—Until other provision is made in this behalf under this Constitution, all the laws in force immediately before the commencement of this Constitution and applicable to any public service or any post which continues to exist after the commencement of this Constitution, as an all-India service or as service or post under the Union or a State shall continue in force so far as consistent with the provisions of this Constitution.

314. [Provision for protection of existing officers of certain services.].— Omitted by the Constitution (Twenty-eighth Amendment) Act, 1972, s. 3 (w.e.f. 29-8-1972).

Chapter II.— Public Service Commissions

315. Public Service Commissions for the Union and for the States.—(1) Subject to the provisions of this article, there shall

221

be a Public Service Commission for the Union and a Public Service Commission for each State.

(2) Two or more States may agree that there shall be one Public Service Commission for that group of States, and if a resolution to that effect is passed by the House or, where there are two Houses, by each House of the Legislature of each of those States, Parliament may by law provide for the appointment of a Joint State Public Service Commission (referred to in this Chapter as Joint Commission) to serve the needs of those States.

(3) Any such law as aforesaid may contain such incidental and consequential provisions as may be necessary or desirable for giving effect to the purposes of the law.

(4) The Public Service Commission for the Union, if requested so to do by the Governor [1]*** of a State, may, with the approval of the President, agree to serve all or any of the needs of the State.

(5) References in this Constitution to the Union Public Service Commission or a State Public Service Commission shall, unless the context otherwise requires, be construed as references to the Commission serving the needs of the Union or, as the case may be, the State as respects the particular matter in question.

316. **Appointment and term of office of members.**—(1) The Chairman and other members of a Public Service Commission shall be appointed, in the case of the Union Commission or a Joint Commission, by the President, and in the case of a State Commission, by the Governor of the State:

Provided that as nearly as may be one-half of the members of every Public Service Commission shall be persons who at the dates of their respective appointments have held office for at least ten years either under the Government of India or under the Government of a State, and in computing the said period of ten years any period before the commencement of this Constitution during which a person has held office under the Crown in India or under the Government of an Indian State shall be included.

---

1 The words "or Rajpramukh" omitted by the Constitution (Seventh Amendment) Act, 1956, s. 29 and Sch. (w.e.f. 1-11-1956).

[1][(1A) If the office of the Chairman of the Commission becomes vacant or if any such Chairman is by reason of absence or for any other reason unable to perform the duties of his office, those duties shall, until some person appointed under clause (1) to the vacant office has entered on the duties thereof or, as the case may be, until the Chairman has resumed his duties, be performed by such one of the other members of the Commission as the President, in the case of the Union Commission or a Joint Commission, and the Governor of the State in the case of a State Commission, may appoint for the purpose.]

(2) A member of a Public Service Commission shall hold office for a term of six years from the date on which he enters upon his office or until he attains, in the case of the Union Commission, the age of sixty-five years, and in the case of a State Commission or a Joint Commission, the age of [2][sixty-two years], whichever is earlier:

Provided that—

(a) a member of a Public Service Commission may, by writing under his hand addressed, in the case of the Union Commission or a Joint Commission, to the President, and in the case of a State Commission, to the Governor [3]*** of the State, resign his office;

(b) a member of a Public Service Commission may be removed from his office in the manner provided in clause (1) or clause (3) of article 317.

(3) A person who holds office as a member of a Public Service Commission shall, on the expiration of his term of office, be ineligible for re-appointment to that office.

317. **Removal and suspension of a member of a Public Service Commission.**—(1) Subject to the provisions of clause (3), the Chairman or any other member of a Public Service Commission shall only be removed from his office by order of the President

1 Ins. by the Constitution (Fifteenth Amendment) Act, 1963, s. 11 (w.e.f. 5-10-1963).
2 Subs. by the Constitution (Forty-first Amendment) Act, 1976, s. 2, for "sixty years" (w.e.f. 7-9-1976).
3 The words "or Rajpramukh" omitted by the Constitution (Seventh Amendment) Act, 1956, s. 29 and Sch. (w.e.f. 1-11-1956).

on the ground of misbehaviour after the Supreme Court, on reference being made to it by the President, has, on inquiry held in accordance with the procedure prescribed in that behalf under article 145, reported that the Chairman or such other member, as the case may be, ought on any such ground to be removed.

(2) The President, in the case of the Union Commission or a Joint Commission, and the Governor [1]*** in the case of a State Commission, may suspend from office the Chairman or any other member of the Commission in respect of whom a reference has been made to the Supreme Court under clause (1) until the President has passed orders on receipt of the report of the Supreme Court on such reference.

(3) Notwithstanding anything in clause (1), the President may by order remove from office the Chairman or any other member of a Public Service Commission if the Chairman or such other member, as the case may be,—

(*a*) is adjudged an insolvent; or

(*b*) engages during his term of office in any paid employment outside the duties of his office; or

(*c*) is, in the opinion of the President, unfit to continue in office by reason of infirmity of mind or body.

(4) If the Chairman or any other member of a Public Service Commission is or becomes in any way concerned or interested in any contract or agreement made by or on behalf of the Government of India or the Government of a State or participates in any way in the profit thereof or in any benefit or emolument arising therefrom otherwise than as a member and in common with the other members of an incorporated company, he shall, for the purposes of clause (1), be deemed to be guilty of misbehaviour.

318. **Power to make regulations as to conditions of service of members and staff of the Commission.**—In the case of the Union Commission or a Joint Commission, the President and, in the case of a State Commission, the Governor [1]*** of the State may by regulations—

---

1 The words "or Rajpramukh" omitted by the Constitution (Seventh Amendment) Act, 1956, s. 29 and Sch. (w.e.f. 1-11-1956).

(a) determine the number of members of the Commission and their conditions of service; and

(b) make provision with respect to the number of members of the staff of the Commission and their conditions of service:

Provided that the conditions of service of a member of a Public Service Commission shall not be varied to his disadvantage after his appointment.

319. Prohibition as to the holding of offices by members of Commission on ceasing to be such members.—On ceasing to hold office—

(a) the Chairman of the Union Public Service Commission shall be ineligible for further employment either under the Government of India or under the Government of a State;

(b) the Chairman of a State Public Service Commission shall be eligible for appointment as the Chairman or any other member of the Union Public Service Commission or as the Chairman of any other State Public Service Commission, but not for any other employment either under the Government of India or under the Government of a State;

(c) a member other than the Chairman of the Union Public Service Commission shall be eligible for appointment as the Chairman of the Union Public Service Commission or as the Chairman of a State Public Service Commission, but not for any other employment either under the Government of India or under the Government of a State;

(d) a member other than the Chairman of a State Public Service Commission shall be eligible for appointment as the Chairman or any other member of the Union Public Service Commission or as the Chairman of that or any other State Public Service Commission, but not for any other employment either under the Government of India or under the Government of a State.

320. **Functions of Public Service Commissions.**—(1) It shall be the duty of the Union and the State Public Service Commissions to conduct examinations for appointments to the services of the Union and the services of the State respectively.

(2) It shall also be the duty of the Union Public Service Commission, if requested by any two or more States so to do, to assist those States in framing and operating schemes of joint recruitment for any services for which candidates possessing special qualifications are required.

(3) The Union Public Service Commission or the State Public Service Commission, as the case may be, shall be consulted—

> (*a*) on all matters relating to methods of recruitment to civil services and for civil posts;
>
> (*b*) on the principles to be followed in making appointments to civil services and posts and in making promotions and transfers from one service to another and on the suitability of candidates for such appointments, promotions or transfers;
>
> (*c*) on all disciplinary matters affecting a person serving under the Government of India or the Government of a State in a civil capacity, including memorials or petitions relating to such matters;
>
> (*d*) on any claim by or in respect of a person who is serving or has served under the Government of India or the Government of a State or under the Crown in India or under the Government of an Indian State, in a civil capacity, that any costs incurred by him in defending legal proceedings instituted against him in respect of acts done or purporting to be done in the execution of his duty should be paid out of the Consolidated Fund of India, or, as the case may be, out of the Consolidated Fund of the State;
>
> (*e*) on any claim for the award of a pension in respect of injuries sustained by a person while serving under the Government of India or the Government of a State or under the Crown in India or under the Government of

an Indian State, in a civil capacity, and any question as to the amount of any such award,

and it shall be the duty of a Public Service Commission to advise on any matter so referred to them and on any other matter which the President, or, as the case may be, the Governor [1]*** of the State, may refer to them:

Provided that the President as respects the all-India services and also as respects other services and posts in connection with the affairs of the Union, and the Governor [2]***, as respects other services and posts in connection with the affairs of a State, may make regulations specifying the matters in which either generally, or in any particular class of case or in any particular circumstances, it shall not be necessary for a Public Service Commission to be consulted.

(4) Nothing in clause (3) shall require a Public Service Commission to be consulted as respects the manner in which any provision referred to in clause (4) of article 16 may be made or as respects the manner in which effect may be given to the provisions of article 335.

(5) All regulations made under the proviso to clause (3) by the President or the Governor [3]*** of a State shall be laid for not less than fourteen days before each House of Parliament or the House or each House of the Legislature of the State, as the case may be, as soon as possible after they are made, and shall be subject to such modifications, whether by way of repeal or amendment, as both Houses of Parliament or the House or both Houses of the Legislature of the State may make during the session in which they are so laid.

321. Power to extend functions of Public Service Commissions.— An Act made by Parliament or, as the case may be, the Legislature of a State may provide for the exercise of additional functions by

1 The words "or Rajpramukh" omitted by the Constitution (Seventh Amendment) Act, 1956, s. 29 and Sch. (w.e.f. 1-11-1956).
2 The words "or Rajpramukh, as the case may be" omitted by s. 29 and Sch. *ibid.* (w.e.f. 1-11-1956).
3 The words "or Rajpramukh" omitted by the Constitution (Seventh Amendment) Act, 1956, s. 29 and Sch. (w.e.f. 1-11-1956).

the Union Public Service Commission or the State Public Service Commission as respects the services of the Union or the State and also as respects the services of any local authority or other body corporate constituted by law or of any public institution.

322. **Expenses of Public Service Commissions.**—The expenses of the Union or a State Public Service Commission, including any salaries, allowances and pensions payable to or in respect of the members or staff of the Commission, shall be charged on the Consolidated Fund of India or, as the case may be, the Consolidated Fund of the State.

323. **Reports of Public Service Commissions.**—(1) It shall be the duty of the Union Commission to present annually to the President a report as to the work done by the Commission and on receipt of such report the President shall cause a copy thereof together with a memorandum explaining, as respects the cases, if any, where the advice of the Commission was not accepted, the reasons for such non-acceptance to be laid before each House of Parliament.

(2) It shall be the duty of a State Commission to present annually to the Governor [1]*** of the State a report as to the work done by the Commission, and it shall be the duty of a Joint Commission to present annually to the Governor [1]*** of each of the States the needs of which are served by the Joint Commission a report as to the work done by the Commission in relation to that State, and in either case the Governor [1]***, shall, on receipt of such report, cause a copy thereof together with a memorandum explaining, as respects the cases, if any, where the advice of the Commission was not accepted, the reasons for such non-acceptance to be laid before the Legislature of the State.

---

1 The words "or Rajpramukh, as the case may be" omitted by s. 29 and Sch. *ibid.* (w.e.f. 1-11-1956).

[1]PART XIV A

TRIBUNALS

323A. **Administrative tribunals.**—(1) Parliament may, by law, provide for the adjudication or trial by administrative tribunals of disputes and complaints with respect to recruitment and conditions of service of persons appointed to public services and posts in connection with the affairs of the Union or of any State or of any local or other authority within the territory of India or under the control of the Government of India or of any corporation owned or controlled by the Government.

(2) A law made under clause (1) may—

(*a*) provide for the establishment of an administrative tribunal for the Union and a separate administrative tribunal for each State or for two or more States;

(*b*) specify the jurisdiction, powers (including the power to punish for contempt) and authority which may be exercised by each of the said tribunals;

(*c*) provide for the procedure (including provisions as to limitation and rules of evidence) to be followed by the said tribunals;

(*d*) exclude the jurisdiction of all courts, except the jurisdiction of the Supreme Court under article 136, with respect to the disputes or complaints referred to in clause (1);

(*e*) provide for the transfer to each such administrative tribunal of any cases pending before any court or other authority immediately before the establishment of such tribunal as would have been within the jurisdiction of such tribunal if the causes of action on which such suits or proceedings are based had arisen after such establishment;

---

1 Part XV A ins. by the Constitution (Forty-second Amendment) Act, 1976, s. 46 (w.e.f. 3-1-1977).

(*f*) repeal or amend any order made by the President under clause (3) of article 371D;

(*g*) contain such supplemental, incidental and consequential provisions (including provisions as to fees) as Parliament may deem necessary for the effective functioning of, and for the speedy disposal of cases by, and the enforcement of the orders of, such tribunals.

(3) The provisions of this article shall have effect notwithstanding anything in any other provision of this Constitution or in any other law for the time being in force.

323B. **Tribunals for other matters.**—(1) The appropriate Legislature may, by law, provide for the adjudication or trial by tribunals of any disputes, complaints, or offences with respect to all or any of the matters specified in clause (2) with respect to which such Legislature has power to make laws.

(2) The matters referred to in clause (1) are the following, namely:—

(*a*) levy, assessment, collection and enforcement of any tax;

(*b*) foreign exchange, import and export across customs frontiers;

(*c*) industrial and labour disputes;

(*d*) land reforms by way of acquisition by the State of any estate as defined in article 31A or of any rights therein or the extinguishment or modification of any such rights or by way of ceiling on agricultural land or in any other way;

(*e*) ceiling on urban property;

(*f*) elections to either House of Parliament or the House or either House of the Legislature of a State, but excluding the matters referred to in article 329 and article 329A;

(*g*) production, procurement, supply and distribution of food-stuffs (including edible oilseeds and oils) and such other goods as the President may, by public notification, declare to be essential goods for the purpose of this article and control of prices of such goods;

¹[(*h*) rent, its regulation and control and tenancy issues including the right, title and interest of landlords and tenants;]

²[(*i*)] offences against laws with respect to any of the matters specified in sub-clauses (*a*) to ³[(*h*)] and fees in respect of any of those matters;

⁴[(*j*)] any matter incidental to any of the matters specified in sub-clauses (*a*) to ⁵[(*i*)].

(3) A law made under clause (1) may—

    (*a*) provide for the establishment of a hierarchy of tribunals;

    (*b*) specify the jurisdiction, powers (including the power to punish for contempt) and authority which may be exercised by each of the said tribunals;

    (*c*) provide for the procedure (including provisions as to limitation and rules of evidence) to be followed by the said tribunals;

    (*d*) exclude the jurisdiction of all courts, except the jurisdiction of the Supreme Court under article 136, with respect to all or any of the matters falling within the jurisdiction of the said tribunals;

    (*e*) provide for the transfer to each such tribunal of any cases pending before any court or any other authority immediately before the establishment of such tribunal as would have been within the jurisdiction of such tribunal if the causes of action on which such suits or proceedings are based had arisen after such establishment;

    (*f*) contain such supplemental, incidental and consequential provisions (including provisions as to fees) as the appropriate Legislature may deem necessary for the effective functioning of, and for the speedy disposal

---

1 Ins. by the Constitution (Seventy-fifth Amendment) Act, 1993, s. 2 (w.e.f. 15-5-1994).
2 Sub-clause (h) re-lettered as sub-clause (i) by s. 2, *ibid.* (w.e.f. 15-5-1994).
3 Subs. by s. 2, *ibid.*, for cl. "(*g*)" (w.e.f. 15-5-1994).
4 Sub-clause (i) re-lettered as sub-clause (j) by the Constitution (Seventy-fifth Amendment) Act, 1993, s. 2 (w.e.f. 15-5-1994).
5 Subs. by s. 2, *ibid*, for "(*h*)" (w.e.f. 15-5-1994).

of cases by, and the enforcement of the orders of, such tribunals.

(4) The provisions of this article shall have effect notwithstanding anything in any other provision of this Constitution or in any other law for the time being in force.

Explanation.—In this article, "appropriate Legislature", in relation to any matter, means Parliament or, as the case may be, a State Legislature competent to make laws with respect to such matter in accordance with the provisions of Part XI.]

PART XV

ELECTIONS

324. **Superintendence, direction and control of elections to be vested in an Election Commission.**—(1) The superintendence, direction and control of the preparation of the electoral rolls for, and the conduct of, all elections to Parliament and to the Legislature of every State and of elections to the offices of President and Vice-President held under this Constitution [1]*** shall be vested in a Commission (referred to in this Constitution as the Election Commission).

(2) The Election Commission shall consist of the Chief Election Commissioner and such number of other Election Commissioners, if any, as the President may from time to time fix and the appointment of the Chief Election Commissioner and other Election Commissioners shall, subject to the provisions of any law made in that behalf by Parliament, be made by the President.

(3) When any other Election Commissioner is so appointed the Chief Election Commissioner shall act as the Chairman of the Election Commission.

---

1 The words "including the appointment of election tribunals for the decision of doubts and disputes arising out of or in connection with elections to Parliament and to the Legislatures of States" omitted by the Constitution (Nineteenth Amendment) Act, 1966, s. 2 (w.e.f. 11-12-1966).

(4) Before each general election to the House of the People and to the Legislative Assembly of each State, and before the first general election and thereafter before each biennial election to the Legislative Council of each State having such Council, the President may also appoint after consultation with the Election Commission such Regional Commissioners as he may consider necessary to assist the Election Commission in the performance of the functions conferred on the Commission by clause (1).

(5) Subject to the provisions of any law made by Parliament, the conditions of service and tenure of office of the Election Commissioners and the Regional Commissioners shall be such as the President may by rule determine:

Provided that the Chief Election Commissioner shall not be removed from his office except in like manner and on the like grounds as a Judge of the Supreme Court and the conditions of service of the Chief Election Commissioner shall not be varied to his disadvantage after his appointment:

Provided further that any other Election Commissioner or a Regional Commissioner shall not be removed from office except on the recommendation of the Chief Election Commissioner.

(6) The President, or the Governor [1]*** of a State, shall, when so requested by the Election Commission, make available to the Election Commission or to a Regional Commissioner such staff as may be necessary for the discharge of the functions conferred on the Election Commission by clause (1).

325. **No person to be ineligible for inclusion in, or to claim to be included in a special, electoral roll on grounds of religion, race, caste or sex.**—There shall be one general electoral roll for every territorial constituency for election to either House of Parliament or to the House or either House of the Legislature of a State and no person shall be ineligible for inclusion in any such roll or claim to be included in any special electoral roll for any such constituency on grounds only of religion, race, caste, sex or any of them.

---

1 The words "or Rajpramukh" omitted by the Constitution (Seventh Amendment) Act, 1956, s. 29 and Sch. (w.e.f. 1-11-1956).

326. **Elections to the House of the People and to the Legislative Assemblies of States to be on the basis of adult suffrage.**—The elections to the House of the People and to the Legislative Assembly of every State shall be on the basis of adult suffrage; that is to say, every person who is a citizen of India and who is not less than [1][eighteen years] of age on such date as may be fixed in that behalf by or under any law made by the appropriate Legislature and is not otherwise disqualified under this Constitution or any law made by the appropriate Legislature on the ground of non-residence, unsoundness of mind, crime or corrupt or illegal practice, shall be entitled to be registered as a voter at any such election.

327. **Power of Parliament to make provision with respect to elections to Legislatures.**—Subject to the provisions of this Constitution, Parliament may from time to time by law make provision with respect to all matters relating to, or in connection with, elections to either House of Parliament or to the House or either House of the Legislature of a State including the preparation of electoral rolls, the delimitation of constituencies and all other matters necessary for securing the due constitution of such House or Houses.

328. **Power of Legislature of a State to make provision with respect to elections to such Legislature.**—Subject to the provisions of this Constitution and in so far as provision in that behalf is not made by Parliament, the Legislature of a State may from time to time by law make provision with respect to all matters relating to, or in connection with, the elections to the House or either House of the Legislature of the State including the preparation of electoral rolls and all other matters necessary for securing the due constitution of such House or Houses.

329. **Bar to interference by courts in electoral matters.**—[2][Notwithstanding anything in this Constitution [3]***—]

---

1 Subs. by the Constitution (Sixty-first Amendment) Act, 1988, s. 2, for "twenty-one years" (w.e.f. 28-3-1989).
2 Subs. by the Constitution (Thirty-ninth Amendment) Act, 1975, s. 3, for certain words (w.e.f. 10-8-1975).
3 The words, figures and letter "but subject to the provisions of article 329A" omitted by the Constitution (Forty-fourth Amendment) Act, 1978, s. 35 (w.e.f. 20-6-1979).

    (*a*)   the validity of any law relating to the delimitation of constituencies or the allotment of seats to such constituencies, made or purporting to be made under article 327 or article 328, shall not be called in question in any court;

    (*b*)   no election to either House of Parliament or to the House or either House of the Legislature of a State shall be called in question except by an election petition presented to such authority and in such manner as may be provided for by or under any law made by the appropriate Legislature.

[1]**329a.**   [*Special provision as to elections to Parliament in the case of Prime Minister and Speaker*.].—*Omitted by the Constitution (Forty-fourth Amendment) Act, 1978, s. 36 (w.e.f. 20-6-1979).*

PART XVI

SPECIAL PROVISIONS
RELATING TO CERTAIN CLASSES

330.   **Reservation of seats for Scheduled Castes and Scheduled Tribes in the House of the People.**—(1) Seats shall be reserved in the House of the People for —

    (*a*)   the Scheduled Castes;

    [2][(*b*) the Scheduled Tribes except the Scheduled Tribes in the autonomous districts of Assam; and]

    (*c*)   the Scheduled Tribes in the autonomous districts of Assam.

(2) The number of seats reserved in any State [3][or Union territory] for the Scheduled Castes or the Scheduled Tribes under clause (1) shall bear, as nearly as may be, the same proportion to the

---

1 Ins. by the Constitution (Thirty-ninth Amendment) Act, 1975, s. 4 (w.e.f. 10-8-1975).

2 Subs. by the Constitution (Fifty-first Amendment) Act, 1984, s. 2, for sub-clause (*b*) (w.e.f. 16-6-1986).

3 Ins. by the Constitution (Seventh Amendment) Act, 1956, s. 29 and Sch. (w.e.f. 1-11-1956).

total number of seats allotted to that State ²[or Union territory] in the House of the People as the population of the Scheduled Castes in the State ²[or Union territory] or of the Scheduled Tribes in the State ²[or Union territory] or part of the State ²[or Union territory], as the case may be, in respect of which seats are so reserved, bears to the total population of the State ²[or Union territory].

¹[(3) Notwithstanding anything contained in clause (2), the number of seats reserved in the House of the People for the Scheduled Tribes in the autonomous districts of Assam shall bear to the total number of seats allotted to that State a proportion not less than the population of the Scheduled Tribes in the said autonomous districts bears to the total population of the State.]

²[*Explanation.*—In this article and in article 332, the expression "population" means the population as ascertained at the last preceding census of which the relevant figures have been published:

Provided that the reference in this *Explanation* to the last preceding census of which the relevant figures have been published shall, until the relevant figures for the first census taken after the year ³[2026] have been published, be construed as a reference to the ⁴[2001] census.]

331.   **Representation of the Anglo-Indian Community in the House of the People.**—Notwithstanding anything in article 81, the President may, if he is of opinion that the Anglo-Indian community is not adequately represented in the House of the People, nominate not more than two members of that community to the House of the People.

332.   **Reservation of seats for Scheduled Castes and Scheduled Tribes in the Legislative Assemblies of the States.**—(1) Seats

---

1 Ins. by the Constitution (Thirty-first Amendment) Act, 1973, s. 3 (w.e.f. 17-10-1973).

2 Ins. by the Constitution (Forty-second Amendment) Act, 1976, s. 47 (w.e.f. 3-1-1977).

3 Subs. by the Constitution (Eighty-fourth Amendment) Act, 2001, s. 6, for "2000" (w.e.f. 21-2-2002).

4 Subs. by the Constitution (Eighty-seventh Amendment) Act, 2003, s. 5, for "1991" (w.e.f. 22-6-2003).

shall be reserved for the Scheduled Castes and the Scheduled Tribes, [1][except the Scheduled Tribes in the autonomous districts of Assam], in the Legislative Assembly of every State [2]***.

(2) Seats shall be reserved also for the autonomous districts in the Legislative Assembly of the State of Assam.

(3) The number of seats reserved for the Scheduled Castes or the Scheduled Tribes in the Legislative Assembly of any State under clause (1) shall bear, as nearly as may be, the same proportion to the total number of seats in the Assembly as the population of the Scheduled Castes in the State or of the Scheduled Tribes in the State or part of the State, as the case may be, in respect of which seats are so reserved, bears to the total population of the State.

[3][(3A) Notwithstanding anything contained in clause (3), until the taking effect, under article 170, of the re-adjustment, on the basis of the first census after the year [4][2026], of the number of seats in the Legislative Assemblies of the States of Arunachal Pradesh, Meghalaya, Mizoram and Nagaland, the seats which shall be reserved for the Scheduled Tribes in the Legislative Assembly of any such State shall be,—

    (a) if all the seats in the Legislative Assembly of such State in existence on the date of coming into force of the Constitution (Fifty-seventh Amendment) Act, 1987 (hereafter in this clause referred to as the existing Assembly) are held by members of the Scheduled Tribes, all the seats except one;

    (b) in any other case, such number of seats as bears to the total number of seats, a proportion not less than the number (as on the said date) of members belonging to the Scheduled Tribes in the existing Assembly bears to the total number of seats in the existing Assembly.]

---

1   Subs. by the Constitution (Fifty-first Amendment) Act, 1984, s. 3, for certain words (w.e.f. 16-6-1986).

2   The words and letters "specified in Part A or Part B of the First Schedule" omitted by the Constitution (Seventh Amendment) Act, 1956, s. 29 and Sch. (w.e.f. 1-11-1956).

3   Ins. by the Constitution (Fifty-seventh Amendment) Act, 1987, s. 2 (w.e.f. 21-9-1987).

4   Subs. by the Constitution (Eighty-fourth Amendment) Act, 2001, s. 7, for "2000" (w.e.f. 21-2-2002).

¹[(3B) Notwithstanding anything contained in clause (3), until the re-adjustment, under article 170, takes effect on the basis of the first census after the year ²[2026], of the number of seats in the Legislative Assembly of the State of Tripura, the seats which shall be reserved for the Scheduled Tribes in the Legislative Assembly shall be, such number of seats as bears to the total number of seats, a proportion not less than the number, as on the date of coming into force of the Constitution (Seventy-second Amendment) Act, 1992, of members belonging to the Scheduled Tribes in the Legislative Assembly in existence on the said date bears to the total number of seats in that Assembly.]

(4) The number of seats reserved for an autonomous district in the Legislative Assembly of the State of Assam shall bear to the total number of seats in that Assembly a proportion not less than the population of the district bears to the total population of the State.

(5) The constituencies for the seats reserved for any autonomous district of Assam shall not comprise any area outside that district ³***.

(6) No person who is not a member of a Scheduled Tribe of any autonomous district of the State of Assam shall be eligible for election to the Legislative Assembly of the State from any constituency of that district ¹***:

⁴[Provided that for elections to the Legislative Assembly of the State of Assam, the representation of the Scheduled Tribes and non-Scheduled Tribes in the constituencies included in the Bodoland Territorial Areas District, so notified, and existing prior to the constitution of Bodoland Territorial Areas District, shall be maintained.]

333. Representation of the Anglo-Indian community in the Legislative Assemblies of the States.—Notwithstanding

---

1 Ins. by the Constitition (Seventy-second Amendment) Act, 1992, s. 2 (w.e.f. 5-12-1992).

2 Subs. by the Constitution (Eighty-fourth Amendment) Act, 2001, s. 7, for "2000" (w.e.f. 21-2-2002).

3 Certain words omitted by the North-Eastern Areas (Reorganisation) Act, 1971 (81 of 1971), s. 71 (w.e.f. 21-1-1972).

4 Ins. by the Constitution (Ninetieth Amendment) Act, 2003, s. 2 (w.e.f. 28-9-2003).

anything in article 170, the Governor [1]*** of a State may, if he is of opinion that the Anglo-Indian community needs representation in the Legislative Assembly of the State and is not adequately represented therein, [2][nominate one member of that community to the Assembly].

334. [3][**Reservation of seats and special representation to cease after certain period**].—Notwithstanding anything in the foregoing provisions of this Part, the provisions of this Constitution relating to—

(*a*) the reservation of seats for the Scheduled Castes and the Scheduled Tribes in the House of the People and in the Legislative Assemblies of the States; and

(*b*) the representation of the Anglo-Indian community in the House of the People and in the Legislative Assemblies of the States by nomination,

shall cease to have effect on the expiration of a period of [4][eighty years in respect of clause (*a*) and seventy years in respect of clause (*b*)] from the commencement of this Constitution:

Provided that nothing in this article shall affect any representation in the House of the People or in the Legislative Assembly of a State until the dissolution of the then existing House or Assembly, as the case may be.

335. **Claims of Scheduled Castes and Scheduled Tribes to services and posts**.—The claims of the members of the Scheduled Castes and the Scheduled Tribes shall be taken into consideration, consistently with the maintenance of efficiency of

---

1 The words "or Rajpramukh" omitted by the Constitution (Seventh Amendment) Act, 1956, s. 29 and Sch. (w.e.f. 1-11-1956).

2 Subs. by the Constitution (Twenty-third Amendment) Act, 1969, s. 4, for "nominate such number of members of the community to the Assembly as he considers appropriate" (w.e.f. 23-1-1970).

3 Subs. by the Constitution (One hundred and fourth Amendment) Act, 2019, s. 2, for marginal heading (w.e.f. 25-1-2020).

4 Subs. by s. 2, *ibid.*, for "seventy years" (w.e.f. 25-1-2020). The words "seventy years" subs. for "sixty years" by the Constitution (Ninety-fifth Amendment) Act, 2009, s.2 (w.e.f. 25-1-2010). The words "sixty years" subs. for "fifty years" by the Constitution (Seventy-ninth Amendment) Act, 1999, s. 2 (w.e.f. 25-1-2000). The words "fifty years" subs. for "forty years" by the Constitution (Sixty-second Amendment) Act, 1989, s. 2 (w.e.f. 20-12-1989). The words "forty years" subs. for "thirty years" by the Constitution (Forty-fifth Amendment) Act, 1980, s. 2 (w.e.f. 25-1-1980).

administration, in the making of appointments to services and posts in connection with the affairs of the Union or of a State:

[1][Provided that nothing in this article shall prevent in making of any provision in favour of the members of the Scheduled Castes and the Scheduled Tribes for relaxation in qualifying marks in any examination or lowering the standards of evaluation, for reservation in matters or promotion to any class or classes of services or posts in connection with the affairs of the Union or of a State.]

336. Special provision for Anglo-Indian community in certain services.—(1) During the first two years after the commencement of this Constitution, appointments of members of the Anglo-Indian community to posts in the railway, customs, postal and telegraph services of the Union shall be made on the same basis as immediately before the fifteenth day of August, 1947.

During every succeeding period of two years, the number of posts reserved for the members of the said community in the said services shall, as nearly as possible, be less by ten per cent. than the numbers so reserved during the immediately preceding period of two years:

Provided that at the end of ten years from the commencement of this Constitution all such reservations shall cease.

(2) Nothing in clause (1) shall bar the appointment of members of the Anglo-Indian community to posts other than, or in addition to, those reserved for the community under that clause if such members are found qualified for appointment on merit as compared with the members of other communities.

337. Special provision with respect to educational grants for the benefit of Anglo-Indian community.—During the first three financial years after the commencement of this Constitution, the same grants, if any, shall be made by the Union and by each State [2]*** for the benefit of the Anglo-Indian community in respect of education as were made in the financial year ending on the thirty-first day of March, 1948.

---

1 Ins. by the Constitution (Eighty-second Amendment) Act, 2000, s. 2 (w.e.f. 8-9-2000).
2 The words and letters "specified in Part A or Part B of the First Schedule" omitted by the Constitution (Seventh Amendment) Act, 1956, s. 29 and Sch. (w.e.f. 1-11-1956).

During every succeeding period of three years the grants may be less by ten per cent. than those for the immediately preceding period of three years:

Provided that at the end of ten years from the commencement of this Constitution such grants, to the extent to which they are a special concession to the Anglo-Indian community, shall cease:

Provided further that no educational institution shall be entitled to receive any grant under this article unless at least forty per cent. of the annual admissions therein are made available to members of communities other than the Anglo-Indian community.

338. [1][**National Commission for Scheduled Castes**].—[2][[3][(1) There shall be a Commission for the Scheduled Castes to be known as the National Commission for the Scheduled Castes.

(2) Subject to the provisions of any law made in this behalf by Parliament, the Commission shall consist of a Chairperson, Vice-Chairperson and three other Members and the conditions of service and tenure of office of the Chairperson, Vice-Chairperson and other Members so appointed shall be such as the President may by rule determine.]

(3) The Chairperson, Vice-Chairperson and other Members of the Commission shall be appointed by the President by warrant under his hand and seal.

(4) The Commission shall have the power to regulate its own procedure.

(5) It shall be the duty of the Commission—

    (a) to investigate and monitor all matters relating to the safeguards provided for the Scheduled Castes [4]*** under this Constitution or under any other law for the time being in force or under any order of the Government and to evaluate the working of such safeguards;

---

1 Subs. by the Constitution (Eighty-ninth Amendment) Act, 2003, s. 2, for the marginal heading (w.e.f. 19-2-2004).

2 Subs. by the Constitution (Sixty-fifth Amendment) Act, 1990, s. 2, for cls. (1) and (2) (w.e.f. 12-3-1992).

3 Subs. by the Constitution (Eighty-ninth Amendment) Act, 2003, s. 2, for cls. (1) and (2) (w.e.f. 19-2-2004).

4 The words "and Scheduled Tribes" omitted by the Constitution (Eighty-ninth Amendment) Act, 2003, s. 2 (w.e.f. 19-2-2004).

(*b*) to inquire into specific complaints with respect to the deprivation of rights and safeguards of the Scheduled Castes [1]***;

(*c*) to participate and advise on the planning process of socio-economic development of the Scheduled Castes [1]*** and to evaluate the progress of their development under the Union and any State;

(*d*) to present to the President, annually and at such other times as the Commission may deem fit, reports upon the working of those safeguards;

(*e*) to make in such reports recommendations as to the measures that should be taken by the Union or any State for the effective implementation of those safeguards and other measures for the protection, welfare and socio-economic development of the Scheduled Castes [1]***; and

(*f*) to discharge such other functions in relation to the protection, welfare and development and advancement of the Scheduled Castes [1]*** as the President may, subject to the provisions of any law made by Parliament, by rule specify.

(6) The President shall cause all such reports to be laid before each House of Parliament along with a memorandum explaining the action taken or proposed to be taken on the recommendations relating to the Union and the reasons for the non-acceptance, if any, of any of such recommendations.

(7) Where any such report, or any part thereof, relates to any matter with which any State Government is concerned, a copy of such report shall be forwarded to the Governor of the State who shall cause it to be laid before the Legislature of the State along with a memorandum explaining the action taken or proposed to be taken on the recommendations relating to the State and the reasons for the non-acceptance, if any, of any of such recommendations.

(8) The Commission shall, while investigating any matter referred to in sub-clause (*a*) or inquiring into any complaint referred to in sub-clause (*b*) of clause (5), have all the powers

of a civil court trying a suit and in particular in respect of the following matters, namely :—

(a) summoning and enforcing the attendance of any person from any part of India and examining him on oath;

(b) requiring the discovery and production of any document;

(c) receiving evidence on affidavits;

(d) requisitioning any public record or copy thereof from any court or office;

(e) issuing commissions for the examination of witnesses and documents;

(f) any other matter which the President may, by rule, determine.

(9) The Union and every State Government shall consult the Commission on all major policy matters affecting Scheduled Castes [1]***].

[2][(10)] In this article, references to the Scheduled Castes [1]*** shall be construed as including references [3]*** to the Anglo-Indian community.

[4][338A. **National Commission for Scheduled Tribes.**—(1) There shall be a Commission for the Scheduled Tribes to be known as the National Commission for the Scheduled Tribes.

(2) Subject to the provisions of any law made in this behalf by Parliament, the Commission shall consist of a Chairperson, Vice-Chairperson and three other Members and the conditions of service and tenure of office of the Chairperson, Vice-Chairperson and other Members so appointed shall be such as the President may by rule determine.

---

1 The words "and Scheduled Tribes" omitted by the Constitution (Eighty-ninth Amendment) Act, 2003, s. 2 (w.e.f. 19-2-2004).

2 Cl. (3) renumbered as cl. (10) by the Constitution (Sixty-fifth Amendment) Act, 1990, s. 2 (w.e.f. 12-3-1992).

3 The words, brackets and figures "to such other backward classes as the President may, on receipt of the report of a Commission appointed under cl. (1) of article 340, by order specify and also" omitted by the Constitution (One Hundred and Second Amendment) Act, 2018, s. 2 (w.e.f. 15-8-2018).

4 Art.338A ins. by the Constitution (Eighty-ninth Amendment) Act, 2003, s. 3 (w.e.f. 19-2-2004).

(3) The Chairperson, Vice-Chairperson and other Members of the Commission shall be appointed by the President by warrant under his hand and seal.

(4) The Commission shall have the power to regulate its own procedure.

(5) It shall be the duty of the Commission—

(*a*) to investigate and monitor all matters relating to the safeguards provided for the Scheduled Tribes under this Constitution or under any other law for the time being in force or under any order of the Government and to evaluate the working of such safeguards;

(*b*) to inquire into specific complaints with respect to the deprivation of rights and safeguards of the Scheduled Tribes;

(*c*) to participate and advise on the planning process of socio-economic development of the Scheduled Tribes and to evaluate the progress of their development under the Union and any State;

(*d*) to present to the President, annually and at such other times as the Commission may deem fit, reports upon the working of those safeguards;

(*e*) to make in such reports recommendations as to the measures that should be taken by the Union or any State for the effective implementation of those safeguards and other measures for the protection, welfare and socio-economic development of the Scheduled Tribes; and

(*f*) to discharge such other functions in relation to the protection, welfare and development and advancement of the Scheduled Tribes as the President may, subject to the provisions of any law made by

Parliament, by rule specify.

(6) The President shall cause all such reports to be laid before each House of Parliament along with a memorandum explaining the action taken or proposed to be taken on the recommendations relating to the Union and the reasons for the non-acceptance, if any, of any such recommendations.

(7) Where any such report, or any part thereof, relates to any matter with which any State Government is concerned, a copy of such report shall be forwarded to the Governor of the State who shall cause it to be laid before the Legislature of the State along with a memorandum explaining the action taken or proposed to be taken on the recommendations relating to the State and the reasons for the non-acceptance, if any, of any of such recommendations.

(8) The Commission shall, while investigating any matter referred to in sub-clause (*a*) or inquiring into any complaint referred to in sub-clause (*b*) of clause (5), have all the powers of a civil court trying a suit and in particular in respect of the following matters, namely:—

(*a*) summoning and enforcing the attendance of any person from any part of India and examining him on oath;

(*b*) requiring the discovery and production of any document;

(*c*) receiving evidence on affidavits;

(*d*) requisitioning any public record or copy thereof from any court or office;

(*e*) issuing commissions for the examination of witnesses and documents;

(*f*) any other matter which the President may, by rule, determine.

(9) The Union and every State Government shall consult the Commission on all major policy matters affecting Scheduled Tribes.]

¹[**338B. National Commission for Backward Classes.**—(1) There shall be a Commission for the socially and educationally backward classes to be known as the National Commission for Backward Classes.

(2) Subject to the provisions of any law made in this behalf by Parliament, the Commission shall consist of a Chairperson,

---

1 Art. 338B ins. by the Constitution (One Hundred and Second Amendment) Act, 2018, s. 3 (w.e.f. 15-8-2018).

Vice-Chairperson and three other Members and the conditions of service and tenure of office of the Chairperson, Vice-Chairperson and other Members so appointed shall be such as the President may by rule determine.

(3) The Chairperson, Vice-Chairperson and other Members of the Commission shall be appointed by the President by warrant under his hand and seal.

(4) The Commission shall have the power to regulate its own procedure.

(5) It shall be the duty of the Commission—

(a) to investigate and monitor all matters relating to the safeguards provided for the socially and educationally backward classes under this Constitution or under any other law for the time being in force or under any order of the Government and to evaluate the working of such safeguards;

(b) to inquire into specific complaints with respect to the deprivation of rights and safeguards of the socially and educationally backward classes;

(c) to participate and advise on the socio-economic development of the socially and educationally backward classes and to evaluate the progress of their development under the Union and any State;

(d) to present to the President, annually and at such other times as the Commission may deem fit, reports upon the working of those safeguards;

(e) to make in such reports the recommendations as to the measures that should be taken by the Union or any State for the effective implementation of those safeguards and other measures for the protection, welfare and socio-economic development of the socially and educationally backward classes; and

(f) to discharge such other functions in relation to the protection, welfare and development and advancement of the socially and educationally backward classes as the President may, subject to the provisions of any law made by Parliament, by rule specify.

(6) President shall cause all such reports to be laid before each House of Parliament along with a memorandum explaining the action taken or proposed to be taken on the recommendations relating to the Union and the reasons for the non-acceptance, if any, of any such recommendations.

(7) Where any such report, or any part thereof, relates to any matter with which any State Government is concerned, a copy of such report shall be forwarded to the State Government which shall cause it to be laid before the Legislature of the State along with a memorandum explaining the action taken or proposed to be taken on the recommendations relating to the State and the reasons for the non-acceptance, it any, of any such recommendations.

(8) Commission shall, while investigating any matter referred to in sub-clause (*a*) or inquiring into any complaint referred to in sub-clause (*b*) of clause (5), have all the powers of a civil court trying a suit and in particular in respect of the following matters, namely :—

    (*a*) summoning and enforcing the attendance of any person from any part of India and examining him on oath;

    (*b*) requiring the discovery and production of any document;

    (*c*) receiving evidence on affidavits;

    (*d*) requisitioning any public record or copy thereof from any court or office;

    (*e*) issuing commissions for the examination of witnesses and documents;

    (*f*) other matter which the President may by rule, determine.

(9) The Union and every State Government shall consult the Commission on all major policy matters affecting the socially and educationally backward classes:]

[1][Provided that nothing in this clause shall apply for the purposes of clause (3) of article 342A.]

---

1 Ins. by the Constitution (One Hundred and Fifth Amendment) Act, 2021, s. 2 (w.e.f. 15-9-2021).

339. **Control of the Union over the administration of Scheduled Areas and the welfare of Scheduled Tribes.**—(1) The President may at any time and shall, at the expiration of ten years from the commencement of this Constitution by order appoint a Commission to report on the administration of the Scheduled Areas and the welfare of the Scheduled Tribes in the States [1]***. The order may define the composition, powers and procedure of the Commission and may contain such incidental or ancillary provisions as the President may consider necessary or desirable.

(2) The executive power of the Union shall extend to the giving of directions to [2][a State] as to the drawing up and execution of schemes specified in the direction to be essential for the welfare of the Scheduled Tribes in the State.

340. **Appointment of a Commission to investigate the conditions of backward classes.**—(1) The President may by order appoint a Commission consisting of such persons as he thinks fit to investigate the conditions of socially and educationally backward classes within the territory of India and the difficulties under which they labour and to make recommendations as to the steps that should be taken by the Union or any State to remove such difficulties and to improve their condition and as to the grants that should be made for the purpose by the Union or any State and the conditions subject to which such grants should be made, and the order appointing such Commission shall define the procedure to be followed by the Commission.

(2) A Commission so appointed shall investigate the matters referred to them and present to the President a report setting out the facts as found by them and making such recommendations as they think proper.

(3) The President shall cause a copy of the report so presented together with a memorandum explaining the action taken thereon to be laid before each House of Parliament.

---

1 The words and letters for "specified in Part A or Part B of the First Schedule" omitted by the Constitution (Seventh Amendment) Act, 1956, s. 29 and Sch. (w.e.f. 1-11-1956).
2 Subs. by s. 29 and Sch. *ibid.* for "any such State" (w.e.f. 1-11-1956).

341.   Scheduled Castes.—(1) The President [1][may with respect to any State [2][or Union territory], and where it is a State [3]***, after consultation with the Governor [4]*** thereof], by public notification[5], specify the castes, races or tribes or parts of or groups within castes, races or tribes which shall for the purposes of this Constitution be deemed to be Scheduled Castes in relation to that State [2][or Union territory, as the case may be.]

(2) Parliament may by law include in or exclude from the list of Scheduled Castes specified in a notification issued under clause (1) any caste, race or tribe or part of or group within any caste, race or tribe, but save as aforesaid a notification issued under the said clause shall not be varied by any subsequent notification.

342.   Scheduled Tribes.—(1) The President [6][may with respect to any State [7][or Union territory], and where it is a State [8]***, after consultation with the Governor [8]*** thereof], by public notification[9], specify the tribes or tribal communities or parts of or groups within tribes or tribal communities which shall for the purposes of this Constitution be deemed to be Scheduled Tribes in relation to that State [7][or Union territory, as the case may be.]

---

1 Subs. by the Constitution (First Amendment) Act, 1951, s. 10, for "may, after consultation with the Governor or Rajpramukh of a State" (w.e.f. 18-6-1951).

2 Ins. by the Constitution (Seventh Amendment) Act, 1956, s. 29 and Sch. (w.e.f. 1-11-1956).

3 The words and letters "specified in Part A or Part B of the First Schedule" omitted by s. 29 and Sch., *ibid*. (w.e.f. 1-11-1956).

4 The words "or Rajpramukh" omitted by s. 29 and Sch., *ibid*. (w.e.f. 1-11-1956).

5 See the Constitution (Scheduled Castes) Order, 1950 (C.O. 19), the Constitution (Scheduled Castes) (Union Territories) Order, 1951 (C.O. 32), the Constitution (Jammu and Kashmir) Scheduled Castes Order, 1956 (C.O. 52), the Constitution (Dadra and Nagar Haveli) (Scheduled Castes) Order, 1962 (C.O. 64), the Constitution (Pondicherry) Scheduled Castes Order, 1964 (C.O. 68), the Constitution (Goa, Daman and Diu) Scheduled Castes Order, 1968 (C.O. 81) and the Constitution (Sikkim) Scheduled Castes Order, 1978 (C.O. 110).

6 Subs. by the Constitution (First Amendment) Act, 1951, s. 11, for "may, after consultation with the Governor or Rajpramukh of State" (w.e.f. 18-6-1951).

7 Ins. by the Constitution (Seventh Amendment) Act, 1956, s. 29 and Sch. (w.e.f. 1-11-1956).

8 Certain words omitted by s. 29 and Sch., *ibid*, (w.e.f. 1-11-1956).

9 See the Constitution (Scheduled Tribes) Order, 1950 (C.O. 22), the Constitution (Scheduled Tribes) (Union Territories) Order, 1951 (C.O. 33), the Constitution (Andaman and Nicobar Islands) (Scheduled Tribes) Order, 1959 (C.O. 58), Constitution (Dadra and Nagar Haveli) (Scheduled Tribes) Order, 1962 (C.O. 65), the Constitution (Scheduled Tribes) (Uttar Pradesh) Order, 1967 (C.O. 78), the Constitution (Goa, Daman and Diu) Scheduled Tribes Order, 1968 (C.O. 82), the Constitution (Nagaland) Scheduled Tribes Order, 1970 (C.O. 88) the Constitution (Sikkim) Scheduled Tribes Order, 1978 (C.O. 111).

(2) Parliament may by law include in or exclude from the list of Scheduled Tribes specified in a notification issued under clause (1) any tribe or tribal community or part of or group within any tribe or tribal community, but save as aforesaid a notification issued under the said clause shall not be varied by any subsequent notification.

[1][**342A. Socially and educationally backward classes.**—(1) The President may with respect to any State or Union territory, and where it is a State, after consultation with the Governor thereof, by public notification, specify [2][the socially and educationally backward classes in the Central List which shall for the purposes of the Central Government] be deemed to be socially and educationally backward classes in relation to that State or Union territory, as the case may be.

(2) Parliament may by law include in or exclude from the Central List of socially and educationally backward classes specified in a notification issued under clause (1) any socially and educationally backward class, but save as aforesaid a notification issued under the said clause shall not be varied by any subsequent notification.] [3][*Explanation.*—For the purposes of clauses (1) and (2), the expression "Central List" means the list of socially and educationally backward classes prepared and maintained by and for the Central Government.

(3) Notwithstanding any contained in clauses (1) and (2), every State or Union territory may, by law, prepare and maintain, for its own purposes, a list of socially and educationally backward classes, entries in which may be different from the Central List.]

---

1 Art. 342A ins. by the Constitution (One Hundred and Second Amendment) Act, 2018, s. 4 (w.e.f. 15-8-2018).

2 Subs. by the Constitution (One Hundred and Fifth Amendment) Act, 2021, s. 3, for "the socially and educationally backward classes which shall for the purposes of this Constitution" (w.e.f. 15-9-2021).

3 Ins. by the Constitution (One Hundred and Fifth Amendment) Act, 2021, s. 3 (w.e.f. 15-9-2021).

PART XVII

OFFICIAL LANGUAGE

Chapter I.—Language of the Union

343.   **Official language of the Union.**—(1) The official language of the Union shall be Hindi in Devanagari script.

The form of numerals to be used for the official purposes of the Union shall be the international form of Indian numerals.

(2) Notwithstanding anything in clause (1), for a period of fifteen years from the commencement of this Constitution, the English language shall continue to be used for all the official purposes of the Union for which it was being used immediately before such commencement:

Provided that the President may, during the said period, by order1 authorise the use of the Hindi language in addition to the English language and of the Devanagari form of numerals in addition to the international form of Indian numerals for any of the official purposes of the Union.

(3) Notwithstanding anything in this article, Parliament may by law provide for the use, after the said period of fifteen years, of—

(*a*)   the English language, or

(*b*)   the Devanagari form of numerals,

for such purposes as may be specified in the law.

344.   **Commission and Committee of Parliament on official language.**—(1) The President shall, at the expiration of five years from the commencement of this Constitution and thereafter at the expiration of ten years from such commencement, by order constitute a Commission which shall consist of a Chairman and such other members representing the different languages specified in the Eighth Schedule as the President may appoint, and the order shall define the procedure to be followed by the Commission.

---

1   *See* C.O. 41.

(2) It shall be the duty of the Commission to make recommendations to the President as to—

(a) the progressive use of the Hindi language for the official purposes of the Union;

(b) restrictions on the use of the English language for all or any of the official purposes of the Union;

(c) the language to be used for all or any of the purposes mentioned in article 348;

(d) the form of numerals to be used for any one or more specified purposes of the Union;

(e) any other matter referred to the Commission by the President as regards the official language of the Union and the language for communication between the Union and a State or between one State and another and their use.

(3) In making their recommendations under clause (2), the Commission shall have due regard to the industrial, cultural and scientific advancement of India, and the just claims and the interests of persons belonging to the non-Hindi speaking areas in regard to the public services.

(4) There shall be constituted a Committee consisting of thirty members, of whom twenty shall be members of the House of the People and ten shall be members of the Council of States to be elected respectively by the members of the House of the People and the members of the Council of States in accordance with the system of proportional representation by means of the single transferable vote.

(5) It shall be the duty of the Committee to examine the recommendations of the Commission constituted under clause (1) and to report to the President their opinion thereon.

(6) Notwithstanding anything in article 343, the President may, after consideration of the report referred to in clause (5), issue directions in accordance with the whole or any part of that report.

Chapter II.—Regional Languages

345. Official language or languages of a State.—Subject to the provisions of articles 346 and 347, the Legislature of a State may by law adopt any one or more of the languages in use in the State or Hindi as the language or languages to be used for all or any of the official purposes of that State:

Provided that, until the Legislature of the State otherwise provides by law, the English language shall continue to be used for those official purposes within the State for which it was being used immediately before the commencement of this Constitution.

346. Official language for communication between one State and another or between a State and the Union.—The language for the time being authorised for use in the Union for official purposes shall be the official language for communication between one State and another State and between a State and the Union:

Provided that if two or more States agree that the Hindi language should be the official language for communication between such States, that language may be used for such communication.

347. Special provision relating to language spoken by a section of the population of a State.—On a demand being made in that behalf the President may, if he is satisfied that a substantial proportion of the population of a State desire the use of any language spoken by them to be recognised by that State, direct that such language shall also be officially recognised throughout that State or any part thereof for such purpose as he may specify.

Chapter III.—Language of the Supreme Court, High Courts, etc.

348. Language to be used in the Supreme Court and in the High Courts and for Acts, Bills, etc.—(1) Notwithstanding anything in the foregoing provisions of this Part, until Parliament by law otherwise provides—

(*a*) all proceedings in the Supreme Court and in every High Court,

(*b*) the authoritative texts—

(*i*) of all Bills to be introduced or amendments thereto to be moved in either House of Parliament or in the House or either House of the Legislature of a State,

(*ii*) of all Acts passed by Parliament or the Legislature of a State and of all Ordinances promulgated by the President or the Governor 1*** of a State, and

(*iii*) of all orders, rules, regulations and bye-laws issued under this Constitution or under any law made by Parliament or the Legislature of a State,

shall be in the English language.

(2) Notwithstanding anything in sub-clause (*a*) of clause (1), the Governor ¹*** of a State may, with the previous consent of the President, authorise the use of the Hindi language, or any other language used for any official purposes of the State, in proceedings in the High Court having its principal seat in that State:

Provided that nothing in this clause shall apply to any judgment, decree or order passed or made by such High Court.

(3) Notwithstanding anything in sub-clause (*b*) of clause (1), where the Legislature of a State has prescribed any language other than the English language for use in Bills introduced in, or Acts passed by, the Legislature of the State or in Ordinances promulgated by the Governor ²*** of the State or in any order, rule, regulation or bye-law referred to in paragraph (*iii*) of that sub-clause, a translation of the same in the English language published under the authority of the Governor ²*** of the State in the Official Gazette of that State shall be deemed to be the authoritative text thereof in the English language under this article.

---

1 The words "or Rajpramukh" omitted by the Constitution (Seventh Amendment) Act, 1956, s. 29 and Sch. (w.e.f. 1-11-1956).

2 The words "or Rajpramukh" omitted by the Constitution (Seventh Amendment) Act, 1956, s. 29 and Sch. (w.e.f. 1-11-1956).

The Constitution of India

349. **Special procedure for enactment of certain laws relating to language.**—During the period of fifteen years from the commencement of this Constitution, no Bill or amendment making provision for the language to be used for any of the purposes mentioned in clause (1) of article 348 shall be introduced or moved in either House of Parliament without the previous sanction of the President, and the President shall not give his sanction to the introduction of any such Bill or the moving of any such amendment except after he has taken into consideration the recommendations of the Commission constituted under clause (1) of article 344 and the report of the Committee constituted under clause (4) of that article.

Chapter IV.—Special Directives

350. **Language to be used in representations for redress of grievances.**—Every person shall be entitled to submit a representation for the redress of any grievance to any officer or authority of the Union or a State in any of the languages used in the Union or in the State, as the case may be.

[1][**350A.** **Facilities for instruction in mother-tongue at primary stage.**—It shall be the endeavour of every State and of every local authority within the State to provide adequate facilities for instruction in the mother-tongue at the primary stage of education to children belonging to linguistic minority groups; and the President may issue such directions to any State as he considers necessary or proper for securing the provision of such facilities.

350B. **Special Officer for linguistic minorities.**—(1) There shall be a Special Officer for linguistic minorities to be appointed by the President.

(2) It shall be the duty of the Special Officer to investigate all matters relating to the safeguards provided for linguistic minorities under this Constitution and report to the President upon those matters at such intervals as the President may direct,

---

1 Arts. 350A and 350B ins. by s.21., *ibid.* (w.e.f. 1-11-1956).

and the President shall cause all such reports to be laid before each House of Parliament, and sent to the Governments of the States concerned.]

351. **Directive for development of the Hindi language.**—It shall be the duty of the Union to promote the spread of the Hindi language, to develop it so that it may serve as a medium of expression for all the elements of the composite culture of India and to secure its enrichment by assimilating without interfering with its genius, the forms, style and expressions used in Hindustani and in the other languages of India specified in the Eighth Schedule, and by drawing, wherever necessary or desirable, for its vocabulary, primarily on Sanskrit and secondarily on other languages.

PART XVIII

EMERGENCY PROVISIONS

352. **Proclamation of Emergency.**—(1) If the President is satisfied that a grave emergency exists whereby the security of India or of any part of the territory thereof is threatened, whether by war or external aggression or ¹[armed rebellion], he may, by Proclamation, make a declaration to that effect ²[in respect of the whole of India or of such part of the territory thereof as may be specified in the Proclamation.]

³[*Explanation.*—A Proclamation of Emergency declaring that the security of India or any part of the territory thereof is threatened by war or by external aggression or by armed rebellion may be made before the actual occurrence of war or of any such aggression or rebellion, if the President is satisfied that there is imminent danger thereof.]

---

1 Subs. by the Constitution (Forty-fourth Amendment) Act, 1978, s. 37, for "internal disturbance" (w.e.f. 20-6-1979).
2 Ins. by the Constitution (Forty-second Amendment) Act, 1976, s. 48 (w.e.f. 3-1-1977).
3 Ins. by the Constitution (Forty-fourth Amendment) Act, 1978, s. 37 (w.e.f. 20-6-1979).

[(2) A Proclamation issued under clause (1) may be varied or revoked by a subsequent Proclamation.

(3) The President shall not issue a Proclamation under clause (1) or a Proclamation varying such Proclamation unless the decision of the Union Cabinet (that is to say, the Council consisting of the Prime Minister and other Ministers of Cabinet rank appointed under article 75) that such a Proclamation may be issued has been communicated to him in writing.

(4) Every Proclamation issued under this article shall be laid before each House of Parliament and shall, except where it is a Proclamation revoking a previous Proclamation, cease to operate at the expiration of one month unless before the expiration of that period it has been approved by resolutions of both Houses of Parliament:

Provided that if any such Proclamation (not being a Proclamation revoking a previous Proclamation) is issued at a time when the House of the People has been dissolved, or the dissolution of the House of the People takes place during the period of one month referred to in this clause, and if a resolution approving the Proclamation has been passed by the Council of States, but no resolution with respect to such Proclamation has been passed by the House of the People before the expiration of that period, the Proclamation shall cease to operate at the expiration of thirty days from the date on which the House of the People first sits after its reconstitution, unless before the expiration of the said period of thirty days a resolution approving the Proclamation has been also passed by the House of the People.

(5) A Proclamation so approved shall, unless revoked, cease to operate on the expiration of a period of six months from the date of the passing of the second of the resolutions approving the Proclamation under clause (4):

Provided that if and so often as a resolution approving the continuance in force of such a Proclamation is passed by both Houses of Parliament the Proclamation shall, unless revoked, continue in force for a further period of six months from the

---

1 Subs. by s. 37, *ibid.*, for cls. (2), (2A) and (3) (w.e.f. 20-6-1979).

date on which it would otherwise have ceased to operate under this clause:

Provided further that if the dissolution of the House of the People takes place during any such period of six months and a resolution approving the continuance in force of such Proclamation has been passed by the Council of States but no resolution with respect to the continuance in force of such Proclamation has been passed by the House of the People during the said period, the Proclamation shall cease to operate at the expiration of thirty days from the date on which the House of the People first sits after its reconstitution unless before the expiration of the said period of thirty days, a resolution approving the continuance in force of the Proclamation has been also passed by the House of the People.

(6) For the purposes of clauses (4) and (5), a resolution may be passed by either House of Parliament only by a majority of the total membership of that House and by a majority of not less than two-thirds of the Members of that House present and voting.

(7) Notwithstanding anything contained in the foregoing clauses, the President shall revoke a Proclamation issued under clause (1) or a Proclamation varying such Proclamation if the House of the People passes a resolution disapproving, or, as the case may be, disapproving the continuance in force of, such Proclamation.

(8) Where a notice in writing signed by not less than one-tenth of the total number of members of the House of the People has been given, of their intention to move a resolution for disapproving, or, as the case may be, for disapproving the continuance in force of, a Proclamation issued under clause (1) or a Proclamation varying such Proclamation,—

(a)   to the Speaker, if the House is in session; or

(b)   to the President, if the House is not in session,

a special sitting of the House shall be held within fourteen days from the date on which such notice is received by the Speaker, or, as the case may be, by the President, for the purpose of considering such resolution.]

¹[(9) The power conferred on the President by this article shall include the power to issue different Proclamations on different grounds, being war or external aggression or ²[armed rebellion] or imminent danger of war or external aggression or ²[armed rebellion], whether or not there is a Proclamation already issued by the President under clause (1) and such Proclamation is in operation.

¹*   *   *   *   *   *   *   *]

353. Effect of Proclamation of Emergency.—While a Proclamation of Emergency is in operation, then—

(a) notwithstanding anything in this Constitution, the executive power of the Union shall extend to the giving of directions to any State as to the manner in which the executive power thereof is to be exercised;

(b) the power of Parliament to make laws with respect to any matter shall include power to make laws conferring powers and imposing duties, or authorising the conferring of powers and the imposition of duties, upon the Union or officers and authorities of the Union as respects that matter, notwithstanding that it is one which is not enumerated in the Union List:

³[Provided that where a Proclamation of Emergency is in operation only in any part of the territory of India,—

(i) the executive power of the Union to give directions under clause (a), and

(ii) the power of Parliament to make laws under clause (b),

shall also extend to any State other than a State in which or in any part of which the Proclamation of Emergency is in operation if and in so far as the security of India or any part of the territory thereof is threatened by activities in or in relation to the part of the territory of India in which the Proclamation of Emergency is in operation.]

---

1 Cls. (4) and (5) were ins. by the Constitution (Thirty-eighth Amendment) Act, 1975, s. 5 (with retrospective effect) and subsequently cl. (4) renumbered as cl. (9) and cl. (5) omitted by the Constitution (Forty-fourth Amendment) Act, 1978, s. 37 (w.e.f. 20-6-1979).
2 Subs. by s. 37, *ibid.* for "internal disturbance" (w.e.f. 20-6-1979).
3 Added by the Constitution (Forty-second Amendment) Act, 1976, s. 49 (w.e.f. 3-1-1977).

354. **Application of provisions relating to distribution of revenues while a Proclamation of Emergency is in operation.**—(1) The President may, while a Proclamation of Emergency is in operation, by order direct that all or any of the provisions of articles 268 to 279 shall for such period, not extending in any case beyond the expiration of the financial year in which such Proclamation ceases to operate, as may be specified in the order, have effect subject to such exceptions or modifications as he thinks fit.

(2) Every order made under clause (1) shall, as soon as may be after it is made, be laid before each House of Parliament.

355. **Duty of the Union to protect States against external aggression and internal disturbance.**—It shall be the duty of the Union to protect every State against external aggression and internal disturbance and to ensure that the Government of every State is carried on in accordance with the provisions of this Constitution.

356. **Provisions in case of failure of constitutional machinery in States.**—(1) If the President, on receipt of a report from the Governor [1]*** of a State or otherwise, is satisfied that a situation has arisen in which the Government of the State cannot be carried on in accordance with the provisions of this Constitution, the President may by Proclamation—

> (*a*) assume to himself all or any of the functions of the Government of the State and all or any of the powers vested in or exercisable by the Governor [2]*** or any body or authority in the State other than the Legislature of the State;
>
> (*b*) declare that the powers of the Legislature of the State shall be exercisable by or under the authority of Parliament;
>
> (*c*) make such incidental and consequential provisions as appear to the President to be necessary or desirable

---

1 The words "or Rajpramukh" omitted by the Constitution (Seventh Amendment) Act, 1956, s. 29 and Sch. (w.e.f. 1-11-1956).

2 The words "or Rajpramukh, as the case may be" omitted by the Constitution (Seventh Amendment) Act, 1956, s. 29 and Sch. (w.e.f. 1-11-1956).

for giving effect to the objects of the Proclamation, including provisions for suspending in whole or in part the operation of any provisions of this Constitution relating to any body or authority in the State:

Provided that nothing in this clause shall authorise the President to assume to himself any of the powers vested in or exercisable by a High Court, or to suspend in whole or in part the operation of any provision of this Constitution relating to High Courts.

(2) Any such Proclamation may be revoked or varied by a subsequent Proclamation.

(3) Every Proclamation under this article shall be laid before each House of Parliament and shall, except where it is a Proclamation revoking a previous Proclamation, cease to operate at the expiration of two months unless before the expiration of that period it has been approved by resolutions of both Houses of Parliament:

Provided that if any such Proclamation (not being a Proclamation revoking a previous Proclamation) is issued at a time when the House of the People is dissolved or the dissolution of the House of the People takes place during the period of two months referred to in this clause, and if a resolution approving the Proclamation has been passed by the Council of States, but no resolution with respect to such Proclamation has been passed by the House of the People before the expiration of that period, the Proclamation shall cease to operate at the expiration of thirty days from the date on which the House of the People first sits after its reconstitution unless before the expiration of the said period of thirty days a resolution approving the Proclamation has been also passed by the House of the People.

(4) A Proclamation so approved shall, unless revoked, cease to operate on the expiration of a period of [1][six months from the date of issue of the Proclamation]:

---

1 Subs. by the Constitution (Forty-second Amendment) Act, 1976, s. 50, for "six months" (w.e.f. 3-1-1977) and further subs. by the Constitution (Forty-fourth Amendment) Act, 1978, s. 38, for "one year from the date of the passing of the second of the resolutions approving the Proclamation under clause (3)" (w.e.f. 20-6-1979).

Provided that if and so often as a resolution approving the continuance in force of such a Proclamation is passed by both Houses of Parliament, the Proclamation shall, unless revoked, continue in force for a further period of ¹[six months] from the date on which under this clause it would otherwise have ceased to operate, but no such Proclamation shall in any case remain in force for more than three years:

Provided further that if the dissolution of the House of the People takes place during any such period of ²[six months] and a resolution approving the continuance in force of such Proclamation has been passed by the Council of States, but no resolution with respect to the continuance in force of such Proclamation has been passed by the House of the People during the said period, the Proclamation shall cease to operate at the expiration of thirty days from the date on which the House of the People first sits after its reconstitution unless before the expiration of the said period of thirty days a resolution approving the continuance in force of the Proclamation has been also passed by the House of the People:

²[Provided also that in the case of the Proclamation issued under clause (1) on the 11th day of May, 1987 with respect to the State of Punjab, the reference in the first proviso to this clause to "three years" shall be construed as a reference to ³[five years].]

⁴[(5) Notwithstanding anything contained in clause (4), a resolution with respect to the continuance in force of a Proclamation approved under clause (3) for any period beyond the expiration of one year from the date of issue of such Proclamation shall not be passed by either House of Parliament unless—

(*a*) a Proclamation of Emergency is in operation, in the whole of India or, as the case may be, in the whole or

---

1 Subs. by s. 50, *ibid.*, for "six months" (w.e.f. 3-1-1977) and further subs. by s. 38, *ibid.*, for "one year", respectively (w.e.f. 20-6-1979).

2 Ins. by the Constitution (Sixty-fourth Amendment) Act, 1990, s. 2 (w.e.f. 16-4-1990).

3 Subs. by the Constitution (Sixty-seventh Amendment) Act, 1990, s. 2 (w.e.f. 4-10-1990) and further subs. by the Constitution (Sixty-eighth Amendment) Act, 1991, s. 2 (w.e.f. 12-3-1991).

4 Ins. by the Constitution (Thirty-eighth Amendment) Act, 1975, s. 6 (with retrospective effect) and subsequently subs. by the Constitution (Forty-fourth Amendment) Act, 1978, s. 38, for cl. (5) (w.e.f. 20-6-1979).

any part of the State, at the time of the passing of such resolution, and

(*b*) the Election Commission certifies that the continuance in force of the Proclamation approved under clause (3) during the period specified in such resolution is necessary on account of difficulties in holding general elections to the Legislative Assembly of the State concerned:]

[1][Provided that nothing in this clause shall apply to the Proclamation issued under clause (1) on the 11th day of May, 1987 with respect to the State of Punjab.]

357. **Exercise of legislative powers under Proclamation issued under article 356.**—(1) Where by a Proclamation issued under clause (1) of article 356, it has been declared that the powers of the Legislature of the State shall be exercisable by or under the authority of Parliament, it shall be competent—

(*a*) for Parliament to confer on the President the power of the Legislature of the State to make laws, and to authorise the President to delegate, subject to such conditions as he may think fit to impose, the power so conferred to any other authority to be specified by him in that behalf;

(*b*) for Parliament, or for the President or other authority in whom such power to make laws is vested under sub-clause (*a*), to make laws conferring powers and imposing duties, or authorising the conferring of powers and the imposition of duties, upon the Union or officers and authorities thereof;

(*c*) for the President to authorise when the House of the People is not in session expenditure from the Consolidated Fund of the State pending the sanction of such expenditure by Parliament.

[2][(2) Any law made in exercise of the power of the Legislature of the State by Parliament or the President or other authority

---

1 Proviso omitted by the Constitution (Sixty-third Amendment) Act, 1989, s. 2 (w.e.f. 6- 1-1990) and subsequently ins. by the Constitution (Sixty-fourth Amendment) Act, 1990, s. 2 (w.e.f. 16-4-1990).
2 Subs. by the Constitution (Forty-second Amendment) Act, 1976, s. 51 (w.e.f. 3-1-1977).

referred to in sub-clause (*a*) of clause (1) which Parliament or the President or such other authority would not, but for the issue of a Proclamation under article 356, have been competent to make shall, after the Proclamation has ceased to operate, continue in force until altered or repealed or amended by a competent Legislature or other authority.]

358. **Suspension of provisions of article 19 during emergencies.**— [1][(1)] [2][While a Proclamation of Emergency declaring that the security of India or any part of the territory thereof is threatened by war or by external aggression is in operation], nothing in article 19 shall restrict the power of the State as defined in Part III to make any law or to take any executive action which the State would but for the provisions contained in that Part be competent to make or to take, but any law so made shall, to the extent of the incompetency, cease to have effect as soon as the Proclamation ceases to operate, except as respects things done or omitted to be done before the law so ceases to have effect:

[3][Provided that [4][where such Proclamation of Emergency] is in operation only in any part of the territory of India, any such law may be made, or any such executive action may be taken, under this article in relation to or in any State or Union territory in which or in any part of which the Proclamation of Emergency is not in operation, if and in so far as the security of India or any part of the territory thereof is threatened by activities in or in relation to the part of the territory of India in which the Proclamation of Emergency is in operation.]

[5][(2) Nothing in clause (1) shall apply—

    (*a*)   to any law which does not contain a recital to the effect that such law is in relation to the Proclamation of Emergency in operation when it is made; or

---

1 Art. 358 re-numbered as cl. (1) by the Constitution (Forty-fourth Amendment) Act, 1978, s. 39 (w.e.f. 20-6-1979).
2 Subs. by s. 39, *ibid*, for "While a Proclamation of Emergency is in operation" (w.e.f. 20-6-1979).
3 Added by the Constitution (Forty-second Amendment) Act, 1976, s. 52 (w.e.f. 3-1-1977).
4 Subs. by the Constitution (Forty-fourth Amendment) Act, 1978, s. 39, for "where a Proclamation of Emergency" (w.e.f. 20-6-1979).
5 Ins. by s. 39, *ibid*. (w.e.f. 20-6-1979).

(*b*) to any executive action taken otherwise than under a law containing such a recital.]

359. Suspension of the enforcement of the rights conferred by Part III during emergencies.—(1) Where a Proclamation of Emergency is in operation, the President may by order declare that the right to move any court for the enforcement of such of [1][the rights conferred by Part III (except articles 20 and 21)] as may be mentioned in the order and all proceedings pending in any court for the enforcement of the rights so mentioned shall remain suspended for the period during which the Proclamation is in force or for such shorter period as may be specified in the order.

[2][(1A) While an order made under clause (1) mentioning any of [1][the rights conferred by Part III (except articles 20 and 21)] is in operation, nothing in that Part conferring those rights shall restrict the power of the State as defined in the said Part to make any law or to take any executive action which the State would but for the provisions contained in that Part be competent to make or to take, but any law so made shall, to the extent of the incompetency, cease to have effect as soon as the order aforesaid ceases to operate, except as respects things done or omitted to be done before the law so ceases to have effect:]

[3][Provided that where a Proclamation of Emergency is in operation only in any part of the territory of India, any such law may be made, or any such executive action may be taken, under this article in relation to or in any State or Union territory in which or in any part of which the Proclamation of Emergency is not in operation, if and in so far as the security of India or any part of the territory thereof is threatened by activities in or in relation to the part of the territory of India in which the Proclamation of Emergency is in operation.]

[4][(1B) Nothing in clause (1A) shall apply—

---

1 Subs. by the Constitution (Forty-fourth Amendment) Act, 1978, s. 40, for "the rights conferred by Part III" (w.e.f. 20-6-1979).
2 Ins. by the Constitution (Thirty-eighth Amendment) Act, 1975, s. 7 (with retrospective effect).
3 Added by the Constitution (Forty-second Amendment) Act, 1976, s. 53 (w.e.f. 3-1-1977).
4 Ins. by the Constitution (Forty-fourth Amendment) Act, 1978, s. 40 (w.e.f. 20-6-1979).

(*a*) to any law which does not contain a recital to the effect that such law is in relation to the Proclamation of Emergency in operation when it is made; or

(*b*) to any executive action taken otherwise than under a law containing such a recital.]

(2) An order made as aforesaid may extend to the whole or any part of the territory of India:

[1][Provided that where a Proclamation of Emergency is in operation only in a part of the territory of India, any such order shall not extend to any other part of the territory of India unless the President, being satisfied that the security of India or any part of the territory thereof is threatened by activities in or in relation to the part of the territory of India in which the Proclamation of Emergency is in operation, considers such extension to be necessary.]

(3) Every order made under clause (1) shall, as soon as may be after it is made, be laid before each House of Parliament.

[2]**359A.** [*Application of this Part to the State of Punjab.*].—*Omitted by the Constitution (Sixty-third Amendment) Act,* 1989, *s.* 3 *(w.e.f.* 6-1-1990).

360. **Provisions as to financial emergency.**—(1) If the President is satisfied that a situation has arisen whereby the financial stability or credit of India or of any part of the territory thereof is threatened, he may by a Proclamation make a declaration to that effect.

[3][(2) A Proclamation issued under clause (1)—

(*a*) may be revoked or varied by a subsequent Proclamation;

(*b*) shall be laid before each House of Parliament;

(*c*) shall cease to operate at the expiration of two months, unless before the expiration of that period it has been approved by resolutions of both Houses of Parliament:

Provided that if any such Proclamation is issued at a time when the House of the People has been dissolved or the dissolution

---

1 Added by the Constitution (Forty-second Amendment) Act, 1976, s. 53 (w.e.f. 3-1-1977).

2 Ins. by the Constitution (Fifty-ninth Amendment) Act, 1988, s. 3 (w.e.f. 30-3-1988) and ceased to operate on the expiry of a period of two years from the commencement of that Act, *i.e.* 30th day of March, 1988.

3 Subs. by the Constitution (Forty-fourth Amendment) Act, 1978, s. 41, for cl. (2) (w.e.f. 20-6-1979).

of the House of the People takes place during the period of two months referred to in sub-clause (c), and if a resolution approving the Proclamation has been passed by the Council of States, but no resolution with respect to such Proclamation has been passed by the House of the People before the expiration of that period, the Proclamation shall cease to operate at the expiration of thirty days from the date on which the House of the People first sits after its reconstitution unless before the expiration of the said period of thirty days a resolution approving the Proclamation has been also passed by the House of the People.]

(3) During the period any such Proclamation as is mentioned in clause (1) is in operation, the executive authority of the Union shall extend to the giving of directions to any State to observe such canons of financial propriety as may be specified in the directions, and to the giving of such other directions as the President may deem necessary and adequate for the purpose.

(4) Notwithstanding anything in this Constitution—

    (a) any such direction may include—

        (i) a provision requiring the reduction of salaries and allowances of all or any class of persons serving in connection with the affairs of a State;

        (ii) a provision requiring all Money Bills or other Bills to which the provisions of article 207 apply to be reserved for the consideration of the President after they are passed by the Legislature of the State;

    (b) it shall be competent for the President during the period any Proclamation issued under this article is in operation to issue directions for the reduction of salaries and allowances of all or any class of persons serving in connection with the affairs of the Union including the Judges of the Supreme Court and the High Courts.

[1][(5)   *   *   *   *   *]

---

1 Ins. by the Constitution (Thirty-eighth Amendment) Act, 1975, s. 8 (with retrospective effect) and omitted by the Constitution (Forty-fourth Amendment) Act, 1978, s. 41 (w.e.f. 20-6-1979).

PART XIX

MISCELLANEOUS

361. **Protection of President and Governors and Rajpramukhs.**—
(1) The President, or the Governor or Rajpramukh of a State, shall not be answerable to any court for the exercise and performance of the powers and duties of his office or for any act done or purporting to be done by him in the exercise and performance of those powers and duties:

Provided that the conduct of the President may be brought under review by any court, tribunal or body appointed or designated by either House of Parliament for the investigation of a charge under article 61:

Provided further that nothing in this clause shall be construed as restricting the right of any person to bring appropriate proceedings against the Government of India or the Government of a State.

(2) No criminal proceedings whatsoever shall be instituted or continued against the President, or the Governor [1]*** of a State, in any court during his term of office.

(3) No process for the arrest or imprisonment of the President, or the Governor [1]*** of a State, shall issue from any court during his term of office.

(4) No civil proceedings in which relief is claimed against the President, or the Governor [1]*** of a State, shall be instituted during his term of office in any court in respect of any act done or purporting to be done by him in his personal capacity, whether before or after he entered upon his office as President, or as Governor [1]*** of such State, until the expiration of two months next after notice in writing has been delivered to the President or the Governor [1]***, as the case may be, or left at his office stating the nature of the proceedings, the cause of action therefor, the

---

1 The words "or Rajpramukh" omitted by the Constitution (Seventh Amendment) Act, 1956, s. 29 and Sch. (w.e.f. 1-11-1956).

name, description and place of residence of the party by whom such proceedings are to be instituted and the relief which he claims.

[361A. **Protection of publication of proceedings of Parliament and State Legislatures.**—(1) No person shall be liable to any proceedings, civil or criminal, in any court in respect of the publication in a newspaper of a substantially true report of any proceedings of either House of Parliament or the Legislative Assembly, or, as the case may be, either House of the Legislature, of a State, unless the publication is proved to have been made with malice:

Provided that nothing in this clause shall apply to the publication of any report of the proceedings of a secret sitting of either House of Parliament or the Legislative Assembly, or, as the case may be, either House of the Legislature, of a State.

(2) Clause (1) shall apply in relation to reports or matters broadcast by means of wireless telegraphy as part of any programme or service provided by means of a broadcasting station as it applies in relation to reports or matters published in a newspaper.

Explanation.—In this article, "newspaper" includes a news agency report containing material for publication in a newspaper.]

[361B. **Disqualification for appointment on remunerative political post.**—A member of a House belonging to any political party who is disqualified for being a member of the House under paragraph 2 of the Tenth Schedule shall also be disqualified to hold any remunerative political post for duration of the period commencing from the date of his disqualification till the date on which the term of his office as such member would expire or till the date on which he contests an election to a House and is declared elected, whichever is earlier.

Explanation. — For the purposes of this article,—

(a) the expression "House" has the meaning assigned to it in clause (a) of paragraph 1 of the Tenth Schedule;

(b) the expression "remunerative political post" means any office—

---

1 Art. 361A ins. by the Constitution (Forty-fourth Amendment) Act, 1978, s. 42 (w.e.f. 20-6-1979).
2 Art. 361B ins. by the Constitution (Ninety-first Amendment) Act, 2003, s. 4 (w.e.f. 1-1-2004).

      (*i*)   under the Government of India or the Government of a State where the salary or remuneration for such office is paid out of the public revenue of the Government of India or the Government of the State, as the case may be; or

      (*ii*)   under a body, whether incorporated or not, which is wholly or partially owned by the Government of India or the Government of State, and the salary or remuneration for such office is paid by such body,

except where such salary or remuneration paid is compensatory in nature.]

362.   [*Rights and privileges of Rulers of Indian States*.].—*Omitted by the Constitution (Twenty-sixth Amendment) Act*, 1971, s. 2 (w.e.f. 28-12-1971).

363.   **Bar to interference by courts in disputes arising out of certain treaties, agreements, etc.**—(1) Notwithstanding anything in this Constitution but subject to the provisions of article 143, neither the Supreme Court nor any other court shall have jurisdiction in any dispute arising out of any provision of a treaty, agreement, covenant, engagement, *sanad* or other similar instrument which was entered into or executed before the commencement of this Constitution by any Ruler of an Indian State and to which the Government of the Dominion of India or any of its predecessor Governments was a party and which has or has been continued in operation after such commencement, or in any dispute in respect of any right accruing under or any liability or obligation arising out of any of the provisions of this Constitution relating to any such treaty, agreement, covenant, engagement, *sanad* or other similar instrument.

(2) In this article—

    (*a*) "Indian State" means any territory recognised before the commencement of this Constitution by His Majesty or the Government of the Dominion of India as being such a State; and

    (*b*) "Ruler" includes the Prince, Chief or other person recognised before such commencement by His Majesty or the Government of the Dominion of India as the Ruler of any Indian State.

¹[**363A. Recognition granted to Rulers of Indian States to cease and privy purses to be abolished.**—Notwithstanding anything in this Constitution or in any law for the time being in force—

(*a*) the Prince, Chief or other person who, at any time before the commencement of the Constitution (Twenty-sixth Amendment) Act, 1971, was recognised by the President as the Ruler of an Indian State or any person who, at any time before such commencement, was recognised by the President as the successor of such ruler shall, on and from such commencement, cease to be recognised as such Ruler or the successor of such Ruler;

(*b*) on and from the commencement of the Constitution (Twenty- sixth Amendment) Act, 1971, privy purse is abolished and all rights, liabilities and obligations in respect of *privy purse* are extinguished and accordingly the Ruler or, as the case may be, the successor of such Ruler, referred to in clause (*a*) or any other person shall not be paid any sum as *privy purse*.]

364. Special provisions as to major ports and aerodromes.—(1) Notwithstanding anything in this Constitution, the President may by public notification direct that as from such date as may be specified in the notification—

(*a*) any law made by Parliament or by the Legislature of a State shall not apply to any major port or aerodrome or shall apply thereto subject to such exceptions or modifications as may be specified in the notification, or

(*b*) any existing law shall cease to have effect in any major port or aerodrome except as respects things done or omitted to be done before the said date, or shall in its application to such port or aerodrome have effect subject to such exceptions or modifications as may be specified in the notification.

---

1 Art. 363A ins. by the Constitution (Twenty-sixth Amendment) Act, 1971, s. 3 (w.e.f. 28-12-1971).

(2) In this article—

    (*a*) "major port" means a port declared to be a major port by or under any law made by Parliament or any existing law and includes all areas for the time being included within the limits of such port;

    (*b*) "aerodrome" means aerodrome as defined for the purposes of the enactments relating to airways, aircraft and air navigation.

365. **Effect of failure to comply with, or to give effect to, directions given by the Union.**—Where any State has failed to comply with, or to give effect to, any directions given in the exercise of the executive power of the Union under any of the provisions of this Constitution, it shall be lawful for the President to hold that a situation has arisen in which the Government of the State cannot be carried on in accordance with the provisions of this Constitution.

366. **Definitions.**—In this Constitution, unless the context otherwise requires, the following expressions have the meanings hereby respectively assigned to them, that is to say—

(1) "agricultural income" means agricultural income as defined for the purposes of the enactments relating to Indian income-tax;

(2) "an Anglo-Indian" means a person whose father or any of whose other male progenitors in the male line is or was of European descent but who is domiciled within the territory of India and is or was born within such territory of parents habitually resident therein and not established there for temporary purposes only;

(3) "article" means an article of this Constitution;

(4) "borrow" includes the raising of money by the grant of annuities, and "loan" shall be construed accordingly;

[1][(4A)*   *   *   *]

(5) "clause" means a clause of the article in which the expression occurs;

---

1 Cl. (4A) was ins. by the Constitution (Forty-second Amendment) Act, 1976, s. 54 (w.e.f. 1-2-1977) and subsequently omitted by the Constitution (Forty-third Amendment) Act, 1977, s. 11 (w.e.f. 13-4-1978).

(6) "corporation tax" means any tax on income, so far as that tax is payable by companies and is a tax in the case of which the following conditions are fulfilled:—

    (*a*) that it is not chargeable in respect of agricultural income;

    (*b*) that no deduction in respect of the tax paid by companies is, by any enactments which may apply to the tax, authorised to be made from dividends payable by the companies to individuals;

    (*c*) that no provision exists for taking the tax so paid into account in computing for the purposes of Indian income-tax the total income of individuals receiving such dividends, or in computing the Indian income-tax payable by, or refundable to, such individuals;

(7) "corresponding Province", "corresponding Indian State" or "corresponding State" means in cases of doubt such Province, Indian State or State as may be determined by the President to be the corresponding Province, the corresponding Indian State or the corresponding State, as the case may be, for the particular purpose in question;

(8) "debt" includes any liability in respect of any obligation to repay capital sums by way of annuities and any liability under any guarantee, and "debt charges" shall be construed accordingly;

(9) "estate duty" means a duty to be assessed on or by reference to the principal value, ascertained in accordance with such rules as may be prescribed by or under laws made by Parliament or the Legislature of a State relating to the duty, of all property passing upon death or deemed, under the provisions of the said laws, so to pass;

(10) "existing law" means any law, Ordinance, order, bye-law, rule or regulation passed or made before the commencement of this Constitution by any Legislature, authority or person having power to make such a law, Ordinance, order, bye-law, rule or regulation;

(11) "Federal Court" means the Federal Court constituted under the Government of India Act, 1935;

(12) "goods" includes all materials, commodities, and articles;

¹[(12A) "goods and services tax" means any tax on supply of goods, or services or both except taxes on the supply of the alcoholic liquor for human consumption];

(13) "guarantee" includes any obligation undertaken before the commencement of this Constitution to make payments in the event of the profits of an undertaking falling short of a specified amount;

(14) "High Court" means any Court which is deemed for the purposes of this Constitution to be a High Court for any State and includes—

(a) any Court in the territory of India constituted or reconstituted under this Constitution as a High Court, and

(b) any other Court in the territory of India which may be declared by Parliament by law to be a High Court for all or any of the purposes of this Constitution;

(15) "Indian State" means any territory which the Government of the Dominion of India recognised as such a State;

(16) "Part" means a Part of this Constitution;

(17) "pension" means a pension, whether contributory or not, of any kind whatsoever payable to or in respect of any person, and includes retired pay so payable; a gratuity so payable and any sum or sums so payable by way of the return, with or without interest thereon or any other addition thereto, of subscriptions to a provident fund;

(18) "Proclamation of Emergency" means a Proclamation issued under clause (1) of article 352;

(19) "public notification" means a notification in the Gazette of India, or, as the case may be, the Official Gazette of a State;

(20) "railway" does not include—

(a) a tramway wholly within a municipal area, or

(b) any other line of communication wholly situate in one State and declared by Parliament by law not to be a railway;

²[(21)*　　*　*　　*]

---

1 Ins. by the Constitution (One Hundred and First Amendment) Act, 2016, s. 14(i) (w.e.f. 16-9-2016).
2 Cl. (21) omitted by the Constitution (Seventh Amendment) Act, 1956, s. 29 and Sch. (w.e.f. 1-11-1956).

¹[(22) "Ruler" means the Prince, Chief or other person who, at any time before the commencement of the Constitution (Twenty-sixth Amendment) Act, 1971, was recognised by the President as the Ruler of an Indian State or any person who, at any time before such commencement, was recognised by the President as the successor of such Ruler;]

(23) "Schedule" means a Schedule to this Constitution;

(24) "Scheduled Castes" means such castes, races or tribes or parts of or groups within such castes, races or tribes as are deemed under article 341 to be Scheduled Castes for the purposes of this Constitution;

(25) "Scheduled Tribes" means such tribes or tribal communities or parts of or groups within such tribes or tribal communities as are deemed under article 342 to be Scheduled Tribes for the purposes of this Constitution;

(26) "securities" includes stock;

²* * *

³[(26A) "Services" means anything other than goods;

(26B) "State" with reference to articles 246A, 268, 269, 269A and article 279A includes a Union territory with Legislature];

⁴[(26C) "socially and educationally backward classes" means such backward classes as are so deemed under article 342A for the purposes of the Central Government or the State or Union territory, as the case may be];

(27) "sub-clause" means a sub-clause of the clause in which the expression occurs;

(28) "taxation" includes the imposition of any tax or impost, whether general or local or special, and "tax" shall be construed accordingly;

---

1 Subs. by the Constitution (Twenty-sixth Amendment) Act, 1971, s. 4 (w.e.f. 28-12-1971).
2 Cl. (26A) was ins. by the Constitution (Forty-second Amendment) Act, 1976, s. 54 (w.e.f. 1-2-1977) and subsequently omitted by the Constitution (Forty-third Amendment) Act, 1977, s. 11 (w.e.f. 13-4-1978).
3 Ins. by the Constitution (One Hundred and First Amendment) Act, 2016, s. 14(ii) (w.e.f. 16-9-2016).
4 Cl. (26C) was ins. by the Constitution (One Hundred and Second Amendment) Act, 2018, s.5 (w.e.f. 14-8-2018) and subsequently subs. by the Constitution (One Hundred and Fifth Amendment) Act, 2021, s. 4 (w.e.f. 15-9-2021).

(29) "tax on income" includes a tax in the nature of an excess profits tax;

[1][(29A) "tax on the sale or purchase of goods" includes—

(a) a tax on the transfer, otherwise than in pursuance of a contract, of property in any goods for cash, deferred payment or other valuable consideration;

(b) a tax on the transfer of property in goods (whether as goods or in some other form) involved in the execution of a works contract;

(c) a tax on the delivery of goods on hire-purchase or any system of payment by instalments;

(d) a tax on the transfer of the right to use any goods for any purpose (whether or not for a specified period) for cash, deferred payment or other valuable consideration;

(e) a tax on the supply of goods by any unincorporated association or body of persons to a member thereof for cash, deferred payment or other valuable consideration;

(f) a tax on the supply, by way of or as part of any service or in any other manner whatsoever, of goods, being food or any other article for human consumption or any drink (whether or not intoxicating), where such supply or service, is for cash, deferred payment or other valuable consideration,

and such transfer, delivery or supply of any goods shall be deemed to be a sale of those goods by the person making the transfer, delivery or supply and a purchase of those goods by the person to whom such transfer, delivery or supply is made;]

[2][(30) "Union territory" means any Union territory specified in the First Schedule and includes any other territory comprised within the territory of India but not specified in that Schedule.]

367. **Interpretation.**—(1) Unless the context otherwise requires, the General Clauses Act, 1897, shall, subject to any adaptations and modifications that may be made therein under article 372, apply for the interpretation of this Constitution as it applies for

1 Cl.(29A) ins. by the Constitution (Forty-sixth Amendment) Act, 1982, s. 4 (w.e.f. 2-2-1983).
2 Subs. by the Constitution (Seventh Amendment) Act, 1956, s. 29 and Sch. for cl. (30) (w.e.f. 1-11-1956).

the interpretation of an Act of the Legislature of the Dominion of India.

(2) Any reference in this Constitution to Acts or laws of, or made by, Parliament, or to Acts or laws of, or made by, the Legislature of a State [1]***, shall be construed as including a reference to an Ordinance made by the President or, to an Ordinance made by a Governor [2]***, as the case may be.

(3) For the purposes of this Constitution "foreign State" means any State other than India:

Provided that, subject to the provisions of any law made by Parliament, the President may by order[3] declare any State not to be a foreign State for such purposes as may be specified in the order.

[4][(4) *   *   *   *]

PART XX

AMENDMENT OF THE CONSTITUTION

368.   [5][**Power of Parliament to amend the Constitution and procedure therefor].**— [6][(1) Notwithstanding anything in this Constitution, Parliament may in exercise of its constituent power amend by way of addition, variation or repeal any provision of this Constitution in accordance with the procedure laid down in this article.]

[7][(2)] An amendment of this Constitution may be initiated only by the introduction of a Bill for the purpose in either House of Parliament, and when the Bill is passed in each House by a

---

1 The words and letters "specified in Part A or Part B of the First Schedule" omitted by s. 29 and Sch., *ibid*. (w.e.f. 1-11-1956).

2 The words "or Rajpramukh" omitted by s. 29 and Sch., *ibid*. (w.e.f. 1-11-1956).

3 *See* the Constitution (Declaration as to Foreign States) Order, 1950 (C.O. 2).

4 Added by the Constitution (Application to Jammu and Kashmir) Order, 2019 (C.O. 272) (w.e.f. 5-8-2019). For the text of this C.O., *see* Appendix II.

5 Marginal heading subs. by the Constitution (Twenty-fourth Amendment) Act, 1971, s. 3, for "Procedure for amendment of the Constitution" (w.e.f. 5-11-1971).

6 Ins. by s. 3, *ibid*. (w.e.f. 5-11-1971).

7 Art. 368 re-numbered as cl. (2) thereof by s. 3, *ibid*. (w.e.f. 5-11-1971).

majority of the total membership of that House and by a majority of not less than two-thirds of the members of that House present and voting, ¹[it shall be presented to the President who shall give his assent to the Bill and thereupon] the Constitution shall stand amended in accordance with the terms of the Bill:

Provided that if such amendment seeks to make any change in—

(a) article 54, article 55, article 73, ²[article 162, article 241 or article 279A]; or

(b) Chapter IV of Part V, Chapter V of Part VI, or Chapter I of Part XI; or

(c) any of the Lists in the Seventh Schedule; or

(d) the representation of States in Parliament; or

(e) the provisions of this article,

the amendment shall also require to be ratified by the Legislatures of not less than one-half of the States ³*** by resolutions to that effect passed by those Legislatures before the Bill making provision for such amendment is presented to the President for assent.

⁴[(3) Nothing in article 13 shall apply to any amendment made under this article.]

⁵[(4) No amendment of this Constitution (including the provisions of Part III) made or purporting to have been made under this article [whether before or after the commencement of section 55 of the Constitution (Forty-second Amendment) Act, 1976] shall be called in question in any court on any ground.

(5) For the removal of doubts, it is hereby declared that there shall be no limitation whatever on the constituent power of Parliament to amend by way of addition, variation or repeal the provisions of this Constitution under this article.]

---

1 Subs. by s. 3, *ibid.*, (w.e.f. 5-11-1971).

2 Subs. by the Constitution (One Hundred and First Amendment) Act, 2016, s. 15, for the words and figures "article 162 or article 241" (w.e.f. 16-9-2016).

3 The words and letters "specified in Part A and Part B of the First Schedule" omitted by the Constitution (Seventh Amendment) Act, 1956, s. 29 and Sch. (w.e.f. 1-11-1956).

4 Ins. by the Constitution (Twenty-fourth Amendment) Act, 1971, s. 3 (w.e.f. 5-11-1971).

5 Ins. by the Constitution (Forty-second Amendment) Act, 1976, s. 55 (w.e.f. 3-1-1977). This section has been declared invalid by the Supreme Court in *Minerva Mills Ltd. and Others Vs. Union of India and Others* AIR 1980 SC 1789.

PART XXI

¹[TEMPORARY, TRANSITIONAL AND SPECIAL PROVISIONS]

369.   **Temporary power to Parliament to make laws with respect to certain matters in the State List as if they were matters in the Concurrent List.**—Notwithstanding anything in this Constitution, Parliament shall, during a period of five years from the commencement of this Constitution, have power to make laws with respect to the following matters as if they were enumerated in the Concurrent List, namely:—

(*a*)   trade and commerce within a State in, and the production, supply and distribution of, cotton and woollen textiles, raw cotton (including ginned cotton and unginned cotton or *kapas*), cotton seed, paper (including newsprint), food-stuffs (including edible oilseeds and oil), cattle fodder (including oil-cakes and other concentrates), coal (including coke and derivatives of coal), iron, steel and mica;

(*b*)   offences against laws with respect to any of the matters mentioned in clause (*a*), jurisdiction and powers of all courts except the Supreme Court with respect to any of those matters, and fees in respect of any of those matters but not including fees taken in any court,

but any law made by Parliament, which Parliament would not but for the provisions of this article have been competent to make, shall, to the extent of the incompetency, cease to have effect on the expiration of the said period, except as respects things done or omitted to be done before the expiration thereof.

²*[370.   **Temporary provisions with respect to the State of Jammu**

---

1   Subs. by the Constitution (Thirteenth Amendment) Act, 1962, s. 2, for "TEMPORARY AND TRANSITIONAL PROVISIONS" (w.e.f. 1-12-1963).

2   In exercise of the powers conferred by clause (3) of article 370 read with clause (1) of article 370 of the Constitution of India, the President, on the recommendation of Parliament, is pleased to declare that, as from the 6th August, 2019 all clauses of said article 370 shall cease to be operative except the following which shall read as under, namely:—

and Kashmir.—(1) Notwithstanding anything in this Constitution,—

    (*a*) the provisions of article 238 shall not apply in relation to the State of Jammu and Kashmir;

    (*b*) the power of Parliament to make laws for the said State shall be limited to—

        (*i*) those matters in the Union List and the Concurrent List which, in consultation with the Government of the State, are declared by the President to correspond to matters specified in the Instrument of Accession governing the accession of the State to the Dominion of India as the matters with respect to which the Dominion Legislature may make laws for that State; and

        (*ii*) such other matters in the said Lists as, with the concurrence of the Government of the State, the President may by order specify.

    Explanation.—For the purposes of this article, the Government of the State means the person for the time being recognised by the President as the Maharaja of Jammu and Kashmir acting on the advice of the

---

"370. All provisions of this Constitution, as amended from time to time, without any modifications or exceptions, shall apply to the State of Jammu and Kashmir notwithstanding anything contrary contained in article 152 or article 308 or any other article of this Constitution or any other provision of the Constitution of Jammu and Kashmir or any law, document, judgment, ordinance, order, by-law, rule, regulation, notification, custom or usage having the force of law in the territory of India, or any other instrument, treaty or agreement as envisaged under article 363 or otherwise.".

[See Appendix III (C.O.273)].

* In exercise of the powers conferred by clause (3) of the Constitution of India, the President, on the recommendation of the Constituent Assembly of the State of Jammu and Kashmir, declared that, as from the 17th day of November, 1952, the said art. 370 shall be operative with the modification that for the *Explanation* in cl. (1) thereof, the following *Explanation* is substituted, namely:—

"*Explanation.*—For the purposes of this article, the Government of the State means the person for the time being recognised by the President on the recommendation of the Legislative Assembly of the State as the *Sadar-I Riyasat of Jammu and Kashmir, acting on the advice of the Council of Ministers of the State for the time being in office.".

(C.O. 44, dated the 15th November, 1952).

*Now "Governor".

Council of Ministers for the time being in office under the Maharaja's Proclamation dated the fifth day of March, 1948;

(*c*) the provisions of article 1 and of this article shall apply in relation to that State;

(*d*) such of the other provisions of this Constitution shall apply in relation to that State subject to such exceptions and modifications as the President may by order*[1] specify:

Provided that no such order which relates to the matters specified in the Instrument of Accession of the State referred to in paragraph (*i*) of sub-clause (*b*) shall be issued except in consultation with the Government of the State:

Provided further that no such order which relates to matters other than those referred to in the last preceding proviso shall be issued except with the concurrence of that Government.

(2) If the concurrence of the Government of the State referred to in paragraph (*ii*) of sub-clause (*b*) of clause (1) or in the second proviso to sub-clause (*d*) of that clause be given before the Constituent Assembly for the purpose of framing the Constitution of the State is convened, it shall be placed before such Assembly for such decision as it may take thereon.

(3) Notwithstanding anything in the foregoing provisions of this article, the President may, by public notification, declare that this article shall cease to be operative or shall be operative only with such exceptions and modifications and from such date as he may specify:

Provided that the recommendation of the Constituent Assembly of the State referred to in clause (2) shall be necessary before the President issues such a notification.

²[**371.** **Special provision with respect to the States of** ³ * * * **Maharashtra and Gujarat.**—⁴[(1)* * * * *]

---

* *See* the Constitution (Application to Jammu and Kashmir) Order, 2019 (C.O. 272) in Appendix II. The Constitution (Application to Jammu and Kashmir) Order, 1954 (C.O.48) stands superseded *vide* C.O.272 (w.e.f.5-8-2019).

2 Subs. by the Constitution (Seventh Amendment) Act, 1956, s. 22, for art. 371 (w.e.f. 1-11-1956).

3 The words "Andhra Pradesh", omitted by the Constitution (Thirty-second Amendment) Act, 1973, s. 2 (w.e.f. 1-7-1974).

4 Cl. (1) omitted by s. 2, *ibid.* (w.e.f. 1-7-1974).

(2) Notwithstanding anything in this Constitution, the President may by order made with respect to ¹[the State of Maharashtra or Gujarat], provide for any special responsibility of the Governor for—

(*a*) the establishment of separate development boards for Vidarbha, Marathwada, ²[and the rest of Maharashtra or, as the case may be], Saurashtra, Kutch and the rest of Gujarat with the provision that a report on the working of each of these boards will be placed each year before the State Legislative Assembly;

(*b*) the equitable allocation of funds for developmental expenditure over the said areas, subject to the requirements of the State as a whole; and

(*c*) an equitable arrangement providing adequate facilities for technical education and vocational training, and adequate opportunities for employment in services under the control of the State Government, in respect of all the said areas, subject to the requirements of the State as a whole.]

³[**371A. Special provision with respect to the State of Nagaland.**—(1) Notwithstanding anything in this Constitution,—

(*a*) no Act of Parliament in respect of—

(*i*) religious or social practices of the Nagas,

(*ii*) Naga customary law and procedure,

(*iii*) administration of civil and criminal justice involving decisions according to Naga customary law,

(*iv*) ownership and transfer of land and its resources,

shall apply to the State of Nagaland unless the Legislative Assembly of Nagaland by a resolution so decides;

(*b*) the Governor of Nagaland shall have special responsibility with respect to law and order in the

---

1 Subs. by the Bombay Reorganisation Act, 1960 (11 of 1960), s. 85, for "the State of Bombay" (w.e.f. 1-5-1960).

2 Subs. by s. 85, *ibid.*, for "the rest of Maharashtra" (w.e.f. 1-5-1960).

3 Art. 371A ins. by the Constitution (Thirteenth Amendment) Act, 1962, s. 2 (w.e.f. 1-12-1963).

State of Nagaland for so long as in his opinion internal disturbances occurring in the Naga Hills-Tuensang Area immediately before the formation of that State continue therein or in any part thereof and in the discharge of his functions in relation thereto the Governor shall, after consulting the Council of Ministers, exercise his individual judgment as to the action to be taken:

Provided that if any question arises whether any matter is or is not a matter as respects which the Governor is under this sub-clause required to act in the exercise of his individual judgment, the decision of the Governor in his discretion shall be final, and the validity of anything done by the Governor shall not be called in question on the ground that he ought or ought not to have acted in the exercise of his individual judgment:

Provided further that if the President on receipt of a report from the Governor or otherwise is satisfied that it is no longer necessary for the Governor to have special responsibility with respect to law and order in the State of Nagaland, he may by order direct that the Governor shall cease to have such responsibility with effect from such date as may be specified in the order;

(c) in making his recommendation with respect to any demand for a grant, the Governor of Nagaland shall ensure that any money provided by the Government of India out of the Consolidated Fund of India for any specific service or purpose is included in the demand for a grant relating to that service or purpose and not in any other demand;

(d) as from such date as the Governor of Nagaland may by public notification in this behalf specify, there shall be established a regional council for the Tuensang district consisting of thirty-five members and the Governor shall in his discretion make rules providing for—

(i) the composition of the regional council and the manner in which the members of the regional council shall be chosen:

283

Provided that the Deputy Commissioner of the Tuensang district shall be the Chairman *ex officio* of the regional council and the Vice-Chairman of the regional council shall be elected by the members thereof from amongst themselves;

(*ii*) the qualifications for being chosen as, and for being, members of the regional council;

(*iii*) the term of office of, and the salaries and allowances, if any, to be paid to members of, the regional council;

(*iv*) the procedure and conduct of business of the regional council;

(*v*) the appointment of officers and staff of the regional council and their conditions of services; and

(*vi*) any other matter in respect of which it is necessary to make rules for the constitution and proper functioning of the regional council.

(2) Notwithstanding anything in this Constitution, for a period of ten years from the date of the formation of the State of Nagaland or for such further period as the Governor may, on the recommendation of the regional council, by public notification specify in this behalf,—

(*a*) the administration of the Tuensang district shall be carried on by the Governor;

(*b*) where any money is provided by the Government of India to the Government of Nagaland to meet the requirements of the State of Nagaland as a whole, the Governor shall in his discretion arrange for an equitable allocation of that money between the Tuensang district and the rest of the State;

(*c*) no Act of the Legislature of Nagaland shall apply to Tuensang district unless the Governor, on the recommendation of the regional council, by public notification so directs and the Governor in giving such direction with respect to any such Act may direct that the Act shall in its application to the Tuensang district or any part thereof have effect subject to such exceptions or modifications as the Governor may specify on the recommendation of the regional council: Provided that any direction given under this sub-clause may be given so as to have retrospective effect;

(d) the Governor may make regulations for the peace, progress and good government of the Tuensang district and any regulations so made may repeal or amend with retrospective effect, if necessary, any Act of Parliament or any other law which is for the time being applicable to that district;

(e) (i) one of the members representing the Tuensang district in the Legislative Assembly of Nagaland shall be appointed Minister for Tuensang affairs by the Governor on the advice of the Chief Minister and the Chief Minister in tendering his advice shall act on the recommendation of the majority of the members as aforesaid[1];

(ii) the Minister for Tuensang affairs shall deal with, and have direct access to the Governor on, all matters relating to the Tuensang district but he shall keep the Chief Minister informed about the same;

(f) notwithstanding anything in the foregoing provisions of this clause, the final decision on all matters relating to the Tuensang district shall be made by the Governor in his discretion;

(g) in articles 54 and 55 and clause (4) of article 80, references to the elected members of the Legislative Assembly of a State or to each such member shall include references to the members or member of

---

1 Paragraph 2 of the Constitution (Removal of Difficulties) Order No. X provides (w.e.f. 1-12-1963) that article 371A of the Constitution of India shall have effect as if the following proviso were added to paragraph (i) of sub-clause (e) of clause (2) thereof, namely:—
"Provided that the Governor may, on the advice of the Chief Minister, appoint any person as Minister for Tuensang affairs to act as such until such time as persons are chosen in accordance with law to fill the seats allocated to the Tuensang district, in the Legislative Assembly of Nagaland.".

the Legislative Assembly of Nagaland elected by the regional council established under this article;

(b) in article 170—

(i) clause (1) shall, in relation to the Legislative Assembly of Nagaland, have effect as if for the word "sixty", the word "forty- six" had been substituted;

(ii) in the said clause, the reference to direct election from territorial constituencies in the State shall include election by the members of the regional council established under this article;

(iii) in clauses (2) and (3), references to territorial constituencies shall mean references to territorial constituencies in the Kohima and Mokokchung districts.

(3) If any difficulty arises in giving effect to any of the foregoing provisions of this article, the President may by order do anything (including any adaptation or modification of any other article) which appears to him to be necessary for the purpose of removing that difficulty:

Provided that no such order shall be made after the expiration of three years from the date of the formation of the State of Nagaland.

Explanation..—In this article, the Kohima, Mokokchung and Tuensang districts shall have the same meanings as in the State of Nagaland Act, 1962.]

[371B]. **Special provision with respect to the State of Assam.**— Notwithstanding anything in this Constitution, the President may, by order made with respect to the State of Assam, provide for the constitution and functions of a committee of the Legislative Assembly of the State consisting of members of that Assembly elected from the tribal areas specified in [2][Part I] of the table appended to paragraph 20 of the Sixth Schedule and such number of other members of that Assembly as may be

---

1 Art.371B ins. by the Constitution (Twenty-second Amendment) Act, 1969, s. 4 (w.e.f. 25-9-1969).
2 Subs. by the North-Eastern Areas (Reorganisation) Act, 1971 (81 of 1971), s. 71, for "Part A" (w.e.f. 21-1-1972).

specified in the order and for the modifications to be made in the rules of procedure of that Assembly for the constitution and proper functioning of such committee.]

¹[371C. **Special provision with respect to the State of Manipur.**—(1) Notwithstanding anything in this Constitution, the President may, by order made with respect to the State of Manipur, provide for the constitution and functions of a committee of the Legislative Assembly of the State consisting of members of that Assembly elected from the Hill Areas of that State, for the modifications to be made in the rules of business of the Government and in the rules of procedure of the Legislative Assembly of the State and for any special responsibility of the Governor in order to secure the proper functioning of such committee.

(2) The Governor shall annually, or whenever so required by the President, make a report to the President regarding the administration of the Hill Areas in the State of Manipur and the executive power of the Union shall extend to the giving of directions to the State as to the administration of the said areas.

Explanation.—In this article, the expression "Hill Areas" means such areas as the President may, by order, declare to be Hill areas.]

²[371D. **Special provisions with respect to ³[the State of Andhra Pradesh or the State of Telangana].**—⁴[(1) The President may by order made with respect to the State of Andhra Pradesh or the State of Telangana, provide, having regard to the requirement of each State, for equitable opportunities and facilities for the people belonging to different parts of such State, in the matter of public employment and in the matter of education, and different provisions may be made for various parts of the States.]

(2) An order made under clause (1) may, in particular,—

(*a*) require the State Government to organise any class or classes of posts in a civil service of, or any class

1 Art. 371C ins. by the Constitution (Twenty-seventh Amendment) Act, 1971, s. 5 (w.e.f. 15-2-1972).
2 Arts. 371D and 371E ins. by the Constitution (Thirty-second Amendment) Act, 1973, s. 3 (w.e.f. 1-7-1974).
3 Subs. by the Andhra Pradesh Reorganisation Act, 2014 (6 of 2014), s. 97, for "the State of Andhra Pradesh" (w.e.f. 2-6-2014).
4 Subs. by s. 97, *ibid.* for cl. (1) (w.e.f. 2-6-2014).

or classes of civil posts under, the State into different local cadres for different parts of the State and allot in accordance with such principles and procedure as may be specified in the order the persons holding such posts to the local cadres so organised;

(b) specify any part or parts of the State which shall be regarded as the local area—

(i) for direct recruitment to posts in any local cadre (whether organised in pursuance of an order under this article or constituted otherwise) under the State Government;

(ii) for direct recruitment to posts in any cadre under any local authority within the State; and

(iii) for the purposes of admission to any University within the State or to any other educational institution which is subject to the control of the State Government;

(c) specify the extent to which, the manner in which and the conditions subject to which, preference or reservation shall be given or made—

(i) in the matter of direct recruitment to posts in any such cadre referred to in sub-clause (b) as may be specified in this behalf in the order;

(ii) in the matter of admission to any such University or other educational institution referred to in sub-clause (b) as may be specified in this behalf in the order,

to or in favour of candidates who have resided or studied for any period specified in the order in the local area in respect of such cadre, University or other educational institution, as the case may be.

(3) The President may, by order, provide for the constitution of an Administrative Tribunal for ¹[the State of Andhra Pradesh and for the State of Telangana] to exercise such jurisdiction,

---

1 Subs. by the Andhra Pradesh Reorganisation Act, 2014 (6 of 2014), s. 97, for "the State of Andhra Pradesh" (w.e.f. 2-6-2014).

powers and authority [including any jurisdiction, power and authority which immediately before the commencement of the Constitution (Thirty-second Amendment) Act, 1973, was exercisable by any court (other than the Supreme Court) or by any tribunal or other authority] as may be specified in the order with respect to the following matters, namely:—

(a) appointment, allotment or promotion to such class or classes of posts in any civil service of the State, or to such class or classes of civil posts under the State, or to such class or classes of posts under the control of any local authority within the State, as may be specified in the order;

(b) seniority of persons appointed, allotted or promoted to such class or classes of posts in any civil service of the State, or to such class or classes of civil posts under the State, or to such class or classes of posts under the control of any local authority within the State, as may be specified in the order;

(c) such other conditions of service of persons appointed, allotted or promoted to such class or classes of posts in any civil service of the State or to such class or classes of civil posts under the State or to such class or classes of posts under the control of any local authority within the State, as may be specified in the order.

(4) An order made under clause (3) may—

(a) authorise the Administrative Tribunal to receive representations for the redress of grievances relating to any matter within its jurisdiction as the President may specify in the order and to make such orders thereon as the Administrative Tribunal deems fit;

(b) contain such provisions with respect to the powers and authorities and procedure of the Administrative Tribunal (including provisions with respect to the powers of the Administrative Tribunal to punish for contempt of itself) as the President may deem necessary;

(c) provide for the transfer to the Administrative Tribunal of such classes of proceedings, being proceedings relating

289

to matters within its jurisdiction and pending before any court (other than the Supreme Court) or tribunal or other authority immediately before the commencement of such order, as may be specified in the order;

(d) contain such supplemental, incidental and consequential provisions (including provisions as to fees and as to limitation, evidence or for the application of any law for the time being in force subject to any exceptions or modifications) as the President may deem necessary.

*(5) The Order of the Administrative Tribunal finally disposing of any case shall become effective upon its confirmation by the State Government or on the expiry of three months from the date on which the order is made, whichever is earlier:

Provided that the State Government may, by special order made in writing and for reasons to be specified therein, modify or annul any order of the Administrative Tribunal before it becomes effective and in such a case, the order of the Administrative Tribunal shall have effect only in such modified form or be of no effect, as the case may be.

(6) Every special order made by the State Government under the proviso to clause (5) shall be laid, as soon as may be after it is made, before both Houses of the State Legislature.

(7) The High Court for the State shall not have any powers of superintendence over the Administrative Tribunal and no court (other than the Supreme Court) or tribunal shall exercise any jurisdiction, power or authority in respect of any matter subject to the jurisdiction, power or authority of, or in relation to, the Administrative Tribunal.

(8) If the President is satisfied that the continued existence of the Administrative Tribunal is not necessary, the President may by order abolish the Administrative Tribunal and make such provisions in such order as he may deem fit for the transfer and disposal of cases pending before the Tribunal immediately before such abolition.

---

* In P. Sambamurthy and Others Vs. State of Andhra Pradesh and Others (1987) 1 S.C.C. 362, the Supreme Court declared cl. (5) of art. 371D along with the proviso to be unconstitutional and void.

(9) Notwithstanding any judgment, decree or order of any court, tribunal or other authority,—

    (*a*)   no appointment, posting, promotion or transfer of any person—

        (*i*)   made before the 1st day of November, 1956, to any post under the Government of, or any local authority within, the State of Hyderabad as it existed before that date; or

        (*ii*) made before the commencement of the Constitution (Thirty-second Amendment) Act, 1973, to any post under the Government of, or any local or other authority within, the State of Andhra Pradesh; and

    (*b*)   no action taken or thing done by or before any person referred to in sub-clause (*a*),

shall be deemed to be illegal or void or ever to have become illegal or void merely on the ground that the appointment, posting, promotion or transfer of such person was not made in accordance with any law, then in force, providing for any requirement as to residence within the State of Hyderabad or, as the case may be, within any part of the State of Andhra Pradesh, in respect of such appointment, posting, promotion or transfer.

(10) The provisions of this article and of any order made by the President thereunder shall have effect notwithstanding anything in any other provision of this Constitution or in any other law for the time being in force.

371E.   **Establishment of Central University in Andhra Pradesh.**— Parliament may by law provide for the establishment of a University in the State of Andhra Pradesh.]

[371F.]   **Special provisions with respect to the State of Sikkim.**— Notwithstanding anything in this Constitution,—

    (*a*)   the Legislative Assembly of the State of Sikkim shall consist of not less than thirty members;

    (*b*)   as from the date of commencement of the Constitution (Thirty- sixth Amendment) Act, 1975 (hereafter in this article referred to as the appointed day)—

---

1   Art. 371 ins. by the Constitution (Thirty-sixth Amendment) Act, 1975, s. 3 (w.e.f. 26-4-1975).

(*i*) the Assembly for Sikkim formed as a result of the elections held in Sikkim in April, 1974 with thirty-two members elected in the said elections (hereinafter referred to as the sitting members) shall be deemed to be the Legislative Assembly of the State of Sikkim duly constituted under this Constitution;

(*ii*) the sitting members shall be deemed to be the members of the Legislative Assembly of the State of Sikkim duly elected under this Constitution; and

(*iii*) the said Legislative Assembly of the State of Sikkim shall exercise the powers and perform the functions of the Legislative Assembly of a State under this Constitution;

(*c*) in the case of the Assembly deemed to be the Legislative Assembly of the State of Sikkim under clause (*b*), the references to the period of ¹[five years], in clause (1) of article 172 shall be construed as references to a period of ²[four years] and the said period of 2[four years] shall be deemed to commence from the appointed day;

(*d*) until other provisions are made by Parliament by law, there shall be allotted to the State of Sikkim one seat in the House of the People and the State of Sikkim shall form one parliamentary constituency to be called the parliamentary constituency for Sikkim;

(*e*) the representative of the State of Sikkim in the House of the People in existence on the appointed day shall be elected by the members of the Legislative Assembly of the State of Sikkim;

(*f*) Parliament may, for the purpose of protecting the rights and interests of the different sections of the population of Sikkim make provision for the number

---

1 Subs. by the Constitution (Forty-second Amendment) Act, 1976, s. 56, for "five years (w.e.f. 3-1-1977) and further subs. by the Constitution (Forty-fourth Amendment) Act, 1978, s. 43, for "six years" (w.e.f. 6-9-1979).

2 Subs. by s. 56, *ibid.*, for "four years" (w.e.f. 3-1-1977) and further subs. by s. 43, *ibid.*, for "five years", respectively (w.e.f. 6-9-1979).

of seats in the Legislative Assembly of the State of Sikkim which may be filled by candidates belonging to such sections and for the delimitation of the assembly constituencies from which candidates belonging to such sections alone may stand for election to the Legislative Assembly of the State of Sikkim;

(g) the Governor of Sikkim shall have special responsibility for peace and for an equitable arrangement for ensuring the social and economic advancement of different sections of the population of Sikkim and in the discharge of his special responsibility under this clause, the Governor of Sikkim shall, subject to such directions as the President may, from time to time, deem fit to issue, act in his discretion;

(h) all property and assets (whether within or outside the territories comprised in the State of Sikkim) which immediately before the appointed day were vested in the Government of Sikkim or in any other authority or in any person for the purposes of the Government of Sikkim shall, as from the appointed day, vest in the Government of the State of Sikkim;

(i) the High Court functioning as such immediately before the appointed day in the territories comprised in the State of Sikkim shall, on and from the appointed day, be deemed to be the High Court for the State of Sikkim;

(j) all courts of civil, criminal and revenue jurisdiction, all authorities and all officers, judicial, executive and ministerial, throughout the territory of the State of Sikkim shall continue on and from the appointed day to exercise their respective functions subject to the provisions of this Constitution;

(k) all laws in force immediately before the appointed day in the territories comprised in the State of Sikkim or any part thereof shall continue to be in force therein until amended or repealed by a competent Legislature or other competent authority;

(*l*) for the purpose of facilitating the application of any such law as is referred to in clause (*k*) in relation to the administration of the State of Sikkim and for the purpose of bringing the provisions of any such law into accord with the provisions of this Constitution, the President may, within two years from the appointed day, by order, make such adaptations and modifications of the law, whether by way of repeal or amendment, as may be necessary or expedient, and thereupon, every such law shall have effect subject to the adaptations and modifications so made, and any such adaptation or modification shall not be questioned in any court of law;

(*m*) neither the Supreme Court nor any other court shall have jurisdiction in respect of any dispute or other matter arising out of any treaty, agreement, engagement or other similar instrument relating to Sikkim which was entered into or executed before the appointed day and to which the Government of India or any of its predecessor Governments was a party, but nothing in this clause shall be construed to derogate from the provisions of article 143;

(*n*) the President may, by public notification, extend with such restrictions or modifications as he thinks fit to the State of Sikkim any enactment which is in force in a State in India at the date of the notification;

(*o*) if any difficulty arises in giving effect to any of the foregoing provisions of this article, the President may, by order,* do anything (including any adaptation or modification of any other article) which appears to him to be necessary for the purpose of removing that difficulty: Provided that no such order shall be made after the expiry of two years from the appointed day;

(*p*) all things done and all actions taken in or in relation to the State of Sikkim or the territories comprised therein during the period commencing on the appointed day

---

*   *See* the Constitution (Removal of Difficulties) Order No. XI (C.O. 99).

and ending immediately before the date on which the Constitution (Thirty-sixth Amendment) Act, 1975, receives the assent of the President shall, in so far as they are in conformity with the provisions of this Constitution as amended by the Constitution (Thirty-sixth Amendment) Act, 1975, be deemed for all purposes to have been validly done or taken under this Constitution as so amended.]

[1][**371G. Special provision with respect to the State of Mizoram.**— Notwithstanding anything in this Constitution,—

    (*a*)   no Act of Parliament in respect of—

        (*i*)   religious or social practices of the Mizos,

        (*ii*) Mizo customary law and procedure,

        (*iii*) administration of civil and criminal justice involving decisions according to Mizo customary law,

        (*iv*) ownership and transfer of land,

shall apply to the State of Mizoram unless the Legislative Assembly of the State of Mizoram by a resolution so decides:

Provided that nothing in this clause shall apply to any Central Act in force in the Union territory of Mizoram immediately before the commencement of the Constitution (Fifty-third Amendment) Act, 1986;

    (*b*)   the Legislative Assembly of the State of Mizoram shall consist of not less than forty members.]

[2][**371H. Special provision with respect to the State of Arunachal Pradesh.**—Notwithstanding anything in this Constitution,—

    (*a*)   the Governor of Arunachal Pradesh shall have special responsibility with respect to law and order in the State of Arunachal Pradesh and in the discharge of his functions in relation thereto, the Governor shall, after consulting the Council of Ministers, exercise his individual judgment as to the action to be taken:

---

1 Art. 371G ins. by the Constitution (Fifty-third Amendment) Act, 1986.s. 2 (w.e.f. 20-2-1987).
2 Art. 371H ins. by the Constitution (Fifty-fifth Amendment) Act, 1986, s. 2 (w.e.f. 20-2-1987).

Provided that if any question arises whether any matter is or is not a matter as respects which the Governor is under this clause required to act in the exercise of his individual judgment, the decision of the Governor in his discretion shall be final, and the validity of anything done by the Governor shall not be called in question on the ground that he ought or ought not to have acted in the exercise of his individual judgment:

Provided further that if the President on receipt of a report from the Governor or otherwise is satisfied that it is no longer necessary for the Governor to have special responsibility with respect to law and order in the State of Arunachal Pradesh, he may by order direct that the Governor shall cease to have such responsibility with effect from such date as may be specified in the order;

(b) the Legislative Assembly of the State of Arunachal Pradesh shall consist of not less than thirty members.]

[1][371-I. **Special provision with respect to the State of Goa.**— Notwithstanding anything in this Constitution, the Legislative Assembly of the State of Goa shall consist of not less than thirty members.]

[2][371J. **Special provisions with respect to the State of Karnataka.**— (1) The President may, by order made with respect to the State of Karnataka, provide for any special responsibility of the Governor for—

(a) establishment of a separate development board for Hyderabad-Karnataka region with the provision that a report on the working of the board will be placed each year before the State Legislative Assembly;

(b) equitable allocation of funds for developmental expenditure over the said region, subject to the requirements of the State as a whole; and

(c) equitable opportunities and facilities for the people belonging to the said region, in matters of public

---

1 Art.37-I ins. by the Constitution (Fifty-sixth Amendment) Act, 1987, s. 2 (w.e.f. 30-5-1987).
2 Art.371J ins. by the Constitution (Ninety-eighth Amendment) Act, 2012, s. 2 (w.e.f. 1-10-2013).

employment, education and vocational training, subject to the requirements of the State as a whole.

(2) An order made under sub-clause (*c*) of clause (1) may provide for—

    (*a*) reservation of a proportion of seats educational and vocational training institutions in the Hyderabad-Karnataka region for students who belong to that region by birth or by domicile; and

    (*b*) identification of posts or classes of posts under the State Government and in any body or organisation under the control of the State Government in the Hyderabad-Karnataka region and reservation of a proportion of such posts for persons who belong to that region by birth or by domicile and for appointment thereto by direct recruitment or by promotion or in any other manner as may be specified in the order.]

372. Continuance in force of existing laws and their adaptation.— (1) Notwithstanding the repeal by this Constitution of the enactments referred to in article 395 but subject to the other provisions of this Constitution, all the law in force in the territory of India immediately before the commencement of this Constitution shall continue in force therein until altered or repealed or amended by a competent Legislature or other competent authority.

(2) For the purpose of bringing the provisions of any law in force in the territory of India into accord with the provisions of this Constitution, the President may by order* make such adaptations and modifications of such law, whether by way of repeal or amendment, as may be necessary or expedient, and provide

---

* See the Adaptation of Laws Order, 1950, dated the 26th January, 1950, Gazette of India, Extraordinary, p. 449, as amended by notification No. S.R.O. 115, dated the 5th June, 1950, Gazette of India, Extraordinary, Part II, Section 3, p. 51, notification No. S.R.O. 870, dated the 4th November, 1950, Gazette of India, Extraordinary, Part II, Section 3, p. 903, notification No. S.R.O. 508, dated the 4th April, 1951, Gazette of India, Extraordinary, Part II, Section 3, p. 287, notification No. S.R.O. 1140B, dated the 2nd July, 1952, Gazette of India, Extraordinary, Part II, Section 3, p. 616/1, and the Adaptation of the Travancore-Cochin Land Acquisition Laws Order, 1952, dated the 20th November, 1952, Gazette of India, Extraordinary, Part II, Section 3, p. 923.

that the law shall, as from such date as may be specified in the order, have effect subject to the adaptations and modifications so made, and any such adaptation or modification shall not be questioned in any court of law.

(3) Nothing in clause (2) shall be deemed—

(a) to empower the President to make any adaptation or modification of any law after the expiration of [1][three years] from the commencement of this Constitution; or

(b) to prevent any competent Legislature or other competent authority from repealing or amending any law adapted or modified by the President under the said clause.

Explanation I.—The expression "law in force" in this article shall include a law passed or made by a Legislature or other competent authority in the territory of India before the commencement of this Constitution and not previously repealed, notwithstanding that it or parts of it may not be then in operation either at all or in particular areas.

Explanation II.—Any law passed or made by a Legislature or other competent authority in the territory of India which immediately before the commencement of this Constitution had extra-territorial effect as well as effect in the territory of India shall, subject to any such adaptations and modifications as aforesaid, continue to have such extra-territorial effect.

Explanation III.—Nothing in this article shall be construed as continuing any temporary law in force beyond the date fixed for its expiration or the date on which it would have expired if this Constitution had not come into force.

Explanation IV.—An Ordinance promulgated by the Governor of a Province under section 88 of the Government of India Act, 1935, and in force immediately before the commencement of this Constitution shall, unless withdrawn by the Governor of the corresponding State earlier, cease to operate at the expiration of six weeks from the first meeting after such commencement of

---

1 Subs. by the Constitution (First Amendment) Act, 1951, s. 12 for "two years" (w.e.f. 18-6-1951).

the Legislative Assembly of that State functioning under clause (1) of article 382, and nothing in this article shall be construed as continuing any such Ordinance in force beyond the said period.

¹[**372A.** **Power of the President to adapt laws.**—(1) For the purposes of bringing the provisions of any law in force in India or in any part thereof, immediately before the commencement of the Constitution (Seventh Amendment) Act, 1956, into accord with the provisions of this Constitution as amended by that Act, the President may by order* made before the first day of November, 1957, make such adaptations and modifications of the law, whether by way of repeal or amendment, as may be necessary or expedient, and provide that the law shall, as from such date as may be specified in the order, have effect subject to the adaptations and modifications so made, and any such adaptation or modification shall not be questioned in any court of law.

(2) Nothing in clause (1) shall be deemed to prevent a competent Legislature or other competent authority from repealing or amending any law adapted or modified by the President under the said clause.]

373. **Power of President to make order in respect of persons under preventive detention in certain cases.**—Until provision is made by Parliament under clause (7) of article 22, or until the expiration of one year from the commencement of this Constitution, whichever is earlier, the said article shall have effect as if for any reference to Parliament in clauses (4) and (7) thereof there were substituted a reference to the President and for any reference to any law made by Parliament in those clauses there were substituted a reference to an order made by the President.

374. **Provisions as to Judges of the Federal Court and proceedings pending in the Federal Court or before His Majesty in Council.**—(1) The Judges of the Federal Court holding office immediately before the commencement of this Constitution shall, unless they have elected otherwise, become

---

1 Art. 372A ins. by the Constitution (Seventh Amendment) Act, 1956, s. 23 (w.e.f. 1-11-1956).
* *See* the Adaptation of Laws Order of 1956 and 1957.

on such commencement the Judges of the Supreme Court and shall thereupon be entitled to such salaries and allowances and to such rights in respect of leave of absence and pension as are provided for under article 125 in respect of the Judges of the Supreme Court.

(2) All suits, appeals and proceedings, civil or criminal, pending in the Federal Court at the commencement of this Constitution shall stand removed to the Supreme Court, and the Supreme Court shall have jurisdiction to hear and determine the same, and the judgments and orders of the Federal Court delivered or made before the commencement of this Constitution shall have the same force and effect as if they had been delivered or made by the Supreme Court.

(3) Nothing in this Constitution shall operate to invalidate the exercise of jurisdiction by His Majesty in Council to dispose of appeals and petitions from, or in respect of, any judgment, decree or order of any court within the territory of India in so far as the exercise of such jurisdiction is authorised by law, and any order of His Majesty in Council made on any such appeal or petition after the commencement of this Constitution shall for all purposes have effect as if it were an order or decree made by the Supreme Court in the exercise of the jurisdiction conferred on such Court by this Constitution.

(4) On and from the commencement of this Constitution the jurisdiction of the authority functioning as the Privy Council in a State specified in Part B of the First Schedule to entertain and dispose of appeals and petitions from or in respect of any judgment, decree or order of any court within that State shall cease, and all appeals and other proceedings pending before the said authority at such commencement shall be transferred to, and disposed of by, the Supreme Court.

(5) Further provision may be made by Parliament by law to give effect to the provisions of this article.

375. **Courts, authorities and officers to continue to function subject to the provisions of the Constitution.**—All courts of civil, criminal and revenue jurisdiction, all authorities and all officers, judicial, executive and ministerial, throughout the

territory of India, shall continue to exercise their respective functions subject to the provisions of this Constitution.

376. **Provisions as to Judges of High Courts.**—(1) Notwithstanding anything in clause (2) of article 217, the Judges of a High Court in any Province holding office immediately before the commencement of this Constitution shall, unless they have elected otherwise, become on such commencement the Judges of the High Court in the corresponding State, and shall thereupon be entitled to such salaries and allowances and to such rights in respect of leave of absence and pension as are provided for under article 221 in respect of the Judges of such High Court. [1][Any such Judge shall, notwithstanding that he is not a citizen of India, be eligible for appointment as Chief Justice of such High Court, or as Chief Justice or other Judge of any other High Court.]

(2) The Judges of a High Court in any Indian State corresponding to any State specified in Part B of the First Schedule holding office immediately before the commencement of this Constitution shall, unless they have elected otherwise, become on such commencement the Judges of the High Court in the State so specified and shall, notwithstanding anything in clauses (1) and (2) of article 217 but subject to the proviso to clause (1) of that article, continue to hold office until the expiration of such period as the President may by order determine.

(3) In this article, the expression "Judge" does not include an acting Judge or an additional Judge.

377. **Provisions as to Comptroller and Auditor-General of India.**— The Auditor-General of India holding office immediately before the commencement of this Constitution shall, unless he has elected otherwise, become on such commencement the Comptroller and Auditor-General of India and shall thereupon be entitled to such salaries and to such rights in respect of leave of absence and pension as are provided for under clause (3) of article 148 in respect of the Comptroller and Auditor-General of India and be entitled to continue to hold office until the expiration of his term of office as determined under the

---

1 Added by the Constitution (First Amendment) Act, 1951, s. 13 (w.e.f. 18-6-1951).

provisions which were applicable to him immediately before such commencement.

378. Provisions as to Public Service Commissions.—(1) The members of the Public Service Commission for the Dominion of India holding office immediately before the commencement of this Constitution shall, unless they have elected otherwise, become on such commencement the members of the Public Service Commission for the Union and shall, notwithstanding anything in clauses (1) and (2) of article 316 but subject to the proviso to clause (2) of that article, continue to hold office until the expiration of their term of office as determined under the rules which were applicable immediately before such commencement to such members.

(2) The Members of a Public Service Commission of a Province or of a Public Service Commission serving the needs of a group of Provinces holding office immediately before the commencement of this Constitution shall, unless they have elected otherwise, become on such commencement the members of the Public Service Commission for the corresponding State or the members of the Joint State Public Service Commission serving the needs of the corresponding States, as the case may be, and shall, notwithstanding anything in clauses (1) and (2) of article 316 but subject to the proviso to clause (2) of that article, continue to hold office until the expiration of their term of office as determined under the rules which were applicable immediately before such commencement to such members.

¹**[378A. Special provision as to duration of Andhra Pradesh Legislative Assembly.**—Notwithstanding anything contained in article 172, the Legislative Assembly of the State of Andhra Pradesh as constituted under the provisions of sections 28 and 29 of the States Reorganisation Act, 1956, shall, unless sooner dissolved, continue for a period of five years from the date referred to in the said section 29 and no longer and the expiration of the said period shall operate as a dissolution of that Legislative Assembly.]

---

1 Art. 378A ins. by the Constitution (Seventh Amendment) Act, 1956, s. 24 (w.e.f. 1-11-1956).

379.   *[Provisions as to provisional Parliament and the Speaker and Deputy Speaker thereof.].—Omitted by the Constitution (Seventh Amendment) Act, 1956, s. 29 and Sch. (w.e.f. 1-11-1956).*

380.   *[Provision as to President.].—Omitted by the Constitution (Seventh Amendment) Act, 1956, s. 29 and Sch. (w.e.f. 1-11-1956).*

381.   *[Council of Ministers of the President.].—Omitted by the Constitution (Seventh Amendment) Act, 1956, s. 29 and Sch. (w.e.f. 1-11-1956).*

382.   *[Provisions as to provisional Legislatures for States in Part A of the First Schedule.].—Omitted by the Constitution (Seventh Amendment) Act, 1956, s. 29 and Sch. (w.e.f. 1-11-1956).*

383.   *[Provision as to Governors of Provinces.].—Omitted by the Constitution (Seventh Amendment) Act, 1956, s. 29 and Sch. (w.e.f. 1-11-1956).*

384.   *[Council of Ministers of the Governors.].—Omitted by the Constitution (Seventh Amendment) Act, 1956, s. 29 and Sch. (w.e.f. 1-11-1956).*

385.   *[Provision as to provisional Legislatures in States in Part B of the First Schedule.].—Omitted by the Constitution (Seventh Amendment) Act, 1956, s. 29 and Sch. (w.e.f. 1-11-1956).*

386.   *[Council of Ministers for States in Part B of the First Schedule.].— Omitted by the Constitution (Seventh Amendment) Act, 1956, s. 29 and Sch. (w.e.f. 1-11-1956).*

387.   *[Special provision as to determination of population for the purposes of certain elections.].—Omitted by the Constitution (Seventh Amendment) Act, 1956, s. 29 and Sch. (w.e.f. 1-11-1956).*

388.   *[Provisions as to the filling of casual vacancies in the provisional Parliament and provisional Legislatures of the States.].—Omitted by the Constitution (Seventh Amendment) Act, 1956, s. 29 and Sch. (w.e.f. 1-11-1956).*

389.   *[Provision as to Bills pending in the Dominion Legislatures and in the Legislatures of Provinces and Indian States.] Omitted by the Constitution (Seventh Amendment) Act, 1956, s. 29 and Sch. (w.e.f. 1-11-1956).*

390.   *[Money received or raised or expenditure incurred between the commencement of the Constitution and the 31st day of March, 1950.]—Omitted by the Constitution (Seventh Amendment) Act, 1956, s. 29 and Sch. (w.e.f. 1-11-1956).*

391.   *[Power of the President to amend the First and Fourth Schedules in certain contingencies.].—Omitted by the Constitution (Seventh Amendment) Act, 1956, s. 29 and Sch. (w.e.f. 1-11-1956).*

392. **Power of the President to remove difficulties.**—(1) The President may, for the purpose of removing any difficulties, particularly in relation to the transition from the provisions of the Government of India Act, 1935, to the provisions of this Constitution, by order direct that this Constitution shall, during such period as may be specified in the order, have effect subject to such adaptations, whether by way of modification, addition or omission, as he may deem to be necessary or expedient:

Provided that no such order shall be made after the first meeting of Parliament duly constituted under Chapter II of Part V.

(2) Every order made under clause (1) shall be laid before Parliament.

(3) The powers conferred on the President by this article, by article 324, by clause (3) of article 367 and by article 391 shall, before the commencement of this Constitution, be exercisable by the Governor-General of the Dominion of India.

PART XXII

SHORT TITLE, COMMENCEMENT, [AUTHORITATIVE TEXT IN HINDI] AND REPEALS

393. **Short title.**—This Constitution may be called the Constitution of India.

394. **Commencement.**—This article and articles 5, 6, 7, 8, 9, 60, 324, 366, 367, 379, 380, 388, 391, 392 and 393 shall come into force at once, and the remaining provisions of this Constitution shall come into force on the twenty-sixth day of January, 1950, which day is referred to in this Constitution as the commencement of this Constitution.

²[394A. **Authoritative text in the Hindi language.**—(1) The President shall cause to be published under his authority,—

---

1 Ins. by the Constitution (Fifty-eighth Amendment) Act, 1987, s. 2 (w.e.f. 9-12-1987).
2 Art. 394A ins. by s. 3, *ibid.* (w.e.f. 9-12-1987).

(a) the translation of this Constitution in the Hindi language, signed by the members of the Constituent Assembly, with such modifications as may be necessary to bring it in conformity with the language, style and terminology adopted in the authoritative texts of Central Acts in the Hindi language, and incorporating therein all the amendments of this Constitution made before such publication; and

(b) the translation in the Hindi language of every amendment of this Constitution made in the English language.

(2) The translation of this Constitution and of every amendment thereof published under clause (1) shall be construed to have the same meaning as the original thereof and if any difficulty arises in so construing any part of such translation, the President shall cause the same to be revised suitably.

(3) The translation of this Constitution and of every amendment thereof published under this article shall be deemed to be, for all purposes, the authoritative text thereof in the Hindi language.]

395. **Repeals.**—The Indian Independence Act, 1947, and the Government of India Act, 1935, together with all enactments amending or supplementing the latter Act, but not including the Abolition of Privy Council Jurisdiction Act, 1949, are hereby repealed.

¹FIRST SCHEDULE

[Articles 1 and 4]

I. THE STATES	
Name	*Territories*
1. Andhra Pradesh	²[The territories specified in sub-section (1) of section 3 of the Andhra State Act, 1953, sub-section (1) of section 3 of the States Reorganisation Act, 1956, the First Schedule to the Andhra Pradesh and Madras (Alteration of Boundaries) Act, 1959, and the Schedule to the Andhra Pradesh and Mysore (Transfer of Territory) Act, 1968, but excluding the territories specified in the Second Schedule to the Andhra Pradesh and Madras (Alteration of Boundaries) Act, 1959] ³[and the territories specified in section 3 of the Andhra Pradesh Reorganisation Act, 2014].
2. Assam	The territories which immediately before the commencement of this Constitution were comprised in the Province of Assam, the Khasi States and the Assam Tribal Areas, but excluding the territories specified in the Schedule to the Assam (Alteration of Boundaries) Act, 1951 ⁴[and the territories specified in sub-section (1) of section 3 of the State of Nagaland Act, 1962] ⁵[and the territories specified in sections 5, 6 and 7 of the North- Eastern Areas (Reorganisation) Act, 1971] ⁶[and the territories referred to in Part I of the Second Schedule to the Constitution (One Hundredth Amendment) Act, 2015, notwithstanding anything contained in clause (a) of section 3 of the Constitution (Ninth Amendment) Act, 1960, so far as it relates to the territories referred to in Part I of the Second Schedule to the Constitution (One Hundredth Amendment) Act, 2015.]

---

1 Subs. by the Constitution (Seventh Amendment) Act, 1956, s. 2, for the First Sch. (w.e.f. 1-11-1956).
2 Subs. by the Andhra Pradesh and Mysore (Transfer of Territory) Act, 1968 (36 of 1968), s. 4, for the former entry (w.e.f. 1-10-1968).
3 Ins. by the Andhra Pradesh Reorganisation Act, 2014 (6 of 2014), s. 10 (w.e.f. 2-6-2014).
4 Added by the State of Nagaland Act, 1962 (27 of 1962), s. 4 (w.e.f. 1-12-1963).
5 Added by the North-Eastern Areas (Reorganisation) Act, 1971 (81 of 1971), s. 9 (w.e.f. 21-1-1972).
6 Added by the Constitution (One Hundredth Amendment) Act, 2015, s. 3 (w.e.f. 31-7-2015). For the text of the Act, see Appendix I.

3. Bihar	[1][The territories which immediately before the commencement of this Constitution were either comprised in the Province of Bihar or were being administered as if they formed part of that Province and the territories specified in clause (*a*) of sub-section (1) of section 3 of the Bihar and Uttar Pradesh (Alteration of Boundaries) Act, 1968, but excluding the territories specified in sub-section (1) of section 3 of the Bihar and West Bengal (Transfer of Territories) Act, 1956, and the territories specified in clause (*b*) of sub-section (1) of section 3 of the first mentioned Act [2][and the territories specified in section 3 of the Bihar Reorganisation Act, 2000].]
[3][4. Gujarat	The territories referred to in sub-section (1) of section 3 of the Bombay Reorganisation Act, 1960.]
5. Kerala	The territories specified in sub-section (1) of section 5 of the States Reorganisation Act, 1956.
6. Madhya Pradesh	The territories specified in sub-section (1) of section 9 of the States Reorganisation Act, 1956 [4][and the First Schedule to the Rajasthan and Madhya Pradesh (Transfer of Territories) Act, 1959], [5][but excluding the territories specified in section 3 of the Madhya Pradesh Reorganisation Act, 2000.]
[6][7. Tamil Nadu]	The territories which immediately before the commencement of this Constitution were either comprised in the Province of Madras or were being administered as if they formed part of that Province and the territories specified in section 4 of the States Reorganisation Act, 1956, [7][and the Second Schedule to the Andhra Pradesh and Madras (Alteration of Boundaries) Act, 1959], but excluding the territories specified in sub-section (1) of section 3 and sub-section (1) of section 4 of the Andhra State Act, 1953 and [8][the territories specified in clause (b) of sub-section (1) of section 5, section 6 and clause (d) of sub-section (1) of section 7 of the States Reorganisation Act, 1956 and the territories specified in the First Schedule to the Andhra Pradesh and Madras (Alteration of Boundaries) Act, 1959.]

---

1 Subs. by the Bihar and Uttar Pradesh (Alteration of Boundaries) Act, 1968 (24 of 1968), s. 4, for the former entry (w.e.f. 10-6-1970).
2 Added by the Bihar Reorganisation Act, 2000 (30 of 2000), s. 5 (w.e.f. 15-11-2000).
3 Subs. by the Bombay Reorganisation Act, 1960 (11 of 1960), s. 4 (w.e.f. 1-5-1960).
4 Ins. by the Rajasthan and Madhya Pradesh (Transfer of Territories) Act, 1959 (47 of 1959), s. 4 (w.e.f. 1-10-1959).
5 Added by the Madhya Pradesh Reorganisation Act, 2000 (28 of 2000), s. 5 (w.e.f. 1-11-2000).
6 Subs. by the Madras State (Alteration of Name) Act, 1968 (53 of 1968), s. 5, for "7. Madras" (w.e.f. 14-1-1969).
7 Ins. by the Andhra Pradesh and Madras (Alteration of Boundaries) Act, 1959 (56 of 1959), s. 6 (w.e.f. 1-4-1960).
8 Subs. by s. 6, *ibid.*, for certain words (w.e.f. 1-4-1960).

[1][8. Maharashtra	The territories specified in sub-section (1) of section 8 of the States Reorganisation Act, 1956, but excluding the territories referred to in sub-section (1) of section 3 of the Bombay Reorganisation Act, 1960.]
[2][[3][9.] Karnataka]	The territories specified in sub-section (1) of section 7 of the States Reorganisation Act, 1956 [4][but excluding the territory specified in the Schedule to the Andhra Pradesh and Mysore (Transfer of Territory) Act, 1968.]
[5][10.] [6][Odisha]	The territories which immediately before the commencement of this Constitution were either comprised in the Province of Orissa or were being administered as if they formed part of that Province.
[1][11.] Punjab	The territories specified in section 11 of the States Reorganisation Act, 1956 [7][and the territories referred to in Part II of the First Schedule to the Acquired Territories (Merger) Act, 1960] [8][but excluding the territories referred to in Part II of the First Schedule to the Constitution (Ninth Amendment) Act, 1960] [9][and the territories specified in sub-section (1) of section 3, section 4 and sub-section (1) of section 5 of the Punjab Reorganisation Act, 1966.]
[1][12.] Rajasthan	The territories specified in section 10 of the States Reorganisation Act, 1956 [10][but excluding the territories specified in the First Schedule to the Rajasthan and Madhya Pradesh (Transfer of Territories) Act, 1959].

---

1 Ins. by the Bombay Reorganisation Act, 1960 (11 of 1960), s. 4 (w.e.f. 1-5-1960).

2 Subs. by the Mysore State (Alteration of Name) Act, 1973 (31 of 1973), s. 5, for "9. Mysore" (w.e.f. 1-11-1973).

3 Entries 8 to 14 renumbered as entries 9 to 15 by the Bombay Reorganisation Act, 1960 (11 of 1960), s. 4 (w.e.f. 1-5-1960).

4 Ins. by the Andhra Pradesh and Mysore (Transfer of Territory) Act, 1968 (36 of 1968), s. 4 (w.e.f. 1-10-1968).

5 Entries 8 to 14 renumbered as entries 9 to 15 by the Bombay Reorganisation Act, 1960 (11 of 1960), s. 4 (w.e.f. 1-5-1960).

6 Subs. by the Orissa (Alteration of Name) Act, 2011 (15 of 2011), s. 6, for "Orissa" (w.e.f. 1-11-2011).

7 Ins. by the Acquired Territories (Merger) Act, 1960 (64 of 1960), s. 4 (w.e.f. 17-1-1961).

8 Added by the Constitution (Ninth Amendment) Act, 1960, s. 3 (w.e.f. 17-1-1961).

9 Added by the Punjab Reorganisation Act, 1966 (31 of 1966), s. 7 (w.e.f. 1-11-1966).

10 Ins. by the Rajasthan and Madhya Pradesh (Transfer of Territories) Act, 1959 (47 of 1959), s. 4 (w.e.f. 1-10-1959).

[1][13.] Uttar Pradesh	[2][The territories which immediately before the commencement of this Constitution were either comprised in the Province known as the United Provinces or were being administered as if they formed part of that Province, the territories specified in clause (*b*) of sub-section (1) of section 3 of the Bihar and Uttar Pradesh (Alteration of Boundaries) Act, 1968, and the territories specified in clause (*b*) of sub-section (1) of section 4 of the Haryana and Uttar Pradesh (Alteration of Boundaries) Act, 1979, but excluding the territories specified in clause (*a*) of sub-section (1) of section 3 of the Bihar and Uttar Pradesh (Alteration of Boundaries) Act, 1968, [3][and the territories specified in section 3 of the Uttar Pradesh Reorganisation Act, 2000] and the territories specified in clause (*a*) of sub-section (1) of section 4 of the Haryana and Uttar Pradesh (Alteration of Boundaries) Act, 1979.]
[1][14.] West Bengal	The territories which immediately before the commencement of this Constitution were either comprised in the Province of West Bengal or were being administered as if they formed part of that Province and the territory of Chandernagore as defined in clause (*c*) of section 2 of the Chandernagore (Merger) Act, 1954 and also the territories specified in sub-section (1) of section 3 of the Bihar and West Bengal (Transfer of Territories) Act, 1956 [4][and also the territories referred to in Part III of the First Schedule but excluding the territories referred to in Part III of the Second Schedule to the Constitution (One Hundredth Amendment) Act, 2015, notwithstanding anything contained in clause (*c*) of section 3 of the Constitution (Ninth Amendment) Act, 1960, so far as it relates to the territories referred to in Part III of the First Schedule and the territories referred to in Part III of the Second Schedule to the Constitution (One Hundredth Amendment) Act, 2015.]
[5][6][**	* * * * *

---

1 Entries 8 to 14 renumbered as entries 9 to 15 by the Bombay Reorganisation Act, 1960 (11 of 1960), s. 4 (w.e.f. 1 5 1960)

2 Subs. by the Haryana and Uttar Pradesh (Alteration of Boundaries) Act, 1979 (31 of 1979), s. 5, for the entry against "13. Uttar Pradesh" (w.e.f. 15-9-1983).

3 Ins. by the Uttar Pradesh Reorganisation Act, 2000 (29 of 2000), s. 5 (w.e.f. 9-11-2000).

4 Added by the Constitution (One Hundredth Amendment) Act, 2015, s. 3 (w.e.f. 31-7-2015). For the text of the Act see Appendix I.

5 **Entry 15 relating to Jammu and Kashmir deleted by the Jammu and Kashmir Reorganisation Act, 2019 (34 of 2019), s. 6 (w.e.f. 31-10-2019).

6 Entries 8 to 14 renumbered as 9 to 15 by the Bombay Reorganisation Act, 1960 (11 of 1960), s. 4 (w.e.f. 1-5-1960).

[1][2][15.] Nagaland	The territories specified in sub-section (1) of section 3 of the State of Nagaland Act, 1962.]
[1][3][16.] Haryana	[4][The territories specified in sub-section (1) of section 3 of the Punjab Reorganisation Act, 1966 and the territories specified in clause (a) of sub-section (1) of section 4 of the Haryana and Uttar Pradesh (Alteration of Boundaries) Act, 1979, but excluding the territories specified in clause (v) of sub-section (1) of section 4 of that Act.]]
[1][5][17.] Himachal Pradesh	The territories which immediately before the commencement of this Constitution were being administered as if they were Chief Commissioners' Provinces under the names of Himachal Pradesh and Bilaspur and the territories specified in sub-section (1) of section 5 of the Punjab Reorganisation Act, 1966.]
[1][6][18.] Manipur	The territory which immediately before the commencement of this Constitution was being administered as if it were a Chief Commissioner's Province under the name of Manipur.]
[7][19.] Tripura	The territory which immediately before the commencement of this Constitution was being administered as if it were a Chief Commissioner's Province under the name of Tripura [8][and the territories referred to in Part II of the First Schedule to the Constitution (One Hundredth Amendment) Act, 2015, notwithstanding anything contained in clause (d) of section 3 of the Constitution (Ninth Amendment) Act, 1960, so far as it relates to the territories referred to in Part II of the First Schedule to the Constitution (One Hundredth Amendment) Act, 2015.]
[1][20.] Meghalaya	The territories specified in section 5 of the North-Eastern Areas (Reorganisation) Act, 1971] [2][and the territories referred to in Part I of the First Schedule but excluding the territories referred to in Part II of the Second Schedule to the Constitution (One Hundredth Amendment) Act, 2015.]

1 Entries 16 to 29 renumbered as entries 15 to 28 by the Jammu and Kashmir Reorganisation Act, 2019 (34 of 2019), s. 6 (w.e.f. 31-10-2019).

2 Ins. by the State of Nagaland Act, 1962 (27 of 1962), s. 4 (w.e.f. 1-12-1963).

3 Ins. by the Punjab Reorganisation Act, 1966 (31 of 1966), s. 7 (w.e.f. 1-11-1966) and the entry therein subsequently amended by the Haryana and Uttar Pradesh (Alteration of Boundaries) Act, 1979 (31 of 1979), s. 5 (w.e.f. 15-9-1983).

4 Subs. by the Haryana and Uttar Pradesh (Alteration of Boundaries) Act, 1979 (31 of 1979), s. 5, for the entry against "17. Haryana" (w.e.f. 15-9-1983).

5 Ins. by the State of Himachal Pradesh Act, 1970 (53 of 1970), s. 4 (w.e.f. 25-1-1971).

6 Ins. by the North-Eastern Areas (Reorganisation) Act, 1971 (81 of 1971), s. 9 (w.e.f. 21-1-1972).

7 Entries 16 to 29 renumbered as entries 15 to 28 by the Jammu and Kashmir Reorganisation Act, 2019 (34 of 2019), s. 6 (w.e.f. 31-10-2019).

8 Added by the Constitution (One Hundredth Amendment) Act, 2015, s. 3 (w.e.f. 31-7-2015). For the text of the Act, see Appendix I.

[1][1][21.] Sikkim	The territories which immediately before the commencement of the Constitution (Thirty-sixth Amendment) Act, 1975, were comprised in Sikkim.]
[1][2][22.] Mizoram	The territories specified in section 6 of the North-Eastern Areas (Reorganisation) Act, 1971.]
[1][3][23.] Arunachal Pradesh	The territories specified in section 7 of the North-Eastern Areas (Reorganisation) Act, 1971.]
[1][4][24.] Goa	The territories specified in section 3 of the Goa, Daman and Diu Reorganisation Act, 1987.]
[5][6][25.] Chhattisgarh	The territories specified in section 3 of the Madhya Pradesh Reorganisation Act, 2000.]
[1][7][26.] [8][Uttarakhand]	The territories specified in section 3 of the Uttar Pradesh Reorganisation Act, 2000.]
[1][9][27.] Jharkhand	The territories specified in section 3 of the Bihar Reorganisation Act, 2000.]
[1][10][28.] Telangana	The territories specified in section 3 of the Andhra Pradesh Reorganisation Act, 2014.]
II. THE UNION TERRITORIES	
Name	*Extent*
1. Delhi	The territory which immediately before the commencement of this Constitution was comprised in the Chief Commissioner's Province of Delhi.
[11][* * * * *]	
[12][2.] The Andaman and Nicobar Islands	The territory which immediately before the commencement of this Constitution was comprised in the Chief Commissioner's Province of the Andaman and Nicobar Islands.

1 Ins. by the Constitution (Thirty-sixth Amendment) Act, 1975, s. 2 (w.e.f. 26-4-1975).
2 Ins. by the State of Mizoram Act, 1986 (34 of 1986), s. 4 (w.e.f. 20-2-1987).
3 Ins. by the State of Arunachal Pradesh Act, 1986 (69 of 1986), s. 4 (w.e.f. 20-2-1987).
4 Ins. by the Goa, Daman and Diu Reorganisation Act, 1987 (18 of 1987), s. 5 (w.e.f. 30-5-1987).
5 Entries 16 to 29 renumbered as entries 15 to 28 by the Jammu and Kashmir Reorganisation Act, 2019 (34 of 2019), s. 6 (w.e.f. 31-10-2019).
6 Added by the Madhya Pradesh Reorganisation Act, 2000 (28 of 2000), s. 5 (w.e.f. 1-11-2000).
7 Ins. by the Uttar Pradesh Reorganisation Act, 2000 (29 of 2000), s. 5 (w.e.f. 9-11-2000).
8 Subs. by the Uttaranchal (Alteration of Name) Act, 2006 (52 of 2006), s. 4, for the word "Uttaranchal" (w.e.f. 1-1-2007).
9 Added by the Bihar Reorganisation Act, 2000 (30 of 2000), s. 5 (w.e.f. 15-11-2000).
10 Ins. by the Andhra Pradesh Reorganisation Act, 2014 (6 of 2014) , s. 10 (w.e.f. 2-6-2014).
11 Entry 2 relating to Himachal Pradesh omitted and entries 3 to 10 renumbered as entries 2 to 9 respectively by the State of Himachal Pradesh Act, 1970 (53 of 1970), s. 4 (w.e.f. 25-1-1971) and subsequently entries relating to Manipur and Tripura (i.e. entries 2 and 3) omitted by the North-Eastern Areas (Reorganisation) Act, 1971 (81 of 1971) s. 9 (w.e.f. 21-1-1972).
12 Entries 4 to 9 renumbered as entries 2 to 7 by the North-Eastern Areas (Reorganisation) Act, 1971 (81 of 1971), s. 9 (w.e.f. 21-1-1972).

[1][3.] [2][Lakshadweep]	The territory specified in section 6 of the States Reorganisation Act, 1956.
[3][[1][4.] Dadra and Nagar Haveli and Daman and Diu	The territory which immediately before the eleventh day of August, 1961 was comprised in Free Dadra and Nagar Haveli and the territories specified in section 4 of the Goa, Daman and Diu Reorganisation Act, 1987.]
[4][[1][*]	[3][* * * *]
[5][[1][6.] [6][Puducherry]	The territories which immediately before the sixteenth day of August, 1962, were comprised in the French Establishments in India known as Pondicherry, Karikal, Mahe and Yanam.]
[7][[1][7.] Chandigarh	The territories specified in section 4 of the Punjab Reorganisation Act, 1966.]
[8][* * * * *]	
[1][* * * * *]	
[9][8. Jammu and Kashmir	The territories specified in section 4 of the Jammu and Kashmir Reorganisation Act, 2019.
Ladakh	The territories specified in section 3 of the Jammu and Kashmir Reorganisation Act, 2019.]

1 Entries 4 to 9 renumbered as entries 2 to 7 (respectively) by the North-Eastern Areas (Reorganisation) Act, 1971 (81 of 1971), s. 9 (w.e.f. 21-1-1972).

2 Subs. by the Laccadive, Minicoy and Amindivi Islands (Alteration of Name) Act, 1973 (34 of 1973), s. 5, for "The Laccadive, Minicoy and Amindivi Islands" (w.e.f. 1-11-1973).

3 Entry 4 relating to Dadra and Nagar Haveli was ins. by the Constitution (Tenth Amendment) Act, 1961, s. 2 (w.e.f. 11-8-1961) and subsequently subs. by the Dadra and Nagar Haveli and Daman and Diu (Merger of Union territories) Act, 2019 (44 of 2019), s. 5, for entries 4 and 5 (w.e.f. 26-1-2020).

4 Subs. by the Goa, Daman and Diu (Reorganisation) Act, 1987 (18 of 1987), s. 5, for entry 5 (w.e.f. 30-5-1987).

5 Ins. by the Constitution (Fourteenth Amendment) Act, 1962, s. 3 (with retrospective effect).

6 Subs. by the Pondicherry (Alteration of Name) Act, 2006 (44 of 2006), s. 5 for "Pondicherry" (w.e.f. 1-10-2006).

7 Ins. by the Punjab Reorganisation Act, 1966 (31 of 1966), s. 7 (w.e.f. 1-11-1966).

8 Entry 8 relating to Mizoram omitted and entry 9 relating to Arunachal Pradesh renumbered as entry 8 by the State of Mizoram Act, 1986 (34 of 1986), s. 4 (w.e.f. 20-2-1987) and entry 8 relating to Arunachal Pradesh omitted by the State of Arunachal Pradesh Act, 1986 (69 of 1986) s. 4 (w.e.f. 20-2-1987).

9 Ins. by the Jammu and Kashmir Reorganisation Act, 2019 (34 of 2019), s. 6 (w.e.f. 31-10-2019).

SECOND SCHEDULE

**[Articles 59(3), 65(3), 75(6), 97, 125,
148(3), 158(3), 164 (5), 186 and 221]**

PART A

PROVISIONS AS TO THE PRESIDENT
AND THE GOVERNORS OF STATES [1]***

1. There shall be paid to the President and to the Governors of the States [1]*** the following emoluments per mensem, that is to say:—

   The President   ......   10,000 rupees*.
   The Governor of a State   ......   5,500 rupees**.

2. There shall also be paid to the President and to the Governors of the States [2]*** such allowances as were payable respectively to the Governor-General of the Dominion of India and to the Governors of the corresponding Provinces immediately before the commencement of this Constitution.

3. The President and the Governors of [3][the States] throughout their respective terms of office shall be entitled to the same privileges to which the Governor- General and the Governors of the corresponding Provinces were respectively entitled immediately before the commencement of this Constitution.

4. While the Vice-President or any other person is discharging the functions of, or is acting as, President, or any person is discharging the functions of the Governor, he shall be entitled to the same emoluments, allowances and privileges as the President

---

1 The words and letter "specified in Part A of the First Schedule" omitted by the Constitution (Seventh Amendment) Act, 1956, s. 29 and Sch. (w.e.f. 1-11-1956).
* Now five lakh rupees, *vide* the Finance Act, 2018 (13 of 2018), s. 137. (w.e.f. 1-1-2016).
** Now three lakh fifty thousand rupees, by s. 161, *ibid.* (w.e.f. 1-1-2016).
2 The words "so specified" omitted by the Constitution (Seventh Amendment) Act, 1956, s. 29 and Sch. (w.e.f. 1-11-1956).
3 Subs. by s. 29 and Sch., *ibid.*, for "such states" (w.e.f. 1-11-1956).

or the Governor whose functions he discharges or for whom he
acts, as the case may be.

1*   *   *   *   *

PART C

Provisions as to the Speaker and the Deputy Speaker of the House of the
People and the Chairman and the Deputy Chairman OF THE COUNCIL
OF STATES AND THE SPEAKER AND THE DEPUTY SPEAKER
OF THE LEGISLATIVE ASSEMBLY 2*** AND THE CHAIRMAN
AND THE DEPUTY CHAIRMAN OF THE LEGISLATIVE
COUNCIL OF 3[A STATE]

7.   There shall be paid to the Speaker of the House of the People
and the Chairman of the Council of States such salaries and
allowances as were payable to the Speaker of the Constituent
Assembly of the Dominion of India immediately before the
commencement of this Constitution, and there shall be paid
to the Deputy Speaker of the House of the People and to
the Deputy Chairman of the Council of States such salaries
and allowances as were payable to the Deputy Speaker of the
Constituent Assembly of the Dominion of India immediately
before such commencement.

8.   There shall be paid to the Speaker and the Deputy Speaker
of the Legislative Assembly 4*** and to the Chairman and
the Deputy Chairman of the Legislative Council of 5[a State]
such salaries and allowances as were payable respectively to the
Speaker and the Deputy Speaker of the Legislative Assembly
and the President and the Deputy President of the Legislative
Council of the corresponding Province immediately before
the commencement of this Constitution and, where the

---

1   Part B omitted by s. 29 and Sch., *ibid.* (w.e.f. 1-11-1956).
2   The words and letter "of a State in Part A of the First Schedule" omitted by the Constitution
   (Seventh Amendment) Act, 1956, s. 29 and Sch.(w.e.f. 1-11-1956).
3   Subs. by s. 29 and Sch., *ibid.*, for "any such State." (w.e.f. 1-11-1956).
4   The words and letter "of a State specified in Part A of the First Schedule" omitted by s. 29 and
   Sch., *ibid.* (w.e.f. 1-11-1956).
5   Subs. by s. 29 and Sch., *ibid.*, for "such State" (w.e.f. 1-11-1956).

corresponding Province had no Legislative Council immediately before such commencement, there shall be paid to the Chairman and the Deputy Chairman of the Legislative Council of the State such salaries and allowances as the Governor of the State may determine.

PART D

Provisions as to the Judges of
the Supreme Court and of the HIGH COURTS [1]****

9.   (1) There shall be paid to the Judges of the Supreme Court, in respect of time spent on actual service, salary at the following rates per mensem, that is to say:—

The Chief Justice   ...   [2][10,000 rupees.].*
Any other Judge   ...   [3][9,000 rupees.].*

Provided that if a Judge of the Supreme Court at the time of his appointment is in receipt of a pension (other than a disability or wound pension) in respect of any previous service under the Government of India or any of its predecessor Governments or under the Government of a State or any of its predecessor Governments, his salary in respect of service in the Supreme Court [4][shall be reduced—

(a)   by the amount of that pension, and

(b)   if he has, before such appointment, received in lieu of a portion of the pension due to him in respect of such

1   The words and letter "in States in Part A of the First Schedule" omitted by the Constitution (Seventh Amendment) Act, 1956, s. 25(a) (w.e.f. 1-11-1956).
2   Subs. by the Constitution (Fifty-fourth Amendment) Act, 1986, s. 4, for "5,000 rupees" (w.e.f. 1-4-1986).
*   Now two lakh eighty thousand rupees, *vide* the High Court and Supreme Court Judges (Salaries and Conditions of Service) Amendment Act, 2018 (10 of 2018), s. 6 (w.e.f. 1-1-2016).
3   Subs. by the Constitution (Fifty-fourth Amendment) Act, 1986, s. 4, for "4,000 rupees" (w.e.f. 1-4-1986).
**   Now two lakh fifty thousand rupees, *vide* the High Court and Supreme Court Judges (Salaries and Conditions of Service) Amendment Act, 2018 (10 of 2018), s. 6 (w.e.f. 1-1-2016).
4   Subs. by the Constitution (Seventh Amendment) Act, 1956, s. 25(b), for "shall be reduced by the amount of that pension" (w.e.f. 1-11-1956).

previous service the commuted value thereof, by the amount of that portion of the pension, and

(c) if he has, before such appointment, received a retirement gratuity in respect of such previous service, by the pension equivalent of that gratuity.]

(2) Every Judge of the Supreme Court shall be entitled without payment of rent to the use of an official residence.

(3) Nothing in sub-paragraph (2) of this paragraph shall apply to a Judge who, immediately before the commencement of this Constitution,—

(a) was holding office as the Chief Justice of the Federal Court and has become on such commencement the Chief Justice of the Supreme Court under clause (1) of article 374, or

(b) was holding office as any other Judge of the Federal Court and has on such commencement become a Judge (other than the Chief Justice) of the Supreme Court under the said clause,

during the period he holds office as such Chief Justice or other Judge, and every Judge who so becomes the Chief Justice or other Judge of the Supreme Court shall, in respect of time spent on actual service as such Chief Justice or other Judge, as the case may be, be entitled to receive in addition to the salary specified in sub-paragraph (1) of this paragraph as special pay an amount equivalent to the difference between the salary so specified and the salary which he was drawing immediately before such commencement.

(4) Every Judge of the Supreme Court shall receive such reasonable allowances to reimburse him for expenses incurred in travelling on duty within the territory of India and shall be afforded such reasonable facilities in connection with travelling as the President may from time to time prescribe.

(5) The rights in respect of leave of absence (including leave allowances) and pension of the Judges of the Supreme Court shall be governed by the provisions which, immediately before the commencement of this Constitution, were applicable to the Judges of the Federal Court.

10.   (1) [1][There shall be paid to the Judges of High Courts, in respect of time spent on actual service, salary at the following rates per mensem, that is to say,—

The Chief Justice   ...   [2][9,000 rupees] *

Any other Judge   ...   [3][8,000 rupees]: **

Provided that if a Judge of a High Court at the time of his appointment is in receipt of a pension (other than a disability or wound pension) in respect of any previous service under the Government of India or any of its predecessor Governments or under the Government of a State or any of its predecessor Governments, his salary in respect of service in the High Court shall be reduced—

(a)   by the amount of that pension, and

(b)   if he has, before such appointment, received in lieu of a portion of the pension due to him in respect of such previous service the commuted value thereof, by the amount of that portion of the pension, and

(c)   if he has, before such appointment, received a retirement gratuity in respect of such previous service, by the pension equivalent of that gratuity.]

(2) Every person who immediately before the commencement of this Constitution—

(a)   was holding office as the Chief Justice of a High Court in any Province and has on such commencement become the Chief Justice of the High Court in the corresponding State under clause (1) of article 376, or

---

1   Subs. by the Constitution (Seventh Amendment) Act, 1956, s. 25(c)(i), for sub-paragraph (1) (w.e.f. 1-11-1956).

2   Subs. by the Constitution (Fifty-fourth Amendment) Act, 1986, s. 4, for "4,000 rupees" (w.e.f. 1-4-1986).

*   Now two lakh fifty thousand rupees, *vide* the High Court and Supreme Court Judges (Salaries and Conditions of Service) Amendment Act, 2018 (10 of 2018), s. 2 (w.e.f. 1-1-2016).

3   Subs. by the Constitution (Fifty-fourth Amendment) Act, 1986, s. 4, for "3,500 rupees" (w.e.f. 1-4-1986).

** Now two lakh twenty-five thousand rupees, *vide* the High Court and Supreme Court Judges (Salaries and Conditions of Service) Amendment Act, 2018 (10 of 2018), s. 2 (w.e.f. 1-1-2016).

(*b*) was holding office as any other Judge of a High Court in any Province and has on such commencement become a Judge (other than the Chief Justice) of the High Court in the corresponding State under the said clause,

shall, if he was immediately before such commencement drawing a salary at a rate higher than that specified in sub-paragraph (1) of this paragraph, be entitled to receive in respect of time spent on actual service as such Chief Justice or other Judge, as the case may be, in addition to the salary specified in the said sub-paragraph as special pay an amount equivalent to the difference between the salary so specified and the salary which he was drawing immediately before such commencement.

¹[(3) Any person who, immediately before the commencement of the Constitution (Seventh Amendment) Act, 1956, was holding office as the Chief Justice of the High Court of a State specified in Part B of the First Schedule and has on such commencement become the Chief Justice of the High Court of a State specified in the said Schedule as amended by the said Act, shall, if he was immediately before such commencement drawing any amount as allowance in addition to his salary, be entitled to receive in respect of time spent on actual service as such Chief Justice, the same amount as allowance in addition to the salary specified in sub-paragraph (1) of this paragraph.].

11.   In this Part, unless the context otherwise requires,—

(*a*) the expression "Chief Justice" includes an acting Chief Justice, and a "Judge" includes an *ad hoc* Judge;

(*b*) "actual service" includes—

(*i*) time spent by a Judge on duty as a Judge or in the performance of such other functions as he may at the request of the President undertake to discharge;

(*ii*) vacations, excluding any time during which the Judge is absent on leave; and

---

1 Subs. by the Constitution (Seventh Amendment) Act, 1956, s. 25(c)(ii), for sub-paragraphs (*3*) and (*4*) (w.e.f. 1-11-1956).

(*iii*) joining time on transfer from a High Court to the Supreme Court or from one High Court to another.

PART E

Provisions as to the Comptroller
and Auditor-General of India

12.   (1) There shall be paid to the Comptroller and Auditor-General of India a salary at the rate of [*]four thousand rupees per mensem. (2) The person who was holding office immediately before the commencement of this Constitution as Auditor-General of India and has become on such commencement the Comptroller and Auditor-General of India under article 377 shall in addition to the salary specified in sub-paragraph (1) of this paragraph be entitled to receive as special pay an amount equivalent to the difference between the salary so specified and the salary which he was drawing as Auditor-General of India immediately before such commencement.

(3) The rights in respect of leave of absence and pension and the other conditions of service of the Comptroller and Auditor-General of India shall be governed or shall continue to be governed, as the case may be, by the provisions which were applicable to the Auditor-General of India immediately before the commencement of this Constitution and all references in those provisions to the Governor-General shall be construed as references to the President.

---

*   The Comptroller and Auditor-General of India shall be paid a salary equal to the salary of the Judges of the Supreme Court *vide* s. 3 of the Comptroller and Auditor General (Duties, Powers and Conditions of Service) Act, 1971 (56 of 1971). The salary of Judges of the Supreme Court has been raised to two lakh fifty thousand rupees per mensem by the High Court and Supreme Court Judges (Salaries and Conditions of Service) Amendment Act, 2018 (10 of 2018), s. 6 (w.e.f. 1-1-2016).

THIRD SCHEDULE

[Articles 75(4), 99, 124(6), 148(2), 164(3), 188 and 219]*

Forms of Oaths or Affirmations

I

Form of oath of office for a Minister for the Union:—

"I, A. B., do $\dfrac{\text{swear in the name of God}}{\text{solemnly affirm}}$ that I will bear true faith
and allegiance to the Constitution of India as by law established, ¹[that I will uphold the sovereignty and integrity of India,] that I will faithfully and conscientiously discharge my duties as a Minister for the Union and that I will do right to all manner of people in accordance with the Constitution and the law, without fear or favour, affection or ill-will."

II

Form of oath of secrecy for a Minister for the Union:—

"I, A.B., do $\dfrac{\text{swear in the name of God}}{\text{solemnly affirm}}$ that I will not directly or
indirectly communicate or reveal to any person or persons any matter which shall be brought under my consideration or shall become known to me as a Minister for the Union except as may be required for the due discharge of my duties as such Minister."

²[III

A

Form of oath or affirmation to be made by a candidate for election to Parliament:—

"I, A.B., having been nominated as a candidate to fill a seat in the Council

---

* *See* also arts. 84 (*a*) and 173 (*a*).
1 Ins. by the Constitution (Sixteenth Amendment) Act, 1963, s. 5 (w.e.f. 5-10-1963).
2 Subs. by s. 5, *ibid.*, for Form III. (w.e.f. 5-10-1963).

of States (or the House of the People) do $\dfrac{\text{swear in the name of God}}{\text{solemnly affirm}}$ that I will bear true faith and allegiance to the Constitution of India as by law established and that I will uphold the sovereignty and integrity of India."

B

Form of oath or affirmation to be made by a member of Parliament:—

"I, A.B., having been elected (or nominated) a member of the Council of States (or the House of the People) do $\dfrac{\text{swear in the name of God}}{\text{solemnly affirm}}$ that I will bear true faith and allegiance to the Constitution of India as by law established, that I will uphold the sovereignty and integrity of India and that I will faithfully discharge the duty upon which I am about to enter."]

IV

Form of oath or affirmation to be made by the Judges of the Supreme Court and the Comptroller and Auditor-General of India:—

"I, A.B., having been appointed Chief Justice (or a Judge) of the Supreme Court of India (or Comptroller and Auditor-General of India) do $\dfrac{\text{swear in the name of God}}{\text{solemnly affirm}}$ that I will bear true faith and faith and allegiance to the Constitution of India as by law established, [1][that I will uphold the sovereignty and integrity of India,] that I will duly and faithfully and to the best of my ability, knowledge and judgment perform the duties of my office without fear or favour, affection or ill-will and that I will uphold the Constitution and the laws."

V

Form of oath of office for a Minister for a State:—

"I, A.B., do $\dfrac{\text{swear in the name of God}}{\text{solemnly affirm}}$ that I will bear true faith and allegiance to the Constitution of India as by law established, [2][that I

---

1 Ins. by the Constitution (Sixteenth Amendment) Act, 1963, s. 5 (w.e.f. 5-10-1963).
2 Ins. by the Constitution (Sixteenth Amendment) Act, 1963, s. 5 (w.e.f. 5-10-1963).

will uphold the sovereignty and integrity of India,] that I will faithfully and conscientiously discharge my duties as a Minister for the State of .... and that I will do right to all manner of people in accordance with the Constitution and the law without fear or favour, affection or ill-will."

VI

Form of oath of secrecy for a Minister for a State:—

"I, A.B., do $\dfrac{\text{swear in the name of God}}{\text{solemnly affirm}}$ that I will not directly or indirectly communicate or reveal to any person or persons any matter which shall be brought under my consideration or shall become known to me as a Minister for the State of except as may be required for the due discharge of my duties as such Minister."

[1][VII

A

Form of oath or affirmation to be made by a candidate for election to the Legislature of a State:—

"I, A.B., having been nominated as a candidate to fill a seat in the Legislative Assembly (or Legislative Council), do $\dfrac{\text{swear in the name of God}}{\text{solemnly affirm}}$ that I will bear true faith and allegiance to the Constitution of India as by law established and that I will uphold the sovereignty and integrity of India."

B

Form of oath or affirmation to be made by a member of the Legislature of a State:—

"I, A.B., having been elected (or nominated) a member of the Legislative Assembly (or Legislative Council), do $\dfrac{\text{swear in the name of God}}{\text{solemnly affirm}}$ that I will bear true faith and allegiance to the Constitution of India as by law established, that I will uphold the sovereignty and integrity of India and that I will faithfully discharge the duty upon which I am about to enter."]

---

1 Subs. by s. 5, *ibid.*, for Form VII (w.e.f. 5-10-1963).

VIII

Form of oath or affirmation to be made by the Judges of a High Court:—
"I, A.B., having been appointed Chief Justice (or a Judge) of the High Court at (or of) do $\frac{\text{swear in the name of God}}{\text{solemnly affirm}}$ that I will bear true faith and allegiance to the Constitution of India as by law established, [1][that I will uphold the sovereignty and integrity of India,] that I will duly and faithfully and to the best of my ability, knowledge and judgment perform the duties of my office without fear or favour, affection or ill-will and that I will uphold the Constitution and the laws."

[2]FOURTH SCHEDULE

[Articles 4(1) and 80(2)]

Allocation of seats in the Council of States

To each State or Union territory specified in the first column of the following table, there shall be allotted the number of seats specified in the second column thereof opposite to that State or that Union territory, as the case may be:

TABLE

1.	Andhra Pradesh	[3][11]
[4][2.	Telangana	7]
[5][3.]	Assam	7
[4][4.]	Bihar	[6][16]

---

1   Ins. by the Constitution (Sixteenth Amendment) Act, 1963, s. 5 (w.e.f. 5-10-1963).
2   Fourth Schedule subs. by the Constitution (Seventh Amendment) Act, 1956, s. 3(2), for Fourth Schedule (w.e.f. 1-11-1956).
3   Subs. by the Andhra Pradesh Reorganisation Act, 2014, s. 12, for "18" (w.e.f. 2-6-2014).
4   Ins. by s. 12, *ibid.* (w.e.f. 2-6-2014).
5   Entries 2 to 30 renumbered as entries 3 to 31 respectively by s. 12, *ibid.* (w.e.f. 2-6-2014).
6   Subs. by the Bihar Reorganisation Act, 2000 (30 of 2000), s. 7, for "22" (w.e.f. 15-11-2000).

[1][4][5.]	Jharkhand	6]
[2][3][4][6.]	Goa	1]]
[4][8][4][7.]	Gujarat	11]]
[5][8][4][8.]	Haryana	5]]
[8][4][9.]	Kerala	9
[6][7][10.]]	Madhya Pradesh	[8][11]
[9][1][2][11.]	Chhattisgarh	5]]
[10][1][2][12.]	Tamil Nadu	[11][18]]
[12][1][2][13.]	Maharashtra	19]]
[13][1][2][14.]	Karnataka	12]]
[1][2][15.]	[14][Odisha]	10]
[1][2][16.]	Punjab	[15][7]
[1][2][17.]	Rajasthan	10]
[1][2][18.]	Uttar Pradesh	[16][31]
[17][1][2][19.]	[18][Uttarakhand]	3]]
[1][2][20.]	West Bengal	16]
[19][1][2][**	*	*

---

1 Ins. by s. 7, *ibid*. (w.e.f. 15-11-2000).
2 Entries 4 to 26 renumbered as entries 5 to 27 respectively and entry "4. Goa 1" ins. by the Goa, Daman and Diu Reorganisation Act, 1987 (18 of 1987), s. 6 (a) and (b)(w.e.f. 30-5-1987).
3 Entries 4 to 29 renumbered as entries 5 to 30 by the Bihar Reorganisation Act, 2000 (30 of 2000), s. 7 (w.e.f. 15-11-2000).
4 Subs. by the Bombay Reorganisation Act, 1960 (11 of 1960), s. 6, for entry "4" (w.e.f. 1-5-1960).
5 Ins. by the Punjab Reorganisation Act, 1966 (31 of 1966), s. 9 (w.e.f. 1-11-1966).
6 Entries 4 to 29 renumbered as entries 5 to 30 by the Bihar Reorganisation Act, 2000 (30 of 2000), s. 7 (w.e.f. 15-11-2000).
7 Entries 2 to 30 renumbered as entries 3 to 31 respectively by the Andhra Pradesh Reorganisation Act, 2014, s. 12 (w.e.f. 2-6-2014).
8 Subs. by the Madhya Pradesh Reorganisation Act, 2000 (28 of 2000), s. 7, for "16" (w.e.f. 1-11-2000).
9 Ins. by s. 7, *ibid*. (w.e.f. 1-11-2000).
10 Subs. by the Madras State (Alteration of Name) Act, 1968 (53 of 1968), s. 5, for "8. Madras" (renumbered as *11) (w.e.f. 14-1-1969).
11 Subs. by the Andhra Pradesh and Madras (Alteration of Boundaries) Act, 1959 (56 of 1959), s. 8, for "17" (w.e.f. 1-4-1960).
12 Ins. by the Bombay Reorganisation Act, 1960 (11 of 1960), s. 6 (w.e.f. 1-5-1960).
13 Subs. by the Mysore State (Alteration of Name) Act, 1973 (31 of 1973), s. 5, for "10. Mysore" (w.e.f. 1-11-1973).
14 Subs. by the Orissa (Alteration of Name) Act, 2011 (15 of 2011), s. 7 for "Orissa" (w.e.f. 1-11-2011).
15 Subs. by the Punjab Reorganisation Act, 1966 (31 of 1966), s. 9 for "11" (w.e.f. 1-11-1966).
16 Subs. by the Uttar Pradesh Reorganisation Act, 2000 (29 of 2000), s. 7 for "34" (w.e.f. 9-11-2000).
17 Ins. by s. 7, *ibid*. (w.e.f. 9-11-2000).
18 Subs. by the Uttaranchal (Alteration of Name) Act, 2006 (52 of 2006), s. 5 for "Uttaranchal" (w.e.f. 1-1-2007).
19 Entry 21 relating to Jammu and Kashmir deleted by the Jammu and Kashmir Reorganisation Act, 2019 (34 of 2019), s. 8 (w.e.f. 31-10-2019).

[1][2][1][2][21.]	Nagaland	1]]
[3][4][5][6][22.]	Himachal Pradesh	3]]]
.]		
[3][2][4][23.]	Manipur	1]
[3][2][4][24.]	Tripura	1]]
[3][2][4][25.]	Meghalaya	1]]
[7][3][2][4][26.]	Sikkim	1]]
[8][3][2][4][27.]	Mizoram	1]]
[9][3][2][4][28.]	Arunachal Pradesh	1]]
[3][2][4][29.]	Delhi	3]
[3][2][4][30.]	10[Puducherry]	1]]
[11][3][2][4][31.	Jammu and Kashmir	4]
	Total	12[233]

1 Entries 22 to 31 re-numbered as entries 21 to 30, respectively by the Jammu and Kashmir Reorganisation Act, 2019 (34 of 2019), s. 8 (w.e.f. 31-10-2019).
2 Ins. by the State of Nagaland Act, 1962 (27 of 1962), s. 6 (w.e.f. 1-12-1963).
3 Ins. by the State of Himachal Pradesh Act, 1970 (53 of 1970), s. 5 (w.e.f. 25-1-1971).
4 Entries 4 to 29 renumbered as entries 5 to 30 by the Bihar Reorganisation Act, 2000 (30 of 2000), s. 7 (w.e.f. 15-11-2000).
5 Entries 2 to 30 renumbered as entries 3 to 31 respectively by the Andhra Pradesh Reorganisation Act, 2014 (6 of 2014), s. 12 (w.e.f. 2-6-2014).
6 Entries 22 to 31 renumbered as entries 21 to 30 respectively by the Jammu and Kashmir Reorganisation Act, 2019 (34 of 2019), s. 8 (w.e.f. 31-10-2019).
7 Ins. by the Constitution (Thirty-sixth Amenement) Act, 1975, s. 4 (w.e.f. 26-4-1975).
8 Ins. by the State of Mizoram Act, 1986 (34 of 1986), s. 5 (w.e.f. 20-2-1987).
9 Ins. by the State of Arunachal Pradesh Act, 1986 (69 of 1986), s. 5 (w.e.f. 20-2-1987). 1987).
10 Subs. by the Pondicherry (Alteration of Name) Act, 2006 (44 of 2006) s. 4, for "Pondicherry" (w.e.f. 1-10-2006).
11 Ins. by the Jammu and Kashmir Reorganisation Act, 2019 (34 of 2019), s. 8 (w.e.f. 31-10-2019).
12 Subs. by the Goa, Daman and Diu Reorganisation Act, 1987 (18 of 1987), s. 6, for "232" (w.e.f. 30-5-1987).

FIFTH SCHEDULE

[Article 244(1)]

Provisions as to the Administration and Control of Scheduled Areas and Scheduled Tribes

PART A
General

1. **Interpretation.**—In this Schedule, unless the context otherwise requires, the expression "State" [1]*** does not include the [2][States of Assam [3][, [4][Meghalaya, Tripura and Mizoram.]]]

2. **Executive power of a State in Scheduled Areas.**—Subject to the provisions of this Schedule, the executive power of a State extends to the Scheduled Areas therein.

3. **Report by the Governor [5]*** to the President regarding the administration of Scheduled Areas.**—The Governor [5]*** of each State having Scheduled Areas therein shall annually, or whenever so required by the President, make a report to the President regarding the administration of the Scheduled Areas in that State and the executive power of the Union shall extend to the giving of directions to the State as to the administration of the said areas.

PART B
Administration and Control of Scheduled Areas and Scheduled Tribes

---

1   The words and letters "means a State specified in Part A or Part B of the First Schedule but" omitted by the Constitution (Seventh Amendment) Act, 1956, s. 29 and Sch. (w.e.f. 1-11-1956).

2   Subs. by the North-Eastern Areas (Reorganisation) Act, 1971 (81 of 1971), s. 71, for "State of Assam" (w.e.f. 21-1-1972).

3   Subs. by the Constitution (Forty-ninth Amendment) Act, 1984, s. 3, for "and Meghalaya" (w.e.f. 1-4-1985).

4   Subs. by the State of Mizoram Act, 1986 (34 of 1986), s. 39, for "Meghalaya and Tripura" (w.e.f. 20-2-1987).

5   The words "or Rajpramukh" omitted by the Constitution (Seventh Amendment) Act, 1956, s. 29 and Sch. (w.e.f. 1-11-1956).

4.   **Tribes Advisory Council.**—(1) There shall be established in each State having Scheduled Areas therein and, if the President so directs, also in any State having Scheduled Tribes but not Scheduled Areas therein, a Tribes Advisory Council consisting of not more than twenty members of whom, as nearly as may be, three-fourths shall be the representatives of the Scheduled Tribes in the Legislative Assembly of the State:

Provided that if the number of representatives of the Scheduled Tribes in the Legislative Assembly of the State is less than the number of seats in the Tribes Advisory Council to be filled by such representatives, the remaining seats shall be filled by other members of those tribes.

(2) It shall be the duty of the Tribes Advisory Council to advise on such matters pertaining to the welfare and advancement of the Scheduled Tribes in the State as may be referred to them by the Governor [1]***.

(3) The Governor [2]*** may make rules prescribing or regulating, as the case may be,—

> (*a*) the number of members of the Council, the mode of their appointment and the appointment of the Chairman of the Council and of the officers and servants thereof;
>
> (*b*) the conduct of its meetings and its procedure in general; and
>
> (*c*) all other incidental matters.

5.   **Law applicable to Scheduled Areas.**—(1) Notwithstanding anything in this Constitution, the Governor [1]*** may by public notification direct that any particular Act of Parliament or of the Legislature of the State shall not apply to a Scheduled Area or any part thereof in the State or shall apply to a Scheduled Area or any part thereof in the State subject to such exceptions and modifications as he may specify in the notification and any direction given under this sub-paragraph may be given so as to have retrospective effect.

(2) The Governor may make regulations for the peace and good government of any area in a State which is for the time being a Scheduled Area.

---

1 The words "or Rajpramukh, as the case may be" omitted by the Constitution (Seventh Amendment) Act, 1956, s. 29 and Sch. (w.e.f. 1-11-1956).
2 The words "or Rajpramukh" omitted by s. 29 and Sch., *ibid.* (w.e.f. 1-11-1956).

In particular and without prejudice to the generality of the foregoing power, such regulations may—

(a) prohibit or restrict the transfer of land by or among members of the Scheduled Tribes in such area;

(b) regulate the allotment of land to members of the Scheduled Tribes in such area;

(c) regulate the carrying on of business as money-lender by persons who lend money to members of the Scheduled Tribes in such area.

(3) In making any such regulation as is referred to in sub-paragraph (2) of this paragraph, the Governor [1]*** may repeal or amend any Act of Parliament or of the Legislature of the State or any existing law which is for the time being applicable to the area in question.

(4) All regulations made under this paragraph shall be submitted forthwith to the President and, until assented to by him, shall have no effect.

(5) No regulation shall be made under this paragraph unless the Governor [1]** making the regulation has, in the case where there is a Tribes Advisory Council for the State, consulted such Council.

PART C
Scheduled Areas

6. **Scheduled Areas.**—(1) In this Constitution, the ˙expression "Scheduled Areas" means such areas as the President may by order declare to be Scheduled Areas.

(2) The President may at any time by order *—

(a) direct that the whole or any specified part of a Scheduled Area shall cease to be a Scheduled Area or a part of such an area;

---

1 The words "or Rajpramukh" omitted by the Constitution (Seventh Amendment) Act, 1956, s. 29 and Sch. (w.e.f. 1-11-1956).

* *See* the Scheduled Areas (Part A States) Order, 1950 (C.O. 9), the Scheduled Areas (Part B States) Order, 1950 (C.O.26), the Scheduled Areas (Himachal Pradesh) Order, 1975 (C.O. 102) and the Scheduled Areas (States of Bihar, Gujarat, Madhya Pradesh and Orissa) Order, 1977 (C.O. 109).

** *See* the Madras Scheduled Areas (Cessor) Order, 1950 (C.O. 30) and the Andhra Scheduled Areas (Cessor) Order, 1955 (C.O. 50).

[1][*(aa)*]increase the area of any Scheduled Area in a State after consultation with the Governor of that State;]

(*b*) alter, but only by way of rectification of boundaries, any Scheduled Area;

(*c*) on any alteration of the boundaries of a State or on the admission into the Union or the establishment of a new State, declare any territory not previously included in any State to be, or to form part of, a Scheduled Area;

[2][*(d*) rescind, in relation to any State or States, any order or orders made under this paragraph, and in consultation with the Governor of the State concerned, make fresh orders redefining the areas which are to be Scheduled Areas;]

and any such order may contain such incidental and consequential provisions as appear to the President to be necessary and proper, but save as aforesaid, the order made under sub-paragraph (1) of this paragraph shall not be varied by any subsequent order.

PART D

Amendment of the Schedule

7. **Amendment of the Schedule.**—(1) Parliament may from time to time by law amend by way of addition, variation or repeal any of the provisions of this Schedule and, when the Schedule is so amended, any reference to this Schedule in this Constitution shall be construed as a reference to such Schedule as so amended.

(2) No such law as is mentioned in sub-paragraph (1) of this paragraph shall be deemed to be an amendment of this Constitution for the purposes of article 368.

---

1 Ins. by the Fifth Schedule to the Constitution (Amendment) Act, 1976 (101 of 1976), s. 2 (w.e.f. 7 9 1976).

* *See* the Scheduled Areas (Part A States) Order, 1950 (C.O. 9), the Scheduled Areas (Part B States) Order, 1950 (C.O.26), the Scheduled Areas (Himachal Pradesh) Order, 1975 (C.O. 102) and the Scheduled Areas (States of Bihar, Gujarat, Madhya Pradesh and Orissa) Order, 1977 (C.O. 109).

** *See* the Madras Scheduled Areas (Cessor) Order, 1950 (C.O. 30) and the Andhra Scheduled Areas (Cessor) Order, 1955 (C.O. 50).

2 Ins. by the Fifth Schedule to the Constitution (Amendment) Act, 1976 (101 of 1976), s. 2 (w.e.f. 7-9-1976).

SIXTH SCHEDULE

[Articles 244(2) and 275(1)]

Provisions as to the Administration of Tribal Areas in
¹[the States of Assam, Meghalaya, Tripura and Mizoram]

²**1.** **Autonomous districts and autonomous regions.**—(1) Subject to the provisions of this paragraph, the tribal areas in each item of ³[⁴[Parts I, II and IIA] and in Part III] of the table appended to paragraph 20 of this Schedule shall be an autonomous district.

(2) If there are different Scheduled Tribes in an autonomous district, the Governor may, by public notification, divide the area or areas inhabited by them into autonomous regions.

(3) The Governor may, by public notification,—

    (*a*)   include any area in ³[any of the Parts] of the said table,

    (*b*)   exclude any area from ³[any of the Parts] of the said table,

    (*c*)   create a new autonomous district,

    (*d*)   increase the area of any autonomous district,

    (*e*)   diminish the area of any autonomous district,

    (*f*)   unite two or more autonomous districts or parts thereof so as to form one autonomous district,

    ⁵[(*ff*) alter the name of any autonomous district],

    (*g*)   define the boundaries of any autonomous district:

Provided that no order shall be made by the Governor under clauses (*c*), (*d*), (*e*) and (*f*) of this sub-paragraph except after consideration

---

1 Subs. by the State of Mizoram Act, 1986 (34 of 1986), s. 39, for certain words (w.e.f. 20-2-1987).

2 Paragraph 1 has been amended in its application to the State of Assam by the Sixth Schedule to the Constitution (Amendment) Act, 2003 (44 of 2003), s. 2, so as to insert the following proviso after sub-paragraph (2), namely :—
"Provided that nothing in this sub-paragraph shall apply to the Bodoland Territorial Areas District" (w.e.f. 7-9-2003).

3 Subs. by the North-Eastern Areas (Reorganisation) Act, 1971 (81 of 1971), s. 71(i) and Eighth Sch., for "Part A" (w.e.f. 21-1-1972).

4 Subs. by the Constitution (Forty-ninth Amendment) Act, 1984, s. 4, for "Part I and II" (w.e.f. 1-4-1985).

5 Ins. by the Assam Reorganisation (Meghalaya) Act, 1969 (55 of 1969), s. 74 and Fourth Sch. (w.e.f. 2-4-1970).

of the report of a Commission appointed under sub-paragraph (1) of paragraph 14 of this Schedule:

[1][Provided further that any order made by the Governor under this sub-paragraph may contain such incidental and consequential provisions (including any amendment of paragraph 20 and of any item in any of the Parts of the said Table) as appear to the Governor to be necessary for giving effect to the provisions of the order.]

[2]**2.** **Constitution of District Councils and Regional Councils.—** [3][(1) There shall be a District Council for each autonomous district consisting of not more than thirty members, of whom not more than four persons shall be nominated by the Governor and the rest shall be elected on the basis of adult suffrage.]

(2) There shall be a separate Regional Council for each area constituted an autonomous region under sub-paragraph (2) of paragraph 1 of this Schedule.

(3) Each District Council and each Regional Council shall be a body corporate by the name respectively of "the District Council of (*name of district*)" and "the Regional Council of (*name of region*)",

---

1 Ins. by the North-Eastern Areas (Reorganisation) Act, 1971 (81 of 1971), s. 71(i) and Eighth Sch. (w.e.f. 21-1-1972).

2 Paragraph 2 has been amended in its application to the State of Assam by the Sixth Schedule to the Constitution (Amendment) Act, 2003(44 of 2003), s. 2, so as to insert the following proviso after sub-paragraph (1), namely: —
"Provided that the Bodoland Territorial Council shall consist of not more than forty-six members of whom forty shall be elected on the basis of adult suffrage, of whom thirty shall be reserved for the Scheduled Tribes, five for non-tribal communities, five open for all communities and the remaining six shall be nominated by the Governor having same rights and privileges as other members, including voting rights, from amongst the un-represented communities of the Bodoland Territorial Areas District, of which at least two shall be women:"
Paragraph 2 has been amended in its application to the State of Assam by the Sixth Schedule to the Constitution (Amendment) Act, 1995(42 of 1995), s.2, so as to insert the following proviso in sub-paragraph (3), namely :—
"Provided that the District Council constituted for the North Cachar Hills District shall be called as the North Cachar Hills Autonomous Council and the District Council constituted for the Karbi Anglong District shall be called as the Karbi Anglong Autonomous Council."
Paragraph 2 has been amended in its application to the State of Assam by the Sixth Schedule to the Constitution (Amendment) Act, 2003(44 of 2003), s. 2, so as to insert the following proviso after the existing proviso in sub-paragraph (3), namely:—
"Provided further that the District Council constituted for the Bodoland Territorial Areas District shall be called the Bodoland Territorial Council."

3 Subs. by the Assam Reorganisation (Meghalaya) Act, 1969 (55 of 1969), s. 74 and Fourth Sch., for sub-paragraph (1) (w.e.f. 2-4-1970).

shall have perpetual succession and a common seal and shall by the said name sue and be sued.

(4) Subject to the provisions of this Schedule, the administration of an autonomous district shall, in so far as it is not vested under this Schedule in any Regional Council within such district, be vested in the District Council for such district and the administration of an autonomous region shall be vested in the Regional Council for such region.

(5) In an autonomous district with Regional Councils, the District Council shall have only such powers with respect to the areas under the authority of the Regional Council as may be delegated to it by the Regional Council in addition to the powers conferred on it by this Schedule with respect to such areas.

(6) The Governor shall make rules for the first constitution of District Councils and Regional Councils in consultation with the existing tribal Councils or other representative tribal organisations within the autonomous districts or regions concerned, and such rules shall provide for—

    (*a*)   the composition of the District Councils and Regional Councils and the allocation of seats therein;

    (*b*)   the delimitation of territorial constituencies for the purpose of elections to those Councils;

    (*c*)   the qualifications for voting at such elections and the preparation of electoral rolls therefor;

    (*d*)   the qualifications for being elected at such elections as members of such Councils;

    (*e*)   the term of office of members of [1][Regional Councils];

    (*f*)   any other matter relating to or connected with elections or nominations to such Councils;

    (*g*)   the procedure and the conduct of business [1][(including the power to act notwithstanding any vacancy)] in the District and Regional Councils;

    (*h*)   the appointment of officers and staff of the District and Regional Councils.

---

1 Subs. by the Assam Reorganisation (Meghalaya) Act, 1969 (55 of 1969), s. 74 and Fourth Sch., for "such Councils" (w.e.f. 2-4-1970).

[(6A) The elected members of the District Council shall hold office for a term of five years from the date appointed for the first meeting of the Council after the general elections to the Council, unless the District Council is sooner dissolved under paragraph 16 and a nominated member shall hold office at the pleasure of the Governor:

Provided that the said period of five years may, while a Proclamation of Emergency is in operation or if circumstances exist which, in the opinion of the Governor, render the holding of elections impracticable, be extended by the Governor for a period not exceeding one year at a time and in any case where a Proclamation of Emergency is in operation not extending beyond a period of six months after the Proclamation has ceased to operate:

Provided further that a member elected to fill a casual vacancy shall hold office only for the remainder of the term of office of the member whom he replaces.]

(7) The District or the Regional Council may after its first constitution make rules [with the approval of the Governor] with regard to the matters specified in sub-paragraph (6) of this paragraph and may also make rules [with like approval] regulating—

 (*a*) the formation of subordinate local Councils or Boards and their procedure and the conduct of their business; and

 (*b*) generally all matters relating to the transaction of business pertaining to the administration of the district or region, as the case may be:

Provided that until rules are made by the District or the Regional Council under this sub-paragraph the rules made by the Governor under sub-paragraph (6) of this paragraph shall have effect in respect of elections to, the officers and staff of, and the procedure and the conduct of business in, each such Council.

2* * * *

1 Ins. by the Assam Reorganisation (Meghalaya) Act, 1969 (55 of 1969), s. 74 and Fourth Sch. (w.e.f. 2-4-1970).

2 Second proviso omitted by s. 74 and Fourth Sch. of the Assam Reorganisation (Meghalaya) Act, 1969 (55 of 1969) (w.e.f. 2-4-1970).

¹3. Powers of the District Councils and Regional Councils to make

1 Paragraph 3 has been amended in its application to the State of Assam by the Sixth Schedule to the Constitution (Amendment) Act, 2003 (44 of 2003), s. 2, so as to substitute sub-paragraph (3) as under (w.e.f. 7-9-2003),— "(3) Save as otherwise provided in sub-paragraph (2) of paragraph 3A or sub-paragraph (2) of paragraph 3B, all laws made under this paragraph or sub-paragraph (1) of paragraph 3A or sub-paragraph (1) of paragraph 3B shall be submitted forthwith to the Governor and, until assented to by him, shall have no effect.".

After paragraph 3, the following paragraph has been inserted in its application to the State of Assam by the Sixth Schedule to the Constitution (Amendment) Act, 1995 (42 of 1995), s. 2 (w.e.f. 12-9-1995), namely: —

"3A. **Additional powers of the North Cachar Hills Autonomous Council and the Karbi Anglong Autonomous Council to make laws.**—(1) Without prejudice to the provisions of paragraph 3, the North Cachar Hills Autonomous Council and the Karbi Anglong Autonomous Council within their respective districts, shall have power to make laws with respect to—

    (*a*) industries, subject to the provisions of entries 7 and 52 of List I of the Seventh Schedule;

    (*b*) communications, that is to say, roads, bridges, ferries and other means of communication not specified in List I of the Seventh Schedule; municipal tramways, ropeways, inland waterways and traffic thereon subject to the provisions of List I and List III of the Seventh Schedule with regard to such waterways; vehicles other than mechanically propelled vehicles;

    (*c*) preservation, protection and improvement of stock and prevention of animal diseases; veterinary training and practice; cattle pounds;

    (*d*) primary and secondary education;

    (*e*) agriculture, including agricultural education and research, protection against pests and prevention of plant diseases;

    (*f*) fisheries;

    (*g*) water, that is to say, water supplies, irrigation and canals, drainage and embankments, water storage and water power subject to the provisions of entry 56 of List I of the Seventh Schedule;

    (*h*) social security and social insurance; employment and unemployment;

    (*i*) flood control schemes for protection of villages, paddy fields, markets, towns, etc. (not of technical nature);

    (*j*) theatre and dramatic performances, cinemas subject to the provisions of entry 60 of List I of the Seventh Schedule; sports, entertainments and amusements;

    (*k*) public health and sanitation, hospitals and dispensaries;

    (*l*) minor irrigation;

    (*m*) trade and commerce in, and the production supply and distribution of, food stuffs, cattle fodder, raw cotton and raw jute;

    (*n*) libraries, museums and other similar institutions controlled or financed by the State; ancient and historical monuments and records other than those declared by or under any law made by Parliament to be of national importance; and

    (*o*) alienation of land.

(2) All laws made by the North Cachar Hills Autonomous Council and the Karbi Anglong Autonomous Council under paragraph 3 or under this paragraph shall, in so far as they relate to matters specified in List III of the Seventh Schedule, be submitted forthwith to the Governor who shall reserve the same for the consideration of the President.

(3) When a law is reserved for the consideration of the President, the President shall declare either that he assents to the said law or that he withholds assent therefrom:

Provided that the President may direct the Governor to return the law to the North Cachar Hills Autonomous Council or the Karbi Anglong Autonomous Council, as the case may be, together with a message requesting that the said Council will reconsider the law or any specified provisions thereof and, in particular, will, consider the desirability of introducing any such amendments as he may recommend in his message and, when the law is so returned, the said Council shall consider the law accordingly within a period of six months from the date of receipt of such message and, if the law is again passed by the said Council with or without amendment it shall be presented again to the President for his consideration.".

After paragraph 3A, the following paragraph has been inserted in its application to the State of Assam by the Sixth Schedule to the Constitution (Amendment) Act, 2003 (44 of 2003), s. 2 (w.e.f. 7-9-2003), namely:—

"3B. **Additional powers of the Bodoland Territorial Council to make laws.**—(1) Without prejudice to the provisions of paragraph 3, the Bodoland Territorial Council within its areas shall have power to make laws with respect to :—

(i) agriculture, including agricultural education and research, protection against pests and prevention of plant diseases; (ii) animal husbandry and veterinary, that is to say, preservation, protection and improvement of stock and prevention of animal diseases, veterinary training and practice, cattle pounds; (iii) co-operation; (iv) cultural affairs; (v) education, that is to say, primary education, higher secondary including vocational training, adult education, college education (general); (vi) fisheries; (vii) flood control for protection of village, paddy fields, markets and towns (not of technical nature); (viii) Food and civil supply; (ix) forests (other than reserved forests); (x) handloom and textile; (xi) health and family welfare, (xii) intoxicating liquors, opium and derivatives, subject to the provisions of entry 84 of List I of the Seventh Schedule; (xiii) irrigation; (xiv) labour and employment; (xv) land and revenue; (xvi) library services (financed and controlled by the State Government); (xvii) lotteries (subject to the provisions of entry 40 of List I of the Seventh Schedule), theatres, dramatic performances and cinemas (subject to the provisions of entry 60 of List I of the Seventh Schedule); (xviii) markets and fairs; (xix) municipal corporation, improvement trust, district boards and other local authorities; (xx) museum and archaeology institutions controlled or financed by the State, ancient and historical monuments and records other than those declared by or under any law made by Parliament to be of national importance; (xxi) panchayat and rural development; (xxii) planning and development; (xxiii) printing and stationery; (xxiv) public health engineering; (xxv) public works department; (xxvi) publicity and public relations; (xxvii) registration of births and deaths; (xxviii) relief and rehabilitation; (xxix) sericulture; (xxx) small, cottage and rural industry subject to the provisions of entries 7 and 52 of List I of the Seventh Schedule; (xxxi) social Welfare; (xxxii) soil conservation; (xxxiii) sports and youth welfare; (xxxiv) statistics; (xxxv) tourism; (xxxvi) transport (roads, bridges, ferries and other means of communications not specified in List I of the Seventh Schedule, municipal tramways, ropeways, inland waterways and traffic thereon subject to the provision of List I and List III of the Seventh Schedule with regard to such waterways, vehicles other than mechanically propelled vehicles); (xxxvii) tribal research institute controlled and financed by the State Government; (xxxviii) urban development—town and country planning; (xxxix) weights and measures subject to the provisions of entry 50 of List I of the Seventh Schedule; and (xl) Welfare of plain tribes and backward classes:

Provided that nothing in such laws shall—

    (a)   extinguish or modify the existing rights and privileges of any citizen in respect of his land at the date of commencement of this Act; and

    (b)   disallow and citizen from acquiring land either by way of inheritance, allotment, settlement or by any other way of transfer if such citizen is otherwise eligible for such acquisition of land within the Bodoland Territorial Areas District.

(2) All laws made under paragraph 3 or under this paragraph shall in so far as they relate to matters specified in List III of the Seventh Schedule, be submitted forthwith to the Governor who shall reserve the same for the consideration of the President.

laws.—(1) The Regional Council for an autonomous region in respect of all areas within such region and the District Council for an autonomous district in respect of all areas within the district except those which are under the authority of Regional Councils, if any, within the district shall have power to make laws with respect to—

(*a*) the allotment, occupation or use, or the setting apart, of land, other than any land which is a reserved forest for the purposes of agriculture or grazing or for residential or other non-agricultural purposes or for any other purpose likely to promote the interests of the inhabitants of any village or town:

Provided that nothing in such laws shall prevent the compulsory acquisition of any land, whether occupied or unoccupied, for public purposes ¹[by the Government of the State concerned] in accordance with the law for the time being in force authorising such acquisition;

(*b*) the management of any forest not being a reserved forest;

(*c*) the use of any canal or water-course for the purpose of agriculture;

(*d*) the regulation of the practice of *jhum* or other forms of shifting cultivation;

(*e*) the establishment of village or town committees or councils and their powers;

(*f*) any other matter relating to village or town administration, including village or town police and public health and sanitation;

(*g*) the appointment or succession of Chiefs or Headmen;

(*h*) the inheritance of property;

---

(3) When a law is reserved for the consideration of the President, the President shall declare either that he assents to the said law or that he withholds assent therefrom:

Provided that the President may direct the Governor to return the law to the Bodoland Territorial Council, together with the message requesting that the said Council will reconsider the law or any specified provisions thereof and, in particular, will consider the desirability of introducing any such amendments as he may recommend in his message and, when the law is so returned, the said Council shall consider the law accordingly within a period of six months from the date of receipt of such message and, if the law is again passed by the said Council with or without amendments it shall be presented again to the President for his consideration.".

1   Subs. by the North-Eastern Areas (Reorganisation) Act, 1971 (81 of 1971), s. 71(i) and Eighth Sch., for certain words (w.e.f. 21-1-1972).

¹[(*i*) marriage and divorce;]

(*j*) social customs.

(2) In this paragraph, a "reserved forest" means any area which is a reserved forest under the Assam Forest Regulation, 1891, or under any other law for the time being in force in the area in question.

(3) All laws made under this paragraph shall be submitted forthwith to the Governor and, until assented to by him, shall have no effect.

²4. **Administration of justice in autonomous districts and autonomous regions.**—(1) The Regional Council for an autonomous region in respect of areas within such region and the District Council for an autonomous district in respect of areas within the district other than those which are under the authority of the Regional Councils, if any, within the district may constitute village councils or courts for the trial of suits and cases between the parties all of whom belong to Scheduled Tribes within such areas, other than suits and cases to which the provisions of sub-paragraph (1) of paragraph 5 of this Schedule apply, to the exclusion of any court in the State, and may appoint suitable persons to be members of such village councils or presiding officers of such courts, and may also appoint such officers as may be necessary for the administration of the laws made under paragraph 3 of this Schedule.

(2) Notwithstanding anything in this Constitution, the Regional Council for an autonomous region or any court constituted in that behalf by the Regional Council or, if in respect of any area within an autonomous district there is no Regional Council, the District Council for such district, or any court constituted in that behalf by the District Council, shall exercise the powers of a court of appeal in respect of all suits and cases triable by a village council or court constituted under sub-paragraph (1) of this paragraph within such region or area, as the case may be, other than those to which the provisions of sub-paragraph (1) of paragraph 5 of this Schedule

---

1 Subs. by the Assam Reorganisation (Meghalaya) Act, 1969 (55 of 1969), s. 74 and Fourth Sch., for cl. (i) (w.e.f. 2-4-1970).

2 Paragraph 4 has been amended in its application to the State of Assam by the Sixth Schedule to the Constitution (Amendment) Act, 2003 (44 of 2003), s. 2, (w.e.f. 7-9-2003) so as to insert the following sub-paragraph after sub-paragraph (5), namely:—

"(6) Nothing in this paragraph shall apply to the Bodoland Territorial Council constituted under the proviso to sub-paragraph (3) of paragraph 2 of this Schedule."

apply, and no other court except the High Court and the Supreme Court shall have jurisdiction over such suits or cases.

(3) The High Court [1]*** shall have and exercise such jurisdiction over the suits and cases to which the provisions of sub-paragraph (2) of this paragraph apply as the Governor may from time to time by order specify.

(4) A Regional Council or District Council, as the case may be, may with the previous approval of the Governor make rules regulating—

(a) the constitution of village councils and courts and the powers to be exercised by them under this paragraph;

(b) the procedure to be followed by village councils or courts in the trial of suits and cases under sub-paragraph (1) of this paragraph;

(c) the procedure to be followed by the Regional or District Council or any court constituted by such Council in appeals and other proceedings under sub-paragraph (2) of this paragraph;

(d) the enforcement of decisions and orders of such councils and courts;

(e) all other ancillary matters for the carrying out of the provisions of sub-paragraphs (1) and (2) of this paragraph.

[2][(5) On and from such date as the President may, [3][after consulting the Government of the State concerned], by notification appoint in this behalf, this paragraph shall have effect in relation to such autonomous district or region as may be specified in the notification, as if—

(i) in sub-paragraph (1), for the words "between the parties all of whom belong to Scheduled Tribes within such areas, other than suits and cases to which the provisions of sub-paragraph (1) of paragraph 5 of this Schedule apply,", the words "not being suits and cases of the nature referred to in sub-paragraph (1) of paragraph (5) of this Schedule,

---

1 The words "of Assam" omitted by the North-Eastern Areas (Reorganisation) Act, 1971 (81 of 1971), s. 71(i) and Eighth Sch. (w.e.f. 21-1-1972).

2 Ins. by the Assam Reorganisation (Meghalaya) Act, 1969 (55 of 1969), s. 74 and Fourth Sch. (w.e.f. 2-4-1970).

3 Subs. by the North-Eastern Areas (Reorganisation) Act, 1971 (81 of 1971), s. 71(i) and Eighth Sch., for certain words (w.e.f. 21-1-1972).

which the Governor may specify in this behalf," had been substituted;

(*ii*) sub-paragraphs (2) and (3) had been omitted;

(*iii*) in sub-paragraph (4)—

(*a*) for the words "A Regional Council or District Council, as the case may be, may with the previous approval of the Governor make rules regulating", the words "the Governor may make rules regulating" had been substituted; and

(*b*) for clause (*a*), the following clause had been substituted, namely:—

"(*a*) the constitution of village councils and courts, the powers to be exercised by them under this paragraph and the courts to which appeals from the decisions of village councils and courts shall lie;";

(*c*) for clause (*c*), the following clause had been substituted, namely:—

"(*c*) the transfer of appeals and other proceedings pending before the Regional or District Council or any court constituted by such Council immediately before the date appointed by the President under sub-paragraph (5);"; and

(*d*) in clause (*e*), for the words, brackets and figures "sub-paragraphs (1) and (2)", the word, brackets and figure "sub-paragraph (1)" had been substituted.]

5. **Conferment of powers under the Code of Civil Procedure, 1908, and the Code of Criminal Procedure, 1898[1], on the Regional and District Councils and on certain courts and officers for the trial of certain suits, cases and offences.**—(1) The Governor may, for the trial of suits or cases arising out of any law in force in any autonomous district or region being a law specified in that behalf by the Governor, or for the trial of offences punishable with death, transportation for life, or imprisonment for a term of not less than five years under the Indian Penal Code or under any other law for the time being applicable to such district or region, confer on the

---

1 *See* the Code of Criminal Procedure, 1973 (2 of 1974).

District Council or the Regional Council having authority over such district or region or on courts constituted by such District Council or on any officer appointed in that behalf by the Governor, such powers under the Code of Civil Procedure, 1908, or, as the case may be, the Code of Criminal Procedure, 1898[1], as he deems appropriate, and thereupon the said Council, court or officer shall try the suits, cases or offences in exercise of the powers so conferred.

(2) The Governor may withdraw or modify any of the powers conferred on a District Council, Regional Council, court or officer under sub-paragraph (1) of this paragraph.

(3) Save as expressly provided in this paragraph, the Code of Civil Procedure, 1908, and the Code of Criminal Procedure, 1898[1], shall not apply to the trial of any suits, cases or offences in an autonomous district or in any autonomous region to which the provisions of this paragraph apply.

[1][(4) On and from the date appointed by the President under sub-paragraph (5) of paragraph 4 in relation to any autonomous district or autonomous region, nothing contained in this paragraph shall, in its application to that district or region, be deemed to authorise the Governor to confer on the District Council or Regional Council or on courts constituted by the District Council any of the powers referred to in sub-paragraph (1) of this paragraph.]

[2][6. **Powers of the District Council to establish primary schools, etc.**— (1) The District Council for an autonomous district may establish, construct, or manage primary schools, dispensaries, markets, [3][cattle pounds], ferries, fisheries, roads, road transport and waterways in the district and may, with the previous approval of the Governor, make regulations for the regulation and control thereof and, in particular, may prescribe the language and the manner in which primary education shall be imparted in the primary schools in the district.

(2) The Governor may, with the consent of any District Council, entrust either conditionally or unconditionally to that Council or to

---

1 Ins. by the Assam Reorganisation (Meghalaya) Act, 1969 (55 of 1969), s. 74 and Fourth Sch. (w.e.f. 2-4-1970).
2 Subs. by s. 74 and Fourth Sch., *ibid.* for "paragraph 6" (w.e.f. 2-4-1970).
3 Subs. by the Repealing and Amending Act, 1974 (56 of 1974), s. 4, for "cattle ponds" (w.e.f. 20-12-1974).

its officers functions in relation to agriculture, animal husbandry, community projects, co-operative societies, social welfare, village planning or any other matter to which the executive power of the State [1]*** extends.

7. **District and Regional Funds.**—(1) There shall be constituted for each autonomous district, a District Fund and for each autonomous region, a Regional Fund to which shall be credited all moneys received respectively by the District Council for that district and the Regional Council for that region in the course of the administration of such district or region, as the case may be, in accordance with the provisions of this Constitution.

[2][(2) The Governor may make rules for the management of the District Fund, or, as the case may be, the Regional Fund and for the procedure to be followed in respect of payment of money into the said Fund, the withdrawal of moneys therefrom, the custody of moneys therein and any other matter connected with or ancillary to the matters aforesaid.

(3) The accounts of the District Council or, as the case may be, the Regional Council shall be kept in such form as the Comptroller and Auditor-General of India may, with the approval of the President, prescribe.

(4) The Comptroller and Auditor-General shall cause the accounts of the District and Regional Councils to be audited in such manner as he may think fit, and the reports of the Comptroller and Auditor-General relating to such accounts shall be submitted to the Governor who shall cause them to be laid before the Council.]

8. **Powers to assess and collect land revenue and to impose taxes.**—(1) The Regional Council for an autonomous region in respect of all lands within such region and the District Council for an autonomous district in respect of all lands within the district except those which are in the areas under the authority of Regional Councils, if any, within the district, shall have the power to assess and collect revenue in respect of such lands in accordance with the principles for

---

1 The words "of Assam or Meghalaya, as the case may be," omitted by the North- Eastern Areas (Reorganisation) Act, 1971 (81 of 1971), s. 71(i) and Eighth Sch. (w.e.f. 21-1-1972).
2 Subs. by the Assam Reorganisation (Meghalaya) Act, 1969 (55 of 1969), s. 74 and Fourth Sch., for sub-paragraph (2) (w.e.f. 2-4-1970).

the time being followed [1][by the Government of the State in assessing lands for the purpose of land revenue in the State generally.]

(2) The Regional Council for an autonomous region in respect of areas within such region and the District Council for an autonomous district in respect of all areas in the district except those which are under the authority of Regional Councils, if any, within the district, shall have power to levy and collect taxes on lands and buildings, and tolls on persons resident within such areas.

(3) The District Council for an autonomous district shall have the power to levy and collect all or any of the following taxes within such district, that is to say —

    (*a*) taxes on professions, trades, callings and employments;

    (*b*) taxes on animals, vehicles and boats;

    (*c*) taxes on the entry of goods into a market for sale therein, and tolls on passengers and goods carried in ferries; [2]***

    (*d*) taxes for the maintenance of schools, dispensaries or roads; [3][and]

    [4][(*e*) taxes on entertainment and amusements.]

(4) A Regional Council or District Council, as the case may be, may make regulations to provide for the levy and collection of any of the taxes specified in sub-paragraphs (2) and (3) of this paragraph [5][and every such regulation shall be submitted forthwith to the Governor and, until assented to by him, shall have no effect].

[6]9. **Licences or leases for the purpose of prospecting for, or extraction of, minerals.**—(1) Such share of the royalties accruing

---

1 Subs. by the North-Eastern Areas (Reorganisation) Act, 1971 (81 of 1971), s. 71(i) and Eighth Sch., for certain words (w.e.f. 21-1-1972).

2 The word "and" omitted by the Constitution (One Hundred and First Amendment) Act, 2016, s. 16(*i*) (w.e.f. 16-9-2016).

3 Ins. by s. 16(ii), *ibid*. (w.e.f. 16-9-2016).

4 Ins. by s. 16(iii), *ibid*. (w.e.f. 16-9-2016).

5 Ins. by the Assam Reorganisation (Meghalaya) Act, 1969 (55 of 1969), s. 74 and Fourth Sch. (w.e.f. 2-4-1970).

6 Paragraph 9 has been amended in its application to the States of Tripura and Mizoram by the Sixth Schedule to the Constitution (Amendment) Act, 1988 (67 of 1988), s. 2 (w.e.f. 16-12-1988), so as to insert the following sub-paragraph after sub-paragraph (2), namely:—

"(3) The Governor may, by order, direct that the share of royalties to be made over to a District Council under this paragraph shall be made over to that Council within a period of one year from the date of any agreement under sub-paragraph (1) or, as the case may be, of any determination under sub-paragraph (2).".

each year from licences or leases for the purpose of prospecting for, or the extraction of, minerals granted by [1][the Government of the State] in respect of any area within an autonomous district as may be agreed upon between [6][the Government of the State] and the District Council of such district shall be made over to that District Council.

(2) If any dispute arises as to the share of such royalties to be made over to a District Council, it shall be referred to the Governor for determination and the amount determined by the Governor in his discretion shall be deemed to be the amount payable under sub-paragraph (1) of this paragraph to the District Council and the decision of the Governor shall be final.

[2]10. **Power of District Council to make regulations for the control of money-lending and trading by non-tribals.**—(1) The District Council of an autonomous district may make regulations for the regulation and control of money-lending or trading within the district by persons other than Scheduled Tribes resident in the district.

(2) In particular and without prejudice to the generality of the foregoing power, such regulations may—

> (a) prescribe that no one except the holder of a licence issued in that behalf shall carry on the business of money-lending;
>
> (b) prescribe the maximum rate of interest which may be charged or be recovered by a money-lender;

---

1 Subs. by the North-Eastern Areas (Reorganisation) Act, 1971 (81 of 1971), s. 71(i) and Eighth Sch., for "the Government of Assam" (w.e.f. 21-1-1972).

2 Paragraph 10 has been amended in its application to the States of Tripura and Mizoram by the Sixth Schedule to the Constitution (Amendment) Act, 1988 (67 of 1988) (w.e.f. 16-12-1988) s.2, as under—

> (a) in the heading, the words "by non-tribals" shall be omitted;
>
> (b) in sub-paragraph (1), the words "other than Scheduled Tribes" shall be omitted;
>
> (c) in sub-paragraph (2), for clause (d), the following clause shall be substituted, namely:—
>
> "(d) prescribe that no person resident in the district shall carry on any trade, whether wholesale or retail, except under a licence issued in that behalf by the District Council:".

Paragraph 10 has been amended in its application to the State of Assam by the Sixth Schedule to the Constitution (Amendment) Act, 2003 (44 of 2003), s. 2 (w.e.f. 7-9-2003), so as to insert the following sub-paragraph after sub-paragraph (3), namely:—

"(4) Nothing in this paragraph shall apply to the Bodoland Territorial Council constituted under the proviso to sub-paragraph (3) of paragraph 2 of this Schedule.".

(c) provide for the maintenance of accounts by money-lenders and for the inspection of such accounts by officers appointed in that behalf by the District Council;

(d) prescribe that no person who is not a member of the Scheduled Tribes resident in the district shall carry on wholesale or retail business in any commodity except under a licence issued in that behalf by the District Council :

Provided that no regulations may be made under this paragraph unless they are passed by a majority of not less than three-fourths of the total membership of the District Council:

Provided further that it shall not be competent under any such regulations to refuse the grant of a licence to a money-lender or a trader who has been carrying on business within the district since before the time of the making of such regulations.

(3) All regulations made under this paragraph shall be submitted forthwith to the Governor and, until assented to by him, shall have no effect.

11. **Publication of laws, rules and regulations made under the Schedule.**—All laws, rules and regulations made under this Schedule by a District Council or a Regional Council shall be published forthwith in the Official Gazette of the State and shall on such publication have the force of law.

¹12. ²**[Application of Acts of Parliament and of the Legislature of the State of Assam to autonomous districts and autonomous**

---

1 Paragraph 12 has been amended to its application to the State of Assam by the Sixth Schedule to the Constitution (Amendment) Act, 1995 (42 of 1995), s. 2 (w.e.f. 12-9-1995) as under,- "in paragraph 12, in sub-paragraph (1), for the words and figure 'matters specified in paragraph 3 of this Schedule', the words, figures and letter 'matters specified in paragraph 3 or paragraph 3A of this Schedule' shall be substituted."

Paragraph 12 has been amended in its application to the State of Assam by the Sixth Schedule to the Constitution (Amendment) Act, 2003 (44 of 2003), s. 2 (w.e.f. 7-9-2003), as under,— "in paragraph 12, in sub-paragraph (1), in clause (a), for the words, figures and letter 'matters specified in paragraph 3 or paragraph 3A of this Schedule', the words, figures and letters 'matters specified in paragraph 3 or paragraph 3A or paragraph 3B of this Schedule' shall be substituted."

2 Subs by the North-Eastern Areas (Reorganisation) Act, 1971 (81 of 1971), s. 71(i) and Eighth Sch., for the heading (w.e.f. 21-1-1972).

regions in the State of Assam].— (1) Notwithstanding anything in this Constitution, —

(a) no Act of the ¹[Legislature of the State of Assam] in respect of any of the matters specified in paragraph 3 of this Schedule as matters with respect to which a District Council or a Regional Council may make laws, and no Act of the ¹[Legislature of the State of Assam] prohibiting or restricting the consumption of any non-distilled alcoholic liquor shall apply to any autonomous district or autonomous region ²[in that State] unless in either case the District Council for such district or having jurisdiction over such region by public notification so directs, and the District Council in giving such direction with respect to any Act may direct that the Act shall in its application to such district or region or any part thereof have effect subject to such exceptions or modifications as it thinks fit;

(b) the Governor may, by public notification, direct that any Act of Parliament or of the ¹[Legislature of the State of Assam] to which the provisions of clause (a) of this sub-paragraph do not apply shall not apply to an autonomous district or an autonomous region ²[in that State], or shall apply to such district or region or any part thereof subject to such exceptions or modifications as he may specify in the notification.

(2) Any direction given under sub-paragraph (1) of this paragraph may be given so as to have retrospective effect.

³[12A. **Application of Acts of Parliament and of the Legislature of the State of Meghalaya to autonomous districts and autonomous regions in the State of Meghalaya.**—Notwithstanding anything in this Constitution,—

(a) if any provision of a law made by a District or Regional Council in the State of Meghalaya with respect to any matter specified in sub-paragraph (1) of paragraph 3 of

---

1 Subs. by the North-Eastern Areas (Reorganisation) Act, 1971 (81 of 1971), s. 71(i) and Eighth Sch., for "Legislature of the State" (w.e.f. 21-1-1972).
2 Ins. by s. 71(i) and Eighth Sch., *ibid.* (w.e.f. 21-1-1972).
3 Subs. by s. 71(i) and Eighth Sch., *ibid.*, for paragraph 12A (w.e.f. 21-1-1972).

this Schedule or if any provision of any regulation made by a District Council or a Regional Council in that State under paragraph 8 or paragraph 10 of this Schedule, is repugnant to any provision of a law made by the Legislature of the State of Meghalaya with respect to that matter, then, the law or regulation made by the District Council or, as the case may be, the Regional Council whether made before or after the law made by the Legislature of the State of Meghalaya, shall, to the extent of repugnancy, be void and the law made by the Legislature of the State of Meghalaya shall prevail;

(*b*) the President may, with respect to any Act of Parliament, by notification, direct that it shall not apply to an autonomous district or an autonomous region in the State of Meghalaya, or shall apply to such district or region or any part thereof subject to such exceptions or modifications as he may specify in the notification and any such direction may be given so as to have retrospective effect.]

¹[12AA. **Application of Acts of Parliament and of the Legislature of the State of Tripura to the autonomous districts and autonomous regions in the State of Tripura.**—Notwithstanding anything in this Constitution,—

(*a*) no Act of the Legislature of the State of Tripura in respect of any of the matters specified in paragraph 3 of this Schedule as matters with respect to which a District Council or a Regional Council may make laws, and no Act of the Legislature of the State of Tripura prohibiting or restricting the consumption of any non-distilled alcoholic liquor shall apply to the autonomous district or an autonomous region in that State unless, in either case, the District Council for that district or having jurisdiction over such region by public notification so directs, and the District Council in giving such direction with respect to

---

1 Paragraph 12AA ins. by the Constitution (Forty-ninth Amendment) Act, 1984, s. 4 (w.e.f. 1-4-1985) and subsequently subs. by the Sixth Schedule to the Constitution (Amendment) Act, 1988 (67 of 1988), s. 2 (w.e.f. 16-12-1988).

any Act may direct that the Act shall, in its application to that district or such region or any part thereof have effect subject to such exceptions or modifications as it thinks fit;

(b) the Governor may, by public notification, direct that any Act of the Legislature of the State of Tripura to which the provisions of clause (a) of this sub-paragraph do not apply, shall not apply to the autonomous district or an autonomous region in that State, or shall apply to that district or such region, or any part thereof, subject to such exceptions or modifications, as he may specify in the notification;

(c) the President may, with respect to any Act of Parliament, by notification, direct that it shall not apply to the autonomous district or an autonomous region in the State of Tripura, or shall apply to such district or region or any part thereof, subject to such exceptions or modifications as he may specify in the notification and any such direction may be given so as to have retrospective effect.]

¹[12B. **Application of Acts of Parliament and of the Legislature of the State of Mizoram to autonomous districts and autonomous regions in the State of Mizoram.**—Notwithstanding anything in this Constitution,—

(a) no Act of the Legislature of the State of Mizoram in respect of any of the matters specified in paragraph 3 of this Schedule as matters with respect to which a District Council or a Regional Council may make laws, and no Act of the Legislature of the State of Mizoram prohibiting or restricting the consumption of any non-distilled alcoholic liquor shall apply to any autonomous district or autonomous region in that State unless, in either case, the District Council for such district or having jurisdiction over such region, by public notification, so directs, and the District Council, in giving such direction with respect to any Act, may direct that the Act shall, in its application

---

1 Subs. by the Sixth Schedule to the Constitution (Amendment) Act, 1988 (67 of 1988), s. 2, for paragraph 12AA (w.e.f. 16-12-1988).

to such district or region or any part thereof, have effect subject to such exceptions or modifications as it thinks fit;

(*b*) the Governor may, by public notification, direct that any Act of the Legislature of the State of Mizoram to which the provisions of clause (*a*) of this sub-paragraph do not apply, shall not apply to an autonomous district or an autonomous region in that State, or shall apply to such district or region, or any part thereof, subject to such exceptions or modifications, as he may specify in the notification;

(*c*) the President may, with respect to any Act of Parliament, by notification, direct that it shall not apply to an autonomous district or an autonomous region in the State of Mizoram, or shall apply to such district or region or any part thereof, subject to such exceptions or modifications as he may specify in the notification and any such direction may be given so as to have retrospective effect.]

13. **Estimated receipts and expenditure pertaining to autonomous districts to be shown separately in the annual financial statement.**—The estimated receipts and expenditure pertaining to an autonomous district which are to be credited to, or is to be made from, the Consolidated Fund of the State [1]*** shall be first placed before the District Council for discussion and then after such discussion be shown separately in the annual financial statement of the State to be laid before the Legislature of the State under article 202.

[2]14. **Appointment of Commission to inquire into and report on the administration of autonomous districts and autonomous regions.**—(1) The Governor may at any time appoint a Commission to examine and report on any matter specified by him relating to the administration of the autonomous districts and autonomous regions in the State, including matters specified in clauses (*c*), (*d*),

---

1 The words "of Assam" omitted by the North-Eastern Areas (Reorganisation) Act, 1971 (81 of 1971), s. 71(i) and Eighth Sch. (w.e.f. 21-1-1972).

2 Paragraph 14 has been amended in its application to the State of Assam by the Sixth Schedule to the Constitution (Amendment) Act, 1995 (42 of 1995), s. 2 (w.e.f.12.9.1995) as under:—
'in paragraph 14, in sub-paragraph (2), the words "with the recommendations of the Governor with respect thereto" shall be omitted.'.

(*e*) and (*f*) of sub-paragraph (3) of paragraph 1 of this Schedule, or may appoint a Commission to inquire into and report from time to time on the administration of autonomous districts and autonomous regions in the State generally and in particular on—

    (*a*) the provision of educational and medical facilities and communications in such districts and regions;

    (*b*) the need for any new or special legislation in respect of such districts and regions; and

    (*c*) the administration of the laws, rules and regulations made by the District and Regional Councils;

and define the procedure to be followed by such Commission.

(2) The report of every such Commission with the recommendations of the Governor with respect thereto shall be laid before the Legislature of the State by the Minister concerned together with an explanatory memorandum regarding the action proposed to be taken thereon by [1][the Government of the State.]

(3) In allocating the business of the Government of the State among his Ministers the Governor may place one of his Ministers specially in charge of the welfare of the autonomous districts and autonomous regions in the State.

[2]15. **Annulment or suspension of acts and resolutions of District and Regional Councils.**—(1) If at any time the Governor is satisfied that an act or resolution of a District or a Regional Council is likely to endanger the safety of India [3][or is likely to be prejudicial to public order], he may annul or suspend such act or resolution and take such steps as he may consider necessary (including the suspension of the Council and the assumption to himself of all or any of the powers vested in or exercisable by the Council) to

---

1 Subs. by the North-Eastern Areas (Reorganisation) Act, 1971 (81 of 1971), s. 71(i) and Eighth Sch., for "the Government of Assam" (w.e.f. 21-1-1972).

2 Paragraph 15 has been amended in its application to the States of Tripura and Mizoram by the Sixth Schedule to the Constitution (Amendment) Act, 1988 (67 of 1988), s. 2 (w.e.f. 16-12-1988), as under,—

    'In paragraph 15, in sub-paragraph (2), -

      (*a*) in the opening paragraph, for the words "by the Legislature of the State", the words "by him" shall be substituted;

      (*b*) the proviso shall be omitted.'.

3 Ins. by the Assam Reorganisation (Meghalaya) Act, 1969 (55 of 1969), s. 74 and Fourth Sch. (w.e.f. 2-4-1970).

prevent the commission or continuance of such act, or the giving of effect to such resolution.

(2) Any order made by the Governor under sub-paragraph (1) of this paragraph together with the reasons therefor shall be laid before the Legislature of the State as soon as possible and the order shall, unless revoked by the Legislature of the State, continue in force for a period of twelve months from the date on which it was so made:

Provided that if and so often as a resolution approving the continuance in force of such order is passed by the Legislature of the State, the order shall unless cancelled by the Governor continue in force for a further period of twelve months from the date on which under this paragraph it would otherwise have ceased to operate.

¹16. **Dissolution of a District or a Regional Council.—** ²[(1)] The Governor may on the recommendation of a Commission appointed under paragraph 14 of this Schedule by public notification order the dissolution of a District or a Regional Council, and—

(a) direct that a fresh general election shall be held immediately for the reconstitution of the Council, or

(b) subject to the previous approval of the Legislature of the State assume the administration of the area under the authority of such Council himself or place the administration of such area under the Commission appointed under the said paragraph or any other body considered suitable by him for a period not exceeding twelve months:

Provided that when an order under clause (a) of this paragraph has been made, the Governor may take the action referred to in clause (b) of this paragraph with regard to the administration of the

---

1 Paragraph 16 has been amended in its application to the States of Tripura and Mizoram by the Sixth Schedule to the Constitution (Amendment) Act, 1988 (67 of 1988) s. 2 (w.e.f. 16-12-1988), as under:—

'(a) in sub-paragraph (1), the words "subject to the previous approval of the Legislature of the State" occurring in clause (b), and the second proviso shall be omitted;

(b) for sub-paragraph (3), the following sub-paragraph shall be substituted, namely:—

"(3) Every order made under sub-paragraph (1) or sub-paragraph (2) of this paragraph, along with the reasons therefor shall be laid before the Legislature of the State.".'.

2 Paragraph 16 renumbered as sub-paragraph (1) thereof by the Assam Reorganisation (Meghalaya) Act, 1969 (55 of 1969), s. 74 and Fourth Sch. (w.e.f. 2-4-1970).

area in question pending the reconstitution of the Council on fresh general election:

Provided further that no action shall be taken under clause (*b*) of this paragraph without giving the District or the Regional Council, as the case may be, an opportunity of placing its views before the Legislature of the State.

¹[(2) If at any time the Governor is satisfied that a situation has arisen in which the administration of an autonomous district or region cannot be carried on in accordance with the provisions of this Schedule, he may, by public notification, assume to himself all or any of the functions or powers vested in or exercisable by the District Council or, as the case may be, the Regional Council and declare that such functions or powers shall be exercisable by such person or authority as he may specify in this behalf, for a period not exceeding six months:

Provided that the Governor may by a further order or orders extend the operation of the initial order by a period not exceeding six months on each occasion.

(3) Every order made under sub-paragraph (2) of this paragraph with the reasons therefor shall be laid before the Legislature of the State and shall cease to operate at the expiration of thirty days from the date on which the State Legislature first sits after the issue of the order, unless, before the expiry of that period it has been approved by that State Legislature.]

²17. **Exclusion of areas from autonomous districts in forming constituencies in such districts.**—For the purposes of elections to ³[the Legislative Assembly of Assam or Meghalaya] ⁴[or Tripura] ⁵[or Mizoram], the Governor may by order declare that

---

1 Added by the Assam Reorganisation (Meghalaya) Act, 1969 (55 of 1969), s. 74 and Fourth Sch. (w.e.f. 2-4-1970).
2 Paragraph 17 has been amended in its application to the State of Assam by the Sixth Schedule to the Constitution (Amendment) Act, 2003 (44 of 2003), s. 2 (w.e.f. 7-9-2003), so as to insert the following proviso, namely:—
   "Provided that nothing in this paragraph shall apply to the Bodoland Territorial Areas District.".
3 Subs. by the North-Eastern Areas (Reorganisation) Act, 1971 (81 of 1971), s. 71(*i*) and Eighth Sch., for "the Legislative Assembly of Assam" (w.e.f. 21-1-1972).
4 Ins. by the Constitution (Forty-ninth Amendment) Act, 1984, s. 4 (w.e.f. 1-4-1985).
5 Ins. by the State of Mizoram Act, 1986 (34 of 1986), s. 39 (w.e.f. 20-2-1987).

any area within an autonomous district [1][in the State of Assam or Meghalaya [4][or Tripura] [5][or Mizoram], as the case may be,] shall not form part of any constituency to fill a seat or seats in the Assembly reserved for any such district but shall form part of a constituency to fill a seat or seats in the Assembly not so reserved to be specified in the order.

[2][18.*   *   *   *   *]

[3]19. **Transitional provisions.**—(1) As soon as possible after the commencement of this Constitution the Governor shall take steps for the constitution of a District Council for each autonomous district in the State under this Schedule and, until a District Council is so constituted for an autonomous district, the administration of such district shall be vested in the Governor and the following provisions shall apply to the administration of the areas within such district instead of the foregoing provisions of this Schedule, namely:—

(a) no Act of Parliament or of the Legislature of the State shall apply to any such area unless the Governor by public notification so directs; and the Governor in giving such a direction with respect to any Act may direct that the Act shall, in its application to the area or to any specified part thereof, have effect subject to such exceptions or modifications as he thinks fit;

(b) the Governor may make regulations for the peace and good government of any such area and any regulations so made may repeal or amend any Act of Parliament or of

---

1 Ins. by the North-Eastern Areas (Reorganisation) Act, 1971 (81 of 1971), s. 71(*i*) and Eighth Sch., for "the Legislative Assembly of Assam" (w.e.f. 21-1-1972).

2 Paragraph 18 omitted by s. 71(*i*) and Eighth Sch., *ibid.* (w.e.f. 21-1-1972).

3 Paragraph 19 has been amended in its application to the State of Assam by the Sixth Schedule to the Constitution (Amendment) Act, 2003 (44 of 2003), s. 2 (w.e.f. 7-9-2003), so as to insert the following sub-paragraph after sub-paragraph (3), namely :—

'(4) As soon as possible after the commencement of this Act an Interim Executive Council for Bodoland Territorial Areas District in Assam shall be formed by the Governor from amongst leaders of the Bodo movement, including the signatories to the Memorandum of Settlement, and shall provide adequate representation to the non-tribal communities in that area:

Provided that Interim Council shall be for a period of six months during which endeavour to hold the election to the Council shall be made.

Explanation.—For the purposes of this sub-paragraph, the expression "Memorandum of Settlement" means the Memorandum signed on the 10th day of February, 2003 between Government of India, Government of Assam and Bodo Liberation Tigers.'.

the Legislature of the State or any existing law which is for the time being applicable to such area.

(2) Any direction given by the Governor under clause (*a*) of sub-paragraph (1) of this paragraph may be given so as to have retrospective effect.

(3) All regulations made under clause (*b*) of sub-paragraph (1) of this paragraph shall be submitted forthwith to the President and, until assented to by him, shall have no effect.

[1][20. **Tribal areas.**—(1) The areas specified in Parts I, II [2][, IIA] and III of the table below shall respectively be the tribal areas within the State of Assam, the State of Meghalaya [2][, the State of Tripura] and the [3][State] of Mizoram.

(2) [4][Any reference in Part I, Part II or Part III of the table below] to any district shall be construed as a reference to the territories comprised within the autonomous district of that name existing immediately before the day appointed under clause (*b*) of section 2 of the North-Eastern Areas (Reorganisation) Act, 1971:

Provided that for the purposes of clauses (*e*) and (*f*) of sub-paragraph (1) of paragraph 3, paragraph 4, paragraph 5, paragraph 6, sub-paragraph (2), clauses (*a*), (*b*) and (*d*) of sub-paragraph (3) and sub-paragraph (4) of paragraph 8 and clause (*d*) of sub-paragraph (2) of paragraph 10 of this Schedule, no part of the area comprised within the municipality of Shillong shall be deemed to be within the [5][Khasi Hills District].

[2][(3) The reference in Part IIA in the table below to the "Tripura Tribal Areas District" shall be construed as a reference to the territory comprising the tribal areas specified in the First Schedule to the Tripura Tribal Areas Autonomous District Council Act, 1979.]

Table

1 Paragraph 20 subs. by the North Eastern Areas (Reorganisation) Act, 1971 (81 of 1971), s. 71(*i*) and Eighth Sch., for paragraph 20 (w.e.f. 21-1-1972).
2 Ins. by the Constitution (Forty-ninth Amendment) Act, 1984, s. 4 (w.e.f. 1-4-1985).
3 Subs. by the State of Mizoram Act, 1986 (34 of 1986), s. 39, for "Union territory" (w.e.f. 20-2-1987).
4 Subs. by the Constitution (Forty-ninth Amendment) Act, 1984, s. 4, for "Any reference in the table below" (w.e.f. 1-4-1985).
5 Subs. by the Government of Meghalaya Notification No. DCA 31/72/11, dated the 14th June, 1973, Gazette of Meghalaya, Pt. VA, dated 23-6-1973, p. 200.

Part I

1. The North Cachar Hills District.
2. ¹[The Karbi Anglong District.]
²[3. The Bodoland Territorial Areas District.]

Part II

³[1. Khasi Hills District.
2. Jaintia Hills District.]
3. The Garo Hills District.

⁴[PART IIA]

Tripura Tribal Areas District]

Part III

⁵*   *   *

⁶[1. The Chakma District.
⁷[2. The Mara District.
3. The Lai District.]]

---

1   Subs. by the Government of Assam Notification No. TAD/R/115/74/47, dated 14-10-1976 for "The Mikir Hills District".
2   Ins. by the Sixth Schedule to the Constitution (Amendment) Act, 2003 (44 of 2003), s. 2 (w.e.f. 7-9-2003).
3   Subs. by the Government of Meghalaya Notification No. DCA 31/72/11, dated the 14th June, 1973, Gazette of Meghalaya, Pt. VA, dated 23-6-1973, p. 200.
4   Ins. by the Constitution (Forty-ninth Amendment) Act, 1984, s. 4 (w.e.f. 1-4-1985).
5   The words "The Mizo District." omitted by the Government of Union Territories (Amendment) Act, 1971 (83 of 1971), s. 13 (w.e.f. 16-2-1972).
6   Ins. by the Mizoram District Councils (Miscellaneous Provisions) Order, 1972, published in the Mizoram Gazette, 1972, dated the 5th May, 1972, Vol. I, Pt. II, p.17 (w.e.f. 29-4-1972).
7   Subs. by the Sixth Schedule to the Constitution (Amendment) Act, 1988 (67 of 1988), s. 2, for serial numbers 2 and 3 and the entries relating thereto (w.e.f. 16-12-1988).

[20A. **Dissolution of the Mizo District Council.**—(1) Notwithstanding anything in this Schedule, the District Council of the Mizo District existing immediately before the prescribed date (hereinafter referred to as the Mizo District Council) shall stand dissolved and cease to exist.

(2) The Administrator of the Union territory of Mizoram may, by one or more orders, provide for all or any of the following matters, namely:—

(*a*) the transfer, in whole or in part, of the assets, rights and liabilities of the Mizo District Council (including the rights and liabilities under any contract made by it) to the Union or to any other authority;

(*b*) the substitution of the Union or any other authority for the Mizo District Council, or the addition of the Union or any other authority, as a party to any legal proceedings to which the Mizo District Council is a party;

(*c*) the transfer or re-employment of any employees of the Mizo District Council to or by the Union or any other authority, the terms and conditions of service applicable to such employees after such transfer or re-employment;

(*d*) the continuance of any laws, made by the Mizo District Council and in force immediately before its dissolution, subject to such adaptations and modifications, whether by way of repeal or amendment, as the Administrator may make in this behalf, until such laws are altered, repealed or amended by a competent Legislature or other competent authority;

(*e*) such incidental, consequential and supplementary matters as the Administrator considers necessary.

Explanation.—In this paragraph and in paragraph 20B of this Schedule, the expression "prescribed date" means the date on which the Legislative Assembly of the Union territory of Mizoram is duly constituted under and in accordance with the provisions of the Government of Union Territories Act, 1963.]

---

1 Paragraph 20A subs. by the North-Eastern Areas (Reorganisation) Act, 1971 (81 of 1971), s.14, for paragraph 20 and further subs. by the Government of Union Territories (Amendment) Act, 1971 (83 of 1971), s. 13, for paragraph 20A (w.e.f. 16-2-1972).

¹[20B. **Autonomous regions in the Union territory of Mizoram to be autonomous districts and transitory provisions consequent thereto.**—(1) Notwithstanding anything in this Schedule,—

> (*a*) every autonomous region existing immediately before the prescribed date in the Union territory of Mizoram shall, on and from that date, be an autonomous district in that Union territory (hereafter referred to as the corresponding new district) and the Administrator thereof may, by one or more orders, direct that such consequential amendments as are necessary to give effect to the provisions of this clause shall be made in paragraph 20 of this Schedule (including Part III of the table appended to that paragraph) and thereupon the said paragraph and the said Part III shall be deemed to have been amended accordingly;

> (*b*) every Regional Council of an autonomous region in the Union territory of Mizoram existing immediately before the prescribed date (hereafter referred to as the existing

---

1 1.Subs. by the Government of Union Territories (Amendment) Act, 1971 (83 of 1971), s. 13, for paragraph 20A (w.e.f. 16-2-1972).

* After paragraph 20B, the following paragraph has been inserted in its application to the State of Assam by the Sixth Schedule to the Constitution of India (Amendment) Act,1995 (42 of 1995), s.2 (w.e.f. 12-2-1995), namely:-

"20BA. **Exercise of discretionary powers by the Governor in the discharge of his functions.**—The Governor in the discharge of his functions under sub-paragraphs (2) and (3) of paragraph 1, sub-paragraphs (1), (6), sub-paragraph (6A) excluding the first proviso and sub-paragraph (7) of paragraph 2, sub-paragraph (3) of paragraph 3, sub-paragraph (4) of paragraph 4, paragraph 5, sub-paragraph (1) of paragraph 6, sub-paragraph (2) of paragraph 7, sub-paragraph (4) of paragraph 8, sub-paragraph (3) of paragraph 9, sub-paragraph (3) of paragraph 10, sub-paragraph (1) of paragraph 14, sub-paragraph (1) of paragraph 15 and sub-paragraphs (1) and (2) of paragraph 16 of this Schedule, shall, after consulting the Council of Ministers and the North Cachar Hills Autonomous Council or the Karbi Anglong Autonomous Council, as the case may be, take such action as he considers necessary in his discretion.".

* After paragraph 20B, the following paragraph has been inserted in its application to the State of Tripura and Mizoram, by the Sixth Schedule to the Constitution (Amendment) Act, 1988 (67 of 1988), s.2 (16-12-1988), namely:-

"20BB. **Exercise of discretionary powers by the Governor in the discharge of his functions.**—The Governor, in the discharge of his functions under sub- paragraphs (2) and (3) of paragraph 1, sub-paragraphs (1) and (7) of paragraph 2, sub-paragraph (3) of paragraph 3, sub-paragraph (4) of paragraph 4, paragraph 5, sub-paragraph (1) of paragraph 6, sub-paragraph (2) of paragraph 7, sub-paragraph (3) of paragraph 9, sub-paragraph (1) of paragraph 14, sub-paragraph (1) of paragraph 15 and sub-paragraphs (1) and (2) of paragraph 16 of this Schedule, shall, after consulting the Council of Ministers, and if he thinks it necessary, the District Council or the Regional Council concerned, take such action as he considers necessary in his discretion.".

Regional Council) shall, on and from that date and until a District Council is duly constituted for the corresponding new district, be deemed to be the District Council of that district (hereafter referred to as the corresponding new District Council).

(2) Every member whether elected or nominated of an existing Regional Council shall be deemed to have been elected or, as the case may be, nominated to the corresponding new District Council and shall hold office until a District Council is duly constituted for the corresponding new district under this Schedule.

(3) Until rules are made under sub-paragraph (7) of paragraph 2 and sub- paragraph (4) of paragraph 4 of this Schedule by the corresponding new District Council, the rules made under the said provisions by the existing Regional Council and in force immediately before the prescribed date shall have effect in relation to the corresponding new District Council subject to such adaptations and modifications as may be made therein by the Administrator of the Union territory of Mizoram.

(4) The Administrator of the Union territory of Mizoram may, by one or more orders, provide for all or any of the following matters, namely:—

(*a*) the transfer in whole or in part of the assets, rights and liabilities of the existing Regional Council (including the rights and liabilities under any contract made by it) to the corresponding new District Council;

(*b*) the substitution of the corresponding new District Council for the existing Regional Council as a party to the legal proceedings to which the existing Regional Council is a party;

(*c*) the transfer or re-employment of any employees of the existing Regional Council to or by the corresponding new District Council, the terms and conditions of service applicable to such employees after such transfer or re-employment;

(*d*) the continuance of any laws made by the existing Regional Council and in force immediately before the prescribed date, subject to such adaptations and modifications, whether by way of repeal or amendment, as the Administrator may make in this behalf until such laws are altered, repealed or amended by a competent Legislature or other competent authority;

(*e*) such incidental, consequential and supplementary matters as the Administrator considers necessary.

[20C. **Interpretation.**—Subject to any provision made in this behalf, the provisions of this Schedule shall, in their application to the Union territory of Mizoram, have effect—

(1) as if references to the Governor and Government of the State were references to the Administrator of the Union territory appointed under article 239, references to State (except in the expression "Government of the State") were references to the Union territory of Mizoram and references to the State Legislature were references to the Legislative Assembly of the Union territory of Mizoram;

(2) as if—

(*a*) in sub-paragraph (5) of paragraph 4, the provision for consultation with the Government of the State concerned had been omitted;

(*b*) in sub-paragraph (2) of paragraph 6, for the words "to which the executive power of the State extends", the words "with respect to which the Legislative Assembly of the Union territory of Mizoram has power to make laws" had been substituted;

(*c*) in paragraph 13, the words and figures "under article 202" had been omitted.]

21. **Amendment of the Schedule.**—(1) Parliament may from time to time by law amend by way of addition, variation or repeal any of the provisions of this Schedule and, when the Schedule is so amended, any reference to this Schedule in this Constitution shall be construed as a reference to such Schedule as so amended.

(2) No such law as is mentioned in sub-paragraph (1) of this paragraph shall be deemed to be an amendment of this Constitution for the purposes of article 368.

---

1 Subs. by the Government of Union Territories (Amendment) Act, 1971 (83 of 1971), s. 13, for paragraph 20A (w.e.f. 16-2-1972).

SEVENTH SCHEDULE

(Article 246)

List I—Union List

1. Defence of India and every part thereof including preparation for defence and all such acts as may be conducive in times of war to its prosecution and after its termination to effective demobilisation.

2. Naval, military and air forces; any other armed forces of the Union.

¹[2A. Deployment of any armed force of the Union or any other force subject to the control of the Union or any contingent or unit thereof in any State in aid of the civil power; powers, jurisdiction, privileges and liabilities of the members of such forces while on such deployment.]

3. Delimitation of cantonment areas, local self-government in such areas, the constitution and powers within such areas of cantonment authorities and the regulation of house accommodation (including the control of rents) in such areas.

4. Naval, military and air force works.

5. Arms, firearms, ammunition and explosives.

6. Atomic energy and mineral resources necessary for its production.

7. Industries declared by Parliament by law to be necessary for the purpose of defence or for the prosecution of war.

8. Central Bureau of Intelligence and Investigation.

9. Preventive detention for reasons connected with Defence, Foreign Affairs, or the security of India; persons subjected to such detention.

10. Foreign affairs; all matters which bring the Union into relation with any foreign country.

11. Diplomatic, consular and trade representation.

12. United Nations Organisation.

13. Participation in international conferences, associations and other bodies and implementing of decisions made thereat.

---

1 Ins. by the Constitution (Forty-second Amendment) Act, 1976, s. 57 (w.e.f. 3-1-1977).

14. Entering into treaties and agreements with foreign countries and implementing of treaties, agreements and conventions with foreign countries.

15. War and peace.

16. Foreign jurisdiction.

17. Citizenship, naturalisation and aliens.

18. Extradition.

19. Admission into, and emigration and expulsion from, India; passports and visas.

20. Pilgrimages to places outside India.

21. Piracies and crimes committed on the high seas or in the air; offences against the law of nations committed on land or the high seas or in the air.

22. Railways.

23. Highways declared by or under law made by Parliament to be national highways.

24. Shipping and navigation on inland waterways, declared by Parliament by law to be national waterways, as regards mechanically propelled vessels; the rule of the road on such waterways.

25. Maritime shipping and navigation, including shipping and navigation on tidal waters; provision of education and training for the mercantile marine and regulation of such education and training provided by States and other agencies.

26. Lighthouses, including lightships, beacons and other provision for the safety of shipping and aircraft.

27. Ports declared by or under law made by Parliament or existing law to be major ports, including their delimitation, and the constitution and powers of port authorities therein.

28. Port quarantine, including hospitals connected therewith; seamen's and marine hospitals.

29. Airways; aircraft and air navigation; provision of aerodromes; regulation and organisation of air traffic and of aerodromes; provision for aeronautical education and training and regulation of such education and training provided by States and other agencies.

30. Carriage of passengers and goods by railway, sea or air, or by national waterways in mechanically propelled vessels.

31. Posts and telegraphs; telephones, wireless, broadcasting and other like forms of communication.

32. Property of the Union and the revenue therefrom, but as regards property situated in a State ¹*** subject to legislation by the State, save in so far as Parliament by law otherwise provides.

²[33* * * * *]

34. Courts of wards for the estates of Rulers of Indian States.

35. Public debt of the Union.

36. Currency, coinage and legal tender; foreign exchange.

37. Foreign loans.

38. Reserve Bank of India.

39. Post Office Savings Bank.

40. Lotteries organised by the Government of India or the Government of a State.

41. Trade and commerce with foreign countries; import and export across customs frontiers; definition of customs frontiers.

42. Inter-State trade and commerce.

43. Incorporation, regulation and winding up of trading corporations, including banking, insurance and financial corporations, but not including co-operative societies.

44. Incorporation, regulation and winding up of corporations, whether trading or not, with objects not confined to one State, but not including universities.

45. Banking.

46. Bills of exchange, cheques, promissory notes and other like instruments.

47. Insurance.

48. Stock exchanges and futures markets.

49. Patents, inventions and designs; copyright; trade-marks and merchandise marks.

50. Establishment of standards of weight and measure.

51. Establishment of standards of quality for goods to be exported out of India or transported from one State to another.

---

1 The words and letters "specified in Part A or Part B of the First Schedule" omitted by the Constitution (Seventh Amendment) Act, 1956, s. 29 and Sch. (w.e.f. 1-11-1956).
2 Entry 33 omitted by s. 26, *ibid.* (w.e.f. 1-11-1956).

52. Industries, the control of which by the Union is declared by Parliament by law to be expedient in the public interest.

53. Regulation and development of oilfields and mineral oil resources; petroleum and petroleum products; other liquids and substances declared by Parliament by law to be dangerously inflammable.

54. Regulation of mines and mineral development to the extent to which such regulation and development under the control of the Union is declared by Parliament by law to be expedient in the public interest.

55. Regulation of labour and safety in mines and oilfields.

56. Regulation and development of inter-State rivers and river valleys to the extent to which such regulation and development under the control of the Union is declared by Parliament by law to be expedient in the public interest.

57. Fishing and fisheries beyond territorial waters.

58. Manufacture, supply and distribution of salt by Union agencies; regulation and control of manufacture, supply and distribution of salt by other agencies.

59. Cultivation, manufacture, and sale for export, of opium.

60. Sanctioning of cinematograph films for exhibition.

61. Industrial disputes concerning Union employees.

62. The institutions known at the commencement of this Constitution as the National Library, the Indian Museum, the Imperial War Museum, the Victoria Memorial and the Indian War Memorial, and any other like institution financed by the Government of India wholly or in part and declared by Parliament by law to be an institution of national importance.

63. The institutions known at the commencement of this Constitution as the Benares Hindu University, the Aligarh Muslim University and the ¹[Delhi University; the University established in pursuance of article 371E;] any other institution declared by Parliament by law to be an institution of national importance.

64. Institutions for scientific or technical education financed by the Government of India wholly or in part and declared by Parliament by law to be institutions of national importance.

---

1 Subs. by the Constitution (Thirty-second Amendment) Act, 1973, s. 4, for "Delhi University, and" (w.e.f. 1-7-1974).

65. Union agencies and institutions for—
   (a) professional, vocational or technical training, including the training of police officers; or
   (b) the promotion of special studies or research; or
   (c) scientific or technical assistance in the investigation or detection of crime.
66. Co-ordination and determination of standards in institutions for higher education or research and scientific and technical institutions.
67. Ancient and historical monuments and records, and archaeological sites and remains, [1][declared by or under law made by Parliament] to be of national importance.
68. The Survey of India, the Geological, Botanical, Zoological and Anthropological Surveys of India; Meteorological organisations.
69. Census.
70. Union Public Service; All-India Services; Union Public Service Commission.
71. Union pensions, that is to say, pensions payable by the Government of India or out of the Consolidated Fund of India.
72. Elections to Parliament, to the Legislatures of States and to the offices of President and Vice-President; the Election Commission.
73. Salaries and allowances of members of Parliament, the Chairman and Deputy Chairman of the Council of States and the Speaker and Deputy Speaker of the House of the People.
74. Powers, privileges and immunities of each House of Parliament and of the members and the Committees of each House; enforcement of attendance of persons for giving evidence or producing documents before committees of Parliament or commissions appointed by Parliament.
75. Emoluments, allowances, privileges, and rights in respect of leave of absence, of the President and Governors; salaries and allowances of the Ministers for the Union; the salaries, allowances, and rights in respect of leave of absence and other conditions of service of the Comptroller and Auditor- General of India.
76. Audit of the accounts of the Union and of the States.

---

1 Subs. by the Constitution (Seventh Amendment) Act, 1956, s. 27, for "declared by Parliament by law" (w.e.f. 1-11-1956).

77. Constitution, organisation, jurisdiction and powers of the Supreme Court (including contempt of such Court), and the fees taken therein; persons entitled to practise before the Supreme Court.

78. Constitution and organisation [1][(including vacations)] of the High Courts except provisions as to officers and servants of High Courts; persons entitled to practise before the High Courts.

[2][79. Extension of the jurisdiction of a High Court to, and exclusion of the jurisdiction of a High Court from, any Union territory.]

80. Extension of the powers and jurisdiction of members of a police force belonging to any State to any area outside that State, but not so as to enable the police of one State to exercise powers and jurisdiction in any area outside that State without the consent of the Government of the State in which such area is situated; extension of the powers and jurisdiction of members of a police force belonging to any State to railway areas outside that State.

81. Inter-State migration; inter-State quarantine.

82. Taxes on income other than agricultural income.

83. Duties of customs including export duties.

[3][84. Duties of excise on the following goods manufactured or produced in India, namely:—

    (*a*) petroleum crude;

    (*b*) high speed diesel;

    (*c*) motor spirit (commonly known as petrol);

    (*d*) natural gas;

    (*e*) aviation turbine fuel; and

    (*f*) tobacco and tobacco products.]

85. Corporation tax.

86. Taxes on the capital value of the assets, exclusive of agricultural land, of individuals and companies; taxes on the capital of companies.

87. Estate duty in respect of property other than agricultural land.

88. Duties in respect of succession to property other than agricultural land.

---

1 Ins. by the Constitution (Fifteenth Amendment) Act, 1963, s. 12 (with retrospective effect).

2 Subs. by the Constitution (Seventh Amendment) Act, 1956, s. 29 and Sch. for entry 79 (w.e.f. 1-11-1956).

3 Subs. by the Constitution (One Hundred and First Amendment) Act, 2016, s. 17(*a*)(*i*) for entry 84 (w.e.f. 16-9-2016).

89.   Terminal taxes on goods or passengers, carried by railway, sea or air; taxes on railway fares and freights.

90.   Taxes other than stamp duties on transactions in stock exchanges and futures markets.

91.   Rates of stamp duty in respect of bills of exchange, cheques, promissory notes, bills of lading, letters of credit, policies of insurance, transfer of shares, debentures, proxies and receipts.

¹[92. *   *   *   *   *]

²[92A. Taxes on the sale or purchase of goods other than newspapers, where such sale or purchase takes place in the course of inter-State trade or commerce.]

³[92B. Taxes on the consignments of goods (whether the consignment is to the person making it or to any other person), where such consignment takes place in the course of inter-State trade or commerce.]

⁴[92C. *   *   *   *   *]

93.   Offences against laws with respect to any of the matters in this List.

94.   Inquires, surveys and statistics for the purpose of any of the matters in this List.

95.   Jurisdiction and powers of all courts, except the Supreme Court, with respect to any of the matters in this List; admiralty jurisdiction.

96.   Fees in respect of any of the matters in this List, but not including fees taken in any court.

97.   Any other matter not enumerated in List II or List III including any tax not mentioned in either of those Lists.

---

1   Entry 92 omitted by the Constitution (One Hundred and First Amendment) Act, 2016, s. 17(a)(ii) (w.e.f. 16-9-2016).
2   Ins. by the Constitution (Sixth Amendment) Act, 1956, s. 2 (w.e.f. 11-9-1956).
3   Ins.by the Constitution (Forty-sixth Amendment) Act, 1982, s. 5 (w.e.f. 2-2-1983).
4   Entry 92C was ins. by the Constitution (Eighty-eighth Amendment) Act, 2003, s. 4 (date not notified) and omitted by the Constitution (One Hundred and First Amendment) Act, 2016, s. 17(a)(ii) (w.e.f. 16-9-2016).

List II—State List

1.   Public order (but not including [1][the use of any naval, military or air force or any other armed force of the Union or of any other force subject to the control of the Union or of any contingent or unit thereof] in aid of the civil power).

[2][2.   Police (including railway and village police) subject to the provisions of entry 2A of List I.]

3.   [3]*** Officers and servants of the High Court; procedure in rent and revenue courts; fees taken in all courts except the Supreme Court.

4.   Prisons, reformatories, Borstal institutions and other institutions of a like nature, and persons detained therein; arrangements with other States for the use of prisons and other institutions.

5.   Local government, that is to say, the constitution and powers of municipal corporations, improvement trusts, districts boards, mining settlement authorities and other local authorities for the purpose of local self-government or village administration.

6.   Public health and sanitation; hospitals and dispensaries.

7.   Pilgrimages, other than pilgrimages to places outside India.

8.   Intoxicating liquors, that is to say, the production, manufacture, possession, transport, purchase and sale of intoxicating liquors.

9.   Relief of the disabled and unemployable.

10.   Burials and burial grounds; cremations and cremation grounds.

[4][11*   *   *   *   *]

12.   Libraries, museums and other similar institutions controlled or financed by the State; ancient and historical monuments and records other than those [5][declared by or under law made by Parliament] to be of national importance.

13.   Communications, that is to say, roads, bridges, ferries, and other means of communication not specified in List I; municipal tramways; ropeways; inland waterways and traffic thereon subject to

---

1   Subs. by the Constitution (Forty-second Amendment) Act, 1976, s. 57, for certain words (w.e.f. 3-1-1977).

2   Subs. by s. 57, for entry 2, *ibid.* (w.e.f. 3-1-1977).

3   Certain words omitted by s. 57, *ibid.* (w.e.f. 3-1-1977).

4   Entry 11 omitted by s. 57, *ibid.* (w.e.f. 3-1-1977).

5   Subs. by the Constitution (Seventh Amendment) Act, 1956, s. 27, for "declared by Parliament by law" (w.e.f. 1-11-1956).

the provisions of List I and List III with regard to such waterways; vehicles other than mechanically propelled vehicles.

14. Agriculture, including agricultural education and research, protection against pests and prevention of plant diseases.

15. Preservation, protection and improvement of stock and prevention of animal diseases; veterinary training and practice.

16. Pounds and the prevention of cattle trespass.

17. Water, that is to say, water supplies, irrigation and canals, drainage and embankments, water storage and water power subject to the provisions of entry 56 of List I.

18. Land, that is to say, rights in or over land, land tenures including the relation of landlord and tenant, and the collection of rents; transfer and alienation of agricultural land; land improvement and agricultural loans; colonization.

[1][19* * * * *
20* * * *]

21. Fisheries.

22. Courts of wards subject to the provisions of entry 34 of List I; encumbered and attached estates.

23. Regulation of mines and mineral development subject to the provisions of List I with respect to regulation and development under the control of the Union.

24. Industries subject to the provisions of [2][entries 7 and 52] of List I.

25. Gas and gas-works.

26. Trade and commerce within the State subject to the provisions of entry 33 of List III.

27. Production, supply and distribution of goods subject to the provisions of entry 33 of List III.

28. Markets and fairs.

[3][29* * * * *]

30. Money-lending and money-lenders; relief of agricultural indebtedness.

31. Inns and inn-keepers.

---

1 Entries 19 and 20 omitted by the Constitution (Forty-second Amendment) Act, 1976, s. 57 (w.e.f. 3-1-1977).

2 Subs. by the Constitution (Seventh Amendment) Act, 1956, s. 28 for "entry 52" (w.e.f. 1-11-1956).

3 Entry 29 omitted by the Constitution (Forty-second Amendment) Act, 1976, s. 57 (w.e.f. 3-1-1977).

32. Incorporation, regulation and winding up of corporations, other than those specified in List I, and universities; unincorporated trading, literary, scientific, religious and other societies and associations; co-operative societies.

33. Theatres and dramatic performances; cinemas subject to the provisions of entry 60 of List I; sports, entertainments and amusements.

34. Betting and gambling.

35. Works, lands and buildings vested in or in the possession of the State.

¹[36* * * * *]

37. Elections to the Legislature of the State subject to the provisions of any law made by Parliament.

38. Salaries and allowances of members of the Legislature of the State, of the Speaker and Deputy Speaker of the Legislative Assembly and, if there is a Legislative Council, of the Chairman and Deputy Chairman thereof.

39. Powers, privileges and immunities of the Legislative Assembly and of the members and the committees thereof, and, if there is a Legislative Council, of that Council and of the members and the committees thereof; enforcement of attendance of persons for giving evidence or producing documents before committees of the Legislature of the State.

40. Salaries and allowances of Ministers for the State.

41. State public services; State Public Service Commission.

42. State pensions, that is to say, pensions payable by the State or out of the Consolidated Fund of the State.

43. Public debt of the State.

44. Treasure trove.

45. Land revenue, including the assessment and collection of revenue, the maintenance of land records, survey for revenue purposes and records of rights, and alienation of revenues.

46. Taxes on agricultural income.

47. Duties in respect of succession to agricultural land.

48. Estate duty in respect of agricultural land.

---

1 Entry 36 omitted by the Constitution (Seventh Amendment) Act, 1956, s. 26 (w.e.f. 1-11-1956).

49.   Taxes on lands and buildings.

50.   Taxes on mineral rights subject to any limitations imposed by Parliament by law relating to mineral development.

51.   Duties of excise on the following goods manufactured or produced in the State and countervailing duties at the same or lower rates on similar goods manufactured or produced elsewhere in India:—

   (*a*)   alcoholic liquors for human consumption;

   (*b*)   opium, Indian hemp and other narcotic drugs and narcotics,

but not including medicinal and toilet preparations containing alcohol or any substance included in sub-paragraph (*b*) of this entry.

¹[52.   *   *   *   *   *]

53.   Taxes on the consumption or sale of electricity.

²[54.   Taxes on the sale of petroleum crude, high speed diesel, motor spirit (commonly known as petrol), natural gas, aviation turbine fuel and alcoholic liquor for human consumption, but not including sale in the course of inter-State trade or commerce or sale in the course of international trade or commerce of such goods.]

³[55.   *   *   *   *   *]

56.   Taxes on goods and passengers carried by road or on inland waterways.

57.   Taxes on vehicles, whether mechanically propelled or not, suitable for use on roads, including tramcars subject to the provisions of entry 35 of List III.

58.   Taxes on animals and boats.

59.   Tolls.

60.   Taxes on professions, trades, callings and employments.

61.   Capitation taxes.

⁴[62.   Taxes on entertainments and amusements to the extent levied and collected by a Panchayat or a Municipality or a Regional Council or a District Council.]

---

1   Entry 52 omitted by the Constitution (One Hundred and First Amendment) Act, 2016, s. 17(*b*) (*i*) (w.e.f. 16-9-2016).

2   Subs. by the Constitution (Sixth Amendment) Act, 1956, s. 2 (w.e.f. 11-9-1956) and further subs. by the Constitution (One Hundred and First Amendment) Act, 2016, s. 17(*b*)(*ii*) (w.e.f. 16-9-2016).

3   Entry 55 omitted by the Constitution (One Hundred and First Amendment) Act, 2016, s. 17(*b*) (*iii*) (w.e.f. 16-9-2016).

4   Subs. by the Constitution (One Hundred and First Amendment) Act, 2016, s. 17(*b*) (*iv*), for entry 62 (w.e.f. 16-9-2016).

63. Rates of stamp duty in respect of documents other than those specified in the provisions of List I with regard to rates of stamp duty.

64. Offences against laws with respect to any of the matters in this List.

65. Jurisdiction and powers of all courts, except the Supreme Court, with respect to any of the matters in this List.

66. Fees in respect of any of the matters in this List, but not including fees taken in any court.

List III—Concurrent List

1. Criminal law, including all matters included in the Indian Penal Code at the commencement of this Constitution but excluding offences against laws with respect to any of the matters specified in List I or List II and excluding the use of naval, military or air forces or any other armed forces of the Union in aid of the civil power.

2. Criminal procedure, including all matters included in the Code of Criminal Procedure at the commencement of this Constitution.

3. Preventive detention for reasons connected with the security of a State, the maintenance of public order, or the maintenance of supplies and services essential to the community; persons subjected to such detention.

4. Removal from one State to another State of prisoners, accused persons and persons subjected to preventive detention for reasons specified in entry 3 of this List.

5. Marriage and divorce; infants and minors; adoption; wills, intestacy and succession; joint family and partition; all matters in respect of which parties in judicial proceedings were immediately before the commencement of this Constitution subject to their personal law.

6. Transfer of property other than agricultural land; registration of deeds and documents.

7. Contracts, including partnership, agency, contracts of carriage, and other special forms of contracts, but not including contracts relating to agricultural land.

8. Actionable wrongs.

9. Bankruptcy and insolvency.

10. Trust and Trustees.

11. Administrators-general and official trustees.

[11A. Administration of Justice; constitution and organisation of all courts, except the Supreme Court and the High Courts.]

12. Evidence and oaths; recognition of laws, public acts and records, and judicial proceedings.

13. Civil procedure, including all matters included in the Code of Civil Procedure at the commencement of this Constitution, limitation and arbitration.

14. Contempt of court, but not including contempt of the Supreme Court.

15. Vagrancy; nomadic and migratory tribes.

16. Lunacy and mental deficiency, including places for the reception or treatment of lunatics and mental deficients.

17. Prevention of cruelty to animals.

[17A. Forests.

17B. Protection of wild animals and birds.]

18. Adulteration of foodstuffs and other goods.

19. Drugs and poisons, subject to the provisions of entry 59 of List I with respect to opium.

20. Economic and social planning.

[20A. Population control and family planning.]

21. Commercial and industrial monopolies, combines and trusts.

22. Trade unions; industrial and labour disputes.

23. Social security and social insurance; employment and unemployment.

24. Welfare of labour including conditions of work, provident funds, employers' liability, workmen's compensation, invalidity and old age pensions and maternity benefits.

[25. Education, including technical education, medical education and universities, subject to the provisions of entries 63, 64, 65 and 66 of List I; vocational and technical training of labour.]

26. Legal, medical and other professions.

27. Relief and rehabilitation of persons displaced from their original place of residence by reason of the setting up of the Dominions of India and Pakistan.

---

1 Entries 11A, 17A, 17B and 26A ins. by the Constitution (Forty-second Amendment) Act, 1976, s. 57 (c) (i),(ii) and (iii)(w.e.f. 3-1-1977).

2 Subs. by the Constitution (Forty-second Amendment) Act, 1976, s. 57 (c) (iv) for entry 25 (w.e.f. 3-1-1977).

28. Charities and charitable institutions, charitable and religious endowments and religious institutions.

29. Prevention of the extension from one State to another of infectious or contagious diseases or pests affecting men, animals or plants.

30. Vital statistics including registration of births and deaths.

31. Ports other than those declared by or under law made by Parliament or existing law to be major ports.

32. Shipping and navigation on inland waterways as regards mechanically propelled vessels, and the rule of the road on such waterways, and the carriage of passengers and goods on inland waterways subject to the provisions of List I with respect to national waterways.

1[33. Trade and commerce in, and the production, supply and distribution of,—

    (*a*) the products of any industry where the control of such industry by the Union is declared by Parliament by law to be expedient in the public interest, and imported goods of the same kind as such products;

    (*b*) foodstuffs, including edible oilseeds and oils;

    (*c*) cattle fodder, including oilcakes and other concentrates;

    (*d*) raw cotton, whether ginned or unginned, and cotton seed; and

    (*e*) raw jute.]

2[33A. Weights and measures except establishment of standards.]

34. Price control.

35. Mechanically propelled vehicles including the principles on which taxes on such vehicles are to be levied.

36. Factories

37. Boilers.

38. Electricity.

39. Newspapers, books and printing presses.

40. Archaeological sites and remains other than those 3[declared by or under law made by Parliament] to be of national importance.

41. Custody, management and disposal of property (including agricultural land) declared by law to be evacuee property.

---

1 Subs. by the Constitution (Third Amendment) Act, 1954, s. 2 for entry 33 (w.e.f. 22-2-1955).
2 Ins. by the Constitution (Forty-second Amendment) Act, 1976, s. 57 (w.e.f. 3-1-1977).
3 Subs. by the Constitution (Seventh Amendment) Act, 1956, s. 27, for "declared by Parliament by law" (w.e.f. 1-11-1956).

¹[42. Acquisition and requisitioning of property.]

43. Recovery in a State of claims in respect of taxes and other public demands, including arrears of land-revenue and sums recoverable as such arrears, arising outside that State.

44. Stamp duties other than duties or fees collected by means of judicial stamps, but not including rates of stamp duty.

45. Inquiries and statistics for the purposes of any of the matters specified in List II or List III.

46. Jurisdiction and powers of all courts, except the Supreme Court, with respect to any of the matters in this List.

47. Fees in respect of any of the matters in this List, but not including fees taken in any court.

EIGHTH SCHEDULE

[Articles 344(1) and 351]

Languages

1. Assamese.
2. Bengali.
²[3. Bodo.
4. Dogri.]
³[5.] Gujarati.
⁴[6.] Hindi.
³[7.] Kannada.
³[8.] Kashmiri.
⁵[³[9.] Konkani.]
¹[10. Maithili.]
⁶[11.] Malayalam.

---

1 Subs. by s. 26, *ibid.*, for entry 42 (w.e.f. 1-11-1956).
2 Entries 3and 4 ins. by the Constitution (Ninety-second Amendment) Act, 2003, s. 2 (w.e.f. 7-1-2004).
3 Entry 3 renumbered as entry 5 by s. 2, *ibid.* (w.e.f. 7-1-2004).
4 Entries 4 to 7 renumbered as entries 6 to 9 by s. 2, *ibid.* (w.e.f. 7-1-2004).
5 Ins. by the Constitution (Seventy-first Amendment) Act, 1992, s.2 (w.e.f. 31-8-1992).
6 Entry 8 renumbered as entry 11 by the Constitution (Ninety-second Amendment) Act, 2003, s.

4[1[12.]   Manipuri.]
6[13.]   Marathi.
4[6[14.]   Nepali.]
6[15.]   2[Odia].
6[16.]   Punjabi.
6[17.]   Sanskrit.
3[18.   Santhali.]
4[5[19.]   Sindhi.]
6[20.]   Tamil.
4[21.]   Telugu.
4[22.]   Urdu.

7[NINTH SCHEDULE

(Article 31B)

1.   The Bihar Land Reforms Act, 1950 (Bihar Act XXX of 1950).

2.   The Bombay Tenancy and Agricultural Lands Act, 1948 (Bombay Act LXVII of 1948).

3.   The Bombay Maleki Tenure Abolition Act, 1949 (Bombay Act LXI of 1949).

4.   The Bombay Taluqdari Tenure Abolition Act, 1949 (Bombay Act LXII of 1949).

5.   The Panch Mahals Mehwassi Tenure Abolition Act, 1949 (Bombay Act LXIII of 1949).

6.   The Bombay Khoti Abolition Act, 1950 (Bombay Act VI of 1950).

7.   The Bombay Paragana and Kulkarni Watan Abolition Act, 1950 (Bombay Act LX of 1950).

---

2 (w.e.f. 7-1-2004).

1 Entries 9 to 14 renumbered as entries 12 to 17 by s. 2, *ibid.* (w.e.f. 7-1-2004).

2 Subs. by the Constitution (Ninety-sixth Amendment) Act, 2011, s. 2, for "Oriya" (w.e.f. 23-9-2011).

3 Ins. by the Constitution (Ninety-second Amendment) Act, 2003, s. 2 (w.e.f. 7-1-2004).

4 Ins. by the Constitution (Twenty-first Amendment) Act, 1967, s. 2 (w.e.f. 10-4-1967).

5 Entry 15 renumbered as entry 19 by the Constitution (Ninety-second Amendment) Act, 2003, s. 2 (w.e.f. 7-1-2004).

6 Entries 16 to 18 renumbered as entries 20 to 22 by s. 2, *ibid.* (w.e.f. 7-1-2004).

7 Ninth schedule (entries 1 to 13) added by the Constitution (First Amendment) Act, 1951, s. 14 (w.e.f. 18-6-1951).

8. The Madhya Pradesh Abolition of Proprietary Rights (Estates, Mahals, Alienated Lands) Act, 1950 (Madhya Pradesh Act I of 1951).

9. The Madras Estates (Abolition and Conversion into Ryotwari) Act, 1948 (Madras Act XXVI of 1948).

10. The Madras Estates (Abolition and Conversion into Ryotwari) Amendment Act, 1950 (Madras Act I of 1950).

11. The Uttar Pradesh Zamindari Abolition and Land Reforms Act, 1950 (Uttar Pradesh Act I of 1951).

12. The Hyderabad (Abolition of Jagirs) Regulation, 1358F (No. LXIX of 1358, Fasli).

13. The Hyderabad Jagirs (Commutation) Regulation, 1359F (No. XXV of 1359, Fasli).]

¹[14. The Bihar Displaced Persons Rehabilitation (Acquisition of Land) Act, 1950 (Bihar Act XXXVIII of 1950).

15. The United Provinces Land Acquisition (Rehabilitation of Refugees) Act, 1948 (U.P. Act XXVI of 1948).

16. The Resettlement of Displaced Persons (Land Acquisition) Act, 1948 (Act LX of 1948).

17. Sections 52A to 52G of the Insurance Act, 1938 (Act IV of 1938), as inserted by section 42 of the Insurance (Amendment) Act, 1950 (Act XLVII of 1950).

18. The Railway Companies (Emergency Provisions) Act, 1951 (Act LI of 1951).

19. Chapter III-A of the Industries (Development and Regulation) Act, 1951 (Act LXV of 1951), as inserted by section 13 of the Industries (Development and Regulation) Amendment Act, 1953 (Act XXVI of 1953).

20. The West Bengal Land Development and Planning Act, 1948 (West Bengal Act XXI of 1948), as amended by West Bengal Act XXIX of 1951.]

²[21. The Andhra Pradesh Ceiling on Agricultural Holdings Act, 1961 (Andhra Pradesh Act X of 1961).

---

1 Entries 14 to 20 added by the Constitution (Fourth Amendment) Act, 1955, s. 5 (w.e.f. 27-4-1955).
2 Entries 21 to 64 and Explanation added by the Constitution (Seventeenth Amendment) Act, 1964, s. 3 (w.e.f. 20-6-1964).

22. The Andhra Pradesh (Telangana Area) Tenancy and Agricultural Lands (Validation) Act, 1961 (Andhra Pradesh Act XXI of 1961).

23. The Andhra Pradesh (Telangana Area) Ijara and Kowli Land Cancellation of Irregular Pattas and Abolition of Concessional Assessment Act, 1961 (Andhra Pradesh Act XXXVI of 1961).

24. The Assam State Acquisition of Lands belonging to Religious or Charitable Institution of Public Nature Act, 1959 (Assam Act IX of 1961).

25. The Bihar Land Reforms (Amendment) Act, 1953 (Bihar Act XX of 1954).

26. The Bihar Land Reforms (Fixation of Ceiling Area and Acquisition of Surplus Land) Act, 1961 (Bihar Act XII of 1962), except section 28 of this Act.

27. The Bombay Taluqdari Tenure Abolition (Amendment) Act, 1954 (Bombay Act I of 1955).

28. The Bombay Taluqdari Tenure Abolition (Amendment) Act, 1957 (Bombay Act XVIII of 1958).

29. The Bombay Inams (Kutch Area) Abolition Act, 1958 (Bombay Act XCVIII of 1958).

30. The Bombay Tenancy and Agricultural Lands (Gujarat Amendment) Act, 1960 (Gujarat Act XVI of 1960).

31. The Gujarat Agricultural Lands Ceiling Act, 1960 (Gujarat Act XXVI of 1961).

32. The Sagbara and Mehwassi Estates (Proprietary Rights Abolition, etc.) Regulation, 1962 (Gujarat Regulation I of 1962).

33. The Gujarat Surviving Alienations Abolition Act, 1963 (Gujarat Act XXXIII of 1963), except in so far as this Act relates to an alienation referred to in sub-clause (*d*) of clause (3) of section 2 thereof.

34. The Maharashtra Agricultural Lands (Ceiling on Holdings) Act, 1961 (Maharashtra Act XXVII of 1961).

35. The Hyderabad Tenancy and Agricultural Lands (Re-enactment, Validation and Further Amendment) Act, 1961 (Maharashtra Act XLV of 1961).

36. The Hyderabad Tenancy and Agricultural Lands Act, 1950 (Hyderabad Act XXI of 1950).

37. The Jenmikaram Payment (Abolition) Act, 1960 (Kerala Act III of 1961).

38. The Kerala Land Tax Act, 1961 (Kerala Act XIII of 1961).

39. The Kerala Land Reforms Act, 1963 (Kerala Act I of 1964).

40. The Madhya Pradesh Land Revenue Code, 1959 (Madhya Pradesh Act XX of 1959).

41. The Madhya Pradesh Ceiling on Agricultural Holdings Act, 1960 (Madhya Pradesh Act XX of 1960).

42. The Madras Cultivating Tenants Protection Act, 1955 (Madras Act XXV of 1955).

43. The Madras Cultivating Tenants (Payment of Fair Rent) Act, 1956 (Madras Act XXIV of 1956).

44. The Madras Occupants of Kudiyiruppu (Protection from Eviction) Act, 1961 (Madras Act XXXVIII of 1961).

45. The Madras Public Trusts (Regulation of Administration of Agricultural Lands) Act, 1961 (Madras Act LVII of 1961).

46. The Madras Land Reforms (Fixation of Ceiling on Land) Act, 1961 (Madras Act LVIII of 1961).

47. The Mysore Tenancy Act, 1952 (Mysore Act XIII of 1952).

48. The Coorg Tenants Act, 1957 (Mysore Act XIV of 1957).

49. The Mysore Village Offices Abolition Act, 1961 (Mysore Act XIV of 1961).

50. The Hyderabad Tenancy and Agricultural Lands (Validation) Act, 1961 (Mysore Act XXXVI of 1961).

51. The Mysore Land Reforms Act, 1961 (Mysore Act X of 1962).

52. The Orissa Land Reforms Act, 1960 (Orissa Act XVI of 1960).

53. The Orissa Merged Territories (Village Offices Abolition) Act, 1963 (Orissa Act X of 1963).

54. The Punjab Security of Land Tenures Act, 1953 (Punjab Act X of 1953).

55. The Rajasthan Tenancy Act, 1955 (Rajasthan Act III of 1955).

56. The Rajasthan Zamindari and Biswedari Abolition Act, 1959 (Rajasthan Act VIII of 1959).

57. The Kumaun and Uttarakhand Zamindari Abolition and Land Reforms Act, 1960 (Uttar Pradesh Act XVII of 1960).

58. The Uttar Pradesh Imposition of Ceiling on Land Holdings Act, 1960 (Uttar Pradesh Act I of 1961).

59. The West Bengal Estates Acquisition Act, 1953 (West Bengal Act I of 1954).

60. The West Bengal Land Reforms Act, 1955 (West Bengal Act X of 1956).

61. The Delhi Land Reforms Act, 1954 (Delhi Act VIII of 1954).

62. The Delhi Land Holdings (Ceiling) Act, 1960 (Central Act 24 of 1960).

63. The Manipur Land Revenue and Land Reforms Act, 1960 (Central Act 33 of 1960).

64. The Tripura Land Revenue and Land Reforms Act, 1960 (Central Act 43 of 1960).

¹[65. The Kerala Land Reforms (Amendment) Act, 1969 (Kerala Act 35 of 1969).

66. The Kerala Land Reforms (Amendment) Act, 1971 (Kerala Act 25 of 1971).]

²[67. The Andhra Pradesh Land Reforms (Ceiling on Agricultural Holdings) Act, 1973 (Andhra Pradesh Act 1 of 1973).

68. The Bihar Land Reforms (Fixation of Ceiling Area and Acquisition of Surplus Land) (Amendment) Act, 1972 (Bihar Act I of 1973).

69. The Bihar Land Reforms (Fixation of Ceiling Area and Acquisition of Surplus Land) (Amendment) Act, 1973 (Bihar Act IX of 1973).

70. The Bihar Land Reforms (Amendment) Act, 1972 (Bihar Act V of 1972).

71. The Gujarat Agricultural Lands Ceiling (Amendment) Act, 1972 (Gujarat Act 2 of 1974).

72. The Haryana Ceiling on Land Holdings Act, 1972 (Haryana Act 26 of 1972).

73. The Himachal Pradesh Ceiling on Land Holdings Act, 1972 (Himachal Pradesh Act 19 of 1973).

74. The Kerala Land Reforms (Amendment) Act, 1972 (Kerala Act 17 of 1972).

75. The Madhya Pradesh Ceiling on Agricultural Holdings (Amendment) Act, 1972 (Madhya Pradesh Act 12 of 1974).

76. The Madhya Pradesh Ceiling on Agricultural Holdings (Second Amendment) Act, 1972 (Madhya Pradesh Act 13 of 1974).

77. The Mysore Land Reforms (Amendment) Act, 1973 (Karnataka Act 1 of 1974).

---

1 Entries 65 and 66 ins. by the Constitution (Twenty-ninth Amendment) Act, 1972, s. 2 (w.e.f. 9-6-1972).

2 Entries 67 to 86 ins. by the Constitution (Thirty-fourth Amendment) Act, 1974, s. 2 (w.e.f. 7-9-1974).

78. The Punjab Land Reforms Act, 1972 (Punjab Act 10 of 1973).

79. The Rajasthan Imposition of Ceiling on Agricultural Holdings Act, 1973 (Rajasthan Act 11 of 1973).

80. The Gudalur Janmam Estates (Abolition and Conversion into Ryotwari) Act, 1969 (Tamil Nadu Act 24 of 1969).

81. The West Bengal Land Reforms (Amendment) Act, 1972 (West Bengal Act XII of 1972).

82. The West Bengal Estates Acquisition (Amendment) Act, 1964 (West Bengal Act XXII of 1964).

83. The West Bengal Estates Acquisition (Second Amendment) Act, 1973 (West Bengal Act XXXIII of 1973).

84. The Bombay Tenancy and Agricultural Lands (Gujarat Amendment) Act, 1972 (Gujarat Act 5 of 1973).

85. The Orissa Land Reforms (Amendment) Act, 1974 (Orissa Act 9 of 1974).

86. The Tripura Land Revenue and Land Reforms (Second Amendment) Act,1974 (Tripura Act 7 of 1974).]

¹[²87* * * * *]

88. The Industries (Development and Regulation) Act, 1951 (Central Act 65 of 1951).

89. The Requisitioning and Acquisition of Immovable Property Act, 1952 (Central Act 30 of 1952).

90. The Mines and Minerals (Regulation and Development) Act, 1957 (Central Act 67 of 1957).

91. The Monopolies and Restrictive Trade Practices Act, 1969 (Central Act 54 of 1969).

[92* * * * *]

93. The Coking Coal Mines (Emergency Provisions) Act, 1971 (Central Act 64 of 1971).

94. The Coking Coal Mines (Nationalisation) Act, 1972 (Central Act 36 of 1972).

---

1 Entries 87 to 124 ins. by the Constitution (Thirty-ninth Amendment) Act, 1975, s. 5 (w.e.f. 10-8-1975).

2 Entries 87 and 92 omitted by the Constitution (Forty-fourth Amendment) Act, 1978, s. 44 (w.e.f. 20-6-1979).

* Rep. by the Competition Act, 2002 (12 of 2003) s. 66 (w.e.f. 1-9-2009).

** Rep. by the Foreign Exchange Management Act, 1999 (42 of 1999), s. 49 (w.e.f. 1-6-2000).

95. The General Insurance Business (Nationalisation) Act, 1972 (Central Act 57 of 1972).

96. The Indian Copper Corporation (Acquisition of Undertaking) Act, 1972 (Central Act 58 of 1972).

97. The Sick Textile Undertakings (Taking Over of Management) Act, 1972 (Central Act 72 of 1972).

98. The Coal Mines (Taking Over of Management) Act, 1973 (Central Act 15 of 1973).

99. The Coal Mines (Nationalisation) Act, 1973 (Central Act 26 of 1973).

"100. The Foreign Exchange Regulation Act, 1973 (Central Act 46 of 1973).

101. The Alcock Ashdown Company Limited (Acquisition of Undertakings) Act, 1973 (Central Act 56 of 1973).

102. The Coal Mines (Conservation and Development) Act, 1974 (Central Act 28 of 1974).

103. The Additional Emoluments (Compulsory Deposit) Act, 1974 (Central Act 37 of 1974).

104. The Conservation of Foreign Exchange and Prevention of Smuggling Activities Act, 1974 (Central Act 52 of 1974).

105. The Sick Textile Undertakings (Nationalisation) Act, 1974 (Central Act 57 of 1974).

106. The Maharashtra Agricultural Lands (Ceiling on Holdings) (Amendment) Act, 1964 (Maharashtra Act XVI of 1965).

107. The Maharashtra Agricultural Lands (Ceiling on Holdings) (Amendment) Act, 1965 (Maharashtra Act XXXII of 1965).

108. The Maharashtra Agricultural Lands (Ceiling on Holdings) (Amendment) Act, 1968 (Maharashtra Act XVI of 1968).

109. The Maharashtra Agricultural Lands (Ceiling on Holdings) (Second Amendment) Act, 1968 (Maharashtra Act XXXIII of 1968).

110. The Maharashtra Agricultural Lands (Ceiling on Holdings) (Amendment) Act, 1969 (Maharashtra Act XXXVII of 1969).

111. The Maharashtra Agricultural Lands (Ceiling on Holdings) (Second Amendment) Act, 1969 (Maharashtra Act XXXVIII of 1969).

112. The Maharashtra Agricultural Lands (Ceiling on Holdings) (Amendment) Act, 1970 (Maharashtra Act XXVII of 1970).

113. The Maharashtra Agricultural Lands (Ceiling on Holdings) (Amendment) Act, 1972 (Maharashtra Act XIII of 1972).

114. The Maharashtra Agricultural Lands (Ceiling on Holdings) (Amendment) Act, 1973 (Maharashtra Act L of 1973).

115. The Orissa Land Reforms (Amendment) Act, 1965 (Orissa Act 13 of 1965).

116. The Orissa Land Reforms (Amendment) Act, 1966 (Orissa Act 8 of 1967).

117. The Orissa Land Reforms (Amendment) Act, 1967 (Orissa Act 13 of 1967).

118. The Orissa Land Reforms (Amendment) Act, 1969 (Orissa Act 13 of 1969).

119. The Orissa Land Reforms (Amendment) Act, 1970 (Orissa Act 18 of 1970).

120. The Uttar Pradesh Imposition of Ceiling on Land Holdings (Amendment) Act, 1972 (Uttar Pradesh Act 18 of 1973).

121. The Uttar Pradesh Imposition of Ceiling on Land Holdings (Amendment) Act, 1974 (Uttar Pradesh Act 2 of 1975).

122. The Tripura Land Revenue and Land Reforms (Third Amendment) Act, 1975 (Tripura Act 3 of 1975).

123. The Dadra and Nagar Haveli Land Reforms Regulation, 1971 (3 of 1971).

124. The Dadra and Nagar Haveli Land Reforms (Amendment) Regulation, 1973 (5 of 1973).]

1[125. Section 66A and Chapter IVA of the Motor Vehicles Act, 1939* (Central Act 4 of 1939).

126. The Essential Commodities Act, 1955 (Central Act 10 of 1955).

127. The Smugglers and Foreign Exchange Manipulators (Forfeiture of Property) Act, 1976 (Central Act 13 of 1976).

128. The Bonded Labour System (Abolition) Act, 1976 (Central Act 19 of 1976).

129. The Conservation of Foreign Exchange and Prevention of Smuggling Activities (Amendment) Act, 1976 (Central Act 20 of 1976).

2130* * * * *

---

1 Entries 125 to 188 ins. by the Constitution (Fortieth Amendment) Act, 1976, s. 3 (w.e.f. 27-5-1976).
* See now the relevant provisions of the Motor Vehicles Act, 1988 (59 of 1988).
2 Entry 130 omitted by the Constitution (Forty-fourth Amendment) Act, 1978, s. 44 (w.e.f. 20-6-1979).

131. The Levy Sugar Price Equalisation Fund Act, 1976 (Central Act 31 of 1976).

132. The Urban Land (Ceiling and Regulation) Act, 1976 (Central Act 33 of 1976).

133. The Departmentalisation of Union Accounts (Transfer of Personnel) Act, 1976 (Central Act 59 of 1976).

134. The Assam Fixation of Ceiling on Land Holdings Act, 1956 (Assam Act I of 1957).

135. The Bombay Tenancy and Agricultural Lands (Vidarbha Region) Act, 1958 (Bombay Act XCIX of 1958).

136. The Gujarat Private Forests (Acquisition) Act, 1972 (Gujarat Act 14 of 1973).

137. The Haryana Ceiling on Land Holdings (Amendment) Act, 1976 (Haryana Act 17 of 1976).

138. The Himachal Pradesh Tenancy and Land Reforms Act, 1972 (Himachal Pradesh Act 8 of 1974).

139. The Himachal Pradesh Village Common Lands Vesting and Utilisation Act, 1974 (Himachal Pradesh Act 18 of 1974).

140. The Karnataka Land Reforms (Second Amendment and Miscellaneous Provisions) Act, 1974 (Karnataka Act 31 of 1974).

141. The Karnataka Land Reforms (Second Amendment) Act, 1976 (Karnataka Act 27 of 1976).

142. The Kerala Prevention of Eviction Act, 1966 (Kerala Act 12 of 1966).

143. The Thiruppuvaram Payment (Abolition) Act, 1969 (Kerala Act 19 of 1969).

144. The Sreepadam Lands Enfranchisement Act, 1969 (Kerala Act 20 of 1969).

145. The Sree Pandaravaka Lands (Vesting and Enfranchisement) Act, 1971 (Kerala Act 20 of 1971).

146. The Kerala Private Forests (Vesting and Assignment) Act, 1971 (Kerala Act 26 of 1971).

147. The Kerala Agricultural Workers Act, 1974 (Kerala Act 18 of 1974).

148. The Kerala Cashew Factories (Acquisition) Act, 1974 (Kerala Act 29 of 1974).

149. The Kerala Chitties Act, 1975 (Kerala Act 23 of 1975).

150. The Kerala Scheduled Tribes (Restriction on Transfer of Lands and Restoration of Alienated Lands) Act, 1975 (Kerala Act 31 of 1975).

151. The Kerala Land Reforms (Amendment) Act, 1976 (Kerala Act 15 of 1976).
152. The Kanam Tenancy Abolition Act, 1976 (Kerala Act 16 of 1976).
153. The Madhya Pradesh Ceiling on Agricultural Holdings (Amendment) Act, 1974 (Madhya Pradesh Act 20 of 1974).
154. The Madhya Pradesh Ceiling on Agricultural Holdings (Amendment) Act, 1975 (Madhya Pradesh Act 2 of 1976).
155. The West Khandesh Mehwassi Estates (Proprietary Rights Abolition, etc.) Regulation, 1961 (Maharashtra Regulation 1 of 1962).
156. The Maharashtra Restoration of Lands to Scheduled Tribes Act, 1974 (Maharashtra Act XIV of 1975).
157. The Maharashtra Agricultural Lands (Lowering of Ceiling on Holdings) and (Amendment) Act, 1972 (Maharashtra Act XXI of 1975).
158. The Maharashtra Private Forest (Acquisition) Act, 1975 (Maharashtra Act XXIX of 1975).
159. The Maharashtra Agricultural Lands (Lowering of Ceiling on Holdings) and (Amendment) Amendment Act, 1975 (Maharashtra Act XLVII of 1975).
160. The Maharashtra Agricultural Lands (Ceiling on Holdings) (Amendment) Act, 1975 (Maharashtra Act II of 1976).
161. The Orissa Estates Abolition Act, 1951 (Orissa Act I of 1952).
162. The Rajasthan Colonisation Act, 1954 (Rajasthan Act XXVII of 1954).
163. The Rajasthan Land Reforms and Acquisition of Landowners' Estates Act, 1963 (Rajasthan Act 11 of 1964).
164. The Rajasthan Imposition of Ceiling on Agricultural Holdings (Amendment) Act, 1976 (Rajasthan Act 8 of 1976).
165. The Rajasthan Tenancy (Amendment) Act, 1976 (Rajasthan Act 12 of 1976).
166. The Tamil Nadu Land Reforms (Reduction of Ceiling on Land) Act, 1970 (Tamil Nadu Act 17 of 1970).
167. The Tamil Nadu Land Reforms (Fixation of Ceiling on Land) Amendment Act, 1971 (Tamil Nadu Act 41 of 1971).
168. The Tamil Nadu Land Reforms (Fixation of Ceiling on Land) Amendment Act, 1972 (Tamil Nadu Act 10 of 1972).

169. The Tamil Nadu Land Reforms (Fixation of Ceiling on Land) Second Amendment Act, 1972 (Tamil Nadu Act 20 of 1972).

170. The Tamil Nadu Land Reforms (Fixation of Ceiling on Land) Third Amendment Act, 1972 (Tamil Nadu Act 37 of 1972).

171. The Tamil Nadu Land Reforms (Fixation of Ceiling on Land) Fourth Amendment Act, 1972 (Tamil Nadu Act 39 of 1972).

172. The Tamil Nadu Land Reforms (Fixation of Ceiling on Land) Sixth Amendment Act, 1972 (Tamil Nadu Act 7 of 1974).

173. The Tamil Nadu Land Reforms (Fixation of Ceiling on Land) Fifth Amendment Act, 1972 (Tamil Nadu Act 10 of 1974).

174. The Tamil Nadu Land Reforms (Fixation of Ceiling on Land) Amendment Act, 1974 (Tamil Nadu Act 15 of 1974).

175. The Tamil Nadu Land Reforms (Fixation of Ceiling on Land) Third Amendment Act, 1974 (Tamil Nadu Act 30 of 1974).

176. The Tamil Nadu Land Reforms (Fixation of Ceiling on Land) Second Amendment Act, 1974 (Tamil Nadu Act 32 of 1974).

177. The Tamil Nadu Land Reforms (Fixation of Ceiling on Land) Amendment Act, 1975 (Tamil Nadu Act 11 of 1975).

178. The Tamil Nadu Land Reforms (Fixation of Ceiling on Land) Second Amendment Act, 1975 (Tamil Nadu Act 21 of 1975).

179. Amendments made to the Uttar Pradesh Zamindari Abolition and Land Reforms Act, 1950 (Uttar Pradesh Act I of 1951) by the Uttar Pradesh Land Laws (Amendment) Act, 1971 (Uttar Pradesh Act 21 of 1971) and the Uttar Pradesh Land Laws (Amendment) Act, 1974 (Uttar Pradesh Act 34 of 1974).

180. The Uttar Pradesh Imposition of Ceiling on Land Holdings (Amendment) Act, 1976 (Uttar Pradesh Act 20 of 1976).

181. The West Bengal Land Reforms (Second Amendment) Act, 1972 (West Bengal Act XXVIII of 1972).

182. The West Bengal Restoration of Alienated Land Act, 1973 (West Bengal Act XXIII of 1973).

183. The West Bengal Land Reforms (Amendment) Act, 1974 (West Bengal Act XXXIII of 1974).

184. The West Bengal Land Reforms (Amendment) Act, 1975 (West Bengal Act XXIII of 1975).

185. The West Bengal Land Reforms (Amendment) Act, 1976 (West Bengal Act XII of 1976).

186. The Delhi Land Holdings (Ceiling) Amendment Act, 1976 (Central Act 15 of 1976).

187. The Goa, Daman and Diu Mundkars (Protection from Eviction) Act, 1975 (Goa, Daman and Diu Act 1 of 1976).

188. The Pondicherry Land Reforms (Fixation of Ceiling on Land) Act, 1973 (Pondicherry Act 9 of 1974).]

[189. The Assam (Temporarily Settled Areas) Tenancy Act, 1971 (Assam Act XXIII of 1971).

190. The Assam (Temporarily Settled Areas) Tenancy (Amendment) Act, 1974 (Assam Act XVIII of 1974).

191. The Bihar Land Reforms (Fixation of Ceiling Area and Acquisition of Surplus Land) (Amendment) Amending Act, 1974 (Bihar Act 13 of 1975).

192. The Bihar Land Reforms (Fixation of Ceiling Area and Acquisition of Surplus Land) (Amendment) Act, 1976 (Bihar Act 22 of 1976).

193. The Bihar Land Reforms (Fixation of Ceiling Area and Acquisition of Surplus Land) (Amendment) Act, 1978 (Bihar Act VII of 1978).

194. The Land Acquisition (Bihar Amendment) Act, 1979 (Bihar Act 2 of 1980).

195. The Haryana Ceiling on Land Holdings (Amendment) Act, 1977 (Haryana Act 14 of 1977).

196. The Tamil Nadu Land Reforms (Fixation of Ceiling on Land) Amendment Act, 1978 (Tamil Nadu Act 25 of 1978).

197. The Tamil Nadu Land Reforms (Fixation of Ceiling on Land) Amendment Act, 1979 (Tamil Nadu Act 11 of 1979).

198. The Uttar Pradesh Zamindari Abolition Laws (Amendment) Act, 1978 (Uttar Pradesh Act 15 of 1978).

199. The West Bengal Restoration of Alienated Land (Amendment) Act, 1978 (West Bengal Act XXIV of 1978).

200. The West Bengal Restoration of Alienated Land (Amendment) Act, 1980 (West Bengal Act LVI of 1980).

201. The Goa, Daman and Diu Agricultural Tenancy Act, 1964 (Goa, Daman and Diu Act 7 of 1964).

---

1   Entries 189 to 202 were ins. by the Constitution (Forty-seventh Amendment) Act, 1984, s. 2 (w.e.f. 26-8-1984).

202. The Goa, Daman and Diu Agricultural Tenancy (Fifth Amendment) Act, 1976 (Goa, Daman and Diu Act 17 of 1976).]

[1][203. The Andhra Pradesh Scheduled Areas Land Transfer Regulation, 1959 (Andhra Pradesh Regulation 1 of 1959).

204. The Andhra Pradesh Scheduled Areas Laws (Extension and Amendment) Regulation, 1963 (Andhra Pradesh Regulation 2 of 1963).

205. The Andhra Pradesh Scheduled Areas Land Transfer (Amendment) Regulation, 1970 (Andhra Pradesh Regulation 1 of 1970).

206. The Andhra Pradesh Scheduled Areas Land Transfer (Amendment) Regulation, 1971 (Andhra Pradesh Regulation 1 of 1971).

207. The Andhra Pradesh Scheduled Areas Land Transfer (Amendment) Regulation, 1978 (Andhra Pradesh Regulation 1 of 1978).

208. The Bihar Tenancy Act, 1885 (Bihar Act 8 of 1885).

209. The Chota Nagpur Tenancy Act, 1908 (Bengal Act 6 of 1908) (Chapter VIII—sections 46, 47, 48, 48A and 49; Chapter X—sections 71, 71A and 71B; and Chapter XVIII—sections 240, 241 and 242).

210. The Santhal Parganas Tenancy (Supplementary Provisions) Act, 1949 (Bihar Act 14 of 1949) except section 53.

211. The Bihar Scheduled Areas Regulation, 1969 (Bihar Regulation 1 of 1969).

212. The Bihar Land Reforms (Fixation of Ceiling Area and Acquisition of Surplus Land) (Amendment) Act, 1982 (Bihar Act 55 of 1982).

213. The Gujarat Devasthan Inams Abolition Act, 1969 (Gujarat Act 16 of 1969).

214. The Gujarat Tenancy Laws (Amendment) Act, 1976 (Gujarat Act 37 of 1976).

215. The Gujarat Agricultural Lands Ceiling (Amendment) Act, 1976 (President's Act 43 of 1976).

216. The Gujarat Devasthan Inams Abolition (Amendment) Act, 1977 (Gujarat Act 27 of 1977).

217. The Gujarat Tenancy Laws (Amendment) Act, 1977 (Gujarat Act 30 of 1977).

218. The Bombay Land Revenue (Gujarat Second Amendment) Act, 1980 (Gujarat Act 37 of 1980).

---

1 Entries 203 to 257 were ins. by the Constitution (Sixty-sixth Amendment) Act, 1990, s. 2 (w.e.f. 7-6-1990).

219. The Bombay Land Revenue Code and Land Tenure Abolition Laws (Gujarat Amendment) Act, 1982 (Gujarat Act 8 of 1982).
220. The Himachal Pradesh Transfer of Land (Regulation) Act, 1968 (Himachal Pradesh Act 15 of 1969).
221. The Himachal Pradesh Transfer of Land (Regulation) (Amendment) Act, 1986 (Himachal Pradesh Act 16 of 1986).
222. The Karnataka Scheduled Castes and Scheduled Tribes (Prohibition of Transfer of Certain Lands) Act, 1978 (Karnataka Act 2 of 1979).
223. The Kerala Land Reforms (Amendment) Act, 1978 (Kerala Act 13 of 1978).
224. The Kerala Land Reforms (Amendment) Act, 1981 (Kerala Act 19 of 1981).
225. The Madhya Pradesh Land Revenue Code (Third Amendment) Act, 1976 (Madhya Pradesh Act 61 of 1976).
226. The Madhya Pradesh Land Revenue Code (Amendment) Act, 1980 (Madhya Pradesh Act 15 of 1980).
227. The Madhya Pradesh Akrishik Jot Uchchatam Seema Adhiniyam, 1981 (Madhya Pradesh Act 11 of 1981).
228. The Madhya Pradesh Ceiling on Agricultural Holdings (Second Amendment) Act, 1976 (Madhya Pradesh Act 1 of 1984).
229. The Madhya Pradesh Ceiling on Agricultural Holdings (Amendment) Act, 1984 (Madhya Pradesh Act 14 of 1984).
230. The Madhya Pradesh Ceiling on Agricultural Holdings (Amendment) Act, 1989 (Madhya Pradesh Act 8 of 1989).
231. The Maharashtra Land Revenue Code, 1966 (Maharashtra Act 41 of 1966), sections 36, 36A and 36B.
232. The Maharashtra Land Revenue Code and the Maharashtra Restoration of Lands to Scheduled Tribes (Second Amendment) Act, 1976 (Maharashtra Act 30 of 1977).
233. The Maharashtra Abolition of Subsisting Proprietary Rights to Mines and Minerals in certain Lands Act, 1985 (Maharashtra Act 16 of 1985).
234. The Orissa Scheduled Areas Transfer of Immovable Property (by Scheduled Tribes) Regulation, 1956 (Orissa Regulation 2 of 1956).
235. The Orissa Land Reforms (Second Amendment) Act, 1975 (Orissa Act 29 of 1976).
236. The Orissa Land Reforms (Amendment) Act, 1976 (Orissa Act 30 of 1976).

237. The Orissa Land Reforms (Second Amendment) Act, 1976 (Orissa Act 44 of 1976).

238. The Rajasthan Colonisation (Amendment) Act, 1984 (Rajasthan Act 12 of 1984).

239. The Rajasthan Tenancy (Amendment) Act, 1984 (Rajasthan Act 13 of 1984).

240. The Rajasthan Tenancy (Amendment) Act, 1987 (Rajasthan Act 21 of 1987).

241. The Tamil Nadu Land Reforms (Fixation of Ceiling on Land) Second Amendment Act, 1979 (Tamil Nadu Act 8 of 1980).

242. The Tamil Nadu Land Reforms (Fixation of Ceiling on Land) Amendment Act, 1980 (Tamil Nadu Act 21 of 1980).

243. The Tamil Nadu Land Reforms (Fixation of Ceiling on Land) Amendment Act, 1981 (Tamil Nadu Act 59 of 1981).

244. The Tamil Nadu Land Reforms (Fixation of Ceiling on Land) Second Amendment Act, 1983 (Tamil Nadu Act 2 of 1984).

245. The Uttar Pradesh Land Laws (Amendment) Act, 1982 (Uttar Pradesh Act 20 of 1982).

246. The West Bengal Land Reforms (Amendment) Act, 1965 (West Bengal Act 18 of 1965).

247. The West Bengal Land Reforms (Amendment) Act, 1966 (West Bengal Act 11 of 1966).

248. The West Bengal Land Reforms (Second Amendment) Act, 1969 (West Bengal Act 23 of 1969).

249. The West Bengal Estate Acquisition (Amendment) Act, 1977 (West Bengal Act 36 of 1977).

250. The West Bengal Land Holding Revenue Act, 1979 (West Bengal Act 44 of 1979).

251. The West Bengal Land Reforms (Amendment) Act, 1980 (West Bengal Act 41 of 1980).

252. The West Bengal Land Holding Revenue (Amendment) Act, 1981 (West Bengal Act 33 of 1981).

253. The Calcutta Thikka Tenancy (Acquisition and Regulation) Act, 1981 (West Bengal Act 37 of 1981).

254. The West Bengal Land Holding Revenue (Amendment) Act, 1982 (West Bengal Act 23 of 1982).

255. The Calcutta Thikka Tenancy (Acquisition and Regulation) (Amendment) Act, 1984 (West Bengal Act 41 of 1984).

256. The Mahe Land Reforms Act, 1968 (Pondicherry Act 1 of 1968).

257. The Mahe Land Reforms (Amendment) Act, 1980 (Pondicherry Act 1 of 1981).]

[1][257A. The Tamil Nadu Backward Classes, Scheduled Castes and Scheduled Tribes (Reservation of Seats in Educational Institutions and of appointments or posts in the Services under the State) Act, 1993 (Tamil Nadu Act 45 of 1994).]

[2][258. The Bihar Privileged Persons Homestead Tenancy Act, 1947 (Bihar Act 4 of 1948).

259. The Bihar Consolidation of Holdings and Prevention of Fragmentation Act, 1956 (Bihar Act 22 of 1956).

260. The Bihar Consolidation of Holdings and Prevention of Fragmentation (Amendment) Act, 1970 (Bihar Act 7 of 1970).

261. The Bihar Privileged Persons Homestead Tenancy (Amendment) Act, 1970 (Bihar Act 9 of 1970).

262. The Bihar Consolidation of Holdings and Prevention of Fragmentation (Amendment) Act, 1973 (Bihar Act 27 of 1975).

263. The Bihar Consolidation of Holdings and Prevention of Fragmentation (Amendment) Act, 1981 (Bihar Act 35 of 1982).

264. The Bihar Land Reforms (Fixation of Ceiling Area and Acquisition of Surplus Land) (Amendment) Act, 1987 (Bihar Act 21 of 1987).

265. The Bihar Privileged Persons Homestead Tenancy (Amendment) Act, 1989 (Bihar Act 11 of 1989).

266. The Bihar Land Reforms (Amendment) Act, 1989 (Bihar Act 11 of 1990).

267. The Karnataka Scheduled Castes and Scheduled Tribes (Prohibition of Transfer of Certain Lands) (Amendment) Act, 1984 (Karnataka Act 3 of 1984).

268. The Kerala Land Reforms (Amendment) Act, 1989 (Kerala Act 16 of 1989).

269. The Kerala Land Reforms (Second Amendment) Act, 1989 (Kerala Act 2 of 1990).

---

1 Entry 257A ins. by the Constitution (Seventy-sixth Amendment) Act, 1994, s. 2 (w.e.f. 31-8-1994).
2 Entries 258 to 284 ins. by the Constitution (Seventy-eighth Amendment) Act, 1995, s. 2 (w.e.f. 30-8-1995).

270. The Orissa Land Reforms (Amendment) Act, 1989 (Orissa Act 9 of 1990).

271. The Rajasthan Tenancy (Amendment) Act, 1979 (Rajasthan Act 16 of 1979).

272. The Rajasthan Colonisation (Amendment) Act, 1987 (Rajasthan Act 2 of 1987).

273. The Rajasthan Colonisation (Amendment) Act, 1989 (Rajasthan Act 12 of 1989).

274. The Tamil Nadu Land Reforms (Fixation of Ceiling on Land) Amendment Act, 1983 (Tamil Nadu Act 3 of 1984).

275. The Tamil Nadu Land Reforms (Fixation of Ceiling on Land) Amendment Act, 1986 (Tamil Nadu Act 57 of 1986).

276. The Tamil Nadu Land Reforms (Fixation of Ceiling on Land) Second Amendment Act, 1987 (Tamil Nadu Act 4 of 1988).

277. The Tamil Nadu Land Reforms (Fixation of Ceiling on Land) (Amendment) Act, 1989 (Tamil Nadu Act 30 of 1989).

278. The West Bengal Land Reforms (Amendment) Act, 1981 (West Bengal Act 50 of 1981).

279. The West Bengal Land Reforms (Amendment) Act, 1986 (West Bengal Act 5 of 1986).

280. The West Bengal Land Reforms (Second Amendment) Act, 1986 (West Bengal Act 19 of 1986).

281. The West Bengal Land Reforms (Third Amendment) Act, 1986 (West Bengal Act 35 of 1986).

282. The West Bengal Land Reforms (Amendment) Act, 1989 (West Bengal Act 23 of 1989).

283. The West Bengal Land Reforms (Amendment) Act, 1990 (West Bengal Act 24 of 1990).

284. The West Bengal Land Reforms Tribunal Act, 1991 (West Bengal Act 12 of 1991).]

Explanation.—Any acquisition made under the Rajasthan Tenancy Act, 1955 (Rajasthan Act 3 of 1955), in contravention of the second proviso to clause (1) of article 31A shall, to the extent of the contravention, be void.]

¹[TENTH SCHEDULE

[Articles 102(2) and 191(2)]

Provisions as to disqualification on ground of defection

1. **Interpretation.**—In this Schedule, unless the context otherwise requires,—

    (*a*) "House" means either House of Parliament or the Legislative Assembly or, as the case may be, either House of the Legislature of a State;

    (*b*) "legislature party", in relation to a member of a House belonging to any political party in accordance with the provisions of paragraph 2 or ²*** paragraph 4, means the group consisting of all the members of that House for the time being belonging to that political party in accordance with the said provisions;

    (*c*) "original political party", in relation to a member of a House, means the political party to which he belongs for the purposes of sub- paragraph (1) of paragraph 2;

    (*d*) "paragraph" means a paragraph of this Schedule.

2. **Disqualification on ground of defection.**—(1) Subject to the provisions of ³[paragraphs 4 and 5], a member of a House belonging to any political party shall be disqualified for being a member of the House—

    (*a*) if he has voluntarily given up his membership of such political party; or

    (*b*) if he votes or abstains from voting in such House contrary to any direction issued by the political party to which he belongs or by any person or authority authorised by it in this behalf, without obtaining, in either case, the prior

---

1 Tenth Schedule added by the Constitution (Fifty-second Amendment) Act, 1985, s. 6 (w.e.f. 1-3-1985).

2 Certain words omitted by the Constitution (Ninety-first Amendment) Act, 2003, s. 5 (w.e.f. 1-1-2004).

3 Subs. by s. 5, *ibid.*, for "paragraphs 3, 4 and 5". (w.e.f. 1-1-2004).

permission of such political party, person or authority and such voting or abstention has not been condoned by such political party, person or authority within fifteen days from the date of such voting or abstention.

Explanation.—For the purposes of this sub-paragraph,—

(*a*) an elected member of a House shall be deemed to belong to the political party, if any, by which he was set up as a candidate for election as such member;

(*b*) a nominated member of a House shall,—

(*i*) where he is a member of any political party on the date of his nomination as such member, be deemed to belong to such political party;

(*ii*) in any other case, be deemed to belong to the political party of which he becomes, or, as the case may be, first becomes, a member before the expiry of six months from the date on which he takes his seat after complying with the requirements of article 99 or, as the case may be, article 188.

(2) An elected member of a House who has been elected as such otherwise than as a candidate set up by any political party shall be disqualified for being a member of the House if he joins any political party after such election.

(3) A nominated member of a House shall be disqualified for being a member of the House if he joins any political party after the expiry of six months from the date on which he takes his seat after complying with the requirements of article 99 or, as the case may be, article 188.

(4) Notwithstanding anything contained in the foregoing provisions of this paragraph, a person who, on the commencement of the Constitution (Fifty- second Amendment) Act, 1985, is a member of a House (whether elected or nominated as such) shall,—

(*i*) where he was a member of political party immediately before such commencement, be deemed, for the purposes of sub-paragraph (1) of this paragraph, to have been elected as a member of such House as a candidate set up by such political party;

(*ii*) in any other case, be deemed to be an elected member of the House who has been elected as such otherwise than as a candidate set up by any political party for the purposes of sub-paragraph (2) of this paragraph or, as the case may be, be deemed to be a nominated member of the House for the purposes of sub-paragraph (3) of this paragraph.

¹*   *   *   *   *

4.   **Disqualification on ground of defection not to apply in case of merger.**—(1) A member of a House shall not be disqualified under sub- paragraph (1) of paragraph 2 where his original political party merges with another political party and he claims that he and any other members of his original political party—

> (a)   have become members of such other political party or, as the case may be, of a new political party formed by such merger; or

> (b)   have not accepted the merger and opted to function as a separate group,

and from the time of such merger, such other political party or new political party or group, as the case may be, shall be deemed to be the political party to which he belongs for the purposes of sub-paragraph (1) of paragraph 2 and to be his original political party for the purposes of this sub-paragraph.

(2) For the purposes of sub-paragraph (1) of this paragraph, the merger of the original political party of a member of a House shall be deemed to have taken place if, and only if, not less than two-thirds of the members of the legislature party concerned have agreed to such merger.

5.   **Exemption.**—Notwithstanding anything contained in this Schedule, a person who has been elected to the office of the Speaker or the Deputy Speaker of the House of the People or the Deputy Chairman of the Council of States or the Chairman or the Deputy Chairman of the Legislative Council of a State or the Speaker or the Deputy Speaker of the Legislative Assembly of a State, shall not be disqualified under this Schedule,—

> (a)   if he, by reason of his election to such office, voluntarily gives up the membership of the political party to which he belonged immediately before such election and does

---

1   Paragraph 3 omitted by the Constitution (Ninety-first Amendment) Act, 2003, s. 5 (w.e.f. 1-1-2004).

not, so long as he continues to hold such office thereafter, rejoin that political party or become a member of another political party; or

(b) if he, having given up by reason of his election to such office his membership of the political party to which he belonged immediately before such election, rejoins such political party after he ceases to hold such office.

6. **Decision on questions as to disqualification on ground of defection.**—(1) If any question arises as to whether a member of a House has become subject to disqualification under this Schedule, the question shall be referred for the decision of the Chairman or, as the case may be, the Speaker of such House and his decision shall be final: Provided that where the question which has arisen is as to whether the Chairman or the Speaker of a House has become subject to such disqualification, the question shall be referred for the decision of such member of the House as the House may elect in this behalf and his decision shall be final.

(2) All proceedings under sub-paragraph (1) of this paragraph in relation to any question as to disqualification of a member of a House under this Schedule shall be deemed to be proceedings in Parliament within the meaning of article 122 or, as the case may be, proceedings in the Legislature of a State within the meaning of article 212.

*7. **Bar of jurisdiction of courts.**—Notwithstanding anything in this Constitution, no court shall have any jurisdiction in respect of any matter connected with the disqualification of a member of a House under this Schedule.

8. **Rules.**—(1) Subject to the provisions of sub-paragraph (2) of this paragraph, the Chairman or the Speaker of a House may make rules for giving effect to the provisions of this Schedule, and in particular, and without prejudice to the generality of the foregoing, such rules may provide for—

(a) the maintenance of registers or other records as to the political parties, if any, to which different members of the House belong;

---

* Paragraph 7 declared invalid for want of ratification in accordance with the proviso to clause (2) of article 368 as per majority opinion in *Kihoto Hollohon Vs. Zachilhu and Others* A.I.R. 1993 SC 412.

(*b*)   the report which the leader of a legislature party in relation to a member of a House shall furnish with regard to any condonation of the nature referred to in clause (*b*) of sub-paragraph (1) of paragraph 2 in respect of such member, the time within which and the authority to whom such report shall be furnished;

(*c*)   the reports which a political party shall furnish with regard to admission to such political party of any members of the House and the officer of the House to whom such reports shall be furnished; and

(*d*)   the procedure for deciding any question referred to in sub-paragraph (1) of paragraph 6 including the procedure for any inquiry which may be made for the purpose of deciding such question.

(2) The rules made by the Chairman or the Speaker of a House under sub-paragraph (1) of this paragraph shall be laid as soon as may be after they are made before the House for a total period of thirty days which may be comprised in one session or in two or more successive sessions and shall take effect upon the expiry of the said period of thirty days unless they are sooner approved with or without modifications or disapproved by the House and where they are so approved, they shall take effect on such approval in the form in which they were laid or in such modified form, as the case may be, and where they are so disapproved, they shall be of no effect.

(3) The Chairman or the Speaker of a House may, without prejudice to the provisions of article 105 or, as the case may be, article 194, and to any other power which he may have under this Constitution direct that any wilful contravention by any person of the rules made under this paragraph may be dealt with in the same manner as a breach of privilege of the House.]

¹[ELEVENTH SCHEDULE

(Article 243G)

1. Agriculture, including agricultural extension.
2. Land improvement, implementation of land reforms, land consolidation and soil conservation.
3. Minor irrigation, water management and watershed development.
4. Animal husbandry, dairying and poultry.
5. Fisheries.
6. Social forestry and farm forestry.
7. Minor forest produce.
8. Small scale industries, including food processing industries.
9. Khadi, village and cottage industries.
10. Rural housing.
11. Drinking water.
12. Fuel and fodder.
13. Roads, culverts, bridges, ferries, waterways and other means of communication.
14. Rural electrification, including distribution of electricity.
15. Non-conventional energy sources.
16. Poverty alleviation programme.
17. Education, including primary and secondary schools.
18. Technical training and vocational education.
19. Adult and non-formal education.
20. Libraries.
21. Cultural activities.
22. Markets and fairs.
23. Health and sanitation, including hospitals, primary health centres and dispensaries.
24. Family welfare.
25. Women and child development.
26. Social welfare, including welfare of the handicapped and mentally retarded.

---

1 Eleventh Schedule added by the Constitution (Seventy-third Amendment) Act, 1992, s. 4 (w.e.f. 24-4-1993).

27.   Welfare of the weaker sections, and in particular, of the Scheduled Castes and the Scheduled Tribes.

28.   Public distribution system.

29.   Maintenance of community assets.]

[TWELFTH SCHEDULE

(Article 243W)

1.   Urban planning including town planning.

2.   Regulation of land-use and construction of buildings.

3.   Planning for economic and social development.

4.   Roads and bridges.

5.   Water supply for domestic, industrial and commercial purposes.

6.   Public health, sanitation conservancy and solid waste management.

7.   Fire services.

8.   Urban forestry, protection of the environment and promotion of ecological aspects.

9.   Safeguarding the interests of weaker sections of society, including the handicapped and mentally retarded.

10.   Slum improvement and upgradation.

11.   Urban poverty alleviation.

12.   Provision of urban amenities and facilities such as parks, gardens, playgrounds.

13.   Promotion of cultural, educational and aesthetic aspects.

14.   Burials and burial grounds; cremations, cremation grounds; and electric crematoriums.

15.   Cattle pounds; prevention of cruelty to animals.

16.   Vital statistics including registration of births and deaths.

17.   Public amenities including street lighting, parking lots, bus stops and public conveniences.

18.   Regulation of slaughter houses and tanneries.]

---

1   Twelfth Schedule added by the Constitution (Seventy-fourth Amendment) Act, 1992, s. 4 (w.e.f. 1-6-1993).

APPENDIX I

THE CONSTITUTION (ONE HUNDREDTH AMENDMENT) ACT, 2015

[28*th May*, 2015.]

An Act further to amend the Constitution of India to give effect to the acquiring of territories by India and transfer of certain territories to Bangladesh in pursuance of the agreement and its protocol entered into between the Governments of India and Bangladesh.

BE it enacted by Parliament in the Sixty-sixth Year of the Republic of India as follows:—

1.   **Short title.**—This Act may be called the Constitution (One Hundredth Amendment) Act, 2015.

2.   **Definitions.**—In this Act,—

    (*a*) "acquired territory" means so much of the territories comprised in the India-Bangladesh agreement and its protocol and referred to in the First Schedule as are demarcated for the purpose of being acquired by India from Bangladesh in pursuance of the agreement and its protocol referred to in clause (*c*);

    (*b*) "appointed day" means such date as the Central Government may, by notification in the Official Gazette, appoint as the date for acquisition of territories from Bangladesh and transfer of the territories to Bangladesh in pursuance of the India-Bangladesh agreement and its protocol, after causing the territories to be so acquired and transferred as referred to in the First Schedule and Second Schedule and demarcated for the purpose;

    (*c*) "India-Bangladesh agreement" means the agreement between the Government of the Republic of India

---

* 31st day of July, 2015, vide notification No. S.O. 2094(E), dated 31st July, 2015.

398

and the Government of the People's Republic of Bangladesh concerning the Demarcation of the Land Boundary between India and Bangladesh and Related Matters dated the 16th day of May, 1974, Exchange of Letters dated the 26th day of December, 1974, the 30th day of December, 1974, the 7th day of October, 1982, the 26th day of March, 1992 and protocol to the said agreement dated the 6th day of September, 2011, entered into between the Governments of India and Bangladesh, the relevant extracts of which are set out in the Third Schedule;

(d) "transferred territory", means so much of the territories comprised in the India-Bangladesh agreement and its protocol and referred to in the Second Schedule as are demarcated for the purpose of being transferred by India to Bangladesh in pursuance of the agreements and its protocol referred to in clause (c).

3.   **Amendment of First Schedule to Constitution.**— As from the appointed day, in the First Schedule to the Constitution,—

(a) in the paragraph relating to the territories of the State of Assam, the words, brackets and figures "and the territories referred to in Part I of the Second Schedule to the Constitution (One Hundredth Amendment) Act, 2015, notwithstanding anything contained in clause (a) of section 3 of the Constitution (Ninth Amendment) Act, 1960, so far as it relates to the territories referred to in Part I of the Second Schedule to the Constitution (One Hundredth Amendment) Act, 2015", shall be added at the end;

(b) in the paragraph relating to the territories of the State of West Bengal, the words, brackets and figures "and also the territories referred to in Part III of the First Schedule but excluding the territories referred to in Part III of the Second Schedule to the Constitution (One Hundredth Amendment) Act, 2015, notwithstanding anything contained in clause (c) of section 3 of the Constitution (Ninth Amendment) Act, 1960, so far as it relates to the territories referred to in Part III of the First Schedule and the territories referred to in Part III of the Second Schedule to the Constitution (One Hundredth Amendment) Act, 2015", shall be added at the end;

(*c*) in the paragraph relating to the territories of the State of Meghalaya, the words, brackets and figures "and the territories referred to in Part I of the First Schedule but excluding the territories referred to in Part II of the Second Schedule to the Constitution (One Hundredth Amendment) Act, 2015", shall be added at the end;

(*d*) in the paragraph relating to the territories of the State of Tripura, the words, brackets and figures "and the territories referred to in Part II of the First Schedule to the Constitution (One Hundredth Amendment) Act, 2015, notwithstanding anything contained in clause (*d*) of section 3 of the Constitution (Ninth Amendment) Act, 1960, so far as it relates to the territories referred to in Part II of the First Schedule to the Constitution (One Hundredth Amendment) Act, 2015", shall be added at the end.

THE FIRST SCHEDULE
[*See* sections 2*(a)*, 2*(b)* and 3]

PART I

The acquired territory in relation to Article 2 of the agreement dated the 16th day of May, 1974 and Article 3 (I) (b) (ii) (iii) (iv) (v) of the protocol dated the 6th day of September, 2011.

PART II

The acquired territory in relation to Article 2 of the agreement dated the 16th day of May, 1974 and Article 3 (I) (c) (i) of the protocol dated the 6th day of September, 2011.

PART III

The acquired territory in relation to Articles 1(12) and 2 of the agreement dated the 16th day of May, 1974 and Articles 2 (II), 3 (I) (a) (iii) (iv) (v) (vi) of the protocol dated the 6th day of September, 2011.

THE SECOND SCHEDULE
[*See* sections 2*(b)*, 2*(d)* and 3]

PART I

The transferred territory in relation to Article 2 of the agreement dated 16th day of May, 1974 and Article 3 (I) (d) (i) (ii) of the protocol dated 6th day of September, 2011.

PART II

The transferred territory in relation to Article 2 of the agreement dated the 16th day of May, 1974 and Article 3 (I) (b) (i) of the protocol dated 6th day of September, 2011.

PART III

The transferred territory in relation to Articles 1(12) and 2 of the agreement dated the 16th day of May, 1974 and Articles 2 (II), 3 (I) (a) (i) (ii) (vi) of the protocol dated the 6th day of September, 2011.

THE THIRD SCHEDULE
[*See* section 2*(c)*]

I. EXTRACTS FROM THE AGREEMENT BETWEEN GOVERNMENT OF THE REPUBLIC OF INDIA AND THE GOVERNMENT OF THE PEOPLE'S REPUBLIC OF BANGLADESH CONCERNING THE DEMARCATION OF THE LAND BOUNDARY BETWEEN INDIA AND BANGLADESH AND RELATED MATTERS DATED THE 16TH DAY OF MAY, 1974

Article 1 (12): ENCLAVES

The Indian enclaves in Bangladesh and the Bangladesh enclaves in India should be exchanged expeditiously, excepting the enclaves mentioned in paragraph 14 without claim to compensation for the additional area going to Bangladesh.

Article 2:

The Governments of India and Bangladesh agree that territories in adverse possession in areas already demarcated in respect of which boundary strip maps are already prepared, shall be exchanged within six months of the signing of the boundary strip maps by the plenipotentiaries. They may sign the relevant maps as early as possible as and, in any case, not later than the 31st December, 1974. Early measures may be taken to print maps in respect of other areas where demarcation has already taken place. These should be printed by the 31st May, 1975 and signed by the plenipotentiaries thereafter in order that the exchange of adversely held possessions in these areas may take place by the 31st December, 1975. In sectors still to be demarcated, transfer of territorial jurisdiction may take place within six months of the signature by plenipotentiaries on the concerned boundary strip maps.

II. EXTRACTS FROM THE PROTOCOL TO THE AGREEMENT BETWEEN THE GOVERNMENT OF THE REPUBLIC OF INDIA AND THE GOVERNMENT OF THE PEOPLE'S REPUBLIC OF BANGLADESH CONCERNING THE DEMARCATION OF THE LAND BOUNDARY BETWEEN INDIA AND BANGLADESH AND RELATED MATTERS, DATED THE 6TH DAY OF SEPTEMBER, 2011

Article 2:

(II) Article 1 Clause 12 of the 1974 Agreement shall be implemented as follows:—

Enclaves

111 Indian Enclaves in Bangladesh and 51 Bangladesh Enclaves in India as per the jointly verified cadastral enclave maps and signed at the level of DGLR&S, Bangladesh and DLR&S, West Bengal (India) in April, 1997, shall be exchanged without claim to compensation for the additional areas going to Bangladesh.

Article 3:

(I)   Article 2 of the 1974 Agreement shall be implemented as follows:—
The Government of India and the Government of Bangladesh
agree that the boundary shall be drawn as a fixed boundary for
territories held in Adverse Possession as determined through joint
survey and fully depicted in the respective adversely possessed land
area Index Map (APL map) finalised by the Land Records and
Survey Departments of both the countries between December,
2010 and August, 2011, which are fully described in clause (a) to (d)
below.
The relevant strip maps shall be printed and signed by the
Plenipotentiaries and transfer of territorial jurisdiction shall be
completed simultaneously with the exchange of enclaves. The
demarcation of the boundary, as depicted in the above-mentioned
Index Maps, shall be as under:—

   (a) **West Bengal Sector**

     (*ii*) *Bousmari – Madhugari (Kushtia-Nadia) area*
The boundary shall be drawn from the existing
Boundary Pillar Nos. 154/5-S to 157/1-S to follow the
centre of old course of river Mathabanga, as depicted
in consolidation map of 1962, as surveyed jointly and
agreed in June, 2011.

     (*ii*) *Andharkota (Kushtia-Nadia) area*
The boundary shall be drawn from existing Boundary
Pillar No. 152/5-S to Boundary Pillar No. 153/1-S
to follow the edge of existing River Mathabanga as
jointly surveyed and agreed in June, 2011.

     (*iii*) *Pakuria (Kushtia-Nadia) area*
The boundary shall be drawn from existing Boundary
Pillar No. 151/1-S to Boundary Pillar No. 152/2-
S to follow the edge of River Mathabanga as jointly
surveyed and agreed in June, 2011.

     (*iv*) *Char Mahishkundi (Kushtia-Nadia) area*
The boundary shall be drawn from existing Boundary
Pillar No. 153/1-S to Boundary Pillar No. 153/9-
S to follow the edge of River Mathabanga as jointly
surveyed and agreed in June, 2011.

(v) *Haripal/Khutadah/Battoli/Sapameri/LNpur*　　(Patari)
(Naogaon-Malda) area

The boundary shall be drawn as line joining from existing Boundary Pillar No. 242/S/13, to Boundary Pillar No. 243/7-S/5 and as jointly surveyed and agreed in June, 2011.

(iv) *Berubari (Panchagarh-Jalpaiguri area)*

The boundary in the area Berubari (Panchagarh-Jalpaiguri) adversely held by Bangladesh, and Berubari and Singhapara-Khudipara (Panchagarh-Jalpaiguri), adversely held by India shall be drawn as jointly demarcated during 1996-1998.

(b) Meghalaya Sector

(i) *Lobachera-Nuncherra*

The boundary from existing Boundary Pillar No. 1315/4-S to Boundary Pillar No. 1315/15-S in Lailong - Balichera, Boundary Pillar No. 1316/1-S to Boundary Pillar No. 1316/11-S in Lailong-Noonchera, Boundary Pillar No. 1317 to Boundary Pillar No. 1317/13-S in Lailong- Lahiling and Boundary Pillar No. 1318/1-S to Boundary Pillar No. 1318/2-S in Lailong- Lobhachera shall be drawn to follow the edge of tea gardens as jointly surveyed and agreed in December, 2010.

(ii) *Pyrdiwah/ Padua Area*

The boundary shall be drawn from existing Boundary Pillar No. 1270/1-S as per jointly surveyed and mutually agreed line till Boundary Pillar No. 1271/1-T. The Parties agree that the Indian Nationals from Pyrdiwah village shall be allowed to draw water from Piyang River near point No. 6 of the agreed Map.

(iii) *Lyngkhat Area*

(aa) *Lyngkhat-I/Kulumcherra and Lyngkhat- II/ Kulumcherra*

The boundary shall be drawn from existing Boundary Pillar No. 1264/4-S to Boundary Pillar No. 1265 and BP No. 1265/6-S to 1265/9-S as per jointly surveyed and mutually agreed line.

(*ab*) *Lyngkhat-III/Sonarhat*

The boundary shall be drawn from existing Boundary Pillar No. 1266/13-S along the nallah southwards till it meets another nallah in the east-west direction, thereafter it shall run along the northern edge of the nallah in east till it meets the existing International Boundary north of Reference Pillar Nos.1267/4-R-B and 1267/3-R-I.

(*iv*) *Dawki/Tamabil area*

The boundary shall be drawn by a straight line joining existing Boundary Pillar Nos. 1275/1-S to Boundary Pillar Nos. 1275/7-S. The Parties agree to fencing on 'zero line' in this area.

(*v*) *Naljuri/Sreepur Area*

(*aa*) Naljuri *I*

The boundary shall be a line from the existing Boundary Pillar No. 1277/2-S in southern direction up to three plots as depicted in the strip Map No. 166 till it meets the nallah flowing from Boundary Pillar No. 1277/5-T, thereafter it will run along the western edge of the nallah in the southern direction up to 2 plots on the Bangladesh side, thereafter it shall run eastwards till it meets a line drawn in southern direction from Boundary Pillar No. 1277/4-S.

(*ab*) *Naljuri III*

The boundary shall be drawn by a straight line from existing Boundary Pillar No. 1278/2-S to Boundary Pillar No. 1279/ 3-S.

(*vi*) *Muktapur/ Dibir Hawor Area*

The Parties agree that the Indian Nationals shall be allowed to visit Kali Mandir and shall also be allowed to draw water and exercise fishing rights in the water body in the Muktapur / Dibir Hawor area from the bank of Muktapur side.

(c) Tripura Sector

Chandannagar-Champarai Tea Garden area in Tripura/ Moulvi Bazar sector

The boundary shall be drawn along Sonaraichhera river from existing Boundary Pillar No. 1904 to Boundary Pillar No. 1905 as surveyed jointly and agreed in July, 2011.

(d) Assam Sector

(*i*) *Kalabari (Boroibari) area in Assam sector*

The boundary shall be drawn from existing Boundary Pillar No. 1066/24-T to Boundary Pillar No. 1067/16-T as surveyed jointly and agreed in August, 2011.

(*ii*) *Pallathal area in Assam sector*

The boundary shall be drawn from existing Boundary Pillar No. 1370/3-S to 1371/ 6-S to follow the outer edge of the tea garden and from Boundary Pillar No. 1372 to 1373/2-S along outer edge of the pan plantation.

III. LIST OF EXCHANGE OF ENCLAVES BETWEEN INDIA AND BANGLADESH IN PURSUANT TO ARTICLE 1 (12) OF THE AGREEMENT DATED 16TH MAY, 1974 AND THE PROTOCOL TO THE AGREEMENT DATED 6TH SEPTEMBER, 2011

A. **EXCHANGEABLE INDIAN ENCLAVES IN BANGLADESH WITH AREA**

Sl.	Name of Chhits No.	Chhit No.	Lying within Police station Bangladesh	Lying within Police station W. Bengal	Area in acres
1	2	3	4	5	6
A. Enclaves with independent chhits					
1.	Garati	75	Pochagar	Haldibari	58.23
2.	Garati	76	Pochagar	Haldibari	0.79
3.	Garati	77	Pochagar	Haldibari	18
4.	Garati	78	Pochagar	Haldibari	958.66
5.	Garati	79	Pochagar	Haldibari	1.74
6.	Garati	80	Pochagar	Haldibari	73.75
7.	Bingimari Part-I	73	Pochagar	Haldibari	6.07
8.	Nazirganja	41	Boda	Haldibari	58.32
9.	Nazirganja	42	Boda	Haldibari	434.29
10.	Nazirganja	44	Boda	Haldibari	53.47
11.	Nazirganja	45	Boda	Haldibari	1.07
12.	Nazirganja	46	Boda	Haldibari	17.95
13.	Nazirganja	47	Boda	Haldibari	3.89

14.	Nazirganja	48	Boda	Haldibari	73.27
15.	Nazirganja	49	Boda	Haldibari	49.05
16.	Nazirganja	50	Boda	Haldibari	5.05
17.	Nazirganja	51	Boda	Haldibari	0.77
18.	Nazirganja	52	Boda	Haldibari	1.04
19.	Nazirganja	53	Boda	Haldibari	1.02
20.	Nazirganja	54	Boda	Haldibari	3.87
21.	Nazirganja	55	Boda	Haldibari	12.18
22.	Nazirganja	56	Boda	Haldibari	54.04
23.	Nazirganja	57	Boda	Haldibari	8.27
24.	Nazirganja	58	Boda	Haldibari	14.22
25.	Nazirganja	60	Boda	Haldibari	0.52
26.	Putimari	59	Boda	Haldibari	122.8
27.	Daikhata Chhat	38	Boda	Haldibari	499.21
28.	Salbari	37	Boda	Haldibari	1188.93
29.	Kajal Dighi	36	Boda	Haldibari	771.44
30.	Nataktoka	32	Boda	Haldibari	162.26
31.	Nataktoka	33	Boda	Haldibari	0.26
32.	Beuladanga Chhat	35	Boda	Haldibari	0.83
33.	Balapara Iagrabar	3	Debiganj	Haldibari	1752.44
34.	Bara Khankikharija Citaldaha	30	Dimla	Haldibari	7.71
35.	Bara Khankikharija Citaldaha	29	Dimla	Haldibari	36.83
36.	Barakhangir	28	Dimla	Haldibari	30.53
37.	Nagarjikobari	31	Dimla	Haldibari	33.41
38.	Kuchlibari	26	Patgram	Mekliganj	5.78
39.	Kuchlibari	27	Patgram	Mekliganj	2.04
40.	Bara Kuchlibari	Fragment of J.L.107 of P.S Mekliganj	Patgram	Mekliganj	4.35
41.	Jamaldaha-Balapukhari	6	Patgram	Mekliganj	5.24
42.	Uponchowki kuchlibari	115/2	Patgram	Mekliganj	0.32
43.	Uponchowki kuchlibari	7	Patgram	Mekliganj	44.04
44.	Bhothnri	11	Patgram	Mekliganj	36.83
45.	Balapukhari	5	Patgram	Mekliganj	55.91
46.	Bara Khangir	4	Patgram	Mekliganj	50.51
47.	Bara Khangir	9	Patgram	Mekliganj	87.42

48.	Chhat Bogdokra	10	Patgram	Mekliganj	41.7
49.	Ratanpur	11	Patgram	Mekliganj	58.91
50.	Bogdokra	12	Patgram	Mekliganj	25.49
51.	Fulker Dabri	Fragment of J.L. 107 of P.S Mekliganj	Patgram	Mekliganj	0.88
52.	Kharkharia	15	Patgram	Mekliganj	60.74
53.	Kharkharia	13	Patgram	Mekliganj	51.62
54.	Lotamari	14	Patgram	Mekliganj	110.92
55.	Bhotbari	16	Patgram	Mekliganj	205.46
56.	Komat Changrabandha	16A	Patgram	Mekliganj	42.8
57.	Komat Changrabandha	17A	Patgram	Mekliganj	16.01
58.	Panisala	17	Patgram	Mekliganj	137.66
59.	Dwarikamari Khasbash	18	Patgram	Mekliganj	36.5
60.	Panisala	153/P	Patgram	Mekliganj	0.27
61.	Panisala	153/O	Patgram	Mekliganj	18.01
62.	Panisala	19	Patgram	Mekliganj	64.63
63.	Panisala	21	Patgram	Mekliganj	51.4
64.	Lotamari	20	Patgram	Mekliganj	283.53
65.	Lotamari	22	Patgram	Mekliganj	98.85
66.	Dwarikamari	23	Patgram	Mekliganj	39.52
67.	Dwarikamari	25	Patgram	Mekliganj	45.73
68.	Chhat Bhothat	24	Patgram	Mekliganj	56.11
69.	Baakata	131	Patgram	Hathabhanga	22.35
70.	Baakata	132	Patgram	Hathabhanga	11.96
71.	Baakata	130	Patgram	Hathibhanga	20.48
72.	Bhogramguri	133	Patgram	Hathibhanga	1.44
73.	Chenakata	134	Patgram	Mekliganj	7.81
74.	Banskata	119	Patgram	Mathabanga	413.81
75.	Banskata	120	Patgram	Mathabanga	30.75
76.	Banskata	121	Patgram	Mathabanga	12.15
77.	Banskata	113	Patgram	Mathabanga	57.86
78.	Banskata	112	Patgram	Mathabanga	315.04
79.	Banskata	114	Patgram	Mathabanga	0.77
80.	Banskata	115	Patgram	Mathabanga	29.2
81.	Banskata	122	Patgram	Mathabanga	33.22
82.	Banskata	127	Patgram	Mathabanga	12.72
83.	Banskata	128	Patgram	Mathabanga	2.33

84.	Banskata	117	Patgram	Mathabanga	2.55
85.	Banskata	118	Patgram	Mathabanga	30.98
86.	Banskata	125	Patgram	Mathabanga	0.64
87.	Banskata	126	Patgram	Mathabanga	1.39
88.	Banskata	129	Patgram	Mathabanga	1.37
89.	Banskata	116	Patgram	Mathabanga	16.96
90.	Banskata	123	Patgram	Mathabanga	24.37
91.	Banskata	124	Patgram	Mathabanga	0.28
92.	Gotamari Chhit	135	Hatibandha	Sitalkuchi	126.59
93.	Gotamari Chhit	136	Hatibandha	Sitalkuchi	20.02
94.	Banapachai	151	Lalmonirhat	Dinhata	217.29
95.	Banapachai Bhitarkuthi	152	Lalmonirhat	Dinhata	81.71
96.	Dasiar Chhara	150	Fulbari	Dinhata	1643.44
97.	Dakurhat-Dakinirkuthi	156	Kurigram	Dinhata	14.27
98.	Kalamati	141	Bhurungamari	Dinhata	21.21
99.	Bhahobganj	153	Bhurungamari	Dinhata	31.58
100.	Baotikursa	142	Bhurungamari	Dinhata	45.63
101.	Bara Coachulka	143	Bhurungamari	Dinhata	39.99
102.	Gaochulka II	147	Bhurungamari	Dinhata	0.9
103.	Gaochulka I	146	Bhurungamari	Dinhata	8.92
104.	Dighaltari II	145	Bhurungamari	Dinhata	8.81
105.	Dighaltari I	144	Bhurungamari	Dinhata	12.31
106.	Chhoto Garaljhora II	149	Bhurungamari	Dinhata	17.85
107.	Chhoto Garaljhora I	148	Bhurungamari	Dinhata	35.74
108.	1 chhit[1]* without name & JL No. at the southern and of JL No. 38 & southern and of JL No. 39 (locally known as Ashokabari **[2])		Patgram	Mathabhanga	3.5
	Enclaves with Fragmented Chhits				
109	(i) Bewladanga	34	Haldibari	Boda	862.46
	(ii) Bewladanga	Fragment	Haldibari	Debiganj	

* Corrected vide 150th (54th) India-Bangladesh Boundary Conference held at Kolkata from 29th September to 2nd October, 2002.
** Corrected *vide* 152nd (56th) India-Bangladesh Boundary Conference held at Kochbihar, India from 18th—20th September, 2003.

110.	(i) Kotbhajni	2	Haldibari	Debiganj	2012.27
	(ii) Kotbhajni	Fragment	Haldibari	Debiganj	
	(iii) Kotbhajni	Fragment	Haldibari	Debiganj	
	(iv) Kotbhajni	Fragment	Haldibari	Debiganj	
111.	(i) Dahala	Khagrabri	Haldibari	Debiganj	2650.35
	(ii) Dahala	Fragment	Haldibari	Debiganj	
	(iii) Dahala	Fragment	Haldibari	Debiganj	
	(iv) Dahala	Fragment	Haldibari	Debiganj	
	(v) Dahala	Fragment	Haldibari	Debiganj	
	(vi) Dahala	Fragment	Haldibari	Debiganj	
					17160.63

The above given details of enclaves have been jointly compared and reconciled with records held by India and Bangladesh during the Indo-Bangladesh Conference held at Calcutta during 9th—12th October, 1996 as well as during joint field inspection at Jalpaiguri (West Bengal) Panchagarh (Bangladesh) sector during 21—24 November, 1996.

Note: Name of enclave in Sl. No. 108 above has been identified as Ashokabari by joint ground verification during field season 1996-97.

Brig. J.R. Peter
Director Land Records & Survey (*Ex-Officio*)
West Bengal, India & Director, Eastern Circle
Survey of India, Calcutta.

Md. Shafi Uddin
Director-General,
Land Records and Surveys,
Bangladesh.

B. EXCHANGEABLE BANGLADESH ENCLAVES IN INDIA WITH AREA

Sl. No.	Name of Chhits	Lying within Police station W. Bengal	Lying within Police station Bangladesh	J.L. No.	Area in acres
1	2	3	4	5	6
A. Enclaves with independent chhits					
1.	Chhit Kuchlibari	Mekliganj	Patgram	22	370.64
2.	Chhit Land of Kuchlibari	Mekliganj	Patgram	24	1.83

3.	Balapukhari	Mekliganj	Patgram	21	331.64
4.	Chhit Land of Panbari No. 2	Mekliganj	Patgram	20	1.13
5.	Chhit Panbari	Mekliganj	Patgram	18	108.59
6.	Dhabalsati Mirgipur	Mekliganj	Patgram	15	173.88
7.	Bamandal	Mekliganj	Patgram	11	2.24
8.	Chhit Dhabalsati	Mekliganj	Patgram	14	66.58
9.	Dhabalsati	Mekliganj	Patgram	13	60.45
10.	Srirampur	Mekliganj	Patgram	8	1.05
11.	Jote Nijjama	Mekliganj	Patgram	3	87.54
12.	Chhit Land of Jagatber No. 3	Mathabhanga	Patgram	37	69.84
13.	Chhit Land of Jagatber No.1	Mathabhanga	Patgram	35	30.66
14.	Chhit Land of Jagatber No. 2	Mathabhanga	Patgram	36	27.09
15.	Chhit Kokoabari	Mathabhanga	Patgram	47	29.49
16.	Chhit Bhandardaha	Mathabhanga	Patgram	67	39.96
17.	Dhabalguri	Mathabhanga	Patgram	52	12.5
18.	Chhit Dhabalguri	Mathabhanga	Patgram	53	22.31
19.	Chhit Land of Dhabalguri No. 3	Mathabhanga	Patgram	70	1.33
20.	Chhit Land of Dhabalguri No. 4	Mathabhanga	Patgram	71	4.55
21.	Chhit Land of Dhabalguri No. 5	Mathabhanga	Patgram	72	4.12
22.	Chhit Land of Dhabalguri No. 1	Mathabhanga	Patgram	68	26.83
23.	Chhit Land of Dhabalguri No. 2	Mathabhanga	Patgram	69	13.95
24.	Mahishmari	Sitalkuchi	Patgram	54	122.77
25.	Bura Saradubi	Sitalkuchi	Hatibandha	13	34.96
26.	Falnapur	Sitalkuchi	Patgram	64	505.56
27.	Amjhol	Sitalkuchi	Hatibandha	57	1.25
28.	Kismat Batrigachh	Dinhata	Kaliganj	82	209.95
29.	Durgapur	Dinhata	Kaliganj	83	20.96
30.	Bansua Khamar Gitaldaha	Dinhata	Lalmonirhat	1	24.54
31.	Poaturkuthi	Dinhata	Lalmonirhat	37	589.94
32.	Paschim Bakalir Chhara	Dinhata	Bhurungamari	38	151.98

33.	Madhya Bakalir Chhara	Dinhata	Bhurungamari	39	32.72
34.	Purba Bakalir Chhara	Dinhata	Bhurungamari	40	12.23
35.	Madhya Masaldanga	Dinhata	Bhurungamari	3	136.66
36.	Madhya Chhit Masaldanga	Dinhata	Bhurungamari	8	11.87
37.	Paschim Chhit Masaldanga	Dinhata	Bhurungamari	7	7.6
38.	Uttar Masaldanga	Dinhata	Bhurungamari	2	27.29
39.	Kachua	Dinhata	Bhurungamari	5	119.74
40.	Uttar Bansjani	Tufanganj	Bhurungamari	1	47.17
41.	Chhat Tilai	Tufanganj	Bhurungamari	17	81.56
B. Enclaves with Fragmented Chhits					
42.	(i) Nalgram	Sitalkuchi	Patgarm	65	1397.34
	(ii) Nalgram (Fragment)	Sitalkuchi	Patgarm	65	
	(iii) Nalgram (Fragment)	Sitalkuchi	Patgarm	65	
43.	(i) Chhit Nalgram	Sitalkuchi	Patgarm	66	49.5
	(ii) Chhit Nalgram (Fragment)	Sitalkuchi	Patgarm	66	
44.	(i) Batrigachh	Dinhata	Kaliganj	81	577.37
	(ii) Batrigachh (Fragment)	Dinhata	Kaliganj	81	
	(iii) Batrigachh (Fragment)	Dinhata	Phulbari	9	
45.	(i) Karala	Dinhata	Phulbari	9	269.91
	(ii) Karala (fragment)	Dinhata	Phulbari	9	
	(iii) Karala (fragment)	Dinhata	Phulbari	8	
46.	(i) Sipprasad Mustati	Dinhata	Phulbari	8	373.2
	(ii) Sipprasad Mustati (Fragment)	Dinhata	Phulbari	6	
47.	(i) Dakshin Masaldanga	Dinhata	Bhurungamari	6	571.38
	(ii) Dakshin Masaldanga (Fragment)	Dinhata	Bhurungamari	6	
	(iii) Dakshin Masaldanga (Fragment)	Dinhata	Bhurungamari	6	
	(iv) Dakshin Masaldanga (Fragment)	Dinhata	Bhurungamari	6	
	(v) Dakshin Masaldanga (Fragment)	Dinhata	Bhurungamari	6	
	(vi) Dakshin Masaldanga (Fragment)	Dinhata	Bhurungamari	6	
48.	(i) Paschim Masaldanga	Dinhata	Bhurungamari	4	29.49
	(ii) Paschim Masaldanga (Fragment)	Dinhata	Bhurungamari	4	

49.	(i) Purba Chhit Masaldanga	Dinhata	Bhurungamari	10	35.01
	(ii) Purba Chhit Masaldanga (Fragment)	Dinhata	Bhurungamari	10	
50.	(i) Purba Masaldanga	Dinhata	Bhurungamari	11	153.89
	(ii) Purba Masaldanga (Fragment)	Dinhata	Bhurungamari	11	
51.	(i) Uttar Dhaldanga	Tufanganj	Bhurungamari	14	24.98
	(ii) Uttar Dhaldanga (Fragment)	Tufanganj	Bhurungamari	14	
	(iii) Uttar Dhaldanga (Fragment)	Tufanganj	Bhurungamari	14	
	Total Area				7,110.02

The above given details of enclaves have been jointly compared and reconciled with records held by India and Bangladesh during the Indo-Bangladesh Conference held at Calcutta during 9th—12th October, 1996 as well as during joint field inspection at Jalpaiguri (West Bengal) – Panchagarh (Bangladesh) sector during 21—24 November, 1996.

Brig. J.R. Peter
Director Land Records & Survey (*Ex officio*)
West Bengal, India & Director, Eastern Circle
Survey of India, Calcutta.

Md. Shafi Uddin
Director General, Land Records
and Surveys, Bangladesh.

APPENDIX II

[1]THE CONSTITUTION
(APPLICATION TO JAMMU AND KASHMIR) ORDER, 2019

C.O. 272

In exercise of the powers conferred by clause (1) of article 370 of the Constitution, the President, with the concurrence of the Government of State of Jammu and Kashmir, is pleased to make the following Order:—

1.   (1) This Order may be called the Constitution (Application to Jammu and Kashmir) Order, 2019.

(2) It shall come into force at once, and shall thereupon supersede the Constitution (Application to Jammu and Kashmir) Order, 1954 as amended from time to time.

2.   All the provisions of the Constitution, as amended from time to time, shall apply in relation to the State of Jammu and Kashmir and the exceptions and modifications subject to which they shall so apply shall be as follows:–

To article 367, there shall be added the following clause, namely:—

"(4) For the purposes of this Constitution as it applies in relation to the State of Jammu and Kashmir–

(*a*) references to this Constitution or to the provisions thereof shall be construed as references to the Constitution or the provisions thereof as applied in relation to the said State;

(*b*) references to the person for the time being recognized by the President on the recommendation of the Legislative Assembly of the State as the Sadar-i-Riyasat of Jammu and Kashmir, acting on the advice of the Council of Ministers of the State for the time being in office, shall be construed as references to the Governor of Jammu and Kashmir;

---

1 Published with the Ministry of Law and Justice, (Legislative Department) notification No. G.S.R. 551 (E), dated the 5th August, 2019, Gazette of India, Extraordinary, Part II, Section 3, Sub-section (i).

(*c*) references to the Government of the said State shall be construed as including references to the Governor of Jammu and Kashmir acting on the advice of his Council of Ministers; and

(*d*) in proviso to clause (3) of article 370 of this Constitution, the expression "Constituent Assembly of the State referred to in clause (2)" shall read "Legislative Assembly of the State".".

APPENDIX III

[1]DECLRATION UNDER ARTICLE 370(3) OF THE CONSTITUTION

C.O. 273

In exercise of the powers conferred by clause (3) of article 370 read with clause (1) of article 370 of the Constitution of India, the President, on the recommendation of Parliament, is pleased to declare that, as from the 6th August, 2019, all clauses of the said article 370 shall cease to be operative except the following which shall read as under, namely:—

"370. All provisions of this Constitution, as amended from time to time, without any modifications or exceptions, shall apply to the State of Jammu and Kashmir notwithstanding anything contrary contained in article 152 or article 308 or any other article of this Constitution or any other provision of the Constitution of Jammu and Kashmir or any law, document, judgement, ordinance, order, by-law, rule, regulation, notification, custom or usage having the force of law in the territory of India, or any other instrument, treaty or agreement as envisaged under article 363 or otherwise.".

---

1 Published with the Ministry of Law and Justice, (Legislative Department) notification No. G.S.R. 562(E), dated the 6th August, 2019, Gazette of India, Extraordinary, Part II, Section 3, Sub-section (i).